Idolatry
A Contemporary Jewish Conversation

Also edited by Alon Goshen-Gottstein:

Judaism's Challenge: Election, Divine Love, and Human Enmity
(2020)

"*Judaism's Challenge* will be of immense interest to anybody wanting to find contemporary meaning, compatible with our modern and liberal sensibilities, in the doctrine of election, and Jewish chosenness.

— Samuel Lebens, University of Haifa, Religious Studies

"Once we accept that God created the vast cosmos, those of us in one extremely tiny corner of the cosmos—who hold ourselves to be the objects of God's special love—are faced with the apparent oddness of the Master of the Universe choosing any subset of humanity as a special treasure. Coming to grips with that apparent oddity is indeed Judaism's Challenge. … On the evidence of the book before us, *Judaism's Challenge* will have a prominent place in this discussion."

— Menachem Kellner, review, *The Lehrhaus*

Idolatry
A Contemporary Jewish Conversation

•

Edited by
Alon Goshen-Gottstein

BOSTON
2023

Library of Congress Cataloging-in-Publication Data

Names: Goshen-Gottstein, Alon, editor.
Title: Idolatry: a contemporary Jewish conversation / edited by Alon Goshen-Gottstein.
Description: Boston: Academic Studies Press, 2023. | Series: Jewish thought, Jewish history: new studies | Includes bibliographical references and index.
Identifiers: LCCN 2022058272 (print) | LCCN 2022058273 (ebook) | ISBN 9798887191379 (hardback) | ISBN 9798887191386 (paperback) | ISBN 9798887191393 (adobe pdf) | ISBN 9798887191409 (epub)
Subjects: LCSH: Idolatry. | God--Biblical teaching. | Gods--Biblical teaching. | Judaism--Relations--Paganism. | Paganism--Relations--Judaism. | Monotheism--Biblical teaching. | Religious tolerance--Judaism. | Judaism |x Doctrines.
Classification: LCC BM729.I36 I36 2023 (print) | LCC BM729.I36 (ebook) | DDC 296.3/1--dc23/eng/20230106
LC record available at https://lccn.loc.gov/2022058272
LC ebook record available at https://lccn.loc.gov/2022058273

Copyright © 2023, Academic Studies Press. All rights reserved

ISBN 9798887191379 (hardback)
ISBN 9798887191386 (paperback)
ISBN 9798887191393 (adobe pdf)
ISBN 9798887191409 (epub)

Book design by PHi Business Solutions.
Cover design by Ivan Grave

Published by Academic Studies Press
1577 Beacon Street
Brookline, MA 02446, USA

press@academicstudiespress.com
www.academicstudiespress.com

For Harold Kasimow—
A great soul whose life is a testimony to the God of life
And a resistance of the idolatry of death.

Contents

Preface and Acknowledgements ix
Alon Goshen-Gottstein

Introduction
I Understanding Idolatry: An Invitation to
 a Contemporary Conversation 1
 Alon Goshen-Gottstein
II Idolatry—Revisiting a Fundamental Concept:
 Project Description 11
 Alon Goshen-Gottstein

1. The Theology and Politics of Idolatry 43
 Reuven Kimelman
2. Monotheism and Idolatry: Theological Challenges and
 Considerations 70
 Michael Fishbane
3. Idolatry on the Other Side of Modernity 93
 Shaul Magid
4. Jewish Feminist Liberation Theology and the
 Modern Criticism of Idols 125
 Melissa Raphael
5. Idolatry as Dehumanization 141
 Rivon Krygier
6. Contemporary Idolatry and a Path to Freedom 151
 Eilon Shamir
7. The Idolatry of Humankind 168
 Jonathan Wittenberg
8. "We Live as Did the Ancients": Reflections on the Ambiguous Role
 of Idolatry in Contemporary Jewish Thought 185
 Arnold Eisen
9. The Dynamism of Idolatry 213
 Haviva Pedaya

10. On Petrification *Michael Marmur*	232
11. The Idolatry of the Written Word *Paul Mendes-Flohr*	253
12. The Concept of Idolatry in Current Times *Hanoch Ben-Pazi*	264
13. The Line between True Religion and Idolatry *Warren Zev Harvey*	282
14. Thinking Idolatry with/against Maimonides: The Case of Christianity *Menachem Kellner*	290
15. Return of the Gods: A Jeux d'Esprit on Idolatry in Judaism *Norman Solomon*	312
16. The Value of Idolatry *Menachem Fisch*	329
Concluding Observations: The Discourse on Idolatry *Alon Goshen-Gottstein*	349
Index	357

Preface and Acknowledgements

I am delighted to present to thinkers, educators, and the educated Jewish public the latest, and final, installment in a series of publications in the area of Jewish theology of religions. Articulating a present-day view of other faiths is a theological-educational, as well as social-political, need. I give thanks to God for having contributed to this area of reflection through several publications. Some of these feature my voice as author; in others, my role has been that of convener of a conversation, to which a broad range of Jewish scholars and thinkers have contributed. The present volume, dedicated to the subject of idolatry and to its contemporary theological-religious relevance, expresses recognition of the group process in its subtitle: "A Contemporary Jewish Conversation."

This conversation follows on from several other projects. The first book that set the stage for later projects was the 2012 *Jewish Theology and World Religions*, co-edited with Eugene Korn and published by the Littman Library. My introductory essay in that publication identified several key issues that a Jewish theology of religions must tackle. Subsequent volumes each focused on one of those issues. Littman Library published in 2020 *Religious Truth: Towards a Jewish Theology of Religions*, dedicated to one of the issues identified. Academic Studies Press published, also in 2020, *Judaism's Challenge: Election, Divine Love, and Human Enmity*. That collection reflected on how Jewish belief in election may be reconceived, as part of a statement or restatement of this dimension of Jewish belief, considered while maintaining awareness of the broader horizons of Jewish relations with other faiths.

The present volume completes the series by focusing on the question of idolatry and its contemporary meaning. This, I believe, is the most important and most challenging conversation. Idolatry is the primary lens through which Judaism sees other religions and is therefore the most challenging topic to consider, in theological and contemporary terms. The question this volume tackles is not whether other religion(s) should be viewed as *avodah zarah*, but rather what *avodah zarah* or "idolatry" means for us today as a theological, moral, and educational category.

There are two particularities to this project, compared to the others referred to above. All the other projects grew out of team projects that had an in-person component. A conference or one or more in-person meetings served as foundation for each of those volumes. This also defined, and to a certain extent limited, the choice of authors for each project. The present volume was carried out using a different methodology. A call for papers was issued and disseminated broadly, and the authors featured here responded to it.

This approach is related to the more prominent role I had in this volume, compared to the previous volumes. In addition to serving as editor, which involved engaging authors in conversations, leading to multiple iterations of almost all the papers, I was also responsible for the conceptual framing of the volume. This project is largely shaped as a follow-up to a volume on idolatry that I published in 2015: *Same God, Other god: Judaism, Hinduism and the Problem of Idolatry* (Palgrave Macmillan). That volume reviewed strategies for viewing other religions in light of the category of *avodah zarah*, and in the process opened up this very category to novel examination. That novel examination lies at the core of the present volume. Having pointed to the challenges, limitations, and need to rethink the category in *Same God, Other god*, I invited scholars and thinkers to reflect on what "idolatry" or *avodah zarah* should mean for us today. This took the form of a concept note, shared with project participants. The concept note summarized some of the key findings of *Same God, Other god*, and set the stage for revisiting the concept.

The present volume opens with the original concept note, which summarizes some of the theses of *Same God, Other god*, and which serve as background to the present project. My overview of the present project and the answers it offers to the question of what is idolatry today follows. It identifies the most important moves made by our authors, and therefore provides the overall orientation for grasping the project's import. This is then followed by Essays by participants follow, grouped into subsections, in light of their specific emphases. Some authors' work is relevant to more than one of the sections of the book, and I had to make a decision relating to the optimal, but by no means exhaustive, classification. The volume concludes with methodological reflections, where I look at some of the processes and dynamics of the book and reflect on the discourse that is featured in it.

Looking at the book as a whole, I am greatly satisfied with the outcome. After several years of working with the authors individually on their essays, while I was engaged in other projects, I only saw the project in its entirety when preparing the volume for publication. A review of the project as a whole made me realize just how significant its outcomes are. There is much research, knowledge, and reflection in these pages. There are significant and original insights throughout. But above all, the project as a whole injects new life into the discussion of idolatry, making it far more relevant as a theological concept with more consequences for our everyday life than the typical application of the category to designate the status of other religions. This, to me, is a major theological achievement, and one that could only be attained by means of group effort. It is, in fact, a way of validating the procedure of convening broader conversations on theological matters. The significant distance and advances that the present project makes in relation to *Same God, Other god* point to the importance and benefits of broader conversations on theological issues. As Paul Mendes-Flohr affirms in his essay in this volume, Talmud Torah is a communal process. I would add that theologizing as a whole is a communal process.

Recognizing that this work is a group process leads me to thank all those who have made it possible. First and foremost, I express my gratitude, friendship, and profound partnership with all contributors to the volume. Only they know how much they have had to put into their essays and what a "difficult" project leader I have been. It has been a privilege for me to have the trust and collaboration of so many important thinkers and scholars, who have allowed me to collaborate with them, even as they collaborated with the project. To all of them, thank you.

Thanks go also to the team at Academic Studies Press. I begin with Kira Nemirovsky, whose communication skills and emotional intelligence have turned many dreary moments of book production into lovely moments of human encounter and friendship. I repeat my gratitude to Gregg Stern and Alessandra Anzani for recognizing the value of these conversations and signing me on to the press. Matthew Charlton has been dependable in driving things forward, as has Kate Yanduganova. A final word of thanks goes to Ivan Grave for the fantastic graphics of the cover.

In conclusion, what do I wish for this book and for the entire series of group conversations? My prayer is that not only is this, and the other volumes, well received by readers, but also that this book and its sister volumes serve to enliven a present-day conversation on matters of Jewish theology, in and of itself and as it relates to other faiths. The issues discussed go to the heart of our faith. May that heart be expanded by means of these conversations.

INTRODUCTION

I   Understanding Idolatry: An Invitation to a Contemporary Conversation

Alon Goshen-Gottstein

Rabbi Johanan teaches that whoever rejects idolatry is a Jew (BT *Megila* 13a). Indeed, for Maimonides, the foundational reason for the commandments is the rejection of idolatry. The prominence of the prohibition on worshipping other gods in the Ten Commandments (Ex. 20:3) provides biblical foundation for the idea that such worship (idolatry, in other words) is a key tenet of Judaism. Indeed, the rabbis consider *avodah zarah* (idolatry) to be one of the three sins from which one should refrain, even at the cost of one's life.

We take the importance of idolatry, *avodah zarah*, for granted. Yet, it is in fact one of the least considered commandments in contemporary thought and education. On the whole, the category serves as a means of rejecting and invalidating other religions and their adherents. Because it functions mainly as a means of excluding others, the attention paid to its significance within, to the reasons for the very prohibition, and to its theoretical and conceptual centrality is minimal. For all its importance in principle, idolatry—quite remarkably—is consigned to secondary place in contemporary religious thought. A number of key sources and rulings are cited time and again. Other religions are pronounced as idolatrous or non-idolatrous, and that is about the extent of the application of the category. Without entering here into the reasons for this situation, the point at hand is that *avodah zarah*, idolatry, is not a significant, generative, creative category that either lends meaning to our religious life or allows us to better grasp Judaism's uniqueness. To a large extent, idolatry has become frozen in a series of rulings and attitudes towards other religions, and for the most part plays no significant role in religious thinking and imagination. For all the theoretical significance attached to it, it is one of Judaism's most inactive theoretical categories.

My own work on idolatry, or *avodah zarah*, grew out of the context of evaluating other religions from a Jewish, primarily halakhic, perspective. In 2015 Palgrave Macmillan published my *Same God, Other god: Judaism, Hinduism, and the Problem of Idolatry*. The book sought to achieve two goals. These were to both evaluate Hinduism in light of *avodah zarah* and, at the same time, to rethink *avodah zarah* in light of a new contemporary dialogue partner—Hinduism. This work was the subject of a discussion panel at the 2017 World Congress of Jewish Studies. Gregg Stern, who attended the session on behalf of Academic Studies Press, suggested doing a volume based on those discussions and, more broadly, on the vital issues raised by my work and by the panel. The result is the present project.

While *Idolatry: A Contemporary Jewish Conversation* has developed out of my earlier work, it has a different and distinct focus. I concluded the body of the discussion of idolatry in *Same God, Other god* with the following statement:

> The common approach to *Avoda Zara* sees it as something cut and dry, easy to define, demanding unequivocal response. For such a view, *Avoda Zara* is not much of a challenge. Once it is defined, it simply has to be avoided. Once it is avoided, it is out of sight and out of mind, no longer challenging the religious system in any meaningful way. The proposed calculus leads to a dynamic view of *Avoda Zara*, where neither practices, nor faith, let alone an entire religion, can be globally defined as *Avoda Zara*. According to the possibility here developed, *Avoda Zara* would apply variously, according to context, need and the spiritual understanding of the performer. This seems to have the disadvantage of confusion and lack of clear categories. But its disadvantage may also be its great advantage. Rather than relegating *Avoda Zara* to the margins of our consciousness and our religious observance, leading us to focus only on the center of our religious life, *Avoda Zara* becomes an ongoing presence. The battle against *Avoda Zara*, both within and without, is a constant one, as we continually seek to improve our spiritual lives. Static definitions of *Avoda Zara* leave us only the option of avoiding it, thereby making it meaningless in our lives, at best an identity marker. An active engagement with *Avoda Zara*, seeking to articulate its meaning, categories, presence and boundaries, makes

Avoda Zara into a meaningful category that intersects with other major categories of meaning—intentionality, morality, spirituality, and more. *Avoda Zara* and going beyond it thus help define our spiritual lives internally, orienting them towards the highest ideals. In this way we do greatest justice to this formative category, by engaging it seriously and giving it the recognition and attention it deserves.[1]

This book picks up where the previous one ended. I consider *Same God, Other god* to have provided various options and possibilities for thinking through what *avodah zarah* is. My concern in that work was to develop a more nuanced application of *avodah zarah* with reference to other religions. The challenge and invitation of what *avodah zarah* means to us as Jews, other than a category for evaluating other religions, is where the present project takes forward the work of *Same God, Other god*. That project sought to move beyond a yes/no answer to the question of how another religion is evaluated and to present more nuanced ways of thinking of other religions and of the category of *avodah zarah*. It therefore seems appropriate that in moving forward in a reflection on what idolatry could or should mean to us today we should maintain the nuance and multivocality that informs Jewish thinking on *avodah zarah*, and that I sought to bring to light. Accordingly, the task of thinking through the contemporary meaning of idolatry should be a matter for a broader Jewish conversation, engaging multiple thinkers across the Jewish spectrum, rather than a position, an opinion, let alone a *pesak* issued by one person. This understanding informs the present project that seeks to stimulate a contemporary Jewish conversation on idolatry, thereby revitalizing the category of *avodah zarah* as an important category for Jewish theological reflection, Jewish spirituality, as well as Jewish identity and self-understanding.

Before I move on, a word is in order regarding the apparent confusion of categories. I have thus far used the terms "idolatry" and *avodah zarah* interchangeably. Are they really the same? What if any is the distinction between them? Which of them is the more authentic Jewish expression? I prefer to leave this question unsettled. Naturally, consideration of *avodah zarah* may be more relevant for Jewish theological thinking, inasmuch as it is a native category. However, if we seek to bring life to a discussion, one possible strategy for doing so could be identifying tensions and theoretical opportunities that arise out of

---

1   Alon Goshen-Gottstein, *Same God, Other god: Judaism, Hinduism, and the Problem of Idolatry* (New York: Palgrave Macmillan, 2015), 203.

the different perspectives that are opened up by the use of different categories. Openness to multiple categories would not be possible were it not for the fact that the term *avodah zarah* itself is also a secondary development, even though it has taken a strong hold in Jewish thinking for two millennia. Still, the Bible does not know this category and speaks of "other gods." "Other gods" have become "foreign worship" (*avodah zarah*), which in turn has been commonly rendered as the worship of idols in other languages. All of which is to say that we should be thinking of the semantic field covered by these different terms. It is a field that brings together approaches to god, true and false religion, otherness and the attitude to the other. The present volume assumes that all these discussions, to which I refer in shorthand, for the sake of convenience, as "idolatry," are relevant for Jewish self-understanding and that therefore there is room for fresh reflection and articulation of what they mean for us today. The invitation issued to participants to join this project is an invitation to engage the broader area and its contemporary theological relevance. I hope that the creative tension between the different expressions by means of which we can refer to this field will open up a creative space for reflection and therefore leave it to each individual to frame his or her contribution with reference to idolatry, *avodah zarah*, or other related expressions.

I would like to now offer an initial overview of some of the possibilities of understanding *avodah zarah* that came up in *Same God, Other god* and that could be relevant to the present project.[2] I will consider here, in brief, what these possibilities could mean for an internal understanding of *avodah zarah* and also introduce some additional theoretical possibilities I did not engage in that project. I offer these as conversation starters for contributors to this volume, who may reference some of this material and build on it, though they need not be circumscribed by these suggestions and may prefer to develop entirely different approaches to what idolatry means.

1. Idolatry as the worship of anything other than God. I believe this is the key definition of *avodah zarah*, formulated clearly by Maimonides, and one that can be harmonized with most others, which in turn can be viewed as means of discerning whom one is worshipping. Accordingly, the prohibition of idolatry is a demand for exclusive worship. The demand for exclusive worship makes most sense in a polytheistic or henotheistic theological framework. What does it mean once we declare there is only one God? Moreover,

---

2   Another important conceptual resource is Moshe Halbertal and Avishai Margalit, *Idolatry* (Cambridge, MA: Harvard University Press, 1992).

what do we mean by worship, and how strictly do we use the term? These two questions could open doors to multiple contemporary applications of the category. There are strategic choices involved. We can pitch worship narrowly (prayer, prostration, ritual acts) and consider the object of worship narrowly (the understanding of some other being as divine). A narrow application will keep the category of *avodah zarah* mostly in the service of evaluating other religions. Or we can apply the terms broadly, in which case serious engagement with certain realities, at the expense of a living relationship with or submission to God, would constitute idolatry. Such broad application could include any form of making something more important, central, value-giving, than God. It could be extended to the state, to ideology, to money, to power—to anything that detracts from the centrality of God as the core of faith and religious life. The difference between narrower and broader application is in part related to whether we remain within the linguistic framework of *avodah zarah*, which favors a narrower application, or speak of idolatry, which may lend itself more readily to broader applications.

2. Idolatry as a fundamental error in relation to God, especially such an error that manifests in wrong worship or intentionality in worship. Maimonides's influential description of the evolution of *avodah zarah*, in *Mishneh Torah*, chapter 1 of the Laws of Idolatry, sees error, even error committed with good intention, as the root of *avodah zarah*.[3] In this view, intention is not key. It is the result, the position that is upheld and the religious life that is practiced as a consequence that count. At various points in Jewish history this approach has been used internally, especially in the context of debates between different and competing schools. Certain practices, like adulation of individuals, are from time to time critiqued as *avodah zarah*. Do we wish to uphold a view of *avodah zarah* that is primarily based on a view of *avodah zarah* as error? Error is the correlate of truth. Are we sure enough of our understanding of truth to ascribe error to another, and if so, within what parameters? What are the broader moral, political, and social implications of emphasizing error as the defining element of idolatry in an age that seeks to overcome divisions, to increase understanding, and to reduce the violent potential of religious difference? How can error as a defining feature of *avodah zarah* be upheld, while containing some of its potential negative consequences? I invite thinkers who are inclined to understand *avodah zarah* in this light to also reflect on these challenges.

---

3   See chapter 6 of Goshen-Gottstein, *Same God, Other god.*

3. *Avodah zarah* as a negative and undesired energetic connection. The champion of this possibility is Nachmanides, who considers the possibility of *avodah zarah* as a means of bonding with harmful and destructive forces.[4] This view assumes the reality of good and bad forces, and the possibility for real influence by these forces, for good and for bad. It assumes our thoughts and actions have consequences, upon ourselves and possibly beyond ourselves. It assumes energy as something real, beyond belief, theology, morality, and the ordering of society. It approaches *avodah zarah* with a measure of objectivity, inasmuch as it is the real contact and its consequences that are the concern of *avodah zarah*, rather than false opinion or action. I am curious if this view will find an echo among participants in this project. It is likely that thinkers who are either kabbalistically attuned or who share so-called new-age sensibilities might be drawn to this understanding. According to this approach, we would have to define what in our life today, both inside religion and in life in general, leads us to God and what makes an opening for something that could be described as non-God, possibly even anti-God.

4. Another tack for understanding idolatry is to associate it with morality. This approach is typically associated with Rabbi Menachem Meiri and has many biblical prooftexts that tie the worship of other gods with moral abominations.[5] The moral criterion could replace the theological criterion. It could also be seen as pointing to the identity of the god that is worshipped, thereby ensuring one is worshipping God and not another. Meiri's approach has been applied mainly in the context in which he used it, namely in the view of contemporary religions. What are its implications if we consider what is wrong with idolatry? At what point can this understanding also furnish an internal understanding of idolatry? And how do we distinguish any number of moral transgressions from the qualitative leap that would lead us to consider a given lifestyle as idolatry? It is likely that this view should be combined with other understandings presented here, especially as we seek to make it work within and to have contemporary relevance. Given the central role that Meiri's view has played in modern Jewish views of other religions, there is room to continue developing the moral criterion as the defining feature of idolatry and to ask about its broader implications for Jewish life, understanding, and spirituality.

5. *Avodah zarah* and affirmation of identity. *Avodah zarah* and its application certainly function as a means of affirming Jewish identity. The strangeness

---

4   See chapter 7 of Goshen-Gottstein, *Same God, Other god.*
5   See chapter 10 of Goshen-Gottstein, *Same God, Other god.*

of the other god and the other religion help set "us" apart from "them." The need for affirming identity and establishing boundaries of otherness are important drivers of the discourse of *avodah zarah* and for the ease, and at times lack of consideration, with which it is applied to other faiths. But perhaps we ought to give more thought to *avodah zarah* as a means of constructing Jewish identity rather than contextualizing or even dismissing this dimension, as we might be inclined to do when *avodah zarah* is viewed purely in relation to other religions. That *avodah zarah* is tied to the relations of self and other comes through very strongly from the halakhic positions that distinguish between how *avodah zarah* applies to Jews and how it applies to non-Jews.[6] According to a central halakhic school, a construct known as *shituf* has been developed, which permits the worship of another being alongside God for non-Jews. Jews alone have the obligation of exclusive, or fully correct and true, worship of God. If so, true worship is deeply tied to the "us" vs. "them" approach. If we uphold this view in relation to others, what does this mean about how we use *avodah zarah* internally. Is there simply a dispensation for non-Jews who are allowed a lower standard in their approach to God or is there something fundamental about the relationship of *avodah zarah* and Jewish identity? Could *avodah zarah* really constitute a means of identity construction? If so, what would this mean for how we apply it internally? Happily, this category has not figured (yet) in contemporary debates between different streams of Judaism, though the potential to do so seems embedded there. Should the close nexus between identity construction and idolatry be upheld, limited, controlled or perhaps deepened, justified, and made a foundation of a contemporary view of *avodah zarah*?

6. Spiritual understanding of *avodah zarah*. Perhaps because of the centrality of the category, or because Judaism for hundreds of years has not had to face out-and-out idolatry (even if some religions were labelled *avodah zarah*), and perhaps for other reasons—there is a history of spiritual application of the category. Spiritual applications are aimed mainly at the individual, apply less to the community, and are rarely if ever applied to another religion.[7] If we seek to keep the category of *avodah zarah* alive and for it to proffer meaning

---

6   See chapters 8 and 9 of Goshen-Gottstein, *Same God, Other god*.
7   The following possibility for a study arises. Can we identify a relationship between spiritual understandings and halakhic views? Are they more predominant in Muslim countries, where the challenge of the religious other as idolatry is lower? Do authors who apply the term spiritually also take up halakhic positions that would reduce the scepter of *avodah zarah* from other religions?

on our lives, then a spiritual view of this category is an important approach. There are two primary spiritual understandings that come to mind. Both of them hark back to the understanding of idolatry as an alternative to God.

- A. The first views ego, vanity, and the human person holding himself in high esteem, at the expense of proper appreciation of God and man's position before God, as idolatry. There are biblical precedents for such an understanding (Isa. 2:7–22), but the idea was most fully developed in Hasidic thought.[8] This view draws on the very real experience of the human person and the human ego being the greatest obstacles to knowledge of God and to having a relationship with Him. The spiritual testimony, I submit, is universally valid and applies today as it did ever. Is it sufficient for developing a contemporary notion of idolatry?
- B. The second view considers money and attachment to it and to material wealth in terms of idolatry. Once again, biblical precedent is amplified in later pietistic literature. And once again, this idea has enormous appeal in an age of globalization, materialism, and consumerism. How can this understanding be put in service of contemporary moral and spiritual needs? Can it exhaust the meaning of idolatry, or must this emerge from the association of this application of idolatry with other ideas, presented above?

7. Political understandings of idolatry. The roots of association of the political with the idolatrous go back to the Ancient Near East where kings of neighboring states and cultures were considered divine and came under prophetic critique. Rabbinic opposition to Roman emperor worship similarly points to the nexus of idolatry, power and politics. If our starting definition is the worship of anything other than God, then contemporary political applications could grow out of historical objections to when power becomes more central than God. Anti-Zionist critique of the State of Israel resorts to such rhetoric. Are these precedents sufficient for developing a contemporary political understanding of idolatry? Does it need to be related to other understandings spelled out above, to give it greater depth and credibility?

8. Some other possibilities came up in the discussion in *Same God, Other god*, and I will mention them in passing. One suggestion saw fixity of ideas and the thought that we can attain knowledge in any stable and final way as an idolatrous approach to religion.[9] Another notion that came up considered

---

8   See Zipi Koifman, "Avoda Zara in Hasidic Thought," *Akdamot* 19 (2007): 65–86 [Hebrew].
9   See in particular the discussion with reference to Herzl Hefter's work in Goshen-Gottstein, *Same God, Other god*, 178 ff.

mental boundaries and limits, whether placed on God or informing one's negative and at times violent view of the other, as forms of idolatry. I leave the elaboration of such possibilities for contributors who are inclined to this line of thinking.

I would like to conclude with some words on what I see as the invitation to the writers. What I have presented above is not meant as the final word and does not seek to be an exhaustive list of understandings of idolatry or *avodah zarah*, even if the list is fairly comprehensive. The list is offered as a way of appreciating the complexity and the scope of possibilities that are already out there. With this broader awareness, authors are invited to state their own understanding of what idolatry is, why it matters, and what it means to our religious thinking today. Put differently, if idolatry is a major dividing point between Jews and non-Jews and, in part, what accounts for Jewish particularity, then we need to understand what we mean by idolatry, why it is problematic, and what it is that Jews avoid when they avoid *avodah zarah*.

Contributors are invited to provide their answers to these questions. The answers should reflect their own theological view, informed as it surely is by their historical research, contextual and theoretical understanding. The more a contributor can not only account for an understanding of idolatry but also relate it to some or most of the possibilities and precedents presented above, the more the position will be grounded in tradition and resound with the authority and credibility for others. It is unlikely that a view of idolatry can be formulated that will affirm all the rich, and at times contradictory, possibilities outlined above. But we can at the very least ask contributors to not only state what idolatry means to them but also how it relates to the history of *avodah zarah* and the Jewish view of other religions.

Perhaps it is not an accident that many thinkers have stopped working with the notion of idolatry. In the process of reaching out to potential contributors for this volume, I had many responses, including by some leading Jewish thinkers, that the category simply does not mean much to them. In addition to the historical reasons alluded to above, there is also a cost for upholding the value of *avodah zarah*. It is a category that comes with a cost; according to tradition it is the cost of life itself. What is the cost we are willing to pay for the use and for maintaining the vitality of the category? The cost may be legal or moral. It may involve willingness to exclude others, perhaps even to uphold violent approaches within tradition to other religions. How do we calculate our understanding of idolatry in relation to the cost it exacts? Do we tailor our understanding of *avodah zarah* in light of the cost we are willing to pay? Does the cost, which in turn touches upon our moral sensibility, provide the boundaries for upholding and developing the category? Where does a contemporary view of idolatry stand in continuity or in discontinuity with some aspects of a traditional view of idolatry?

If I have succeeded in the task of this introductory invitation, then the prospective contributor and the future reader will have become aware of the complexity associated with idolatry, *avodah zarah*, and the othering of gods and their adherents. This complexity has likely deterred many thinkers from deeper engagement with the category. The present volume seeks to bring together multiple voices of thinkers and scholars who are willing to tackle the challenge. They are willing, it is hoped, to not only state what is their understanding of idolatry but also how it relates to the history of tradition, to other views of idolatry, to contemporary reality, and to the price this category exacts.

The present volume promises to be an exciting moment of communal theological reflection, tackling a fundamental theological category and looking at the difficulties and challenges associated with it. I pray that through this collective effort the category of idolatry will receive some of the attention I believe it deserves and that the fruits of this group exercise will be not only an enrichment of our collective theological resources but also the opportunity for self-conscious spiritual deepening of individuals, as they seek to give meaning and to apply to their lives one of Judaism's most formative and fundamental categories.

INTRODUCTION

II   Idolatry—Revisiting a Fundamental Concept: Project Description

Alon Goshen-Gottstein

Background to the Project

The writer's equivalent of שכר מצוה מצוה, the reward of a good deed leads to another (Avot 4:1), is that one book project leads to another. The present project grows out of an earlier project, in which I explored different dimensions of idolatry, as these relate to other religions, particularly Hinduism. In *Same God, Other god: Judaism, Hinduism and the Problem of Idolatry*,[1] I studied a variety of medieval positions relating to idolatry, many of which were articulated initially in relation to Christianity. I then considered their applicability to Hinduism. More broadly, the entire exercise was an occasion to reflect on what is the essential problem with idolatry, how it functions in Jewish legal tradition and in broader Jewish mentality, and what problems, promise, and challenges the category continues to hold for us. The challenge of understanding wherein lies the problem of idolatry takes on new urgency if it is argued, as I explored in this work, that many or most contemporary religions may not be idolatrous. If such a view is taken, what remains of idolatry? Does *avodah zarah* retain any meaning, if it is not a means of delegitimizing other faiths? Recognizing that idolatry, or— referring to its Hebrew equivalent—*avodah zarah*, is a category that must be thought through, restated, and evaluated anew, I set out to engage a broad community of scholars in the exercise of stating or suggesting what *avodah zarah* or

---

1   Alon Goshen-Gottstein, *Same God, Other god: Judaism, Hinduism, and the Problem of Idolatry* (New York: Palgrave Macmillan, 2015).

idolatry means, or could mean, for us today. To that end, a brief introductory position paper was circulated, summarizing some key theses of *Same God, Other god*, and suggesting some possible directions for future reflections. That paper still frames the horizons of the present volume and therefore serves as the introductory essay. The response to the challenge I posed is the volume presented here. Some of the finest minds in present-day Jewish theology and philosophy have contributed to this volume, indicating they all felt the vitality, possibly the urgency, of the question. Some engaged with my earlier work, some responded only to the introductory essay; all shared in the quest to offer a contemporary statement on the meaning of idolatry or *avodah zarah*. It is, therefore, with a sense of gratification and gratitude that I am able to share with the broader public of scholars and thinkers the volume subtitled, "A Contemporary Jewish Conversation." This is what the volume sought to achieve, and what I believe it achieved quite well—advancing a conversation on idolatry in the Jewish community. The ability to engage this topic is a sign of theological and spiritual vitality. Discussing what idolatry is, and stating where the problem lies, is a sign of a healthy and robust spiritual and theological view. The negative expression of idolatry itself points to a religious ideal that the individual thinker seeks to uphold. If idolatry is meaningful, then God, or the fullness of the religious and moral life, are similarly meaningful as ideals and as aspirations. It is therefore a great honor and joy to have facilitated a conversation that demonstrates the spiritual health and vitality shared by our authors in their common quest, across the distinct voices collected in this volume.

The Challenge

The history of this project points to the challenge: articulating what *avodah zarah* or idolatry means for Jewish thought, religion, and spirituality today, beyond a category for evaluating other faiths. The challenge I issued was conceived as emerging from the decoupling of idolatry and the view of many other religions, a decoupling that has ample precedent in the sources and that I sought to further advance and expand. That raised the question of what alternative relevance the category may have and, more significantly, what its religious significance might be for *us*, other than a means by which other faiths are delegitimated. As participants in the project framed their contributions, further articulations of the present challenge emerged, unrelated to the decoupling of the view of other religions from idolatry. In this way, an even more principled approach to the need for a reevaluation of the present-day meaning of *avodah zarah* is affirmed by several of our authors.

Eilon Shamir associates the challenge with the religious significance of being liberated from Egypt, *in every generation*. In every generation, a person must free himself or herself from an outdated perspective. Time and again, we should identify current idols, and seek a personal way of living with God. In other words, the kind of reflection undertaken here is essential to the nature of faith and the reality of idolatry—stating anew what the present idols are that one must resist. Similarly, Michael Fishbane states that it is the very complex dynamics of idolatry, as he describes them, which make it imperative to revisit these issues in every generation.

Haviva Pedaya, too, makes the allusion to the Exodus and the task that confronts every generation. However, she makes the point with a significant addition. The definition of idolatry must be restated because our knowledge of God grows and is different in every generation. Just as the notion of God is not static, so our understanding of idolatry cannot be static. Redefining *avodah zarah* and restating its contemporary relevance is thus a task mandated by the dynamism and progress inherent in the religious life.

An Overview of Approaches

The various contributions and responses to my challenge can be classified as belonging to one of four theoretical approaches.

1. Focusing on something other than God. In line with a fundamental definition of idolatry as worship of a being other than God, several authors view an attitude, an approach or a valuation of other values or realities, other than God, as idolatrous. Several authors appeal to Paul Tillich's reference to idolatry as placing something else, other than God, as one's ultimate concern.[2] Thus, a key halakhic definition maintains its core features, while being expanded from worship in a narrow sense to valuation and to the place a given reality occupies in the life and consciousness of the believer.
2. Proper understanding of God. Following philosophical tradition, and especially the important role Maimonides plays in shaping discourse on idolatry, several of our authors relate to the question of proper understanding of God as the framework within which idolatry is to be understood. The challenges of a proper approach to God are ongoing, and as such as relevant today as

---

2 These include Eisen, Marmur, and Wittenberg.

they were in any generation. The particularities of what constitutes a proper understanding and how it is attained may change, in line with evolving religious understanding. The core perspective, however, remains stable, in relating to God-knowledge at the heart of the concern for idolatry.
3. The problem of fixity. Several of our authors suggest a definition of idolatry that may be best described as emerging from a phenomenology of idolatry, drawing largely from the identification of idolatry as the worship of an idol, an image of the deity fixed in wood and stone. Accordingly, fixity itself is considered as the heart of the concern for idolatry. Consequently, different forms of fixity, as these touch the religious life, are viewed as expressions of idolatry.
4. The third perspective already alludes to the fourth, in which the concern for idolatry shifts from an attitude to God to an attitude to religious ideals associated with God. Whether it is the Torah or true religion, or any other possible religious ideal, any of them can become idolatrous. This, of course, does not define what idolatry is, which would bring us back to the previous definitions, or lead to other contextual understandings. The point, however, is that rather than seeing idolatry in a narrow or focused sense in relation to God, idolatry is understood in relation to the ideals closely associated with God and religion.

The extension of idolatry to centers of the religious life, other than God, is one surprising feature of the project. While some of our authors are very God-centered in their approach to idolatry, others put forth alternative emphases. Many relate to Torah, nationalism, the people of Israel and Judaism as such as coming under the purview of idolatry. Differently put: we ought to be mindful whether idolatry is applied in relation to God or in relation to religion, to Judaism. It remains to be considered whether the broader scope is a sign of the vitality of the category and the meaningful work it can do in relation to other ideals, or whether this is actually a sign of the weakness and lack of meaning, leading to secondary and derivative applications.

These four approaches provide the parameters for our project. Some of our authors may appeal to more than one approach and the perspectives may overlap. For example, the problem of fixity may be related to the concern for proper understanding of God. It is, however, helpful to make an overview of what present-day thinkers consider to be the enduring significance of idolatry or *avodah zarah* in order to recognize these four basic approaches as orienting present-day efforts to cast "positive" meaning in the category, that is, to recognize its enduring religious significance as a category that shapes present-day religious concerns, independently of whatever work it does in relation to other religions.

Looking at this fourfold presentation, I suggest it may be boiled down further to two fundamental perspectives—cognitive and relational. The cognitive perspective refers to understanding and finds the problem of idolatry in wrong religious understanding. The wrong religious understanding relates, in the first instance, to God. But wrong understanding applies also to other values by extension and can refer to attitudes that are considered idolatrous, as expressions of fixity or of other fundamental flaws, as these relate to Torah, to the people of Israel, to the Land of Israel, or to other core religious ideals. The alternative perspective is relational. The problem with idolatry is that it undermines or upsets the appropriate balance or approach to God. It is not the error that is the concern, but the deviation from relationship and its proper practice. Wrong or misplaced relationship with God seems to be more of a concern in relation to God than in relation to other values, where it is not the relationship that comes under examination but the attitude to those values, thereby bringing us back to the cognitive domain. In some cases, however, one can think of relationship with the divine as extending to other values. Other values of the religion could displace God as the center of religious attention, thereby introducing an idolatrous movement into the heart of Judaism. It is even possible to imagine misplaced relational attitudes to other religious ideals that impact the relationship with God negatively. For example, views of Land or nationalism seem to involve a relationship towards those ideals, in a way that goes beyond simply a mistaken understanding or perspective. In sum, the two perspectives—cognitive and relational, and their mutual interactions, primarily in relation to God but also in relation to other religious ideals, define the playing field of idolatry vs. true faith or true religion.

Definitions and Perspectives

Any application of *avodah zarah* or idolatry also assumes a definition by means of which the particular application is made. The different approaches described above assume various definitions of what idolatry is, and by means of these definitions, particular applications can be made. Let us consider some of the definitions that serve the present conversation.

A. The core definition of idolatry described above, the worship of anything other than God, continues to shape many of the discussions. Thus, for Kimelman, anti-idolatry goes to the heart of our relationship with God. It seeks to protect the primacy of the relationship by rejecting any substitute for God.

B. As an extension of this understanding, one can also present idolatry as the worship of the part, at the expense of the whole. Eilon Shamir, similarly, upholds the basic definition, he attributes to Maimonides, where idolatry is a worship of mediators. Such mediators are a part of the whole, and idolatry is therefore understood as a worship of the part, at the expense of the whole. Excessive focus on powers such as money, health, beauty and more can therefore be seen as a present-day expression of idolatry. A parallel application is offered by Jonathan Wittenberg. Understood in a contemporary context, the portion of creation we are in danger of worshipping in this manner today is our own self, separated not only from our divine source, but from the sanctity of all other God-given life. The centrality of serving God and God's creation is displaced by the predominance of the service of ourselves and our own interests. Or, as Haviva Pedaya states, *avodah zarah* is a form of serving oneself and one's desires. This view of what constitutes *avodah zarah* leads her to yet another definition. Engaging in an act (*avodah*) that is foreign (*zar*) to God's existence in the world, by serving one's own interests, is a direct expression of *avodah zarah*.

C. Based on Asa Kasher, Hanoch Ben Pazi arrives at the recognition that everything in the world that is of prominent importance in human life can serve as an idol for the person in question. It is difficult to imagine "any aspect of the world—whether it be an object, a quality, a situation, or an idea," that cannot become an idol. Like Shamir, Ben Pazi relates to the dangers of totality. "The total (read: totalizing) position constitutes the danger of modern idolatry, whether it envisions the totality of the state, the totality of ideology, or the totality of society." Moving, then, from a view of idolatry as *substitution*, namely, substitution of God by something else, these thinkers move to a position of idolatry as a totalizing movement, with its obvious political and ideological connotations.

D. Fixity. Michael Marmur is aware that definitions are petrifications, attempts to trap complexity, and that definitions of idolatry often sacrifice nuance on the strange altar of clarity. Nevertheless, he puts forth a definition of idolatry as a form of petrification, a paralysis, where the written word and the ritual deed have been frozen, turned to stone. There the idol lurks. Idolatry, according to this view, is the fixing of the image of God. The issue is not the substance from which the idol is made, as much as the process where fluid turns to stone.

The problem of fixity may apply to religious values as well as to God himself. The fixity of God is suggested by Magid as a contemporary, kabbalistically oriented understanding of idolatry. Idolatry suggests some stagnant or frozen hierarchical structure in the infinite divisibility of the divine. As it emerges from Magid's analysis, idolatry is also the denial of the human nature of the divine. This is not to say the human is God, but rather that God, like the human, is infinitely divisible and it is the experience or elucidation of that infinite divisibility that makes for the authentic experience of God.

In interesting ways, a similar understanding is echoed by Fishbane. The anthropomorphic depictions of divinity throughout Scripture should not be denied or denigrated as "false images." They have the capacity to engage one's religious consciousness; and, by means of these hermeneutical mediations, evoke new (personal) engagements with the Divine revelations that elicited the original formulations. To forget this overarching consideration (of God's unknowable transcendence *and* the spiritual dimensions of all discernible reality), is to constrict human thought to the surface plane of worldly perception. That leaves us with the "work of our minds" and the potential reification of our predications. This is epistemological idolatry by any other name.

E. Drawing on Maimonides and the philosophical understanding of idolatry, Melissa Raphael reminds us how Maimonides recognized that the most powerful idols are not figures set up in places of worship, but customary erroneous ideas, mediated to the masses in ways that induce ignorance and forgetting. Modernity emancipationists have gone on to identify idolatry, religious and secular, as the medium of false consciousness. Oppression is ideological before it is material. Any serious bid for a redemption from one sort of captivity or another recognizes that idolatrous thought and language, as well as figurative images, give a dangerous artificial life to projections that inhabit and manipulate the imagination. As Rita Gross (cited by Fishbane) makes the point, the debate over what images and pronouns should be used to describe God has given new meaning to idolatry, "usually an empty category in contemporary religious discourse."

F. From position to attitude. One of the important moves that authors make is to shift the uses of idolatry from a distinct position to a broader orientation and attitude. Consequently, it is not that a certain object or a view is defined as idolatry. Rather, idolatry is characterized by an attitude, and that attitude can potentially attach itself to anything. Whatever the value we admire, states Norman Solomon, it is only when admiration and respect become slavish, exclusive, and obsessive do we cross the line to idolatry. Paul Mendes-Flohr, too, refers to an attitude, as it relates to Torah. Idolatry comes in many and varied guises. Common to all its expressions is an attitudinal sensibility, whereby given social and cultural phenomena are venerated as endowed with intrinsic, absolute value. There are two nuances here. The argument against intrinsic value is harder to defend, if one only thinks of religious realities as essentially endowed with spiritual reality, in an innate way. However, I believe what Flohr is after is explicated by the dual reference to intrinsic and absolute. In other words, certain ideals take on absolute value, and that absoluteness may compete with the one reality that ought to be absolute, and that relativizes all else—God's reality.

Rivon Krygier develops the view of idolatry as an attitude, by making us aware that in thinking of idolatry we should not be thinking only of the *object* of belief (the definition and representation of the divine), but even more so of the *subject* of belief (the attitude of the faithful). Idolatry has to be understood within the complete worldview that espouses holiness, morality and self-discipline. Idolatry is deemed reprehensible when it aims to *instrumentalize* the divine, to assist the idolater in escaping the duties of conscience that rest upon every human being created in the image of God. The sacred dimension is thus diverted from its "real" goal by placing it at the service of interests aimed at strengthening the power of the individual, the group, or the nation, and, under certain circumstances, ends up serving as a pretext for inhuman, violent, or humiliating conduct. Consequently, more than a *dedivinization*, idolatry is *dehumanization*. It disfigures God in the same way it disfigures the human being created in God's image.

Idolatry Then and Now

As we move across the spectrum of definitions of idolatry, one significant theoretical issue arises: Is idolatry the same then and now, or has it, and its uses, undergone changes? This question underlies the present project. After all, our starting point is that religions around us should, or may, not be viewed as idolatry, thereby raising the question of what constitutes idolatry today. The very positioning of our conversation in terms of "today" or "contemporary" assumes the possibility that what was idolatry then is different now and that even if we continue to appeal to this category, its applications might differ from the stricter uses that characterized it in the first instance. On this point, we seem to encounter different voices within our project. Not all authors have been explicit with reference to the question of positioning idolatry today in relation to classical uses. But some have, and the work of others can be interrogated further in light of this question.

At the one extreme we find Norman Solomon who makes the point that nothing essential has changed. His description of idolatry's operation today assumes the old gods have returned in new forms. Similarly, Kimelman claims the old temptations are there, making biblical and rabbinic idolatrous references to the individual, and the political applications of idolatry, as relevant as ever.

Others seem to suggest that as religious thought evolves, so does idolatry, and that recognizing progress in religion means that idolatry takes on new theoretical expressions, not merely disguises by means of which the same old forces return to haunt and tempt us. For one, many authors recognize that idolatry is now a force that has to be reckoned with mainly within, as part of religious psychology and spirituality, rather than as an element of interreligious competition. This holds true for Wittenberg, Pedaya, and the thinkers who consider the evolution of religious thought as it impacts our view of God (Kimelman, Raphael). It seems to me this is a development in the reference to idolatry. A more internalized, or more theoretical, or even more nuanced appeal to idolatry is in fact not the same thing under new guise. It is an expression of a more evolved religious consciousness. Religious consciousness still has to struggle with whatever gets in the way of its purity and perfection. Idolatry therefore remains relevant. But it is a different kind of battle, and as such points to the evolution of the battle. Magid, reflecting on the theology of Art Green, raises the question of what idolatry means to the latter, when it is seen in light of the evolution of religious thought. Idolatry, in this understanding, refers to continuing worship in a way that has been overcome through human evolution, an exercise in spiritual obsolescence. While the foundational understanding of idolatry as error may be maintained, it is now couched within an evolutionary awareness that recognizes that though similar, it is, in fact, of a different kind, due to the evolution of religious thought.

While all our authors find continuing significance in *avodah zarah* or idolatry, I am not sure how many of them would be willing to use these terms in a strict sense. The description of some of the uses as moving from "position" to "attitude," or from "worship" to "orientation" is to some extent representative of the entire project. Our authors would have to speak for themselves. However, reading them, I doubt that any of them are ready to attach to idolatry the kind of strictness that led to the death sentence in biblical times, and not only because it is no longer practiced. More fundamentally, all our authors find some middle ground between continuing references to idolatry and the recognition that there is some secondary application, or extension, of the use of idolatry. Even if one speaks of the political domain in terms of idolatry, as Kimelman, Wittenberg, and Eisen do, and even if one recognizes biblical precedent for such usage, I believe these discussions are still at some remove from the full and original usage. Whether this is indeed the case is a matter that not only our authors could continue discussing. It is also a question for readers of the volume, who are encouraged to contemplate the uses here offered in relation to earlier uses and to consider whether, in fact, "idolatry" has not morphed to "idolatrous." The difference between noun and adjective may capture the movement that gave birth to this volume and the range of uses our authors apply.

The Moral Dimension

One of the handles by means of which the subject of idolatry is grasped is considering whom idolatry harms. One could suggest a division between a focus on God and a focus on the human or on society. Of course, one might claim that also with a focus on God, it is the human who is suffering from false religious understanding, rather than God himself being impacted by idolatry. Nevertheless, there is a meaningful distinction between the concerns of idolatry relating, in the first instance, to God, his knowledge, and the relationship with him, and their relating to the human – individual and community. To a large extent, the difference between these perspectives harks back to the differing understandings of Meiri and Maimonides, as these present different understandings of idolatry and draw different conclusions for the religions of their day. The difference between them is significant also for contemporary applications of idolatry. It is interesting that even though many of our authors define idolatry in terms that are borrowed from Maimonides—a testimony to his centrality and to the long shadow that he casts over the history of Jewish halakhah and reflection—in fact, the position they espouse is closer to that of Meiri. Accordingly, even if the *definition* of idolatry is presented in terms of the worship of things other than God, in line with Maimonides's core definition, the *consequences*, the harm that idolatry brings about, is understood in moral terms, thereby echoing Meiri's understanding of *avodah zarah*.[3]

---

3 In *Same God, Other god*, I discuss the theological understanding implicit in Meiri's position. I understand Meiri not simply as putting forth a moral position, but as using the moral realm to reflect a theological understanding. In fact, this makes it easier to translate other definitions of idolatry to Meiri's terms, inasmuch as his position should not be seen simply as a focus on the moral dimension, but as a view that establishes the relationship of the moral and the theological.

Norman Solomon reminds us that already the sages drew moral conclusions from theological understandings.

> The Sages of the Talmud recognized that many forms of behavior, though not halakhically idolatry, shared its essential character: "Who averts his eyes from [giving] charity is an idolater" (BT *Ketubot* 68a); "Who appoints an unsuitable judge is an idolater" (BT *Avodah Zarah* 52a); "Who follows his base instinct is an idolater" (PT *Nedarim* 9:1, 41b); "Who fails to keep his word is an idolater" (BT *Sanhedrin* 92a). In all these cases something, or somebody (avarice, injustice, desire, falsehood) displaces God to direct our behavior.

Haviva Pedaya develops the notion of serving yourself as a form of *avodah zarah*, which in turn gives way to a moral application and to moral consequences. Abuse of others is seen as an expression of *avodah zarah*. Abuse of power, and in particular sexual abuse by religious leaders, is to be understood not simply as a moral weakness, but as a contemporary expression of idolatry. In an important conceptual contribution, she sees idolatry as *betrayal*, evoking the fundamental relational dimension. Reversing the logic, betrayal of God, as in instances of moral abuse, is to be seen as an expression of idolatry.

In a more principled way, all forms of idolatry, from its most primitive expressions, may be considered in terms of their consequences to the human person. Michael Marmur cites Erich Fromm, who offers an internally focused reading of the essence of idolatry. He claims that "the history of mankind up to the present time is primarily the history of idol worship, from the primitive idols of clay and wood to the modern idols of the state, the leader, production and consumption—sanctified by the blessing of an idolized God." For Fromm, "[t]he idol is the alienated form of man's experience of himself." According to Fromm, idolatry is connected to narcissism (man worshipping himself), alienation (the dependence of man on outside powers), and necrophilia (the worship of dead things and destruction). For him, the fight against idolatry is a fight for man's freedom and for a sane society.

Another author who moves along those lines is Eilon Shamir. He also speaks of addiction as a form of idolatry. From a psychological perspective, there is a correlation between the believers and their beliefs. There is a correlative connection between the way we relate to reality/God, and the way we relate to our own souls. For Shamir, idolatry has psychological as well as moral consequences. This is because idolatry means attributing to a partial element of reality more than its natural value, endowing it with more than its natural "place" or weight. Shamir speaks of the price of idolatry that the individual pays. We are inclined to idolize entities such as money, beauty and so on, because it enables us to escape our inner world, our pains and demons. In the short term, these idols "reward" us. But the price is high: we neglect our inner soul, and cannot attain self-integration. This is how these idols enslave us, and nullify growth and self-liberation. And there is a lot of misery in this slavery.

As we move to the implications of idolatry to the human person we, in fact, move from the domain of theology to the domain of psychology. Throughout our project, contemporary applications address the psychological consequences or correlates of idolatry. In fact, one might even suggest that part of the evolution in the understanding of idolatry lies in the move from considering it in relation to the objectivity of the object of worship to its view in relation to the subject and her interior processes.

Idolatry is also to be understood as leading to moral relativism. The point is made by Max Weber, who provides the scaffolding for Eisen's analysis. According to Eisen, Weber believed that monotheistic faith was somehow essential to the moral compass of humanity, while recognizing that adherence to such faith, in his day as in earlier eras, was difficult to achieve and maintain. Weber suggested that the worship of many gods—or no god—carries deleterious moral implications and consequences. In his view, these included a moral relativism that he himself, lacking religious faith, seemed to endorse, albeit reluctantly. Eisen goes on to claim that moral decline or danger is the dominant theme of contemporary Jewish thought concerning idolatry. *Avodah zarah* is rarely taken to mean worship of God in ways other than "ours," or to critique conceptions of God that posit multiple divinities. Idolatry, rather, signifies immoral behavior above all else: the direction of "ultimate concern" to causes, activities or persons who are less than ultimate, including, pre-eminently, the self. Idolatry plays far more of a *moral* than a *religious* role in contemporary Jewish thought. This has ramifications for a view of Judaism, as well as of other religions. Judaism is not the only valid (or "true") religion. All monotheistic faiths are superior to any form of idolatrous worship. This is understood on moral grounds.

Magid reminds us of the broad currency that "ethical monotheism" has enjoyed. In this context, the ethical, often described as humanism, is associated with monotheism, and the unethical, with idolatry. Magid consciously appeals to Meiri as the figurehead of this understanding and relates it to the work of Eliezer Schweid who extends Meiri's notion of an ethical society and monotheism.

To sum up, then, there are multiple pathways by means of which the moral-human-psychological impact of idolatry is derived. These include the fundamental definition of *avodah zarah* offered by Meiri, the analysis of the consequences of idolatry to the human person (Krygier) and, more broadly, the approach to idolatry as an attitude and orientation, rather than a fixed object of worship. This facilitates a view of its consequences in relation to the human person.

The Theological Dimension—Idolatry and God

Let us now consider the alternative conceptual pole—idolatry's relation to God. A focus on God opens up to multiple dimensions of what it is that concerns us, when we discuss idolatry. When we consider the four basic approaches listed above—worship of something other than God, proper understanding of God, and fixity of the divine or religious ideals—all of them relate to God in their respective ways. From the relational perspective, the problem with idolatry is that it compromises our relationship with God. As Kimelman states,

> Anti-idolatry goes to the heart of our relationship with God. It seeks to protect the primacy of the relationship by rejecting any substitute for God. Substitutes encompass any human expression, political expression or alternative claim of divinity that encroaches upon God's exclusive sovereignty. Idolatry is the eclipse of God by means of an alternative reality.

There is, however, he suggests, also a positive dimension to the concern with idolatry. Idolatry is concerned not only with avoiding substitutes to our relationship with God. It is also concerned with protecting our relationship with Him and keeping it alive. "Anti-idolatry can also be positive by keeping the relationship with God alive by not freezing the notion of God in ways that would undermine the relationship."

In similar vein, Marmur relates to Maimonides and Hermann Cohen, on the one hand, and to Franz Rosenzweig, on the other.

> "[F]or Cohen and Maimonides, idolatry is the worship of the wrong God. Since the true God cannot be represented, any representation of God is necessarily a representation of the wrong god." Rosenzweig, in contrast, is not scandalized by a plurality of images of the divine, so long as none of them is given an ultimate

> and unchanging status. *Idolatry comes from the way in which an image is worshipped and not from the thing itself.* Idolatry is the fixing of an image of God, which, Rosenzweig argues, is a denial of divine freedom.

We see how the concern for proper knowledge of God and the concern for fixity are juxtaposed with one another, as alternative perspectives for understanding wherein lies the problem with idolatry.

One might posit the difference as the distinction between the proper *view* of God and the approach to the *living* God, emphasizing not only the relationship with the divine but also the quality of relationship. The concern about a relationship with the living God comes up, alongside the more classical concern about protection from error (such as erroneous theological notions that inform feminist critique), in several essays. Fishbane speaks of the Ba'al Shem Tov's interpretation of the injunction that one should not "turn away" (*ve-sartem*) and serve (*va-avadetem*) other gods" (Deut. 11: 16) to mean that "whenever [or, as soon as] one turns (*ve-sar*) their thought from cleaving (*mi-deveikuto*) to God ... one immediately worships ('*oved*) other gods (*elohim aḥerim*)." If so, idolatry is not about proper theoretical or conceptual understanding of God. It is about maintaining the living relationship of cleaving to him. Fishbane explores the implications of such a perspective to the structure and content of one's theological consciousness.

Kimelman explores this concern in liturgical terms. The liturgy offers us a way of going beyond the fixity of God and maintaining the vitality of our relationship with him by employing a polymorphous approach to God. Recalling Rita Gross's point concerning idolatry in the linguistic domain, we better appreciate Kimelman's description of the many ways in which God is described in the liturgy. A polymorphic God cannot be frozen in one image. More significantly, the relationship with him remains alive, with the help of the multiple images by means of which he is evoked.

Eisen cites Novak and Buber in highlighting the distinction between the living God and the God of the philosophers, who may himself become the focus of an idolatrous religious approach. David Novak and other Jewish thinkers

> maintain that the abstract "God of the philosophers" is not the God of history and covenant to Whom most modern Jewish thinkers (including Novak) remain committed. Heschel declared categorically that philosophy will not lead one to the living God. Buber went so far as to accuse philosophical believers of idolatry

> if they "replace him by the image of images, the idea, [and thus] remove themselves and remove the rest of us furthest from him.... A God who is not a living personality is an idol."

It is helpful to introduce another term to the discussion—faith. Idolatry stands in tension to proper and living faith. As Ben Pazi reminds us, faith is a process, not a fact. The deep meaning of religious faith is coming to know divinity in its infinite and imperceptible sense. This, however, is not a one-time act of faith versus idolatry, but rather the ongoing engagement in a boundless consciousness-based struggle against all actualizing and reductive concepts of divinity. Proper faith is an endless process. Therefore, the deep meaning of idolatry is what defines the process of the refinement of faith.

Approaching idolatry from what may be termed a theocentric (as opposed to the more human-moral) perspective is significant not only for the processes of faith, knowledge, and relationship, as these impact our view of and relationship with God. It also has ramifications for a host of issues that are relevant to the human person, human society, and the world at large. Here is one voice that affirms this association, in relation to present-day ecological concerns.

> The significance of God, the awareness of the sacred in all life and the service of God through showing compassion towards all living beings are absolutely central to a resolution of humankind's most pressing concern, the future of life on earth.

Thus, Jonathan Wittenberg reflecting on the consequences of idolatry in the most expansive way. This leads us, then, to consider other areas in which the wrong, idolatrous, view of God has consequences for dimensions of human life, the human person and human society. Typically, thinkers arrive at these understandings from a God-centered approach to idolatry. As we have seen in some instances above, one might also arrive at these moral-societal implications and understandings of idolatry from the moral-human perspectives on idolatry. Put differently, while these concerns might seem closer to what lies as the heart of Meiri's view of idolatry, one can equally recognize these concerns from a Maimonidean perspective, considering the harm that substitutes for God bring about.

Idolatry and the Human Person

As Zev Harvey notes, whatever it is, idolatry is something profoundly *human*. In Hebrew, the adjective "human" (*enoshi*) is derived from the name "Enosh"

(Gen. 4:26), which is understood in rabbinic tradition as the root of idolatrous practice. Above, we considered the human dimension of the *consequences* of idolatry and discussed what harm it brings about. In what follows, we relate to the human person as the *object* of idolatrous attitudes. Much of what participants in our project consider as contemporary expressions of idolatry, whether defined in theological or in moral terms, does, in fact, relate to an approach to the human person and to human institutions and orientations, such as political structures, racial attitudes, and more.

The historical roots of such views are biblical. As Kimelman teaches us, already the Bible considers worship of the human person, associated with political power, to be an expression of idolatry. For Kimelman, this remains an ever-present component of the danger of idolatry.

An important biblical notion that is germane to a discussion of idolatry is the idea of man's creation in God's image. The majority of authors, about ten in number, reference the idea of *tzelem elokim* in one way or another. This underlines the degree to which the discussion of the application and consequences of idolatry to the human person is a central concern. Moral, psychological, and in some cases ritual concerns come together, as various dimensions of idolatry's relevance to the human person are raised by our authors.

There are various ways of relating the notion of creation in God's image to idolatry. On the positive side, we find Hanoch Ben Pazi's appeal to the self and its core as the yardstick for measuring true faith and for defining idolatry. The deeper meaning of religious faith is a complete allegiance to the truth, which means a turn inward, to the individual's "self." It is therefore not only possible, but also appropriate, to describe faith as the individual's internal allegiance to themselves, and their demand for absolute honesty with themselves. Any action that is not characterized by internal allegiance but rather by allegiance to an external force that is foreign to man and that causes man to act in contradiction of his internal values and beliefs is classified as *avodah zarah*, or idolatry. The deep meaning of idolatry is that internal action is performed not out of internal allegiance but rather out of external compulsion.

As Ben Pazi argues, the basic belief underlying this approach can be the view of the human person as bearing the "inner point," or perhaps the "spark" or the "soul," which is a "part of God above." Serious application of the principle that there is such an inner point leads to linking all honest and direct efforts to serve God to this divine inner point. In this way, a person's primary attentiveness to the divine voice is the inner attentiveness to oneself and one's selfhood. We note here the use of the image of God, but internally, subjectively, and in consciousness rather than simply a reference to others and to human dignity.

However, the notion of humanity's creation in the divine image can also operate in the reverse direction in relation to idolatry. This idea contains *in nuce* the potential idolatrous approach to the human person. While image worship is forbidden, the human person is seen as the image of God, a view that can either point the way to transcending the worship of other images or itself descend into such an idolatrous approach. Heschel, shares Magid, wrote that Jews were forbidden to worship images of God because human beings are themselves the image of God.

One important association of idolatry and the image of God, or a view of the human person, relates to the very definition of how we see a person, and who is included in this definition. Melissa Raphael makes us aware of the implications of this discussion for a view of woman alongside man. Made in the image of God, spelled out by Raphael as "I AM" and "I WILL BE," a woman's true primordial image is inalienable no more or less than a man's, not least because, like any halakhically permitted image, it is unfinished or incomplete.

Contemporary applications will look different from biblical expressions that are more oriented towards worship. Some may be disguised, others require analysis and recognition of their idolatrous approach. One form of a disguised idolatry is found in the present-day linguisic appeal to "idols" as part of popular culture. As Norman Solomon describes, a footballer, a film star, a singer, even the occasional politician might become the focus of the group's existence; their opinion on any matter is the one to follow, their behavior is the model to emulate, their mode of dress dictates fashion. People talk of "gods of stage and screen," a celebrated opera singer is referred to as a "diva" (goddess), pilgrimages are made to shrines such as Graceland as they have from time immemorial been made to the graves of saints. Eilon Shamir makes a similar point. Our culture is full of idolatrous terms, such as "American Idol," "movie stars," "music stars," and so on. He sees these as indications of an unconscious, or semi-conscious, tendency for idolatry that prevails in our culture. Shamir analyzes these uses and suggests we should not dismiss them lightly. One should ask what psychic mechanism leads to such admiration. The use of idolatrous language teaches us something about ourselves, about our culture. As he argues, we need to worship them because they tell an important story about our own lives. The external approach to idolatry is thus linked to its interior consequences.

Like Shamir, Jonathan Wittenberg too considers the role of the self in popular culture, as captured by the "selfie." The preoccupation with our own image is also symbolic of a disturbing concern. In a whole range of ways, we have accepted and embraced a way of life in which it is overwhelmingly ourselves, our own interests, and our self-image that we serve. Put bluntly, today, individually, collectively, as societies but most dangerously as a species, we are at risk of allowing our entire western civilization to become a cult of idolatry of self. Like Shamir who justifies seeing such an attitude as idolatry in view of its worship of a part, rather than the whole, Wittenberg too makes an argument for the worship of the part. The portion of creation we are in danger of worshipping today is our own self, separated not only from our divine source, but from the sanctity of all other God-given life. The dangers inherent in such an attitude are multiple. They include the risk of erosion of commitment to community, with the concomitant loneliness and isolation this entails for many. They also include loss of appreciation for the importance of service of others. At some point on the scale, as the balance tips from committing ourselves to our responsibilities towards demanding our rights, and from serving others to the advancement of our own self, that very self becomes deified, *de facto*, if not *de jure*. It is liable to become what Paul Tillich terms our "ultimate concern"; it is what we worship in practice, if not in stated belief. It is the primary organizing focus of our mind, the motivating ideology that governs our life. Wittenberg self-consciously applies idolatry to contemporary attitude and orientation, even if they lack the theoretical and worship-oriented dimensions that defined idolatry classically.

Reflection and analysis lead to a recognition of idolatry in various other modern expressions, even if these do not appeal to the term. Owen Barfield, as Marmur tells us, references two versions of the modern strain of idolatry— "elevation of the finite individual or collective self" and "degradation of the infinite aspect of selfhood to a false finitude." In both cases, it is the attitude to the human person that provides the contemporary meaning of idolatry. A similar twofold perspective is offered by Eisen. He speculates that there is something in the modern self that wants to keep God at a safe distance so as to pursue the projects of world-mastery and self-direction undisturbed by any higher authority. It would not be too much of a stretch, Eisen says, to call the extreme form of this attitude idolatry of the self. Anthropologist Erving Goffman argued that in today's world human beings enact rituals of "deference" and "demeanor" that were once performed to honor the gods or God, and are now directed at one another or themselves. According to Goffman, "the self is in part a ceremonial thing, a sacred object which must be treated with proper ritual care and in turn must be presented in a proper light to others." Speculating further, Eisen suggests that two very different motives drive idolatry of the modern self, sometimes simultaneously. On the one hand, God is pushed off to the side of modern consciousness because the self has become God in its own eyes. Today's nonbelievers take divine attributes upon themselves, convinced that there are as many gods as there are human beings who confidently assert, as they do, their own divine status and assume total and rightful responsibility for their world. At the other end of this same spectrum, we find human beings so despairing of their own worth in an impersonal, bureaucratized, out-of-control world, spinning in an out-of-the-way corner of a minor galaxy of an infinite universe that they cannot believe that any God that actually existed would take notice of them.

Paul Mendes-Flohr traces the idolatrous turn in relation to the human person. "The Christian system of God-created values corresponding to a God-created soul in man" was displaced by the "self-consciously individual" who seeks to know "the external world through the self and the self through the external world." Hence, "the self became the Godlike creator of the world." Friedrich Nietzsche gave this unabashed "idolatrous" sense of the self rhapsodic affirmation: "The I will be pronounced holy when man has transcended himself, and recognized that he is God, the creator of his own values." Theologian Karl Barth held it was inherent in the very logic of the anthropocentric turn of modern philosophy and culture.

Politics, Nationalism, Racism—Contemporary Expressions of Idolatry

Reference to the human person is highly individual. Considering the culture of the "selfie" or the idol in popular culture addresses *an* individual, whether the self or other. But idolatry also functions in relation to the collective and its sense of self, status, and relation to other. In this context new dimensions of idolatry appear, whether related to the making of the collective as an idolatrous object or whether serving as indications of an idolatrous view of God. Here too, we would be hard-pressed to think of idolatry in a narrow sense, involving worship. Yet, in terms of attitude and in terms of lessons learned from idolatry in the strict sense, there are multiple applications and extensions of an idolatrous attitude that apply to public, political, and social realities.

Biblical reference to idolatry includes a political dimension. As Kimelman and Wittenberg remind us, the Pharaoh is considered in terms of idolatry, thereby establishing a firm connection between idolatry and its political expressions. Later rabbinic objection to emperor worship continues the association, as Solomon, Kimelman, and Raphael remind us. This association of idolatry and rulership opens up to various contemporary applications, even if these do not involve ruler worship. Elements of the attitude to the ruler are considered problematic enough and share sufficient common ground with ancient practices to justify the reference to idolatry.

The essays for this volume were written during the "reign" of Donald Trump. Directly and indirectly, several authors make the association between idolatry and what they saw as problematic aspects of his leadership and attendant public consciousness. Thus, Shamir considers Trump policies, while Eisen explores more directly the association of Trump's presidency and idolatry. As Eisen argues, religion, ancient or modern, is never without a political dimension. Idolatrous faiths without apology make worship of the tribe, city, or state explicit. Here, the attitude of idolatrous faiths extends from the monarch to the collective and to the state, factors to which we shall return presently. Consequently, Eisen queries the religious significance ascribed by Jews to the State of Israel, on the one hand, and American Jewry's commitment to ethnic and religious pluralism, on the other. If, states Eisen, one broadens the notion of the "political" to signify, first, the ways in which *avodah zarah* serves to distinguish between Jews and other peoples, and, secondly, the degree to which Jewish belief and observance are shaped by consideration of what the surrounding gentile state and cultures will approve or tolerate (that is, what their politic is regarding the Jewish minority)—then the salience of the "political dimension" in Judaism is greater still. Significantly, as the case of Trump suggests and as Eisen points out, the distinction between false faith and true, *avodah zarah* and Judaism, is further complicated by the ties that bind Jewish thought about the God of all the world to Jews' particular political loyalties, interests, and conflicts.

From a more theoretical perspective, not shaped by immediate political circumstances, Eliezer Schweid, discussed by Shaul Magid, offers paganism and idolatry as yardsticks for measuring contemporary social thought. Any social theory or system that does not exhibit a collective spirit of responsibility and humanism toward the "other" is considered "pagan" or idolatrous. This, in turn, opens up to the suggestion of Haviva Pedaya: that the use and abuse of others is itself a form of contemporary idolatry.

The political dimension opens up to concerns of group identity and nationalism. Norman Solomon and Haviva Pedaya both consider nationalism in relation to idolatry. Whether we see it as an extension of the older concerns with the worship of the king or the political order, or whether we see it as an idea that has taken a place within the overall system that exceeds its proper proportions, thereby eclipsing God and his centrality, the very idea of nationalism is introduced into the contemporary discussion of idolatry. To be clear, and as both authors clarify, there is nothing inherently wrong with a national identity. However, the threat of idolatry enters as the national feeling becomes an "ism" and as it is translated into political processes, historical movements, and, in particular, as it is associated with a remove from other core religious principles.

Once Israel's success and prosperity are understood as dependent on political or national institutions, rather than on obedience to God's word, God's rule is undermined, amounting to an abandonment of him, that is, idolatry. Pedaya sees this form of idolatry as particular to modernity. Nationalism is akin to religion and uses its language, which, however, is emptied of its true content. This is the grounds for the battle within Judaism concerning the status of Zionism. Pedaya, accordingly, revisits forms of ultra-Orthodox critique of Zionism as idolatry not in order to affirm them as a position, but in order to illustrate how the claim that nationalism can be understood as idolatry is a move that makes sense within a religious worldview. Nationalism requires what the kabbalists call *berur ha-nitzotzot*, the elevation of the sparks of divine reality from within the husks of harsher mundane reality. Going beyond nationalism, Solomon warns of the dangers of ideology. "Ideologies function like gods and celebrities; 'ism' tacked on to a word is a warning sign. But the danger is there; will the 'ism' become an absolute, the exclusive answer to humanity's problems, a god to be unquestioningly obeyed?"

Menachem Fisch alerts us to a point of convergence between classical concerns of *avodah zarah* as a way of categorizing and evaluating other religions and the nationalist concerns, here discussed. The rise in present-day rabbinic voices condemning Christianity as an especially repulsive form of *avodah zarah* is associated with nationalistic perspectives. It shows us how also the status of another faith in present-day Israel is not a purely theoretical issue but one that has taken on specific political coloring.

The further extension of this trajectory of thought relating to idolatry touches upon what authors consider to be racism, and, in the extreme, even upon the very definition of Israel and its particularity. Dovetailing the point just made by Fisch is Michael Marmur's association of idolatry with religiously based racial theories. For Marmur, "to spout racial theories from the standpoint of religious Judaism, as some in Israel and elsewhere are doing in the twenty-first century, is to meet the criteria set out in this paper for idolatry—it is self-aggrandizement and self-flattery. It involves petrifying a dynamic process, making Torah into an inanimate object." As Marmur clarifies, echoing Pedaya and Solomon, it is not that any focus on the Jewish people and Jewish particularism is to be condemned as idolatrous. However, when a petrified reading of the tradition gives rise to narcissism and bigotry, then idolatry may not be far behind.

This, in turn, brings us to Heschel and to his association of racism and idolatry. As we learn from Marmur, one definition offered by Heschel for idolatry is as follows: "Any god who is mine but not yours, any god concerned with me but not you, *is an idol.*" Here, Heschel has identified institutionalized racism as a specific form of his more general understanding of idolatry. If you are worshipping a God who is concerned with you and not with everyone else, you are worshipping no God. Heschel's equation of racism with idolatry, states Eisen, points to the final major role that *avodah zarah* plays in contemporary Jewish thought: the conviction—once more echoing the prophets and the rabbis of old—that worship of other gods is both cause and effect of immorality.

However, once idolatry is associated with Israel's status and uniqueness, we are forced to go to the heart of the notion of election. Is it that only certain extreme expressions of election as superiority should be seen as idolatrous, or might the very notion of election be deemed idolatrous? Here we encounter the radical views of Art Green, as described by Magid. Idolatry is reconceived and lands on the very foundations of normative Judaism. For Green, idolatry is that which serves, affirms, or founds, any fragment for the whole, and misconstrues the parts, or even the sum of the parts, as the whole. Seen in this light, the very Judaism that gave us monotheism is now relegated to its idolatrous fate. It becomes an idol, on this reading, when it views religions hierarchically and exceptionally, whether through a theological rendering of God as other or through a political rendering of Israel exclusively as a biologically determined people. Ultimately, Magid himself arrives at the same conclusion on different metaphysical grounds. He agrees with Green that any religion that creates an absolute hierarchy, based on the idea of divine election, can easily lead to chauvinism, which is an expression of idolatry. While Green claims this is so because of turning away from the One, Magid suggests it is so because such divisions fail to recognize the infinite fragmentation of God in all things.

As a counterpoint to this train of thought, one should take note of Kimelman's original application of the association of idolatry and Israel's election. As Kimelman presents Judaism's struggle against idolatry, he views this as part of its collective mission. This is translated to its history and to the emergence of antisemitism. Jews are hated not because of the potential separation from the One, a position not claimed by Green, but one that could in theory grow out of his theoretical foundations. Rather, Jews are hated because they serve as a reminder to others that God alone is worthy of worship. Seen against the background of the frequent usurpation of divine power and its attribution to the human agent, which is a foundational part of the history of idolatry, the Jew has the role of reminding the world of the ever-present danger of idolatry. If the Jew is hated, it is because he is the denier of divinization of others. Would-be divinizers understand this all too well, which leads to Jew-hatred.

Idolatry and Nature

The association of nature and idolatry seems fundamental to a discussion of a Jewish view of *avodah zarah*. After all, at the heart of many of the forms of *avodah zarah* that Judaism has encountered throughout the ages is the worship of forces of nature. Judaism, runs the common argument, provides an alternative by affirming a God who transcends nature, leading to a prohibition on identifying nature and God and the consequent worship of natural forces. This point remains valid until this day, yet surprisingly finds no expression in our collection. It does not seem to constitute a present-day theological challenge. Other aspects relating to nature take precedence as some of our authors reflect on nature and idolatry.

One of these reflections is the very opposite of what we might consider as idolatry—secularism. Several authors (Pedaya, Fishbane, Shamir) state or allude to the possibility that secularism is, or can become, a form of idolatry. Commenting on a passage from the Zohar, Fishbane relates to seeing reality, that is, nature, while losing sight of the all-embracing divine mystery. It is to see things as just "this" and "that"—secularities without God. This is idolatry plain and simple, says the Zohar. This, in turn, leads to a view in which the world is reduced to thingness—to be used and manipulated. This ties to another dimension of idolatry we shall address presently.

In a different register, the same point is made by Schweid, presented by Magid, and is associated by him with postmodernity. For Schweid, modern secularism is inundated with a theological precept he calls monotheism, without which secular humanism is impossible. As Schweid understands it, postmodernity adopts modernity's secularism but rejects its monotheistic core of viewing the human as that creature who, as the "image of God," can conceptualize that which is beyond nature. This makes secular postmodernity an idolatrous worldview. Disbelief in a God who transcends nature and who is the source of nature and human reason that is bound to nature is polytheism, even if those who hold such views do not relate to the powers of nature as divine. Secular postmodernity is thus a return to idolatry. The human being and society are fully a part of nature and have no innate responsibility to it. Consequently, postmodernity's return to nature is not to live *in* nature as much as *use it* for the human needs. Thus, technology becomes the dominant ideational framework for postmodern society.

This corresponds to how many of our authors see the question of idolatry in relation to nature—as an extension of the earlier discussion of the human person. If idolatry, argues Kimelman, is about usurping the place of God, then a wrong view of the person will eventuate in idolatry. And one such fundamental view of the person relates to human powers, and in particular to how "man," referring to the creation story, rules, controls, or relates to, nature. Drawing on Heschel, Kimelman considers the Sabbath to be an answer to the unlimited exercise of power. The Sabbath teaches us where our control over nature ends and where God's dominion is affirmed. As Marmur describes Heschel's views, Sabbath is the idea that expresses what is most characteristic of Judaism, including the resistance to idolatry, inasmuch as Sabbath epitomizes an alternative to idolatry. Wittenberg extends the argument to the seventh-year sabbatical rest. It is mandated not because it is good for people to take a year off, or because the soil needs to recover for one season out of seven if it is to produce an adequate yield, but because "the earth is mine," affirming divine sovereignty.

There is another way in which nature and idolatry are associated by some of our authors. This has to do with caring for nature and with the contrast between caring and ruling, benefiting from, or using nature—put differently, between lording over nature and being a part of a greater totality. This tension is, of course, related to the biblical notion of the image of God and its applications. Schweid, presented by Magid, affirms that once human beings no longer see themselves as the pinnacle of creation—being created "in the image of God"—a creature that stands in responsible relation to a higher creator, nature simply becomes a tool to use for their benefit. Modernity's relationship to nature leads to Schweid's critique of technology as facilitating the rise of the individual over nature as opposed to seeing oneself as part, and also caretaker, of nature. Pedaya, too, associates care for the world with a critique of technology, all as part of the multi-levelled understanding of idolatry that she puts forth. For her, self-interest is the core of idolatry and its consequences relate to nature as well as to technology. Postmodernity is characterized by an overwhelming focus on technology, first of all internet. This singular concentration can be regarded as idolatry, especially as it often violates the divine calling not to destroy God's world. Fishbane, it should be noted, goes as far as to refer to the *worship* of the technological work of one's hands.

The fullest argument that associates harming nature with idolatry is made by Jonathan Wittenberg. The argument for idolatry is part of a broader argument, wherein the significance of God, the awareness of the sacred in all life, and the service of God through showing compassion towards all living beings are seen as interrelated causes whose ultimate outcome affects the future of life on earth. A present-day attitude, and herein lies the association with idolatry as it draws on the view of the human person, is the absolute right to power we ascribe to ourselves as a species, the anthropocentric exceptionalism of our own kind from the mutual interdependence of all life. Consequently, this awareness of the interconnectedness of all life provides the grounds for *teshuvah*, our return to God, and the deepening of *da'at*, the awareness of the presence of God throughout creation, which are needed to remedy our situation. One realizes that it is not only the usurpation of power by the human that is at the idolatrous root of present-day climate crisis. It is also the lack of knowledge of God, in its fullness. This brings us back to the twofold sense of idolatry, as wrong worship on the one hand and as lack of proper, full, living relationship with God on the other. Reading Wittenberg, especially in a reality shaped by the coronavirus pandemic, one wonders whether the focus upon idolatry as separating ourselves from God might be restated in terms of separating ourselves from the totality, recognized as divine, and the loss of awareness of interconnectivity that establishes the proper relation between the different parts of creation and between them and God.

The Idolatry of Torah

Focus on idolatry within the person points our attention to the individual and to processes that are interior to the individual. This, as we have seen, extends to broader attitudes that impact society in social, political, and other dimensions. Attitudes and understandings impact not only various dimensions of life "out there." They also touch the core of religious life—the Torah, its commandments, the purity and integrity of religion itself. As there can be idolatry in relation to an objective reality "out there," and as there can be idolatry within the human person, there can also be idolatry within, in relation to religion and the religious life. Such idolatry within may derive from several of the fundamental approaches to idolatry, as described earlier. It may be derived from the approach to idolatry that is based on criteria for proper understanding of God. But it can equally draw from the other approaches: concern not to have God replaced nor his place within the overall religious economy eclipsed by other, even religious ideals. It may also be derived from concern with fixity that sets in relation to religious ideals and realities. As Ben Pazi puts it, there is a spiritual-religious danger that man's religious commitment itself can become a kind of idolatry, if it mutates into institutional commitment and commitment to material objects. The trajectory extends further to religious teachings and to specific movements within Judaism, which are criticized as idolatrous.

Zev Harvey cites Rabbi Meir Simcha of Dvinsk who explains Moses's motive in breaking the Tablets of the Torah as follows: "he understood... that [the people] would exchange the calf for the Tables, and continue in their [idolatrous] error." Just as the Israelites had idolized the golden calf, so they could idolize the Tables of the Law. The iconoclastic Moses smashed the Tables of the Law in order to prevent idolatry.

The principle is repeated by Solomon. "What could be more strongly identified with Torah than the Holy Ark containing the Tablets brought down by Moses? Yet when the Israelites turned to the Ark to save them instead of directly to God it saved neither the Israelites nor itself from the Philistines (1 Sam 4: 3–11)." In similar vein, the words of Torah too can become an idol when detached from the context in which they were uttered; words live only in contexts.

Solomon offers a criterion for when Torah becomes an idol. It is when one loses the original context within which its teachings were given. The governing notion seems to be the historical appreciation of its words. A decontextualized reading lends the words of Torah an objective or absolute value that exceeds, one assumes, the divine intention or the proper economy that should characterize the religious system in its entirety. Marmur refers to this as petrification, hardening, and freezing of a living reality. Fixity replaces the living quality that words of Torah should have.

Solomon offers yet a second criterion, by means of which we can recognize idolatry. "The Torah scroll is reduced to a holy icon, paraded and touched and kissed while its commandments are ignored." This may also be seen as an instance of decontextualization. The Torah, as concrete object, is viewed in detachment from what it truly stands for—its instructions and the lifestyle it seeks to implement. If so, religious symbolism can readily degenerate into idolatry, if the purposes of the religion are ignored and the religious life becomes an empty show of exterior adulation.

Torah, then, should be considered not only as the object, but as the teaching in its entirety. Torah too, argues Magid in discussing Green, can become idolatrous, if it teaches anything except the Oneness of being that infuses all creation, a Oneness we can experience through the veil of our fragmentary world. Judaism is idolatry to the extent to which it focuses on its exclusivity and exceptionalism, certainly chauvinism, in relation to God. The separation of Jews, and Judaism from those who practice other religions, or no religion, slides easily into fragmentation of the Oneness of being that produces *perud*—separation and distancing—and idolatry.

Marmur points to Moses Mendelssohn as the originator of a concept to which several authors in this volume relate. In *Jerusalem*, Mendelssohn associates idolatry with the written word and, more specifically, with the printed word. These run the risk of being fixed, in writing or in print, losing their spiritual vitality. For Mendelssohn, the alternative to the written word are rituals. Ceremonies, in Mendelssohn's view, have the virtue of avoiding fixed status, and therefore demonstrate greater immunity to the risks of corruption and manipulation so characteristic of idolatry. This is an interesting juxtaposition. It is, in fact, the very opposite of how Maimonides would have seen matters, as Harvey reports. For Maimonides, rituals and ritual objects can become foci of idolatrous behavior and worship.

A second alternative to idolatry, as stated by Mendelssohn, is found in Paul Mendes-Flohr's presentation. Mendelssohn discerned the idolatrous implications of the humanistic celebration of the written word, which since the invention of the printing press gained an unprecedented cultural status, especially as embellished with the veneer of humanistic learning celebrated by the Enlightenment as the imperial road to truth. Mendelssohn puts forth the alternative. The epistemological consequence of the printed word and its elevated cultural status, Mendelssohn contended, engenders an idolatrous conception of knowledge. Noting that study of the Torah and its commentaries was integral to Jewish communal worship, he presented it as a means to resist the "idolatry" of the word. Talmud Torah should be conducted not privately but as a symposium in which members of the community participate. For Jews, the ever-increasing availability of printed books served to shift the site of knowledge from the synagogue to the privacy of one's home, thus undermining the bonds of community forged by Talmud Torah as a communal activity. Significantly, then, the human person, in dialogue and in community, is the antidote to the idolatry of the word.

One notes with interest that the concern of idolatry, or *avodah zarah*, whose core interest was and should be to protect divine uniqueness, has been extended to the Torah. The line of thought that grows out of Mendelssohn's position seems to operate independently of the concern to protect God and the exclusive worship due to him. Idolatry, in this context, can function as a conceptual structure, emphasizing fixity or other aspects, which can be extended from God to other core values. This perspective may be offset by the similar, yet distinct, approach of Levinas to the holy book, presented by Ben Pazi. Ben Pazi is quite explicit about the conceptual and cultural context within which the discussion takes place. As he describes it, the Jewish model places greater emphasis on the Torah than on God, and on the book than on the experience. This leads to the location of idolatry in ways that are particular to this religious configuration. For Levinas, the thought that immanent sanctity exists in the sacred books amounts to the "idolatry of the Torah." Sanctity does not stem from the object, but rather from specific modes of human activity that sanctify it. Levinas distinguishes between two different approaches to the Holy Scriptures: the Holy Scriptures as independent sacred entities—for example, as a source of religious authority or as writings that provide an experience of revelation—versus a sanctifying approach that describes how humans relate to the Holy Scriptures.

Returning to the notion of the written word, Levinas maintains that the Torah's existence in book form also constitutes a special mode of religion that establishes opposition to idol worship. Relating to the book places one in the position of approaching the object, a book, as something that is to be read. The necessary condition of being a book attests to the reader that sanctity is not found in the Torah but rather in its reading. From Levinas's perspective, the relationship with the Torah is like the relationship with God: "a book thus destined from the start for its Talmudic life." Although there is a book called the Torah that does indeed have a dimension of sanctity, it immediately affirms that its real life is found outside itself, in its reading. Reading the Torah's letters allows renewal, which is the true protection against idolatry. When Levinas uses the expression "hearing the breath of the living God in them [the letters]," he is directing his readers towards God by means of reading beyond the letters in the direction of the infinite. This does not mean that God is embodied in the letters, but that in some way he is nevertheless written in them. The vitality of the letters is found in the lines, between the lines, and in the changing ideas of the readers interpreting them, in all places, and in all the possibilities in which the letters are echoed.

Idolatry and Religious Polemics

Idolatry is a category that frames religious polemics in relation to other faiths. This has been demonstrated at length in *Same God, Other god*. We are now at a point of recognizing how similar dynamics apply also within one faith (Judaism). If idolatry applies within, and if it serves as a means of criticizing practices or attitudes, it can readily serve as a means for criticizing religious movements within Judaism. The critique could either be based on similarity to other faiths or on some of the other criteria suggested above, by means of which idolatry is extended beyond reference to other faiths.

Religious polemics refer to specific practices, especially such that might be considered part of folk religion or such that attribute inherent holiness to places and people. Yeshayahu Leibowitz is both vocal and well-known in this context. As cited by Flohr, Leibowitz insists that the "golden calf" (Exodus 32:2) need not "necessarily have to be of gold. It can be of stone; it can be a place, a country, or even a people, or even an idea (for example, messianic redemption), or a particular personality." Solomon is extensive in his application of this criticism internally, when he speaks of the Hasidic *rebbe*, or *tzaddik*, who are seen as possessing a specially exalted soul. This is then applied to figures such as the Vilna Gaon, the Chasam Sofer, the Chazon Ish, as well as the latest fashionable *rosh yeshiva*. All these are viewed in one grand idolatrous sweep.

But the most salient instance of such internal polemics is the view of Kabbalah as idolatrous. While this polemic has accompanied Kabbalah from its earliest beginnings,[4] I find it striking how often this same critique appears in our project, as it is voiced by contemporary Jewish religious voices. Both authors just quoted extend their view of idolatry to the mystic tradition, to the Kabbalah. Theirs is a rationalistic Judaism, which draws heavily on Maimonides, and considers the kabbalistic tradition in terms of idolatry.

Solomon speaks of the kabbalistic *sefirot* (divine emanations that constitute the manifest Godhead in kabbalistic teaching) as looking like members of an ancient Greek pantheon and goes on to find analogies between different *sefirot* and specific Greek deities. The discussion opens up to methodological considerations. Idolatry within and idolatry outside must be treated by the same criteria. "If you read it as poetry, meant to capture some spiritual essence or experience, you can circumvent the criticism that you are compromising the unity or incorporeality of God. You can do much the same with narratives of Athene, Nike, or Apollo."

The call for theological consistency is the thesis of Kellner's discussion of Maimonides arguing in favor of the concept of idolatry within. Kellner makes the simple but essential point: whatever criteria one applies to other religions in terms of defining idolatry should also be applied within. Accordingly, Kellner notes that the default contemporary view that sees in Christianity an expression of *avodah zarah* is based on Maimonides. If we are willing to base a religious perspective on Maimonides when it comes to other religions, why do we not take Maimonides's views with equal seriousness when it comes to viewing religious phenomena within?

One need not adopt the extreme views of Solomon in order to examine the limits of theological propriety and the ways in which Kabbalah skirts the issue of idolatry. This is illustrated by Elliot Wolfson's work, which is presented by Marmur in this volume. In his analysis of the idolatrous impulse in Kabbalah, Elliot Wolfson has uncovered many of the paradoxes and ironies, which surround this question. For example, "it is precisely the injunction against iconic

---

4   See Alon Goshen-Gottstein, "The Triune and the Decaune God: Christianity and Kabbalah as Objects of Jewish Polemics with Special Reference to Meir ben Simeon of Narbonne's *Milhemet Mitzvah*," in *Religious Polemics in Context*, ed. T. L. Hettema, A. van der Kooij, and J. A. M. Snoek (Assen: Royal Van Gorcum, 2004), 165–197.

figuration of God that unleashed such a powerful visual imagination on the part of kabbalists in their effort to chart the contours of the divine body." Wolfson claims there are occasional indications that the authors of the Zohar were aware that they were pushing the limit of theological discourse to the point of brushing up against the limits of idolatry.

If there is any polemic or conceptual fault line that runs through our essays, it touches on the question of mysticism vs. philosophy, and especially the legacy of Maimonides. Countering the voices we have just heard are voices that consider that the mystical tradition—Kabbalah and Hasidism—actually provides the antidote to the dangers of idolatry that our authors identify. Kimelman appeals to the Ba'al Shem Tov as one resource in establishing the vitality of a relationship with God as the antidote to idolatry. Wittenberg argues that the mystical tradition opens us most deeply to the awareness of God's presence within nature. This awareness is the key to overcoming the idolatrous consequences of human self-assertion and its attendant destructive consequences for nature and for life. Pedaya considers mysticism as a corrective to idolatry, given her particular identification of idolatry with nationalism. Purification of the collective imagination and of the harmful consequences of casting religion in nationalistic terms is achieved by a return to the spiritual reality, mediated with the help of the mystical tradition. Clearly, different authors employ different definitions of idolatry, in light of which the mystical tradition will be found on one or the other side of the divide between idolatrous or ideal religion.

It is not only that different authors take conflicting stances on mysticism and that these are fed by their respective approaches to the Maimonidean perspective. The polemic found within these essays works both ways. In the same way that Kabbalah is attacked by some authors, so is Maimonides. Magid correctly recognizes that the periodic accusation of Kabbalah as potentially "idolatrous" is born from a Maimonidean perspective. His own response is as polemical. For him, the depersonalizing nature of Maimonideanism is dangerous to the extent to which it creates a categorical separation between the human and the divine that threatens the personhood of God and, by extension, the divine nature of the human.

This leads us to the consideration of the spiritual and intellectual resources that inform the various perspectives our authors bring to bear, in an attempt to articulate a contemporary understanding of idolatry. It is clear that differing perspectives owe to different spiritual personalities, which are in turn shaped by competing spiritual resources within Judaism. This is a matter that deserves description, and which I will take up in my concluding essay.

This introductory essay has presented an overview of key positions relating to idolatry. It provides us with conceptual keys and a broader framework within which to appreciate the following individual essays. The concluding essay will examine the project as a whole from a methodological perspective and draw conclusions relating to the process as well as to the outcome of these essays. We shall return, then, to the question of influences and resources as part of the methodological discussion in the concluding chapter.

CHAPTER 1

The Theology and Politics of Idolatry

Reuven Kimelman

1. Idolatry

The word "idolatry" has a constricted and an expansive meaning in Judaism. The constricted meaning focuses on the literal meaning of the rabbinic expression *avodah zarah* (hereafter, AZ), and specific biblical examples. Parallel biblical expressions are *eish zarah* (Ex. 30:9, 37), *qetoret zarah* (Lev. 10:1), and *ish zar* (Num. 17:5), namely, unauthorized fire, unauthorized incense, and unauthorized personnel. So, for example, the case involving Korah and his cohorts was an authorized act, but performed by unauthorized personnel (Num. 17:3–5). The actions leading to the death of the two sons of Aaron, Nadab and Abihu, were a wrong act,[1] but performed by authorized personnel. Besides right personnel and act, the other two factors are the right time and the right place. AZ therefore is best rendered as unauthorized or improper worship.[2] The point is that "God ought to be worshipped according to the rituals established by Him."[3]

The expanded meaning of AZ ranges from the worship of idols, the worship of many gods, and the worship of a god beside the one God, to the worship of the one God through idols and images, and any unauthorized worship of even the one God. The expansive meaning of AZ holds that only God is to be

---

1 See Lev. 10:2, 16:1 (LXX); and Num. 3:4, 26:61 with Jacob Milgrom, *Leviticus* (AB 3), 3 vols. (New York: Doubleday, 1991–2001), 1:598.
2 See Moshe Habertal and Avishai Margalit, *Idolatry* (Cambridge, MA: Harvard University Press, 1988), 237–241; and Yaron Eliav, "Viewing the Sculptural Environment: Shaping the Second Commandment," in *The Talmud Yerushalmi and Graeco-Roman Culture*, ed. Peter Schäfer, 3 vols. (Tübingen: Mohr-Siebeck, 1998–2002), 3:411–433, esp. 426.
3 José Faur, "The Biblical Idea of Idolatry," *JQR* 69 (1978): 1–15.

worshipped, and thus AZ is the worship of any being other than God.⁴ This essay spells out the theological and political implications of the expansive meaning of AZ, namely, the worship of beings other than God.

2. Idolatry versus Polymorphism

The biblical concern with the negation of idolatry and the proper relationship with God involves the proper conceptualization of God. According to the reformulation of the Thirteen Principles of Maimonides in the liturgical hymn *Yigdal*, God's corporeality or materiality is excluded.⁵ This is most problematic for a biblically based religion reveling in anthropomorphism and anthropopathism albeit rejecting iconicism.⁶ The problem is twofold: if God has no materiality and cannot be represented by an image, how can God be imagined? If God cannot be imagined, how can God be worshipped?⁷

Yigdal's concern with theological correctness run the risk of undermining a living relationship with God. Without a living relationship, worship can border on idolatry as much as the limiting of God to a single image can freeze that relationship. God is to be associated with multiple images to reflect the fluidity and richness made possible by a polymorphous view of God. The following deals with divine polymorphism as an antidote to the lure of idolatry.

Biblical and rabbinic literature both relate to God by means of multiple metaphors. Biblically, fire is the preferred representation of God.⁸ According to Ex. 24:17, "the Presence of God appeared in the sight of the Israelites as a

---

4   See Ex. 20:3–5; and Maimonides, *Mishneh Torah*, Laws of Idolatry 2:1.
5   For the rabbinic assessment of God's corporeality, see Alon Goshen-Gottstein, "The Body as Image of God in Rabbinic Literature," HTR 87 (1994): 171–195, with David Aaron, "Shedding Light on God's Body in Rabbinic Midrashim: Reflections on the Theory of a Luminous Adam," HTR 90 (1997): 299–314. The current debate on divine corporeality in rabbinic thought is plagued by overgeneralization. The issue should be divided by rabbi, by century, and by cultural orbit, Israel or Babylonia. Rabbinic thought was no more unanimous than biblical, Second Temple, medieval, or modern Jewish thought.
6   For a comprehensive survey of the issue, see José Costa, "The Body of God in Ancient Rabbinic Judaism: Problems of Interpretation," RHR 227 (2010): 1–33, and the literature cited there, 5f., n. 15.
7   The issue challenged medieval Jewish theology; see Elliot Wolfson, "Sacred Space and Mental Iconography: *Imago Templi* and Contemplation in Rhineland Jewish Pietism," in *Ki Baruch Hu: Ancient Near Eastern, Biblical, and Judaic Studies in Honor of Baruch A. Levine*, ed. R. Chazan, W. Hallo, and L. Schiffman (Winona Lake: Eisenbrauns, 1999), 601–613.
8   See Gen. 15:17b; Ex. 3:2, 13:21f., 19:18, 24:17; Num. 9:15f., 14:14; Deut. 1:33, 4:11f., 4:24, 4:36; Ezek. 1:4, 1:13, 1:27, 8:2; Ps. 78:14; Neh. 9:12.

consuming fire" while Deuteronomy states: "on earth He let you see His great fire" (Deut. 4:36b). Frequently, the voice of God is heard while a fire is seen. Why fire? Fire transcends the classical approach-avoidance dialectic. Whereas it is magnetic and malefic, warming and burning, constructive and destructive, it is also real yet not material, visible yet not tangible, there yet not there, of form yet no fixed form. It is thus eminently representative of God who constantly appears in different forms—a multiple-manifested God.

The other way of dealing with God's appearance is by deploying the illusion of metaphors. An instructive example is the statement about God at the Exodus where God is seemingly represented by the *nesher* ("eagle" or "vulture"): "You have seen what I did to the Egyptians, how I bore you on wings of *nesharim* and brought you to Me" (Ex. 19:4).[9] The metaphor refers to Ex. 14 where the cloud intervened between Egypt and Israel protecting Israel from the onslaught of the Egyptians, as it says:

> The angel of God, who had been going ahead of the Israelite army, now moved and followed behind them; and the pillar of cloud shifted from in front of them and took up a place behind them, and it came between the camp of the Egyptians and the camp of Israel (Ex. 14:19b–20a).

The vertical image of a protective pillar of cloud in chapter 14 becomes the horizontal image of a mother bird carrying her young in chapter 19. By bearing her young on her pinions, the flying mother bird intervenes between any onslaught from below as the pillar of cloud intervened between the Egyptian onslaught from behind. Just when one feels the care of God in the image of a solicitous mother, the image vanishes, as the verse continues with "and brought you to Me." "Me" is not the *nesher*. Its use removes the image of a caring mother bird while retaining the memory of solicitude. For the sake of human imaging, God is like a protective mother to be identified with the mother bird for only a passing moment. God is not packageable in any fixed image, only intimated by multiple images, not captured by any single one. Images are temporary canes to be cast aside lest they become permanent crutches.

Rightfully perceived as polymorphous, God must be grasped through multiple metaphors lest any single metaphor predominate and edge out others. Images of God require ongoing modulation and calibration. Thus, the multiple midrashic

---

9   Alluding to this verse, Deut. 32:11 specifies "like a *nesher*."

comparisons of God to a king of flesh and blood followed by the denial that God is a king of flesh and blood. Comparable yes, identical no. What is initially helpful can be ultimately misleading.

The answer lies in denying that God is really like a human king while affirming that kingship is the best way of grasping the divine, however inadequately. What is required is a theological polymorphism filtered through multiple metaphors as in the piyyut *Kie Anu Amekha* of the Yom Kippurim Ashkenazic liturgy:

> We are Your people; You are our God.
> We are Your children; You are our Father.
> We are Your servants; You are our Master.
> We are Your community; You are our Portion.
> We are Your legacy; You are our Destiny.
> We are Your flock; You are our Shepherd.
> We are Your vineyard; You are our Keeper.
> We are Your masterpiece; You are our Craftsman.
> We are Your lover; You are our Beloved.
> We are Your cherished ones; You are our Intimate One.
> We are Your people; You are our Sovereign.
> We are the ones whom You address; You are the One whom we address.[10]

Over ten metaphors are needed to spell out the meaning of "We are Your people; You are our God." No single metaphor can capture the fluctuating relationship with God. The inadequacy of any single metaphor demands multiple metaphors to approximate the multidimensionality of the divine-human relationship. Univocality misrepresents a multivalent divinity. A single-metaphor deity is susceptible to idolization by solidifying a fluid reality into a fixed one. Even an Unmoved Mover can be fixed generating a single image.[11] A Most Moved Mover, however, revels in fluidity[12] generating multiple images balking at fixity of shape,

---

10 Or: "We are the ones, whom You have spoken for; You are the One whom we have spoken for"; see Deut. 26:17–18.

11 As can any single metaphysical alternative such as non-contingent, necessary existent, Eternal Being, and so on.

12 See Ex. 33:22: "as My Presence *passes by*, I will put you in a cleft of the rock and shield you with My hand *until I have passed by*." God's presence is in motion to be glimpsed passing by. Thus Job's surprise: "Lo, He passes by me, I see Him not; He chances by, I perceive Him not" (Job 9:11). On the fluidity of God in the Bible, see Benjamin Sommer, *The Bodies of God and the World of Ancient Israel* (New York: Cambridge University Press, 2009), chapter 2, which

place, or time. Such a God cannot be limited to a single shape, nor tied down to a single place, nor restricted to a single time. God has a shape but is incorporeal, most accessible in one place yet available in all places, most accessible at specific times yet available at all times.

Except for Stoicism,[13] Greek philosophical monotheists tended to be apologists for image worship.[14] The fact that Greek philosophical monotheism lacked an anti-iconic corollary attests to the absence of a necessary link between monotheism and anti-iconicism.[15] Even an Unmoved Mover is easily susceptible to iconic representation.

The need hence for a multidimensional polymorphous God lest a single-dimension deity become a static single representation. Polymorphism prevents the identification of God with any single image while helping us to relate to a God who transcends all images by making us aware of the inadequacy of any image for capturing the divine. Polymorphism also offers access to a relationship with God that benefits from the luxuriousness of multi-dimensionality. It turns out that divine multi-dimensionality corresponds to human multi-dimensionality allowing for a multi-faceted relationship with God. Multiple images not only undermine one-dimensional idolatry, they also enhance the vitality and meaning of our relationship with God.

This approach to images does not square easily with the picture of divine revelation at Sinai in Deuteronomy. Much was heard, states Deut. 5:20–25; nothing was seen, states Deut. 4:12 and 15. For Deuteronomy, the illusion of seeing the divine leads to the crafting of visual images; the reality of solely hearing the divine eludes the temptation of being taken in by the eyes. Nonetheless, in Ex. 19:21 the people thought that God was subject to gazing and some, according to Ex. 24:10f., may have gotten a glimpse, but even that required the use of similes.[16]

The failure of idolatry seeking to fix what is in flux is highlighted in biblical and rabbinic literature. To make the point of a literal multi-faceted God, Rabbi Levi said:

---

concludes with a discussion of the "multiplicity of divine embodiment and fluidity of divine selfhood" (ibid., 56).

13 See Menahem Stern, *Greek and Latin Authors on Jews and Judaism*, 3 vols. (Jerusalem: The Israel Academy of Sciences and Humanities, 1974–1984), 1:205.

14 Even as late as Plotinus (205–270 CE), *Enneads* 4.3.11. For the literature and the meaning of monotheism in the Greco-Roman world, see Paula Fredriksen, *Paul: The Pagans' Apostle* (New Haven: Yale University Press, 2017), 187, n. 9f.

15 The example of the iconography of the Greek Orthodox Church makes the point insofar as it is presumed to be monotheistic yet extravagantly iconic.

16 This essay does not seek to harmonize these approaches, only to spell out the implications.

> The Holy One, blessed be He, revealed himself to them at Sinai with many faces: with an angry face, with a downcast face, with a dour face, with a joyful face, with a smiling face, and with a radiant face.[17]

At Sinai, God's visage corresponded with the human response. Indeed, a multifaceted God is best positioned to address each person individually:

> The Holy One appeared to them as an image (*eikonion*) with faces on every side. If a thousand people were looking at it, it would be looking back at each of them. So it is with the Holy One. When He spoke, each and every person of Israel said: "God spoke with me," as it is written: "I am the Lord *thy* God" (Ex. 20:2).

To make the point that God appears polymorphically albeit remaining one, R. Ḥiyya bar Abba said: "He appeared to them as appropriate for each and every concern, and so in each and every matter." Thus, the Midrash says:

> Since the Holy One had appeared to them in the sea as a warrior making war (Ex. 15:3), appeared to them on Sinai as a scribe teaching Torah, appeared to them in the days of Solomon as a youth (Song 5:15), and appeared to them in the days of Daniel as an elder (Dan. 7:9, 13, 22); the Holy One said to them: "Even though they saw Me in many forms, I am the one who was in the sea; I am the one who was on Sinai; 'I am the Lord thy God.'"[18]

---

17   For this and the following two sources, see *Midrash Tanḥumah*, ed. S. Buber, *Yitro* 16f.; and *Pesikta de-Rav Kahana* 12:24f., ed. B. Mandelbaum, 223f. For an alternative analysis, see Menahem Kister, "The Manifestation of God in the Midrashic Literature in Light of Christian Texts," *Tarbiz* 81 (2021): 103–142, esp. 112f. [Hebrew]. For the issues involved in biblical and rabbinic literature, see Elliot Wolfson, *Through a Speculum that Shines: Vision and Imagination in Medieval Jewish Mysticism* (Princeton: Princeton University Press, 1994), 15–51; and Steven Fraade, "Hearing and Seeing at Sinai: Interpretive Strategies," in *The Significance of Sinai: Traditions about Sinai and Divine Revelation in Judaism and Christianity*, ed. G. Brooke, H. Najman, and L. Stuckenbruck (Leiden: Brill, 2006), 247–268.

18   This formulation of unity despite apparent diversity is the basis of the liturgical *shir ha-kavod Anim Z'mirot*. It excels in combining polymorphism and polymetaphorism while maintaining the singularity of God. Philosophically, that means: "There is a polarity in everything except God. For all tensions end in God. He is beyond all dichotomies" (Abraham Heschel, *God in Search of Man: A Philosophy of Judaism* [New York: Meridian Books, 1961], 341).

Finally, multiple dimensions correspond to the multiple capacities of the human recipient. One sound does not fit all. As God's appearance is polymorphic so God's voice is polyphonic:

> R. Yose the son of Ḥanina stated further that just as the manna, which was of one substance, could taste differently because of the individual requirements, so could the voice that went forth change for each of them according to the individual's ability to hear it, so that no harm might befall him. Observe that His voice went forth to each Israelite in accordance with the individual's capacity to receive it. The elders, the men, the youths, the little ones, the sucklings—each heard it according to his own capacity. Even Moses heard it according to his capacity, as it is said: "Moses spoke, and God answered him by (with) a voice" (Ex. 19:19), that is, with a voice that Moses was able to comprehend. Thus, it says: "The voice of the Lord was powerful with strength" (Ps. 29:1). "With His strength" is not written in this verse, but "with strength," that is, according to the capacity of each individual.

The voice of revelation modulates according to the capacity of the recipient. Even a divine voice is individually attuned.[19] In both cases, the midrash concludes with "I am the Lord thy God" eliminating any possibility of polytheism, for it is the single God who is both polymorphic and polyphonic. Whatever the case, God appears in the guise of a person always remaining personal.

The following episode relates how difficult it was for others, albeit biblically based, to grasp the biblical-rabbinic understanding of a polymorphic God.

> The Samaritan said to Rabbi Meir: "Is it possible that He Himself, concerning whom it is written 'Do I not fill the heavens and the earth' (Jer. 23:24) was speaking with Moses from between the poles of the ark?" Rabbi Meir responded: "Bring me large mirrors," and he continued: "Look at yourself in what is brought; your reflection in large!" Rabbi Meir said to him: "Bring me small mirrors," and he brought small mirrors. Rabbi Meir said: "Look at yourself in what is brought, your reflection is small!" Rabbi

---

19   See *Avot de-Rabbi Nathan* 2, ed. S. Schechter, 13.

> Meir said to him: "See how if you can change yourself whenever you want, and you are flesh and blood, how much more He who spoke and the world was, blessed is He! And so, when He wishes to be 'Do I not fill the heavens and the earth' (Jer. 23:24), He is. And when He wishes, 'He spoke with Moses from between the poles of the ark.'" Rabbi Ḥanina said: "Sometimes the world and its fullness is not capacious enough for the glory of His divinity, and at other times He speaks with man from between the hairs of his head."[20]

As multiple-sized mirrors, God can be as expansive or as contracted as the situation demands.

As it takes multiple flames to make a fire polymorphous, so it takes multiple metaphors to grasp divine polymorphism. The various guises of God simply reflect the multivalent divine-human relationship. Theological polymorphism deals with a reality exceeding any one perception. It is the biblical answer to the allure of the imaginative power of polytheism. Divine polymorphism safeguards against idolatry as well as against the reification of the divine.

As the grand master of polymorphic theology, Second Isaiah was most articulate regarding both God's transcendence and God's polymorphic immanence. On the one hand, God is eternal (Isa. 40, 41, 43, 48), incomparable (40, 46), and singular (43–46); on the other, God is father (63, 64), husband (54, 62), and pardoner (43, 44, 55).

Isaiah's polymorphic metaphors embrace both genders from warriors at war to women in birth. In one place (Isa. 42:13f.), he begins with: "The Lord goes forth like a warrior, like a fighter He whips up His rage. He yells, He roars aloud, He charges upon His enemies." And then continues: "I have kept silent far too long, kept still and restrained Myself; now I will scream like a woman in labor, I will pant and I will gasp." In the same vein, Isa. 45:9–10 begins with imagining God as a potter and culminates with God as begetter. It states: "Shame on him who argues with his Maker, though naught but a potsherd of earth! Shall the clay say to the potter, 'What are you doing? Your work has no handles?'" And then continues: "Shame on him who asks his father, 'What are you begetting?' Or a woman, 'What are you bearing?'" Elsewhere (49:14–15), consoling Israel that she is not forsaken, Isaiah begins: Zion says, "The Lord has forsaken me, My Lord has forgotten me." And then continues: "Can a woman forget her baby,

---

20 *Genesis Rabbah* 4:4, ed. Theodor-Albeck, 27f.; *Yalkut Shimoni* II:306, ed. Y. Shiloni, 457.

or disown the child of her womb? Though she might forget, I never could forget you." He even uses birth pangs metaphorically. In 66:8, Isaiah states: "Who ever heard the like? Who ever witnessed such events? Can a land pass through travail in a single day? Or is a nation born all at once? Yet Zion travailed and at once bore her children!" And then continues: "Shall I who bring on labor not bring about birth?—says the Lord. Shall I who causes birth shut the womb?— said your God." The process peaks in God identifying as a mother: "As a mother comforts her son so will I comfort you" (Isa. 68:13).

Rather than distributing various images among different gods, biblical polymorphism has them distributed among the different images of the one God. By extension, Isaiah polemicizes against idolatry for all, not just Israel. In fact, chapters 40–46 constitute the Bible's harshest critique of idolatry for anyone. For him, all is included in the One God.

The understanding of a God in flux is the counterpart of a humanity in flux. As Heschel says: "an intention of man toward God produces a counteracting intention of God toward man."²¹ How else to understand the God-Moses relationship as "face to face?"²² Indeed, to all Israel God spoke "face to face on the mountain out of the fire" (Deut. 5:4). Multiple images of God result from the ongoing interaction of the divine and the human. Both are required for their emergence, just like music requires a player and a hearer. It is precisely the absence of attachment to any physical embodiment that allows for multiple images of God. An idol of God reduces God to a single image. It is more than a limitation; it is a falsification.

A relating God is not an immovable, unchanging One. God does not embody perfection by immutability, but by properly adjusting to changing reality. Since the human factor is not fixed, the divine factor cannot be fixed. The appropriate divine image responds to the human reality.²³ Indeed, in kabbalistic thought from R. Meir Ibn Gabbai to R. Israel Baʿal Shem Tov (based on Ps. 121:5, "God is your shadow"), God's response has been understood as shadowing the human response.²⁴ This offers a way of dealing with the various images of God by

---

21 Abraham Heschel, *The Prophets* (Philadelphia: The Jewish Publication Society, 1962), 487.
22 Ex. 33:11; Deut. 34:10; see Gen. 32:31.
23 See Menaḥem Kasher, *Torah Sheleimah*, 42 vols. (Jerusalem: Beth Torah Sheleimah, 1949–1991), 8:153, #188 with note. Ex. 3:14, אֶהְיֶה אֲשֶׁר אֶהְיֶה ("I will be what I will be"), was understood as אֶהְיֶה אֲשֶׁר תִּהְיֶה ("I will be what you shall be"), by exchanging the opening א with the concluding ת based on the substitution cipher or mirror code know as Atbash; see Louis Ginzberg, *Legends of the Jews*, 7 vols. (Philadelphia: The Jewish Publication Society, 1968), 5:421, n. 128.
24 See Moshe Idel, *Kabbalah: New Perspectives* (New Haven: Yale University Press, 1988), 174–178.

different religions. In any case, the goal is "to personalize God and to affirm His presence."[25]

The God of the Bible and the Midrash is thus better characterized by pathos than by perfection.[26] In point of fact, the term perfection is never applied to God, only to His work (Deut. 32:4), His way (Ps. 18:31), and His Torah (Ps. 19:8). Perfection is static, graspable by a single act of the theological imagination; pathos is relational, graspable by a fluctuating theological imagination. As Stern notes in his work on the rabbinic *mashal*:

> The Rabbis were able to portray God's full complexity only by imagining Him in the human image. Why? Because only human behavior presented the Rabbis with a model sufficiently complex to do justice to God. In the king-mashal's narratives, the anthropomorphic imagination of the Rabbis reached its greatest height of achievement.[27]

The idea of a relational God also corresponds to the multiple names of God in the Bible. Multiple names reflect a multiple dimensional reality.[28] Maimonides himself deemed the variety of divine names, except for the Tetragrammaton, to "correspond to the actions existing in the world."[29] A relational God also enables *imitatio Dei*, an impossibility by definition for a non-anthropopathic God. Could anybody imagine an Unmoved Mover clothing the naked such as Adam, visiting the sick such as Abraham, and burying the dead such as Moses? It turns out that the least-imaged God is the most imagined God. The restraint on human-made images releases a torrent of verbal and conceptual images of the divine creating multiple viable, variable portraits of God. This sustains an ongoing living faith.

The psalmist, most famously in Ps. 115:5–8, revels in God's liveliness in contrast to the lifeless, motionless idols.

---

25 David Stern, *Parables in Midrash: Narratives and Exegesis in Rabbinic Literature*, (Cambridge, MA: Harvard University Press, 1991), 98.
26 See Heschel, *The Prophets*, 231.
27 Stern, *Parables in Midrash*, 101.
28 According to the Midrash (*Song of Songs Zuta* 1, ed. S. Buber, 6), it took a seventy-named God to choose a seventy-named Israel.
29 Maimonides, *Guide of the Perplexed* 1:61.

> Our God, who is in heaven, does all He wills
> Their idols are silver and gold, human handiwork.
> They have mouths, but cannot speak; eyes, but cannot see;
> they have ears, but cannot hear; noses, but cannot smell;
> they have hands, but cannot touch; feet, but cannot walk;
> they can utter no sound by their throats.
> Those who fashion them, all who trust in them, shall become like them.[30]

The seven deficiencies of liveliness—mouth, eyes, ears, nose, hands, feet, and voice—namely, the five senses along with motion and speech, are all specified. The psalmist then perceptively equates the worshipper with the object of worship. One becomes what one worships. Worship entails admiration, admiration entails adoration, adoration entails emulation, emulation entails identification, identification entails arrogation. The development from admiration to arrogation begins with the worship of the work of one's hands, slips into the abandonment of the worship of God, and culminates in the worship of self. Jeremiah traced the process backwards: "They have forsaken Me, sacrificed to other gods, and worshipped the works of their hands" (Jer. 1:16b). Wherefore, Jeremiah incredulously asks: "Can a man make gods for himself?" and answers "No-gods are they" (Jer. 16:20). Isaiah (Isa. 44:10–17, 46:5–7) parodies the absurdity of making and worshipping gods of human form and then beseeching them to save their makers though they cannot save themselves. He who worships what he makes ends up worshipping the maker himself. As the adage has it: "There goes a self-made man who worships his creator."

3. Idolatry of the Human

The temptation of idolatry extends most to the human. Greater than the temptation of divinizing our handiwork is the temptation of divinizing the self. Jean-Paul Sartre understood this well when in *Being and Nothingness* he famously claimed, "to be a man means to try to be God." All the more reason for the commandment, "*Thou* shalt have no other gods before Me."

---

30   Also in Deut. 4:28 and Ps. 135:15–17, idols cannot see, hear, taste, or smell. Thus, sacrifice to them is to "sacrifice to the dead" (Ps. 106:28). In contrast, Isaiah says: "O Lord, incline Your ear and hear, open Your eye and see" (Isa. 37:17).

According to the Midrash, the incipient divinization of humanity begins with Adam. The command that there be male and female to be fruitful and multiple was meant to counter the impression that the singleness of man competes with the singleness of God.[31] Subsequently, in the Bible, the divinization of the human is a byproduct of the arrogation of power. Political idolatry entails a self-aggrandizement into divinity. The greater the power the greater the susceptibility to self-idolization.[32]

The prophets already saw this as a corollary of tyranny. Isa. 36:20 describes the vaunted claim of Sennacherib, king of Assyria, saying: "Which among all the gods of those countries saved their countries from me, that the Lord should save Jerusalem from me?" Isa. 14:12–16 mocks the claim to divinity of Nebuchadnezzar, the king of Babylon, pointing out that the bigger they are the harder they fall.

> How are you fallen from heaven, O Shining One, Son of Dawn! How are you felled to earth, O vanquisher of nations! Once you thought in your heart: "I will climb to the sky; higher than the stars of God I will set my throne. I will sit in the mount of assembly, on the summit of Zaphon: I will mount the back of a cloud—I will match the Most High." Instead, you are brought down to Sheol, to the bottom of the Pit. They who behold you stare; they peer at you closely: "Is this the man who shook the earth, who made realms tremble?"

Ezek. 28:2 and 7 ridicules the Prince of Tyre's claim to divinity by attributing his downfall to it:

> Say to the prince of Tyre: Thus said the Lord God: Because you have been so haughty and have said: "I am a god; I sit enthroned like a god in the heart of the seas," whereas you are not a god but a man, though you deemed your mind equal to a god's . . . Thus,

---

31 *Pirkei de-Rabbi Eliezer* 12, ed. D. Luria, 29b; see Rashi on Gen. 2:18. *Pirkei de-Rabbi Eliezer* 11, 28a, has Adam redirecting the impulse of all the creatures to worship him, as he bore God's likeness, toward acclaiming God as king. For a similar move on Adam's part, see *Pesikta De-Rav Kahana* 4:3, ed. B. Mandelbaum, 61, lines 6–8.

32 See *Midrash Mekhilta, Shirta* 8, ed. Horowitz-Rabin, 142f., on Ex. 15:11, with Judah Goldin, *Song at the Sea* (New Haven: Yale University Press, 1971), 193f.; and Michael Fishbane, *The JPS Bible Commentary Haftarot* (Philadelphia: The Jewish Publication Society, 2002), 92f.

> I will bring against you ... the most ruthless of nations ... And they shall strike down your splendor.

Ezek. 29:3 and 8–9 lambasts the Egyptian Pharaoh's outrageous claims to divinity by showing how it sows the seeds of Egypt's ruin.

> Thus said the Lord God: "I am going to deal with you, O Pharaoh king of Egypt, mighty monster, sprawling in your channels, who said: 'The Nile is my own; I made it [or: 'I made myself']." ... Assuredly, thus said the Lord God: "Lo, I will bring a sword against you, and will cut off man and beast from you, so that the land of Egypt shall fall into desolation and ruin. And they shall know that I am the Lord—because he boasted: 'The Nile is mine, and I made it' [or: 'I made myself']."

In each case, the reality of the sovereignty of the Divine King undercuts the illusive claim of the sovereignty of the human king. The sovereignty of God challenges the sovereignty of man, the sovereignty of his achievements, and the sovereignty of his ideals.

This ancient affliction of power plagues modern totalitarian regimes leading to the replacement of God by the personality cult of the leader. The idols are the leader's images that are as ubiquitous as Jesus in Catholic churches. The point is that man is a worshipping animal. If the true God is not worshipped, false gods will be. Neither religion nor politics tolerates a theological vacuum. Take for example the various branches of atheistic Communism. Despite the differences between Russian, Chinese, and North Korean communism, all replaced the worship of God by their führer, be it Stalin, Mao Zedong, or the three generations of Kims. Both sustain a regnant political theology. Each claims the key to history in which obedience to the leader leads to political utopia.

The cult of personality also characterizes the leaders and founders of the four most consequential historical movements that have manifested fateful expressions of antisemitism: Christianity, Islam, Nazism, and Communism, namely, Jesus and Muhammed,[33] Hitler and Stalin. The linkage of the two pairs is initially

---

33 The case of Muhammed must be considered in phenomenological rather than strictly theological terms. While great care is taken in Islam to *not* afford him divine status, actions associated with protecting his status can cross theological boundaries that render his image relevant to the concerns of idolatry. The issue of blasphemy, for example, and how it finds practical expression can serve to diminish the gap between the human and the divine especially when

shocking in the light of the piety of the former and the iniquity of the latter. No two have brought more to the worship of God than Jesus and Muhammed; no two have sought to eliminate more the image of God than Hitler and Stalin. Yet, it is precisely the coalescence of opposites that raises the issue of the connection between the compromising of the singularity of God, or the replacement of God, and the drive to denigrate or eliminate an anti-idolatry Jewry or Judaism.

The Jew as the defier and denier of the divinization of any human authority in the name of the one God harks back to Roman times. Rome deified their leader through emperor worship. Julius Caesar was referred to as *Divus Iulius* ("the divine Julius"), and his adopted son Octavian, or Augustus, as *Divi filius* ("son of the deified one, son of the god"). Although unclear how literally this was taken, within three generations Octavian's great grandson, Gaius Caligula, was outraged at the Jewish refusal to call him a god.[34] According to Philo, the Jews alone in the Roman Empire opposed Caligula since they alone "acknowledge one God who is the Father and Maker of the world."[35] The recognition of God as Maker of the world was then already the antidote to vaunted human claims of divinity. A Jewry that rejects the deification of idols is predisposed to reject the deification of man.

A midrashic anecdote on Hadrian's claim to divinity further underscores the role of Israel in refusing to countenance human deification:

> After Hadrian, the king of Edom, conquered the entire world, he returned to Rome and told his courtiers: "I command you to acclaim me a god, for I have subjugated the entire world." Whereupon they replied: "You do not rule the Holy City and the Temple." He went there, conquered the Holy City, demolished the Temple, and exiled Israel. Upon his return to Rome, he said: "Now that I have destroyed His house, burned down His sanctuary, and exiled His people, acclaim me a god."[36]

---

it is translated into virulent anti-Jewish or anti-Israelism. The massacre of 2015 regarding the French magazine *Charlie Hebdo* bears this out.

34 Philo, *Embassy to Gaius* 353; see Mireille Hadas-Lebel, *Jerusalem against Rome* (Leuven: Peters, 2006), 348–355.

35 Philo, *Legatio* 115.

36 *Midrash Tanḥumah, Bereishit* 7, p. 8. Hadrian has replaced Titus here; see Moshe D. Herr, "Persecutions and Martyrdom in Hadrian's Days," *Scripta Hierosolymitana* 23 (1972): *Studies in History*, ed. D. Asheri and I. Shatzman, 85–125, in particular 116, n. 113.

The destruction of Israel is the sine qua non for acclaiming the emperor a god.[37] Israel alone stands in the way of the deification of the human, king or otherwise. By demolishing the Temple, the Roman emperor can lay claim to displacing God. A Jewry intact, however, undermines Hadrian's claim to divinity despite having conquered the whole wide world.[38]

What is noteworthy is the differing, but complementary, techniques that Christianity and Islam developed for the centering of their founders. In Christianity, images of Jesus are ubiquitous. In Islam, images of Muhammad have become non-existent in the Arab world yet sporadic in Turkey and Iran.[39] As God is not to be portrayed, neither is Muhammed. The application of "blasphemy" to the use of his picture and the entertainment of the possibility of killing the perpetrator raises the veneration of Muhammad beyond the human.[40] It is a short move from criminalizing the blasphemy of religious leaders to that of political leaders. In any case, both Jesus and Muhammad are deemed sui generis in their respective religion. The veneration of them verges, at least, on the superhuman.

What about Moses, the greatest of the prophets, lawgiver, and liberator? Scripture confirms Moses as the most faithful servant of God's household enabling God to speak to him "mouth to mouth" (Num. 12:7–8) and that "Never again did there arise in Israel a prophet like Moses—whom the Lord singled out, face to face" (Deut. 34:10). To prevent these ascriptions from being translatable into superhuman status making for post-mortem homage Scripture emphasizes "no one knows his burial place to this day" (Deut. 34:6).[41] Num. 20:10 even exposes his faults and publicly subjects him to censure. The Midrash has the fiftieth level of divine wisdom withheld from Moses, for "You have made him a little

---

37   Cicero already contrasted the fate of Israel with the fate of Rome; see *Pro Flacco* 28:69 in Stern, *Greek and Latin Authors*, 1:198. The contrasting fortunes of Israel and Rome is a recurring theme in the Midrash.
38   Accordingly, it was precisely the cult of the emperor as divine that was most opposed by the Rabbis; see Ephraim Urbach, "The Rabbinical Laws of Idolatry in the Second and Third Centuries in the Light of Archaeological and Historical Facts," *Israel Exploration Journal* 9 (1959): 149–165, 229–245, especially 238–241.
39   For textual portraits of Muhammad in early Islamic manuscripts, see Suleyman Dost, "Muslims Have Visualized Prophet Muhammad in Words and Calligraphic Art for Centuries," The Conversation.com—150053.
40   In 2020, Samuel Paty was beheaded in France for showing his students caricatures of Muhammed. On the frequency of executions in the Muslim world for blasphemy, see Wikipedia, "Islam and Blasphemy," https://en.wikipedia.org/wiki/Islam_and_blasphemy.
41   See Jeffrey Tigay, *Deuteronomy*, *The JPS Torah Commentary* (Philadelphia: The Jewish Publication Society, 1996), 412, n. 19.

less than Divine" (Ps. 8:6).[42] It also castigates him for killing the Egyptian taskmaster contending that lacking the ability to restore life as God does he lacks the right to take it.[43] In a God-centered world, no human being may encroach on the divine, exercise divine prerogatives, or elude critique. The most that Scripture confers on Moses is the oft-repeated epithet "servant of God."

4. Idolatry and Judeophobia

The four "religions" that historically have been most bent on the destruction of the Jews or Judaism have all been, at one time or another, totalitarian messianic states bent on world conquest. All laid claims to chosenness. The competition over election helps explain how hatred of the Jew became the common denominator of Christianity and Islam[44] and Nazism and Communism. Jew-hatred or, better, Judeophobia creates strange bedfellows.[45] The four world-impacting

---

42 BT *Rosh Hashanah* 21b; and BT *Nedarim* 38a. Nonetheless, the Midrash does flirt with the possibility of Moses temporally functioning as a demi-god; see *Midrash Psalms* 90:5, ed. S. Buber, 388.

43 See the Midrash on the death of Moses, *Bet Ha-Midrasch*, ed. A. Jellinek, 1:119, with Reuven Kimelman, "Terrorism, Political Murder, and Judaism," *Journal of Jewish Education* 62, no. 2 (1996): 6f.

44 On the unique status of Israel in the Islamic imagination, see, for example, Qur'an 2:47 and 122, 7:140, 44:32, 45:16; and the summary in Meir Bar-Asher, *Jews and the Qur'an* (Princeton: Princeton University Press, 2021), 37–40.

45 On the link between the self-perception of chosenness of all four and antisemitism, see Reuven Kimelman, "My Response to Alon Goshen-Gottstein's Luther the Anti-Semite: A Contemporary Jewish Perspective," *Contemporary Jewry* 40 (2020): 85–107, 91–95. The link with Christianity and Islam is obvious. Regarding Hitler, according to a conversation with Hermann Rauschning, Hitler explained his hatred of Jews insisting, "There cannot be two chosen peoples. We are the chosen people" (Hermann Diem, *Das Rätsel des Antisemitismus* [Munich: Chr. Kaiser, 1960], 7). Similar in line with his claim that Jews were in pursuit of world dominance, he could have said "There cannot be two world-dominating peoples." Parroting Hitler, the Nazi propagandist Julius Streicher, who specialized in producing antisemitic books for children such as *Der Giftpilz* [The toadstool], told a group of schoolchildren: "Boys and girls, even if they say that the Jews were once the chosen people, do not believe it, but believe us when we say the Jews are not a chosen people" (Raul Hilberg, *The Destruction of the European Jews*, 3 vols. [New York: Holmes & Meier, 1985], 1:72). A Methodist journal, *Religion in Life* (Summer 1971): 279, accordingly wrote: "It is not surprising that Hitler retaliated against the chosen race by decreeing that it was not the Jewish but the Aryan race that was chosen." Regarding the "theological" factor in the antisemitism of Communist Russia and its rabid anti-Israelism is its belief of having been chosen by history to usher in the economic and social revolution promised by Marxism; see Richard Crossman, ed., *The God that Failed* (New York: Columbia University Press, 2001). Significantly, the titles of the two parts of the book are "The Initiates" and "Worshippers from Afar." Tellingly, on October 21, 1973, the Soviet ambassador to the United Nations, Yakov Malik, was so agitated by the belief in Jewish

movements that came closest to deifying their leader/founder all regarded Jewish existence objectionable. Despite both pairs being otherwise sworn enemies, they converged on a policy of degradation and expulsion of Jewry, or elimination of their religion and/or personhood. All four were aghast at the possibility of Jewish sovereignty. For the antisemite, nothing affirms Jewish chosenness more than Jewish sovereignty. Christianity, Islam, and Communism can tolerate a subjugated, landless Jew. For Nazism, the sheer existence of Jewry threatened its own claims of chosenness. In sum, the Jew is perceived as the eternal barrier against alternative claims of chosenness and leadership idolization, whether of a religious or of a political nature. The greater the craving to supplant the Jews as the chosen people the greater the incentive to eliminate them.

The desire to minimize or eliminate Jewry has little to do with its behavior, or even its perception or non-perception of chosenness. Its very existence threatens the vaunted ideological claims of others on history by blocking their dreams of engulfing the world. Each adopted a form of Judeophobia that perceives the Jew as the mythic impediment to their messianism. For Christianity, it was the Jew as the anti-Christ.[46] For Communism, it was the Jew as the unrepentant capitalist.[47] For Nazism, it was the Jew as the defiler of Aryan purity.[48] For much

---

chosenness that he initiated a debate on Racism and Zionism, declaring, "The Zionists have come forward with the theory of the chosen people, an absurd ideology. That is religious racism." See Denis Prager and Joseph Telushkin, *Why the Jews: The Reason for Antisemitism* (New York: Simon and Schuster, 1983), 41. Malik's envious resentment was matched by the mufti Haj Amin el-Husseini, the organizer of the murder of the Jews of Hebron in 1929, who on November 2, 1943 proclaimed: "The overwhelming egoism which lies in the character of the Jews, their unworthy belief that they are God's chosen nation.... The divine anger and curse that the Holy Quran mentions with reference to the Jews is because of this unique character of the Jews" (cited in Elias Cooper, "Forgotten Palestinian: The Nazi Mufti," *The American Zionist* [March–April 1978]: 26).

46 The anti-Christ is a protean figure in Christianity frequently identified with a theological adversary. Nonetheless, without any basis in Scripture, popular Christianity tended to identify him with the Jew based on the Patristic identification of the anti-Christ with one of the tribe of Dan. Once Jews were wrongfully charged with killing the Christian savior, it easily evolved into Christ-killing and then into deicide, a charge as blasphemous to the Muslim ear as to the Jewish. Nothing grants the Jew supernatural status more than the charge of deicide. On the relationship between the Jew as anti-Christ and as supernatural, see the classic study of Joshua Trachtenberg, *The Devil and the Jews: The Medieval Conception of the Jew and Its Relation to Modern Anti-Semitism* (Philadelphia: The Jewish Publication Society, 2002), 11–53.

47 This harks back to the essay of Marx, "On the Jewish Question." His sinking to Nazi-like Jewish hatred explains Hitler's positive reference to the essay; see Julius Carlebach, *Karl Marx and the Radical Critique of Judaism* (London: Routledge and Kegan Paul, 1978), 355f.

48 It is ironic that the Soviet Union identified Nazism with Zionism, whereas Nazism identified Jewry with Communism. How a stateless people of never more than twenty million can be

of Islam, it has become the Jew as sovereign, especially over Jerusalem. Jewish sovereignty undercuts the claim of Islamic triumphalism as it does for Christian triumphalism. A subjugated Jewry, whether under Islam or Christianity, testified to their claims of supercessionism; a sovereign Jewry undermines the claim.

Once theology is tethered to politics, it rises and falls with it. A theological triumphalism predicated on political success will lash out at political successes that challenge its alleged theological supremacy. This is a problem for all religious ideologies that enter the realm of the political in the wake of worldly success.

In all four cases, the Jew and only the Jew possesses the (supernatural) power to thwart their messianic aspirations. In each case, the Jew and only the Jew bars the path to world domination. This repeated phenomena—not limited to geography, social or economic class, or culture—cannot be reduced to psychological, sociological, economic, or political considerations. Without the theological factor, it defies understanding.[49] Indeed, nothing affirms Jewish chosenness more than Judeophobia.

The more an ideological/religious group claims the mantle of chosenness, for whatever reason, the more it seeks to topple the most prominent contender to the crown. Many groups perceive themselves as chosen, only the Jews/Israel are also perceived as such by others. The irony is that haters of Jews affirm Jewish chosenness more than Jews do.

Judeophobia serves as the flipside of chosenness, not just the chosenness of Israel but the perceived chosenness of the hater. Judeophobia captures the phenomenon better than antisemitism. It is not an "ism" like capitalism, socialism, or nationalism. Otherwise, it would avoid the inflation into a phantasmagoria of fearing the Jew as part of a worldwide cabal. Would anyone think it makes sense to gang up on a local Arab for what an Arab country does in the Middle East, or to attack a local black for what a black country does in Africa, or to take it out against a local Asian for what some country does in Asia? Judeophobia is a hatred unlike any other hatred. As a phobia, it perversely targets any Jew for what Israel is perceived to have done, or any other Jew. Every Jew becomes symbolic of every other Jew. Thriving in the imagination, nourished in non-earthly

---

the bogeyman of the two most powerful murderous empires of modernity defies rationality yet demands explanation.

49 Typical of the inability to grasp, or the inadequate understanding of, the theological factor is Peter Schäfer's final chapter, "Anti-Semitism," in his *Judeophobia: Attitudes toward Jews in the Ancient World* (Cambridge, MA: Harvard University Press, 1997), 187–211. The underestimation of the chosenness factor also characterizes Amos Kiewe's recent perceptive survey in *The Rhetoric of Antisemitism: From the Origins of Christianity and Islam to the Present* (Lanham: Lexington Books, 2021), 1–16.

metaphysical soil, it requires no grounding in empirical reality. Such are the metaphysics of antisemitism.

As the barrier to idolatry, the Jew must be eliminated or denigrated lest the idolization of the leader be thwarted. In all these cases, it is not the actions of Jews that triggers the antipathy, just their sheer existence. Is it coincidental that the only country on earth unabashedly publicly committed to the destruction of another country, a non-contiguous one at that, refers to its own head as "the supreme leader" (*rahbar-e mo'azzam*), an expression comparable to *der Führer*. It also considers itself the vanguard of an Islamic takeover. Indeed, the Shi'i Islam of Iran deems only itself chosen, not all Muslims. In its eyes, Israel alone has the power to hinder the arrival of the hidden imam known as the Mahdi, the twelfth imam. Three factors come into play here: chosenness, the supernatural, and antipathy. The greater the perception of being chosen, the greater one's antipathy to Israel. The more Israel is perceived to be chosen, the more it is perceptible as having supernatural power. The more it is perceived to be supernatural, the greater the antipathy.[50] Thus, the Iranian aspiration to eliminate Israel is only graspable in theological terms. Neither politics, economics, nor nationalism are sufficient factors.

Whereas other countries may be delegitimated, only Israel and Jewry are demonized. Such is the flipside of chosenness. An account of the demonization includes the belief in Jewish exceptionalism. Inwardly, that entails being "a light unto the nations"; outwardly, that entails being subject to a double or triple standard. It is the latter that is behind the UN's obsessive condemnations of Israel. Since the creation of the United Nations Human Rights Council (UNHRC) in 2006, its anti-Israel resolutions equal that of the rest of the world combined. Nonetheless, what is important for our thesis is the correlation between despotic or religiously driven regimes and condemnations of Israel as opposed to the anti-condemnations or abstentions of democratic governments.

Political religions of totalitarian society tend to cultivate worship of their leader with his ubiquitous picture ever in view. In this regard, Kim Jong-un of North Korea and Saddam Hussein of Iraq partake of the same religio-political syndrome. Both had their portrait plastered on every public space throughout their regime. In modernity, the idolatry of flesh and blood is as pervasive as that of it in antiquity. Indeed, it may be endemic to tyranny.

Jewish tradition traces the idolatry-despotism syndrome back to the biblical Nimrod. The statement regarding him, "he began to be a mighty one in the

---

50 See the example of the Emperor Hadrian, above, nn. 36–38.

earth" (Gen. 10:8), was taken as a rebellious exertion of power against God.[51] The two converge in the connotations of "Nimrod," which in Hebrew means "we shall rebel" (against God)[52] and in old English is an epithet for tyrant. The erosion of divine power occurs in tandem with the arrogation of human power. Nimrod is listed as the first human king to "rule from one end of the world to the other, for all the creatures were dwelling in one place as they were afraid of the waters of the flood, and Nimrod was king over them."[53] Using the threat of another flood, he inveigled them to forgo their independence and accept him as protector and king instead of God,[54] thereby establishing the precedent of insinuating despotism under the pretense of protection.[55] Indeed, *The Wisdom of Solomon* 4:16f. attributes the worship of graven images to the desire of despots to be worshipped from afar. In any case, Nimrod is the first human to claim divinity.[56] Foreshadowing the role of the Jew in history as the impediment to the divinization of despots, Abraham both monotheist and iconoclast is the one who defies Nimrod by spurning his claim to divinity.[57]

The paradigm of despotic control with theological overtones is that of Pharaoh of Egypt in the Book of Exodus. His enslavement of Israel was not for their workforce to build store cites but for the reduction of their population (see Ex. 1:8) and finally their elimination. Accordingly, he plotted twice to slay the baby boys (Ex. 1:16 and 22)—something counterproductive for the increase of the workforce. Cannily, Pharaoh understood from the start that the issue was the retention of his status and image versus that of the God of Israel, as he says in his initial salvo: "Who is the Lord that I should heed Him and let Israel go? I do not know the Lord, so I will not let Israel go" (Ex. 5:2). He assumes that knowing the Lord entails letting His people go, an acknowledgement he cannot make yet keep Israel enslaved. Any concession on his part even to allow Israel to worship their God (Ex. 5:18) is an affront to his divine-like claim of total control. His major fear was of Israel taking advantage of the chaos of war to "go up from

---

51   See Alan Mittleman, *The Scepter Shall Not Depart from Judah: Perspectives on the Persistence of the Political in Judaism* (Lanham, MD: Lexington Books, 2000), 96–102; and Carol Bakhos, "Nimrod: The Making of a Nemesis," www.theTorah.com.
52   See *Genesis Rabbah* 41:4, ed. Theodor-Albeck, 408, notes and parallels.
53   *Pirkei de-Rabbi Eliezer* 11, ed. D. Luria, 28b.
54   See Naḥmanides to Gen. 10:8f.
55   See Josephus, *Antiquities*, 1:114, ed. L. Feldman, 40f., n. 291.
56   See Moses Gaster, *The Exempla of the Rabbis* (New York: KTAV, 1968), 2:2, l. 20; and *Pirkei de-Rabbi Eliezer* 24, ed. D. Luria, 56b.
57   See *Midrash ha-Gadol*, ed. M. Margulies, *Bereishit*, p. 205. For the story of Abraham and Nimrod, see Ginzberg, *Legends of the Jews* 1:191–194. See also the example of Caligula, above n. 34f.

the land" (Ex. 1:10). Their unauthorized exodus would attest to the breakdown of the system and undermine his vaunted divine-like status of being in control. His repeated reneging on his commitments of letting them go was motivated by the same need to hold on to power.

Realizing the theological implications, Moses pointedly tells Pharaoh that he would only comply with Pharaoh's request "so that you may know that there is none like the Lord our God" (Ex. 8:6b). This affirmation gets expanded with every set of plagues. So Ex. 8:18b states: "That you may know that I the Lord am in the midst of the land." Or Ex. 9:14b: "So that you may know that there is none like Me in all the world," for "the earth is the Lord's" (Ex. 9:29). Even upon capitulation, Pharaoh cannot let go nor desist from seeking to determine who and what will go. Sensing all along the theo-political import, he rejects his courtiers' plea: "How long shall this one be a snare to us? Let the men go to worship the Lord their God! Are you not aware that Egypt is lost?" (Ex. 10:7). In fact, God let Pharaoh hang on so long as an object-lesson "in order that His fame should resound throughout the world" (Ex. 9:16b). Both God and Pharaoh grasped the theological stakes involved.

One could imagine Hitler borrowing a page from Pharaoh's game plan. He also concocted the threat of the Jews to other Germans to gain their acquiescence and then their cooperation. He also created artificial work camps to disguise programs of mass murder. Most telling is his willingness to impair the German war effort against the Russian advance by commandeering trains meant to resupply German forces and diverting them to transport Jews to the death camps.[58] One could imagine Himmler protesting in the language of Pharaoh's courtiers. In both cases, the plea fell on deaf ears. Both Pharaoh and Hitler saw the conflict in either-or terms. Both perceived the survival of their despotic power as contingent upon the elimination of Israel. Both understood the stakes in theo-political terms.

In sum, as the negation of Israel can descend into a form of idolatry so can the affirmation of Israel rise to a confirmation of God. Entertaining the elimination of Israel can trigger the fantasy of the elimination of God. Opposition to Israel (the witness to God's stake in humanity and the possibility of a collective living relationship with God) goes hand in hand with opposition to an ethical

---

58   This is the thesis of Lucy Dawidowicz's *The War Against the Jews, 1933–1945*. For all the data, see the second volume of Steven Katz, *The Holocaust and New World Slavery: A Comparative History* (Cambridge: Cambridge University Press, 2019).

universal God.⁵⁹ Judeophobia thus needs to be grasped also through a theological prism, for the existence of Israel has been perceived as negating substitute and idolatrous worship patterns of arrogating to other realities authority that is God's alone.

5. Idolatry as a Human Problem

The problem of idolatry transcends the political realm. Hubris is not limited to the political. Whenever humanity overreaches its limits, driven by self-aggrandizing impulses of arrogance, hubris, and power, it inflates its own worth at the expense of that transcendent domain upon which it encroaches. Thus, it attempts to take up the space legitimately occupied by God's presence. God's presence in the world is contingent on humanity's openness and self-limitation. The greater the self-absorption, the less the possibility of divine absorption. There is no room for God in people full of themselves.⁶⁰

According to Gen. 1:28, "the image of God" entails sharing ruling with God. Created in the image of the Boss, man becomes a junior partner in running the world. He is tasked with conquering the earth and conferring names on the animals as God had previously conferred names on the works of creation. The problematic is that junior partners itch to become senior partners. Few aspire to be second-in-command. That is the difficulty in balancing the potential for partnership with the desire to be the controlling partner. Realizing this, the snake held out the promise of divinity by promising the only prerogative withheld—"knowing [that is, to be the source of knowledge, namely, of determining] what is good and what is bad" (Gen. 3:5b). Only one bite from divinity, both indulged only to seek cover fleeing from Divinity. Quashing their quest for divinity, they were punished by the harsh realities of maintaining even their human existence—birth and the need for obtaining sustenance.

The capacity to create human life can delude humanity into illusions of divinity. The first woman's punishment for such delusions was thus excruciating pain in childbirth (Gen. 3:16). Precisely at the divine-like act of giving life, women are wracked by their vulnerability and mortality. Adam, in Gen. 3:17, is also cursed regarding the bringing forth of produce from the earth. The illusions of divinity brought on by bringing forth life from the womb or from the earth are

---

59 See *Midrash Sifrei Numbers*, ed. H. Horowtiz, 84, ed. M. Kahana, 3:578: שכל מי ששונא את ישראל—כאילו שונא את המקום ("Whoever repudiates Israel is as if he repudiated God").
60 כל אדם שיש בו גסות הרוח אמר הקב"ה אין אני והוא יכולין לדור בעולם (BT *Sotah* 5a).

punctured by the harsh realities of mortality and non-divinity. The punishment fits the crime. Both can now realize their gender-based destiny only through the pains of exasperation and desperation, namely עִצָּבוֹן, the common term of both punishments, designating the anguish of bringing forth from the womb and from the earth.[61]

The root of the problem lies in the designation "image of God" itself. In Ancient Near Eastern literature, the expression is one of authority. The king alone was named "the image of the god," which established the godlike nature of the king.[62] What was once the exclusive domain of the king becomes in Genesis the lot of all. What once authorized the rule of one human over others now authorizes the rule of all humans over the world. Humanity itself, as "the image of God" is charged with exercising control over the physical world but not over others.

Mastery over the physical universe, however, kindles the desire for mastery over the moral universe. Indeed, were it not for the Sabbath intervening at the beginning of the second chapter of Genesis between the mandate of executive power over the physical universe and the limitations on humanity on determining what is good and bad in the moral universe, we would have all the makings of the pathology of power that has haunted human achievement down through the generations.[63]

The Sabbath serves as a literary break and as a metaphysical brake on the human ambition of extending the control over the physical universe to the moral universe. It is when the junior partner foregoes the prerogative of rulership in order to pay homage to the rule of the Senior Partner. Otherwise, fulltime rulership, even junior, threatens to create the illusion of total rulership. The periodic prohibition of the human mastery over the realm of nature checks human power from going amok. All human hierarchies are suspended and everyone, master, slave, employer, employee, even domestic animals, are free. By desisting weekly from imposing one's design on God's world, one expands the prospect of appreciating creation, not just manipulating it.[64] Ps. 19 is thus recited on the Sabbath when one is best attuned to perceive that

---

61 Any translation of עִצָּבוֹן (Gen. 3:16f.) will fail to catch the echoes of the preceding עֵץ (Genesis 3:11) and the adjacent עֶצֶב (Gen. 3:16).
62 See Nahum Sarna, *Genesis: The JPS Torah Commentary* (Philadelphia: The Jewish Publication Society, 1989), 12.
63 See Reuven Kimelman, "The Seduction of Eve and the Exegetical Politics of Gender," *Biblical Interpretation* 4, no. 1 (February 1996): 1–39, https://www.academia.edu/38121013/
64 For related explanations of the Sabbath, see Reuven Kimelman, "Review of 'The Sabbath', by Abraham Joshua Heschel," *Shofar* 26, no. 1 (Fall 2007): 187–190, https://www.academia.edu/38121094/

> The heavens declare the glory of God, the sky proclaims His handiwork. Day to day makes utterance, night to night speaks out.
>
> There is no utterance, there are no words; their sound goes unheard. Their voice carries throughout the earth, their words to the end of the world. (Ps. 19:1–4)

The psalm conditions the appreciation of God's handiwork on the capacity to hear its subdued messages. Only on a day free from the bustle of the week and the responsibilities of mastery can one be attuned to the broadcast of heaven reverberating throughout the world.[65]

The other check that Genesis (3:22) imposes on human power is mortality. Without the Sabbath, there would be no experience of the restraint of power; without mortality, there would be no inducement for restraint. Both underscore humanity's non-divinity by imposing limits. The Sabbath restrains the human impetus to play god; death eliminates it.

6. Idolatry and the Liturgy

Our understanding of idolatry is reflected in the Jewish prayer book through the two prayers that initiate and conclude the daily liturgy, Adon Olam and Aleinu. Aleinu defines idolatry, the impact of its elimination, and the nature of exclusive monotheism. The role of defining what is worthy of worship is also assumed by Adon Olam. "There is no other," avers Aleinu; "He has no second," avers Adon Olam. The first half of Aleinu and Adon Olam converge on the affirmation of exclusive monotheism, of God as lord of all, as sovereign from creation.[66]

Both affirmations are anchored in Creation but diverge on the theological implications. For Adon Olam, God's sovereignty, universality, and eternity in the first part make possible the divine solicitude in the second that renders

---

65 See *Siddur of R. Solomon ben Samson of Garmaise including the Siddur of the Haside Ashkenas*, ed. M. Hershler (Jerusalem: Hemed, 1971), 151 [Hebrew].
66 For their roles in the liturgy, see Reuven Kimelman, "The Theology of the Daily Liturgy," in *The Cambridge Companion to Jewish Theology*, ed. Steven Kepnes (Cambridge: Cambridge University Press, 2020), 77–101, esp. 90–94, https://www.academia.edu/44969477/

the prayer the object of divine concern where God becomes "my redeemer, my stronghold, my banner, my bastion, and my cup in time of need." For Aleinu, God's sovereignty, universality, and exclusive monotheism, in the first part generate in the second part the expectation of the universalization of God's kingship with all humanity as the object of divine concern, namely, the redemption of all. Adon Olam advances from God to me; Aleinu advances from us to them. What begins in Adon Olam as a God-individual relationship ends up in Aleinu as a God-humanity relationship. For Aleinu, idolatry is the barrier against the universal acknowledgement of divine kingship; for Adon Olam, the issue is the negation of anything comparable to God. By establishing first God's capacity and then concern, Adon Olam shows that prayer need be neither futile nor frustrating.[67] The combination of God's universal power and personal solicitude obviates any need for an alternative. God is thus characterized by both immanent transcendence and transcendent immanence.[68]

Adon Olam and Aleinu also deal with the two issues of idolatry: the relationship with the living God; the worship of something other than God. The first seeks to counter the eclipse of God; the second the substitutes for God. The alternative between the worship of God and the worship of the gods is the theme of Aleinu. The first part of Aleinu differentiates us, the worshippers of God, from those nations that "bow to naught and emptiness and pray to a god who does not save, whereas we bend, bow, and give thanks before the King over the king of kings, the Holy One, blessed be He."[69] The second part of Aleinu seeks to bridge the gap between us and them by the removal "of all idols from the earth so that all false gods will be totally eliminated; to establish the world as the kingdom of God so that all the people of flesh will call upon Your name."

Note the connection among the removal of idols from the earth, the elimination of false gods, and the establishment of the kingship of God. As the kingship

---

67 Reuven Kimelman, "The Poetics and Theology of Adon Olam," in *On Wings of Prayer Sources of Jewish Worship: Essays in Honor of Professor Stefan C. Reif on the Occasion of his Seventy-Fifth Birthday*, ed. Nuria Calduch-Benages, Michael W. Duggan, and Dalia Marx (Berlin: de Gruyter, 2019), 187–202, https://www.academia.edu/40222022/2.

68 As R. Yochanan says: כָּל מָקוֹם שֶׁאַתָּה מוֹצֵא גְּבוּרָתוֹ/גְדֻלָּתוֹ שֶׁל הַקָּדוֹשׁ בָּרוּךְ הוּא אַתָּה מוֹצֵא עִנְוְותָנוּתוֹ ("Wherever you find expressions of God's transcendence, you find evidence of God's immanence") followed by verses from all three sections of TaNaKh (BT *Megillah* 31a).

69 See Reuven Kimelman, *The Rhetoric of the Jewish Liturgy: A Historical and Literary Commentary to the Prayer Book* (Liverpool: Littman Press, forthcoming), chapter 8, "The Aleinu," section 1.

of God is contingent upon the elimination of false gods, so their elimination is contingent upon the removal of idols. According to Aleinu, this leads to the "turning to You all the wicked of the earth." The removal of false gods creates an ethical opportunity of redirecting the wicked to God.

This corresponds to the other use of "remove" in the last *U'vkhein* section of the Rosh Hashanah Amidah, which is also the origin of Aleinu. There, the line "when You *remove* tyrannical rule from the earth" is followed by "then You, Adonai, alone will reign over all Your creatures."[70] This follows the line: "evil [not evildoers] will be silenced and all wickedness [not the wicked] will dissipate like smoke."[71]

Both employ similar terms in seeking the elimination of evil in order to constitute divine rule. In Aleinu, God is beseeched "to remove the shitty idols[72] from the earth" (לְהַעֲבִיר גִּלּוּלִים מִן הָאָרֶץ) and "to turn the wicked to You." Here, the worship of false gods (אֱלִילִים), literally "puny gods," is dependent upon the existence of their idols (גִּלּוּלִים). Getting rid of the latter eliminates the former—no idols, no gods.[73] In U'vkhein, the precondition for the constituting of divine rule is "that You *remove* tyrannical rule from the earth" (כִּי תַעֲבִיר מֶמְשֶׁלֶת זָדוֹן מִן הָאָרֶץ). For Aleinu, the precondition of divine rule is the removal of idolatry; for the U'vkhein, it is the removal of despotism. Just as Israel had to be liberated from the tyranny of Egyptian rule to make way for Israel's acceptance of divine rule, so humanity has to be liberated from the tyranny of despotism to make way for its acceptance of divine rule.

The correlation between political tyranny and religious falsehood is paralleled by the correlation between the elimination of tyranny and the elimination of idols.[74] The removal of idolatrous political tyranny (*memshelet zadon*) opens the way for the universal reign of God.

The category of idolatry reminds us of the significance of having a relationship with a living God while warning us against replacements and ways of worshipping something other than God. The two are interdependent.

Adon Olam specializes in metaphors capturing the intimacy and, at the same time, the multivalence of the divine-human relationship. It underscores the living relationship with God without which the image of God could flirt with idolatrous trappings. Its use of polymorphism or polymetaphorism shows how

---

70 כִּי תַעֲבִיר מֶמְשֶׁלֶת זָדוֹן מִן הָאָרֶץ וְתִמְלוֹךְ אַתָּה יי לְבַדְּךָ עַל כָּל מַעֲשֶׂיךָ.
71 וְעוֹלָתָה תִּקְפָּץ פִּיהָ. וְכָל הָרִשְׁעָה כֻּלָּהּ כְּעָשָׁן תִּכְלֶה.
72 See Deut. 29:16 with Tigay, *Deuteronomy*, 279; and Ezek. 6:9, 16:36, 18:20, 20:8, 37:23, who couples it with terms for disgusting, detestable, and abominable.
73 לְהַעֲבִיר גִּלּוּלִים מִן הָאָרֶץ וְהָאֱלִילִים כָּרוֹת יִכָּרֵתוּן.
74 See *Sefer Pitron Torah*, ed. E. Urbach, 144, n. 56.

religious expressions can capture the multi-faceted relationship with the living God. In contrast, Aleinu negates the replacement of God by others. Its focus on the exclusive worship of God seeks the removal of all idols and their false gods to pave the way for the ushering in of the universal kingship of God on earth. Israel serves as the vanguard for the implementation of the universal worship of the ethically-concerned God. Adon Olam focuses on our relationship with God; Aleinu focuses on God's relationship with the world. The former resolves the problem of idolatry or multiple gods through polymorphism and polymetaphorism; the latter resolves the problem through the removal and elimination of the false gods and their idols paving the way for the removal of wickedness and the turning to God.

Collectively, humanity cannot exist without worship. Religion abhors a vacuum. The absence of God makes for the presence of idolatry; the absence of idolatry makes for the presence of God and the rejection of man-made alternatives. The more vital the relationship with God the more steeled the resistance to the worshipping of things and humans, whether of ourselves or of others.[75]

---

75 The essay has benefited significantly from the comments of Michael Bohnen of Boston, and rabbis Dovid Shapiro and Alon Goshen-Gottstein of Jerusalem.

CHAPTER 2

Monotheism and Idolatry: Theological Challenges and Considerations

Michael Fishbane

Introduction

We are creatures of the earth, first and foremost: it is our primary existential ground; and the multitude of appearances, both major and minor, comprise the first-order moments of our everyday reality. This panoply of experience impacts our sense of its external diversity—as both visible manifestations and modalities of creative power. Whether out of fascination or fear, both factors (manifestation and power) profoundly influence our perceptions of reality. The archetypes of our soul confirm this primary truth—by absorbing these external forms at the deepest psychic level, and then by reconfiguring them through the many expressions of our creative imagination.[1] It is therefore through its phenomenal bounty—both durative and momentary—that the world speaks to us and comes alive. Over time, tradition and individual talent give these "modes of presence" names and epithets, and thereby characterize them in diverse ways. This interpretative process emerges quite naturally, and is part of our primordial endowment as people who belong to the earth and have thought and language. In addition, our reactions to these various seen and unseen realities constitute our natural religiosity—and inspire more speculative estimations. In what sense or to what degree, one wonders, are these natural manifestations expressive

---

1 For reflections on the fragmentation and personalization of archetypal aggregates, see E. Neumann, *The Origins and History of Consciousness* (original, 1949; Princeton, NJ: University Press, 1970), 320–341.

of physical or even transcendent powers; and how (if at all) are these diverse occasions related?[2] Polytheists focus on the multitude of forms, and the primal forces that engender them; whereas monotheists center on the whole, believing diversity to be an inclusive or integral unity, empowered by one supreme divinity. Equally important are speculations regarding the character (personal or impersonal) of these forms, and the most effective ways of soliciting their powers of protection or sustenance. Such matters have life consequences, and understandably religions give them ideological and institutional priority.

As is evident from a history-of-religions perspective, sacred scriptures and religious hermeneutics are primary means of encoding these issues. Through their authoritative genres, normative topics are featured and evaluated; and cultural and conceptual boundaries are established and sustained. These include programmatic and pedagogical ideals—both theological and ideological—that provide the regulative measures by which religious conformity or deviance is assessed; and by which cultural challenges can be authoritative integrated or rejected. In addition to such positive expressions of identity, polemical juxtaposition and ideological polarization may also have a negative dimension, providing the primary means of constituting forms of "normative inversion."[3] This phrase refers to the practice of identifying those groups that represent the negative cultural antitype (or rejected "other"), whose activities are often portrayed with verbal and emotional animus. Such a dual process of identifying and segregating the "other" remains significant in our time as well—in proportion to the religious groups' perceived need of strong boundaries. Indeed, precisely because conceptual and institutional boundaries are porous and repeatedly challenged by contemporary social realities (through the easy spread of information and physical proximity), some groups dogmatize their differences and turn normative inversion into a way of life. This often results in a hardening of the ideological issues regarding rejected practices, as well as the reuse of this terminology long after authorities reclassified these or related theologies as non-idolatrous—even monotheistic, in certain cases. What is more, such dogmatic allegations were also asserted after these tropes had been appropriated as internal critiques of normative practices. In such instances, warnings against external idolatry were reinterpreted as cautions against certain ways of performing normative worship.

---

2   Still unsurpassed, and of fundamental import, is G. Van Der Leeuw, *Religion is Essence and Manifestation: A Study in Phenomenology* (London: George Allen & Unwin, 1938). Also of enduring probity is the philosophical presentation and study by W. Otto, *The Homeric Gods: The Spiritual Significance of Greek Religion* (New York: Pantheon Books, 1954).
3   For the term, see J. Assmann, *Moses the Egyptian. The Memory of Egypt in Western Monotheism* (Cambridge, MA: Harvard University Press, 1997), 216.

Routinization or formalistic practices were included among such exhortations (diverse examples shall be considered below).

*

Because of the complex dynamics of idolatry, each generation must take up the issues anew, in terms of its perceived normative constraints or values. Because the term evokes borders and distinctions, sub-communities within any particular religion regularly disagree on such matters, just as they have done in the past. The diversity of social solutions therefore provides an index of their assessment of the contemporary situation, and a sense of what constitutes religious or cultural integrity. The ensuing discussion does likewise for Judaism, being an index of my sifting and sorting of the issues. Given the complexity of the subject, the initial task will be to consider the issue of idolatry with an eye to the historical past, and the ways it has been portrayed or invoked in classical texts and traditions. This will provide a conceptual prelude to my attempt to engage these matters for myself and for this time—the postmodern era with its openness to multiple challenges and influences, and with the necessity to assess what can be appropriated with integrity, and what bears the imprint of idolatry and should be recognized and rejected as such. If the strong opprobrium once attached to "idolatry" may have diminished in modern life, it is both a premise and conclusion of this inquiry that it remains a significant category for spiritual and cultural reflection—appropriately parsed and interpreted in contemporary terms. A crucial aspect of modern Jewish theology will be the beneficiary.

How may we proceed? To develop a contemporary Jewish theological approach to the topic, grounded in traditional sources and their interpretation, I shall take the long route through historical texts. This will prevent a conceptual leap to the situation of modernity, and allow us first to consider both programmatic and polemic portrayals of idolatry on their own terms; and then, through a more contemporary formulation of the issues, evaluate their import for modern theology. In the process, the challenge to monotheism will be reformulated and rethought.

An Overview

Because the presentation will develop in several stages, I wish to provide a brief overview of my argument. I take up three topics, each highlighting a particular position in the process—with examples offered to illustrate their specific modality, not to account for every nuance or historical variation. The movement of the discussion is both linear (in the sense of an emergent sequence) and dialectical (in the sense of their internal dynamics). In each instance, one modality of religious consciousness is highlighted, alongside the type of false consciousness related to it—this latter being the particular mode of idolatry involved. Part One begins by introducing the sharp radical difference between biblical monotheistic transcendence and the mythic plenum of the surrounding ancient world—both in terms of the exalted supremacy of one divinity (deemed creator of heaven and earth and totally "other" than them and their elements), and the strong derogation of all types of physical (or featured) cultic representation, including their presumptive divine aspects. This distinction is repeatedly stressed in the biblical sources as an absolute and foundational distinction, whose blatant disregard (specified in terms of turning to "other gods" and their forms of worship) is trenchantly denounced in polemics of many kinds. The second part takes up the religious consequences of this difference, insofar as "radical transcendence" opens a space of absolute theological differentiation between God and the visible powers of the natural world, with two primary consequences: the repeated misrepresentation of the features of the world and a misapprehension of their inherent validity or efficacy (with a consequent backsliding to idolatrous practices). Thinking through these two issues will allow us to think about their conceptual correlates in modern terms. This will prepare the basis for a new theological turn. Accordingly, Part Three attempts to close the theological space between transcendence and immanence through a mystical move—one that shifts from a radical theistic difference between these two aspects, to a recovery of divine plenitude. This turn reconceptualizes the older mythic plenum in monotheistic terms, and introduces new theological engagements with the transcendent mystery of God. In the process, the tasks of the religious life undergo a fundamental epistemological shift, and the meaning of idolatry is reinterpreted.[4] It is toward this fundamental reconsideration that my presentation aims. The preceding generalities provide the overall framework; I now spell out the details.

---

4   Upon completion, I realize that this typology (which moves from a monotheistic rejection of mythic potencies to their mystical retrieval) parallels the dialectic proposed by G. Scholem, in his *Major Trends in Jewish Mysticism* (New York: Schocken Books, 1941), 7–10. This factor notwithstanding, our two dynamics serve different cultural purposes. Thus, my dialectic must be assessed on its own terms.

I. The Mythic Plenum and Monotheistic Aniconism

Cultures often come to self-definition through deliberate contrasts, as do their individual adherents—and over the generations these cultural countertypes (as perceived and as inculcated) provide primary layers of identity. The frequently marked differences between "Egypt" and "Israel" are a striking example of this phenomenon, both in the canonical articulation of the differences in Scripture, and in their ongoing explication throughout Jewish literature. To rethink the issues involved requires one to conceptualize the cultural-ideological issues at stake. Not being able to transcend ourselves, the ensuing evaluation inevitably constitutes a contemporary variant of a multi-millennial process, based on our modern reading of the sources.

Two primary Scriptural moments will set our discussion in motion. The first involves the theomachy (or divine battle) of the plagues; the other concerns the Second Commandment. They are inherently correlated.

Among the notable features of the divinely wrought plagues is that they are presented as counterpoints to the sources of life: blood—as death and the pollution of water (the source of irrigation, arising from the earth itself); pestilence—as the destruction of crops and herds (the natural and animal sources of food); and utter darkness—as the eclipse of the solar luminaries (and the capacity to see by day and navigate by the evening stars). Indeed, more than primary inversions, the plagues constituted a veritable assault on the Egyptian deified powers of sustenance and survival by an unknown god of vagrant slaves, upon whose backs the stones of the immortal pyramids were carried, and through whose labor wheat was threshed and baked. As the Scriptural source stresses, such were horrendous events "the likes of which had never happened in Egypt" (Ex. 9:18 and 10:10)—events that signified the defeat of the local deities, high and low. Such in fact was the pronouncement of the perpetrating God, who said: "I shall wreak judgments against all the gods of the Egyptians" (Ex. 12:12), and as repeated in retrospect by the wandering people years later (Numbers 33:4).[5] For these gods were the named embodiments of the mysteries of sky and water, seeds and flocks—all teeming, spontaneously, as they received vitality from the sun-body of Atum who emitted and begot the gods of air (Shu) and fire (Tefnut), and then Geb (earth) and Nut (heaven), even unto the fourth generation. Out of this primordial, all-generating cosmogonic power (deemed and called *khefer-djesef*, or "the self-generated one") emerged all the

---

5 This polemical motif appears as a *theologoumenon* voiced by Jethro in Ex. 18:11.

biomorphic forms of life and energy. Like the scarab with which Atum was identified, all things emanated or somehow were secreted from his being. If there is any deeper principle here, it is the inherent unity and correlation of things, despite their external forms; and the sense that they communicate an "immediate signification" of meaning.[6] Shapes are what they are, as primary expressions of divinity; and yet, within this mythic plenum, they are but sacred portions of a "single essential substance."[7] Whether you turn to the (just-noted) Helepolitan cosmogonies or those from Memphis;[8] or you read the Coffin texts—similar theogonies (or the mythic accounts of the genesis of the gods) about self-created emergence recur. Listen, for example, to the following hymn to Amon-Re from about 1400 BCE, and thus shortly before the Exodus: "He came forth self-generated, all his limbs speaking to him"; and then more directly: "You have taken on your first form as Re ... You created all that has come into existence and all that exists."

Given the divine inherency presumed in all things, and the direct correlation between the forms of divine representation and their innate reality, is it any wonder that the initial self-presentation of Israel's God at Sinai, pronounces: "I am YHWH who took you out of the land of Egypt" (Ex. 20:2); and immediately thereafter the commandment: "you shall have no other gods (*elohim aḥerim*) besides Me" (Ex. 20:3)? Surely not; for with this conjunction, it is clear that the epithet ("who took you out of ... Egypt") is more than a proclamation of political theology[9] (YHWH as the supreme Lord), and inextricably coupled to its fundamental corollary: the absolute prohibition of theolatry *and* all modes of representation—be they in the heavens or on the earth (Ex. 20:4). Aniconism

---

6   The term recurs in A. Assmann, *Die Legitimität der Fiktion. Eine Beitrag der literarischen Kommunikation* (Munich: W. Fink, 1980).

7   This is the formulation of J. A. Wilson, in *The Intellectual Adventure of Ancient Man* (Chicago IL: The University of Chicago Press, 1946), chapter 3, 68. He also speaks on "consubstantiality" (ibid., 68, 70).

8   For a host of the texts annotated here, see especially S. Sauneron and J. Yoyette, "La naissance du monde selon L'Égypte ancienne," in *La Naissance du monde: Égypte, Akkad, Hourrites et Hittites, Canaan, Israel, Islam, Turcs and Mongols, Iran préislamique, Inde, Siam, Laos, Tibet, Chine*, ed. A. Esnoul (Paris: Éditions du Seuil, 1959), 17–91. For others citations, see also J. Assmann, "Creation through Hieroglyphs: The Cosmic Grammatology of Ancient Egypt," in *The Poetics of Grammar and the Metaphysics of sound and Sign*, ed. D. Shulman and S. La Porta (Leiden: E. J. Brill, 2007), 17–34. See also the summary assessment in Wilson, *The Intellectual Adventure*, 50–61.

9   For a fully developed analysis, see J. Assmann, *Politische Theologie zwischen Ägypten und Israel* (Munich: C. F. von Siemans Stiftung, 1992).

is thus a primary polemic, and cuts far deeper than theological loyalty.[10] It is, in fact, the cultic corollary of a new mode of religious consciousness, one that we may label "radical transcendence." God is "other" than the world, and there is no inherent or objective correlative between the two, in whole or in part.[11] Hence, figurative representations are absolutely prohibited. To drive this point home, a later homily expanded on the brief statement in Ex. 20:4, which only refers to the things in heaven and earth in general terms, filling in the polemical space with a specification of the entire order of creation. In this extended polemic, Moses alludes to all the elements of divine creation in Genesis 1—starting with human forms and moving through the creatures of earth and sky to the heavenly bodies, in what is manifestly a deliberate reversal of the latter sequence. Thus, using the teaching of Genesis 1 as blueprint of potential images and powers, the result is a vigorous prohibition of all forms related to the visible or sensate world (Deut. 4:16–19).[12] And why are they so vigorously prohibited? Because, it is stressed, when God appeared to the people at Sinai, the people saw no image, but only heard a voice (Deut. 4:12 and 15). In contrast to the eye, and the earth-bound imagination, the ear has no spatial correlation. Hearing occurs in time, as something received—and not as something perceived in spatial terms.

Radical theological transcendence thus introduces a revolutionary moment that marks a fundamental cognitive break with the mythic plenum, and its principle of correlation or partial representation of divinities or divine powers. The new mindset is disjoined from seeing within the forms of the world potential figurations or representations of God. Even more, there is no permitted embodiment of God's acts of creation in the phenomenal world. The cognitive disjunction between what is perceived and what (or "Who") one is dependent upon is absolute. To accede to this kind of monotheism imposes a new mode of religious consciousness, one that takes a preeminent role in the hierarchy

---

10 It bears emphasis that the crucial issue in the prohibition of images is the cultic representation of God, *not* the reported figural appearances in prophetic vision *or* the imaginal expressions and depictions of God (in terms of volition, mood, or activity) in poetry and prayer. This distinction is often disregarded or variously obscured.

11 I stress the word "inherent" since there is, of course, one significant exception: the human being was created in the "form and likeness" of God. Certainly, the issue of creation is the distinctive element; though it must be stated, and is significantly overlooked, that the human creature is the only creation not brought into existence by the divine word, or speech. And with respect to this event, we have voluble mythic overtones: in Gen. 1:26 we read: "let us make (*na'aseh*) man;" and in Gen. 2:7 the formulation is: "[The Lord God] formed (*va-yitzer*) the man from the dust of the earth."

12 See already my comments in *Biblical Interpretation in Ancient Israel* (Oxford: The Clarendon Press, 1985), 321–322; and the initial formulation in my "Varia Deuteronomica," *Zeitschrift für die alttestamentliche Wissenschaft* 84 (1972): 349.

of divine commandments. Indeed, the fundamental significance of this theological demand is signaled not only by its primary position among the norms that follow, *but also* by its address to one's personal religious life. The imperative "You shall not have (*lo yiheyeh lekha*) other gods besides Me" (Ex. 20:3), means that one must not have other gods "for yourself (*lekha*)." And with this strong emphasis on the spiritual life of the worshipper, the onus of false worship is focused both on ritual behavior and (on an incorrect or false) theological consciousness. The worshipper is warned to be vigilant regarding the appeal of the mythic plenum, and not be drawn into any seduction to the arresting vitalities of the world. This theological position regarding absolute transcendence, focusing on both its cognitive recognition and its ritual preservation, is the center of the new religion. It is also, I believe, the ideological core for all those who would receive Scripture as a religious document addressed to their theological life (and not solely to their social solidarity). Hence, this issue is also the pivot of the present discussion. To state my point somewhat differently: *the initial theological command against idolatry is concerned with making the spiritual-cognitive event of liberation* (from nature and the mythic plenum) *into a permanent epistemic endowment*. The need to negate any and all forms of representation is thus a foremost necessity of the positive apprehension of transcendent monotheism. Self-monitoring is therefore crucial; the imperative of *lo yihyeh lekha* is addressed to one's theological integrity. I consider this to be a consideration of foundational value, with central bearing on any modern Jewish religious psychology—one that will require an equally radical rethinking of the nature and limits of human expression. Eventually the theological point will be asserted: "To whom (*mi*) will you liken (*tidamyun*) God, and what (*mah*) form (*demut*) compare to Him?" (Isa. 40:18).[13] The challenge to hand, eye, and mind is formidable.

II. The Dialectics of Difference and the Problematics for Monotheism

Let us think further about the spiritual dangers of having "other gods" from this conceptual and theological perspective; for the radical disjunction between the perceptual (or phenomenal) world and the imperceptible (and trans-phenomenal) otherness of God is not easily maintained or sustained—as a significant

---

13   There is no doubt that this, too, is a polemical challenge to Genesis 1—in this case Gen. 1:26. Cf. Isa. 40:25.

amount of Biblical evidence indicates.[14] There is repeated evidence of an ongoing fascination with, and stimulation by, the powers latent and manifest in the forms of the world—in trees and wind; in thunder and rainclouds; in animal life and vegetal growth. The expressions of the world stimulated a natural sense of dependence upon the manifestations of life, and the divine powers inherent therein—and certainly on the divine powers that were traditionally worshipped throughout Canaan. From the beginning, as the prophet Hosea laments, the people's "mouth" was filled with 'the names of the Baalim"—calling them "My Baal" (Hos. 2:19) and asserting: "I will go after my lovers, who supply my bread and my water, my wood and my linen, my oil and my drink" (Hos. 2:7), not knowing who was the true source of vitality and efficacy (Hos. 2:10). Accused of a false religious consciousness, the people followed natural instincts and needs—the tangible expressions of their tangible needs. Jeremiah continues this polemic, accusing the people of defiling the land through lusting after the local gods of the land, lying in worship under sacred trees, and saying, "I love the strangers (*zarim*) and shall follow them (*aḥareihem*)" (Jer. 2:25)[15]—not realizing, beyond their apostasy, that such gods were ultimately futile forces, that could not "save" them in times of need (Jer. 2:28). This heated invective of ignorance and folly (ignorance of the transcendent source of beneficence, and folly in following their physical instincts) was repeatedly conjoined with others, filled to the brim with irony and sarcasm. It is to these polemics especially that we now turn to help us think further about idolatry and its bearing on contemporary theology.

The first text to consider is Isaiah 44—certainly one of the most provocative polemics in Scripture. It is the product of the late, post-exilic prophet Isaiah, who proclaims a theology of pure monotheistic universalism (virtually for the first time). After asserting his primary assertion that the Lord God is the "first" and the "last," and veritably the "only God" (Isa. 44:6 and 8),[16] he proceeds to mock those who create of "form" idols and their product: those who make these objects are "wastrels" (*tohu*) and the upshot "without benefit" (*lo yo'il*)—for they do not realize the folly of their labor and are not ashamed (Isa. 44:9). What they "do" is spiritually ludicrous: they forge iron implements to cut trees,

---

14   I presented a full spectrum of evidence in my essay, "Israel and the Mothers," in *The Other Side of God*, ed. P. Berger (Garden City, New York: Anchor Press and Doubleday, 1981), 28–47.
15   These terms blatantly refer to false gods, specifically the so-called *elohim aḥerim* ("other gods").
16   This theological formulation is also found in Deut. 4:39, toward the conclusion of an apparently post-exilic supplement.

measure their girth and frame an idol from this mass; and then, with double folly, use the wood as fuel to heat their food and warm their bodies, and with the remainder make a "god" and bow down in worship, saying: "Save me, for you are my god" (Isa. 44:17)—never thinking to say: "Surely my right hand acts falsely" (Isa. 44:20). Vitriolic mockery aside, two profound theological matters are involved. One is the "nature" of the cultic object; the other is the "act" of attribution and interpretation. They are both expressions of folly and hubris.

What is so striking in this polemic is the misprision of what it means to be a creature who tries to "act" on one's behalf with a theological intervention—in this instance, the construction of an idol from the world itself with the irony of its double usage (that the wood both gives creaturely warmth and is considered a giver of spiritual salvation). If the first act is merely utilitarian, using the wood of a tree, the second attributes divine agency through another portion of that same earthly object. What the idol-maker does not realize is the category mistake of believing one's act of creation is more than a figure of the human imagination—that attributions and representations are not the "thing itself" (whatever that may be). In contemporary terms, the cognitive error involved in making physical images of God is one of misattribution, and the failure to be properly mindful of one's role in such acts of signification. The idolater fabricates (in a double sense) constructs of the world without taking responsibility for their misappropriation or self-contradictory nature. That is, as a type of *homo faber* (a maker or fabricator), the idolaters forget that they are constituted by the same reality they are recomposing. The principle of transcendence (as I now appropriate it) requires a person to live within the cognitive space of delimitation, with theological cognizance of the creative limitations of all human acts of signification. To disregard this issue is to mistake (or misconceive) the nature of human transcendence (when one falsely thinks they are somehow more that "mere nature"), and thus reify elements constructed from the world, of which we are a natural part.[17] In this double sense, modern idolatry is a willful or ignorant misuse of the work of one's mind. I would therefore suggest that what is involved is both a *forgetting of the divine principle of transcendence* and *not giving proper regard to human limitations*. I shall return to this matter below.

To deepen the cognitive folly ridiculed by Isaiah, we now turn to the second conceptual error of our passage. It is one of hermeneutical hubris: an assertive

---

17 For a profound philosophical consideration of the issue of the human laboring animal as a *homo faber*, and the dangers of reification, see H. Arendt, *The Human Condition* (Chicago, IL: University of Chicago Press, 1958), chapter 19 (on the related issue of "makers" who have conceptual images in mind, see further below).

act of theological attribution and misrepresentation. When the idol-makers say "You are my god," they are "doing" what Austin would call "something with words"—they are engaged in a performative act that transfers reality to an object through speech,[18] all the more problematic for it being an assertion of theological sense and significance; and for having no inner reflexivity wherewith to critique one's action (that is, the maker doesn't have sufficient wisdom to reflect and say "I have burnt half for fuel ... and with the remainder have acted abominably, bowing down to a tree trunk"; Isa. 44:20). From this perspective, the folly of idolatry includes a lack of hermeneutical distance between thought and language, between meaning and its implication. Hence the presumption of the idolater even lacks the sense of shame that such a cognitive perspective brings (Isa. 44:9). Acts of idolatrous representation thus attribute a "false concretion" to the object signified, and presume that this very act of linguistic signification actualizes a transcendent reality. Jeremiah voices the cultic drama of this act when he fulminates against his contemporaries who "say to the tree, 'you are my father (*avi attah*),' and to the stone, 'you have given birth to me (*at yeliditani*)'" (Isa. 44:27).[19] Only a fundamental change of consciousness would result in the retraction: "We shall no longer say 'our gods' (*eloheinu*) to the work of our hands" (Hos. 14:4).[20]

A related polemic drives the preceding issues deeper; for like these texts, which link the folly of the idol-maker with his fallacious results (each being empty and worthless), Ps. 115 also specifies the inconsequence of the idols, but then makes a more telling critique of such worshippers. Referring to the non-Israelite "others" who make idols in the image of themselves, with mouth and eyes and ears and nose, and with arms and legs to boot, the psalmist poignantly adds that not only are these figures incapable of speech or hearing or touch or movement, but that "their makers"—who trust in them—"are just like them" (Ps. 115:4–8). The external acts thus transform the actor reciprocally: false theological presumptions produce correlative mentalities. Instead of producing living gods, they

---

18 See J. L. Austin, *How to Do Things with Words*, ed. J. O Urmson and M. Sbisa (Cambridge, MA: Harvard University Press, 1962).

19 I am reading the Masoretic text with the *ketiv*. The theological counterpoint, for the future, is when the people will say: "You are my father (*avi attah*), the companion of my youth" (Jer. 4:4).

20 The text of the prophet Hosea is replete with idolatrous acts. In other books, of particular note in this context are the acts of divination by means of a "staff" (Ex. 4:12), and ritual offering under sacred trees (Ex. 4:13). In the latter case, one may wonder whether the two poplars mentioned there, *elon* and *elah*, do not refer to male and female deities manifest in these entities.

themselves become mindless "things." This is a hermeneutical critique of a false religious consciousness taken to the extreme: the idolater becomes like the work of his hands, an impotent object. Hence, idol-making is both transformative and constitutive of their makers in equal measure. The hermeneutical act is ineluctably entwined with its physical expression. You are what you make (or what you don't think about when you make it)—as Gershom Scholem adroitly implied, with profound modern concern, when he inaugurated a new computer at the Weitzman Institute of Science in 1965, dubbing it a golem consigned to deadly possibilities, if it merely served as an extension of pure ingenuity, and not humane principles of life.[21]

*

I wish to turn at this point to a related reflection on the conjunction of radical transcendence and aniconism, deepening my discussion of the connection between language and attribution, and thereby bringing into play some other considerations bearing on theology and idolatry.

The worship of the golden calf at the foot of Mount Sinai marks a paradigmatic event of collective idolatry. At the surface and factual level, the narrative reports that with Moses's ascension to God on Mount Sinai, and continued absence, the people were distraught, and asked Aaron to "make gods for us, who will go before us—because we don't know what has happened to Moses, the person Moses who took us up from the land of Egypt" (Ex. 32:1). And if this contrast with the divine self-proclamation at the beginning of the Decalogue, which states "I am the Lord, your God, who took you out of the land of Egypt" (Ex. 20:2), were not sufficiently striking, then also note what the people assert after the idol is made: "These are your gods, O Israel, who took you out of the land of Egypt" (Ex. 32:4). Two substitutions are involved, effecting the inversion of the principles of divine transcendence and aniconism. The first is the substitution of Moses for God; the second, of molten idols for Moses, now called gods (in the plural, thereby activating the inherent multiplicity of the polytheistic term *elohim*). Such displacements—from God to human to physical image—mark the religious (and natural) need for concrete presence. Thus, invisible divine transcendence devolved into a human representation; and the occlusion of the latter resulted in a cultic image. Idolatry thus takes diverse forms, because of the problematics of presence, resulting in cases of faulty

---

21 See G. Scholem, "The Golem of Prague and the Golem of Rehovot," in his *The Messianic Idea in Judaism* (New York: Schocken Books, 1971), 335–340.

attribution (or, as Whitehead would say, of "misplaced concretion"), topped-off by the performative enunciation: "These (*eleh*) are your gods (*eloheykha*)," at the conclusion of the fashioning of the idol. We thus have a striking parallel to what was noted earlier regarding Isaiah, where the act of constructing an image (Isa. 44:12–16) was followed by its proclamation as a god (Isa. 44:17). In both instances, divine transcendence was compromised, to the detriment of human cognition.

*

Going beyond the primary narrative, let us think about this act of designation in contemporary terms, which raises its stakes for modern theology.

As exemplified above, unthinking acts of linguistic designation blend together sign and signification, with the result that there is no conceptual interval perceived between the thing named and its denomination. The thing named is deemed the thing itself, as it were; and, as a result, there is a disregard (or, in Isaiah's locution, a misunderstanding) of the creative interval between the act of speech and the world that it creatively indicates or refers to. Such an elision obscures cognizance (and thus responsibility) for the locutions and their effect. These epistemological consequences are even more significant in a theological context, to the extent that these cases of "naming God" (as an assertion or characterization) are presumptive acts of human attribution; and they border on the idolatrous when they go beyond individual acts of testimony (naming a moment or event of divine manifestation) and purport to be reified or substantive indices of divinity. In such circumstances, idolatry is the counterfeit coin of the worldly realm, falsely presuming that one's mind and language can purchase an ultimate theological truth and meaning. And thus, instead of a person realizing the impossibility of naming or signifying the transcendent "Divine Other"—so utterly beyond imaginal representation (figural or figurative)—one is blinded by hermeneutical hubris. The unnamable horizon of infinitude collapses into the channels of cognitive presumption. Linguistic and cognitive idolatry are the result.

For its part, medieval Jewish philosophy has worn the mantel of radical transcendence and conjured positive assertions about God or theology into topics of new or transformed significance. Thus, the noble path of philosophical theology was deemed a way of negation; that is, its goal was to unsay or negate the natural idols of the mind (or also the anthropomorphic images of tradition), and through this process to purify and redirect the mind towards an absolutely imageless account of God and divine reality. This process of purification of Scriptural images and terms emerged with particular vigor with R. Saadia

Gaon,[22] and achieved its classic expression in Maimonides's celebrated opening seventy chapters of part one of *The Guide of the Perplexed*—where the images of God mentioned in Scripture find their allegorical recalibration in hyper-rational terms. Certainly, this is an intellectual achievement of monumental proportions; and has continued unabated to our age, when a philosopher of the stature of Hermann Cohen substituted rational cognitions and mental structures of God for immediate theological experience and expression.[23] Emptying the mind with legerdemain, the bounty of the world is thereby rationalized and conceptualized—and the modern dangers of instrumental rationality and scientism fill this void. Max Weber famously proclaimed this form of cognitive transcendence to be a first cousin to the "disenchantment" of the world, and the death-knell to the mystery of divine presence.[24] Worship of the technological work of one's hands, based on the reification of mental images, takes place in the desanctified canopy of quantitative time and space. We are thus faced with a theological question. Can a viable version of divine transcendence (radical and ultimate) be formulated that doesn't dilute the wonder and mystery of worldly plenitude, but may actually envelop it and deepen its dimensions? And if so, how might that formulation recalibrate both monotheism and idolatry? I take these questions as a spiritual provocation and intellectual challenge. The ensuing final Part will try to respond in a positive way.

III. Qualifying Unknowable Transcendence and Transforming Divine Plenitude

We yearn to close the gap between ourselves and the divine. Can we do so without falling prey to idolatrous mentalities? The concluding movement of our dialectic aims to reinstall the mystery of transcendence as an expression of divine plenitude. This means constructing a new theological epistemology—a three-step process based on three striking instances of mystical hermeneutics.

---

22 See the instructive essay by S. Rawidowicz, "Saadia's Purification of the Idea of God," in his *Studies in Jewish Thought*, ed. N. N. Glatzer (Philadelphia, PA: The Jewish Publication Society of America, 1974), 246–268.
23 See, in this regard, M. Buber's critique of Herman Cohen, in his "The Love of God and the Idea of the Deity," found in M. Buber, *Eclipse of God: Studies in the Relations between Religion and Philosophy* (New York: Harper & Row, 1952), 52–62.
24 See his famous essay, "Science as a Vocation" (1919), for the term *Entzauberung*, republished in his *From Max Weber: Essays in Sociology*, ed. H. H. Gertz and C. Wright Mills (Oxford: Oxford University Press, 1946), 148.

I begin with a consideration of the people's proclamation in Ex. 32:4, at the completion of the molten calf: "These (*eleh*) are your gods"—as interpreted in the Zohar (I.2a). The significance of the passage lies in its central position near the beginning of the 'Introduction' to the Book of Zohar, thus joining the mystery of creation and idolatry as a primary concern. Just prior to this unit, we are informed about two spiritual realities, which originate in the most hidden, transcendental realm of divinity, but which can also be experienced or perceived here below, in our worldly existence. Both elements are hinted at in Isa. 40:26: "Raise your eyes on high and see who (*mi*) created these (*eleh*)?" In its Scriptural context, this exhortation is to the individual to look upward to heaven and realize "Who" (God) created this cosmic spectacle and its heavenly bodies. But for the mystics of the Zohar, more is at stake. They say, first, that the word *eleh* designates the lowest part (or final "rung") of the divine emanation, which extends earthward and is mirrored in the creation of our universe, whose concluding statement is: "These (*eleh*) are the generations or the heavens and the earth" in Gen. 2:4. Hence, *eleh* symbolizes the perceptual world, emanating from hidden recesses of wonder, which is beyond understanding, at the absolute border of the imaginable. For that reason, the supernatural world is called *mi*. "Who?" is thus a limit-term for absolute mystery.[25] To look upward, to the heights, is therefore to bring one's mind to the hidden wonder of being. The evocative word "Who?" is the ineffable indication of the divine "Beyond."[26]

We are now in a position to read the following:

> Seeking to be revealed, to be named, it [the theological symbol *mi*] covered itself in a marvelously radiant garment and created *eleh*. *Eleh* (אלה) attained the (Divine) Name "*Elohim*" (אלוהים) by joining its letters with those of *mi* [thus: e-l-h + im]. Until it [*mi*] created *eleh*, it did not attain the name *Elohim*. Because of this mystery [of the conjoined names], those who sinned with the golden calf [only] said "These (*eleh*) are your gods, O Israel"

---

25 Zohar II.231b stresses the essentiality of this question and comments on its irreducible nature, when it states that the question—the perception of a supernal divine gradation as *mi*—"ever remains a question (*qayyema tadir le-she'ela*)." Commenting on the radical formulation of this principle in Zohar I.1b, the sixteenth-century kabbalist R. Shimon Lavi made this striking statement: "Regarding whatever cannot be grasped: its question is its answer!" See in his *Ketem Paz* (Djerba: J. Haddad, 1940), I.91a. Elsewhere in Zohar I.1b *mi* is described as a "healing" dimension, "that concealed, supernal rung in which all exists"—through the deferment of all limit and delimitation (proclaiming the positivity of an absolute negative theology).

26 This summation occurs in Zohar I.1b.

(Ex. 32:8). Just as *mi* is combined [primordially] with *eleh*, so the name *Elohim* is forever undergoing [creative] combinations. On the basis of this mystery [of the recombinant names], the universe exists.

How can we understand this passage? One major thrust is that the mystery of existence, indeed, of all being, is the infusion of "mystery" with "things." The actuality of perception, here on earth, is grounded in the multiple things that God created, setting them out in different forms and orders and relationships. This is the external world of reference and comparison—the world to which we point and which we name. *Eleh* is thus a deictic or referential term for things that can be known or indicated. By contrast, *mi* opens the eyes to wonder and mystery, in the way that a question unsettles a formulation. Such attention to the marvel of reality does not (and cannot) name this reality as such, for *mi* is but a mark of speculative awe. What *mi* adds to *eleh* is the transcendent dimension of "otherness" ever latent in all perception, as well as the realization this combination of two elements is the mystery of the Divine Name "*Elohim*." And more: since our worldly perceptions (the domain of *eleh*) are constantly changing, the terms of this sacred name are also constantly mystically recombinant. Thus, although the name *Elohim* is externally one in appearance and sound, it spiritually actualizes every transformation existent in our world. To reduce the world to *eleh* (devoid of *mi*) is therefore to truncate and traduce its all-embracing divine mystery. It is to see things as just "this" and "that"—secularities without God. This is idolatry plain and simple, says the Zohar: the evident achievement of all those for whom the world is reduced to thingness, to be used and manipulated. The idolater's mind makes attributions, but has lost any sense of transcendent magnitude. The counterpoint is spiritual humility. Such spiritual disposition is a first step towards the restoration of existence as a bountiful divine plenitude.

*

We may now take the next step in the epistemological process. To do so, I would like to begin a discussion with the word *anokhi*, the opening divine assertion of the Decalogue ("I am"). It has become an important expression of Hasidic thought, following a question the "Holy Jew" (R. Ya'akov Yitzhak Rabinowitz) asked his student, R. Simhah Bunem Bonhardt of Peschishke, what Biblical passage marks the theological core of Judaism? The latter surmised that it was Isa. 40:26, cited above, which lauds God as the creator of nature. But the master demurred and said that such a proposition might hold for humankind as a whole, but the core of Jewish theology is the word *anokhi* (the divine "I," expressed at

Sinai), since it marks the beginning of a unique spiritual connection between God and humans—which is fundamentally different from a starting point in the world of nature.[27] In terms of our earlier discussions, this insight suggests that the monotheistic breakthrough is marked by a divine self-proclamation that demands exclusive worship together with the rejection of "other gods"; and addresses itself to human subjects. This new theological moment thus catalyzes a strong sense of human transcendence (spiritual and cognitive responsibility), inspired by a supervening transcendent subject.[28] This insight granted, a later disciple of Simhah Bunem, R. Mordechai Yosef Leiner (known as the "Izhbitzer"), gave further import to the word *anokhi* by capitalizing on a minor lexical variation. Pondering why the word *anokhi* (אנוכי) was employed at this juncture, rather than the more common first-person pronoun *ani* (אני), the Izhbitzer remarked that the letter *kaf* (כ) was inserted into the latter word to highlight that all our human conceptions of divinity are fundamentally limited by our mortal mind and imagination. As mortal creatures, we perceive the world and theological realities by linguistic indirection, by comparison and similitude—and this epistemological approach is symbolized by the letter *kaf*, which serves (here and elsewhere) as a stand-in for *ke-* or *kemo* (כ- or כמו, in the sense of "like").[29] Given the limits of our human capacity, nothing transcends this mode of thinking, not even the phenomenon of language itself—insofar as words name things by means of conventional attribution, and do not constitute the designated object "as such." By inserting this letter *kaf* into the divine self-proclamation, we are told that all theology statements (and even interpretation itself) is qualified. Put differently, the signifier *kaf* highlights (for cognition and for theology) that the transcendent truths of divine reality must pass through the limited constructs of the sign-making human mind to be formulated and comprehended. This being so, the world we "know" lies in the shadow of mortal cognition, which filters and mediates the transcendent light of God's creation. Indeed, according to the Izhbitzer, all our theological cognitions and interpretations are "merely a *demut* and *dimyon*" (an "image" and "imaginal figure") of ultimate divine reality and truth. And to underscore this fact, we are also told, Scripture appends the divine injunction: "Don't make for yourself (*lekha*) any idol" (Ex. 20:4)—this being an incisive warning to resist the temptations of theological hubris or presumption.

---

27 The Holy Jew reports this in *Siftei Tzaddik* (s.v. "*bereishit*"), collected in *Sefer Kedushat ha-Yedudi* (Bnai Brak, 1997), 130a.
28 Thinking along the same lines, and concerned with the character of a social-legal covenant, R. Scruton has termed this a "transcendent bond"; see his *The Soul of the World* (Princeton, NJ: Princeton University Press, 2014), 94.
29 See *Mei ha-Shiloaḥ* (Brooklyn, 1984), part 1, 25a, col. 2 (*Yitro*; s.v. "*anokhi*").

Awareness of our epistemological limits is therefore a hedge against idolatries of the imagination. This is a primary consideration for developing a spiritual perspective. The letter *kaf*, inserted into our deepest subjectivity, thus functions as a marker of mystery—of all that transcends our limited hermeneutical abilities.

*

Having briefly considered the relation between transcendent mystery and the constructs of our worldly perceptions, we are in a position to suggest a more robust theological presentation of the issue. With it comes a new formulation of the plenitude of divine reality in the universe and our epistemological delimitations of it. The result will be a reconception of both monotheism and idolatry. The former (monotheism) no longer articulates an absolute theistic difference between divine transcendence and the world, but a non-dualist panentheism wherein God fills the totality of worldly existence though not limited by this omnipresent manifestation. The latter (idolatry) ignores or diminishes this divine dimension, and reduces the world to its all-too-human mental constructs. I believe that this monotheistic alternate is a spiritual transumption of the mythic plenum (and its multitude of divine powers) into a dynamic mystical reality. On this view, a comprehensive divine plenitude is the truth (both manifest and concealed) of perception and existence.

A paradigmatic enunciation of this position is found in a hermeneutical teaching by the Maggid of Mezeritch, R. Dov Ber Friedman.[30] I present it here in line with the overall thrust of the present discussion. It builds on a dynamic correlation between his mystical ontology and the conditions of human epistemology.

According to the Maggid, divine reality is absolute transcendence—infinite and beyond human comprehension (an infinite absolute, in philosophical terms). The primary symbol for this reality is absolute light, because such luminosity is deemed a "pure substance," without variation, gradation, or particulars. This being so, and because of God's beneficent desire that humans have some degree of consciousness of God, this radiance was delimited or compressed for the sake of cognition (otherwise mortals could not "bear" it, as the Maggid was wont to stress). This willful "contraction," says the Maggid, is the decisive creative principle of *tzimtzum*. It is the spiritual investment (so to speak) of divinity into the garment of the physical world—this divine dimension being a component

---

30 The teaching to be discussed below is found in *Maggid Devarav le-Ya'akov*, ed. R. Shatz-Uffenheimer (Jerusalem: Magnes Press, 1976), no. 142, 239–242 (hereinafter *MDL*). Other references are keyed to this edition.

of every particle of existence, their necessary ontological core.³¹ Hence, "The whole world is filled with His Glory" (or more concretely, "The fullness of the world *is* His Glory"); and "there is no place devoid of God."³² However (and this is decisive) this transcendental divine component is spiritually concealed *within* the natural world. The result is the paradox that there is a hidden, radical transcendence to divine immanence. The natural mind only sees and knows things in terms of their external particulars, and therefore does not realize that everything perceived is (in actuality) an expression of God. However, this is not something one could naturally know. Hence, initiation into the truth of reality requires spiritual instruction, and the faithful determination to have spiritual cognizance of the Godhood within being through a proper mental disposition (inculcated while performing the divine commandments, especially). The theological ideal is to know that the "outer" world of nature and the "inner" dimension of spirit are two correlative aspects of one divine disclosure. Or, to put the matter otherwise: the creation is fundamentally a revelation *of* God (understood as both an objective and subjective genitive—that is, a revelation of God, Godself, and a revelation of existence through divine agency).

Let us first consider how the Maggid presents this difference between divine ontology and human epistemology, and then suggest how his understanding of the monotheistic difference—that God's transcendent otherness is within the world and not radically distinct from it—might be reinterpreted for a contemporary theology. The Maggid begins his homily by stating the principle that all created reality is comprised of two simultaneous aspects: the aspects of "front" and "back," or *panim* and *aḥor*, respectively. In rabbinic parlance (and Lurianic Kabbalah), this "bimodal" reality is called *du-partzufin*;³³ and it even has a scriptural formulation in Ps. 139:5, which states that human beings were created *aḥor va-qedem*, both "back and front." This correlation between world reality and human beings allows the Maggid to discuss the dynamic relationship between mystical ontology and human cognition. Presuming both the creative principle of *tzimtzum* noted above, and the spiritual result that the entire world is filled with God's glory, we are instructed about the inner and outer aspects of God's 'transcendent immanence' through the bimodal factor of reality. Thus we learn that the spiritual dimension of divine presence (denoted as its *panim* or "face")

---

31 See the opening teaching in *Maggid Devarav le-Ya'akov*, no. 1, 9–13.
32 The first phrase is from Isa. 6:3; the second an Aramaic formulation ubiquitous in Lurianic and Ḥasidic theosophical literature (and see already in *Pesikta de-Rav Kahana* 1:2). In our passage, see *MDL*, 240, and cf. elsewhere (nos. 26, 52, 87, 145–146, 200, 207).
33 BT *Berakhot* 60a.

is concealed under the cover of the physical nature of existence (denoted as its *aḥor* or "other"). The result is the paradoxical fact that God's worldly "omnipresence" is simultaneously "hidden" from view—the result being a radically transformed sense of the rabbinic locution *hastarat panim* (literally, "concealment of the face"). Whereas earlier rabbinic theology used this expression to convey the mysterious absence of God's guiding providence during times of strife or difficulty; it now specifies God's actual (but concealed) presence in the world. And since there is nothing in existence that is not an expression of divinity, this reality "fills" the mind in every possible way—even though the ignorant perceive the world in the mostly superficial and naturalistic terms.[34] They do not know or understand that the outer husk of existence conceals an inner divine transcendence. Hence, worldly reality is what it seems; and human predications are the sum and substance of life. Only a right-minded hermeneutic can pierce the veil of appearances.

What would constitute such an interpretation, that we might appropriate this teaching in contemporary terms? Beginning with an acknowledgement of the Maggid's teaching that we are creatures suffused within an omnipresent mystery of existence I would propose a shift from mystic theosophy to hermeneutic theology. This conceptual move bypasses his strong metaphysical ontology (which asserts that divine qualities are supra-temporal entities present within existence in a derivative mode), while retaining the importance of spiritual cognition.[35] Towards this end, I shall reformulate the key terms *panim* and *aḥor*. Accordingly, the word *panim* designates the plenitude or panoply of worldly appearances confronting consciousness at every turn.[36] These are the "facets" of phenomenal reality that are both manifest and inferred on the basis of perception or memory (thus taking *panim* to indicate all that Husserl meant when he investigated how things "show themselves" to consciousness, based on our complex embeddedness in the phenomena of experience *and* our analytically transcendent overview of them). Thus, as located creatures with finite minds, perspective is a

---

34 See *MDL*, 240, where we find several striking formulations of this (both positive and negative). The principle is already enunciated in no. 1, 10, in even stronger terms. It is a vital component of the Maggid's theology.
35 This conceptual shift reflects my personal (postmodern) predilection, which acknowledges (with Kant) the conceptual problematics of medieval notions of ontological entities. I grant that some readers may not require this shift. I have tried to correlate my reception of the Maggid's teaching with its structural value and significance.
36 For a primary phenomenology of this sensibility, see E. Minkowski, "La plenitude de la vie—image première," *Tijdschrift voor Filosofie* 24, no. 3 (1962): 507–523.

fundamental symbolic form of our limited understanding and interpretation.[37] It is, moreover, a primary factor in our corresponding recognition that what we perceive is exceeded by an inestimable surplus—a fullness that transcends comprehension. This realization, and the dimensions of the unknown that we infer, point to a transcendent otherness that we shall label (based on the Maggid) *aḥor*. This word designates the transcendent mystery of reality present in the depths of world-being (the *mysterium tremendum et fascinans*—the awesome wonder of things, inspiring both reverence and humility). Human estimations of it constitute the *panim* of conceptual reality. Hence, *aḥor* is the omnipresent mystery of *panim*—its transcendent dimension.[38]

Reformulating this in theological terms, we may state that the plenitude of reality is the multimodal manifestation of God's transcendent creativity, to which we give finite expressions through our lived perceptions and interpretations. As a result, human beings constitute a crossing point, or nexus, between the suffusing bounty of divinity and all hermeneutical predications of the divine.[39] Our minds are filled with God's glory, but limited by our mental structures and traditions; and these provide our (contracted) epistemological expressions of it. God as such is ineffable and absolutely transcendental to all cognition; yet we try to articulate the manifestations of divine immanence for human meaning and signification. Being conscious of our intermediation of God's omnipresent manifestations (recall the cipher *kaf*), our mental predications are reflexively qualified; and having divine transcendence actively in mind, the infinite mystery of reality (recall the word *mi*) may provide a counterpoint to epistemological hubris. Disregard of these matters can result in a reification of our perceptions and an idolatrous bondage to the constructs of our mind—a spiritual danger repeatedly asserted through citations of a teaching of the Ba'al Shem Tov. One particularly compelling formulation was given by his grandson, R. Ephraim of Sudilkov. Building on the Talmudic teaching based on the verse "Do not turn (*tifnu*) to idols" (Lev. 19:4), R. Ephraim first interprets this to mean that persons

---

37 Exemplary is the classic work of E. Panofsky, *Perspective as Symbolic Form* (New York: Zone Books, 1997). But as M. Merleau-Ponty rightly emphasized, "classical perspective is not a law of perceptual behavior. It derives from the cultural order, one of the ways man has invented for projecting before himself the perceived world, *and is not a copy of this world*" (my emphasis). See his *The Prose of the World*, edited by C. Lefort (Evanston, IL: Northwestern University Press, 1973), 51, and the ensuing discussion of representation and style.
38 This is, of course, quite different from the "transcendent otherness" of worldly phenomena— over-against human cognition.
39 I first began to think about the "crossing-point" or "nexus" in my book *Sacred Attunement. A Jewish Theology* (Chicago, IL: University of Chicago Press, 2008).

should not "turn to" or rely upon their own "mind" (*da'atkhem*).⁴⁰ He then cites the warning of his grandfather, the Ba'al Shem Tov, who interprets the injunction that one should not "turn away" (*ve-sartem*) and serve (*ve-'avadetem*) other gods" (Deut. 11:16) to mean that "Whenever (or, as soon as) one turns (*ve-sar*) their thought from cleaving (*mi-deveikuto*) to God . . . one immediately worships (*'oved*) other gods (*elohim aḥerim*)."⁴¹ On this radical view, the structure and content of one's theological consciousness (or religious epistemology) are crucial.

*

The import of these reflections brings me back to my opening remarks, when I spoke about our fundamental embeddedness within the world and its perceptual forms. The revolution of spiritual-religious awareness that I have presented can now be understood to have the following (bimodal) epistemological structure. As distinct from a radical theistic position, that cleaves theological reality into two separate planes (the absolutely transcendent dimension of God, and the concrete worldly realm of creation), the present panentheistic position experiences the omnipresent divine reality within the world as a humanly "mediated immediacy." That is, from this nondualist perspective, God's transcendent mystery is the depth dimension of all phenomenal immanence—never perceived as such, but intuited as the infinite surplus within and beyond cognition.⁴² Stated with respect to our "subjective perception," the infinite plenitude of God-given reality is mediated through one's participatory imagination (and therefore affected by human capacities, limitations, and values).⁴³ Whereas stated with respect to the "objective data" of the world, the phenomena of lived experience (the manifest perceptions of *panim*) are the finite testimonies of an inestimable divine actuality (the primordial dimensions of *aḥor*). The infinite occurrences of existence are thus manifestations of the absolutely transcendent reality of all being—derived from God, "the life of life" (*ḥei ha-ḥayyim*)—as processed through our mortal minds. Accordingly, the emergent images of human thought and imagination are the epistemic constructs of the God-given mystery

---

40   See BT *Shabbat* 149a.
41   See in *Degel Maḥaneh Ephraim* (Jerusalem: Mir Publishers, 1995), 162b (*Kedoshim*; s.v. "*al*").
42   Hence, it is fundamentally different from the perceptions of a "mystical ontology" rooted in medieval Kabbalah.
43   Speaking from a different but related mystical stance, see the reflections of R. Pannikar, *L'Expérience de dieu: Icôns du mystère* (Paris: Albin Michel, 2002), chapter 1.

of existence.[44] In a related manner, the anthropomorphic depictions of divinity throughout Scripture (forms of literary "presence") should not be denied or denigrated as "false images"—to be rejected or reconfigured through allegorical explication. They should rather be deemed *testimonies* of concrete, momentary meetings with God (thus, textual renditions of the "events" or *Geschehen* of this encounter; or "mediated immediacies," using the phrase just proposed).[45] These literary refractions may even, in turn, engage one's religious consciousness; and, by means of these hermeneutical mediations, evoke new (personal) engagements with the divine revelations that elicited the original formulations. To forget this overarching consideration (of God's unknowable transcendence *and* the spiritual dimensions of all discernable reality), is to constrict human thought to the surface plane of worldly perception. We are left with the "work of our minds" and the potential reification of our predications—where nothing qualifies our assertions except the stimulus to find a new or more effective cognitive model.[46] This is epistemological idolatry by any other name.[47] The spiritual challenge is therefore to hold in mind the infinite mystery of God along with our mediations of the God-given occasions of existence,[48] inherently limited and subject to cognitive limitations.[49] Hermeneutic humility is crucial. The alternative has consequences for our soul and our culture.

---

44 The great counterpoint to Weber's notion of *Entzauberung* (noted above, n. 24) is Rilke's verse "But for us existence still can enchant (*verzaubert*); in a hundred / places it's still Origin. A play of pure forces, / which no one sees who doesn't kneel in wonder (*bewundert*). See Rainer Maria Rilke, *Sonnets to Orpheus*, translated by E. Snow (New York: North Point Press, 2002), 78–79 (sonnet II.10).

45 I am obviously indebted to F. Rosenzweig, "A Note on Anthropomorphisms in Response to the *Encyclopedia Judaica*'s Article," in his *God, Man, and the World. Lectures and Essays*, ed. and trans. B. Galli (Syracuse, NY: Syracuse University Press, 1998), 135–145. For the original essay, see *Der Morgen* 4, no. 5 (1928); it was subsequently reprinted in Franz Rosenzweig, *Kleinere Schriften* (Berlin: Schocken Verlag, 1937), 525–533.

46 See Max Weber, "Objective Sociology and Social Science and Social Policy" (1904), in *The Methodology of the Social Sciences*, ed. E. A. Shils and H. H. Finch (New York: The Free Press, 1949), 86 (where he refers to the "*Götterdammerung* of all evaluative perspectives"); and cf. Weber, "Science as a Vocation," 138, on the endless search for ends.

47 Note also the language of Ps. 81:10, "You shall have no strange god in you (*bakh*)," as interpreted in BT *Shabbat* 105b (not a "strange god" in your midst, but within you—personally!).

48 I mean "occasions" in the rich sense employed by A. N. Whitehead, *Process and Reality* (New York: The Free Press, 1978), passim.

49 Thus, both poles (the antinomies of intuited mystery and perceived manifestation) are the products of our always embodied longing for meaning. We cannot escape this this hermeneutical circle. Integrity requires living in the dialectical "middle"—between the wonder of (absolute) unknowability and the utility of our cognitive constructs.

CHAPTER 3

Idolatry on the Other Side of Modernity

Shaul Magid

> Judaism without *devekut* is idolatry.
> —Gershom Scholem

> He who refuses to limit God to the transcendent has a fuller conception of Him than he who does so limit Him. But he who confines God within the immanent means nothing other than Him."
> —Martin Buber

> God is in me, or else not at all.
> —Wallace Stevens

1. Monotheism and Idolatry

Idolatry is a category invented by monotheism. No equivalent term or category to "idolatry" is found in the Hebrew Bible, despite the many prohibitions on image-worship.[1] And so too with monotheism: as Ben Sommer notes, "A narrow, common-sense definition of monotheism is the belief that one God exists

---

1 See, for example, Alon Goshen-Gottstein, *Same God, Other god: Judaism, Hinduism, and the Problem of Idolatry* (New York: Palgrave Macmillan, 2015), 27–30. Elliot Wolfson, in *Giving beyond the Gift: Apophasis and Overcoming Theomania* (New York: Fordham University Press, 2014) offers an in-depth analysis of the codependence of monotheism and idolatry in classical and modern Jewish philosophical sources. While not a subject of this inquiry, Wolfson's thesis greatly informed my analysis.

and that no deities exist other than this one God. If we adapt this definition, we must conclude that the Hebrew Bible is not a monotheistic work, because it acknowledges the existence of many heavenly creatures in addition to YHWH."[2] It is not until we have a more stable "monotheism," beginning to consolidate among the early rabbis of the Mishna and early Christians, that we also find the development of a concept of "idolatry" that is contrasted to monotheism.[3] Early Christians and Jews, approximately at the same time, and perhaps unbeknownst to one another, created the category of "idolatry" and, for the rabbis, *avodah zarah*, to describe and define various forms of worship of surrounding peoples, even though *avodah zarah* may not be a correlate term to idolatry.

The English term "idolatry" is derived from Greek *eidolatriea* (lit. service or worship of images; Latin *idololatria*), which first appears in the writings of the Church Father Tertullian in the third century CE.[4] Tertullian and other Christians articulated *eidolatriea* or *idolatria* with a focus on belief and worship practices, while the rabbis theorized *avodah zarah* somewhat differently, primarily in relation to practice.[5] The Mishna's seeming disinterest in belief in regards to *avodah zarah* mirrors its lack of a sustained discussion on belief in regards to Jewish practice more generally. Alon Goshen-Gottstein compellingly argues that for the rabbis *avodah zarah* is not really about idolatry—they are primarily

---

2   Benjamin Sommer, *The Bodies of God and the World of Ancient Israel* (Cambridge: Cambridge University Press, 2011), 146.
3   It is worth noting that the Greek philosophical tradition, certainly as it coalesced around Aristotle, maintained what one might call a monotheistic worldview in that it held a single force (an "unmoved mover") behind the universe. But calling this monotheism may be problematic if we then include in the same category scriptural notions of a creator God (which Aristotle did not hold to be true) who was also engaged with the world. To some degree Jewish monotheism, as it coalesced around Moses Maimonides and his school, was an accomodationalist position whereby Maimonides was able to wed Aristotelean metaphysics with scriptural theology. Maimonidean monotheism on this reading is thus a scriptural rendering of the Aristotelean teaching that then becomes canonized and is subsequently used to define itself and its other, that is, idolatry.
4   J. C. M. Van Winden, "*Idolum* and *Idolatria* in Tertullian," *Vigiliae Christianae* 36 (1982): 108–114. Van Winden notes, "Jews and Christians confess belief in one God, creator of heaven and earth, to whom we all worship. They saw, however, that 'the nations' gave honour and worship to other beings, to other gods, who were represented in images. The honouring of the gods in these images was the most striking aspect of the heathen regimes. Hence the term *idololatria*" (ibid., 109). For Van Winden, early Christians recognized the existence of pagan gods from their monotheistic viewpoint but viewed them mostly as "impure spirits," fallen angels or, in other iterations, "the devil." So, for many early Christian, idolatry was an expression of devil worship.
5   For example, Tertullian, *de Idol.* 3.1, 11.6; *de Spec.* 10.10; *adv. Prax.* 18. On the battles of early Christianity against idolatry see Robert Grant, *Gods and the One God* (Philadelphia: Westminster Press, 1986), 45–53.

interested in articulating "otherness" in regards to the non-Jews in their midst. The details of such belief were less important than maintaining the "otherness" necessary to ensure continuity and survival.[6] And this otherness was defined primarily by practice.[7]

Even in Christian and Muslim lands in the Middle Ages, for instance, the contrast of "idolatry" and monotheism continued to be productive for Jewish identarian means. For many medieval Jews "idolatry" finds a new home in Christianity. The accusation was that Christianity did not meet the standard of monotheism as the rabbis understood it and it was thus prohibitive for Jews, even in many cases requiring martyrdom. Consistent with the substantial polemics against image-worship among early Christians, earlier rabbinic criticisms of Christianity did not focus on accusations of idolatrous practices.[8] To the degree that the classical rabbinic literature even discusses Christianity at all (mostly regarding Jesus), it is in terms of heresy rather than idolatry.[9] To be sure, certain medieval Jewish authorities—such as Menachem Meiri, a fourteenth-century jurist and glossator—argued against Christianity as idolatry, more accurately *avodah zarah*, describing it instead as an alternative form of monotheism.[10] Meiri was one of the few medieval jurists who argued that idolatry was a historically contextualized phenomena that had, by the fourteenth century, all but disappeared except in certain remote areas of the globe. Instead of trying to recreate it (largely via Jewish attitudes toward the church) Jews should accommodate to the reality that the surrounding society in which they lived was now monotheistic.

More important for our concerns, Meiri argued that because Christianity had created an ethical society, it is not that it is *not* idolatry, but that it *cannot* be

---

6   See Goshen-Gottstein, *Same God, Other god*, 28–29.
7   See also Mira Beth Wasserman, *Jews, Gentiles, and Other Animals* (Philadelphia: University of Pennsylvania Press, 2017), 5: "AZ (*avodah zara*) is the section of the rabbinic corpus that governs relationships between Jews and non-Jews. Ostensibly dedicated to explicating prohibitions of idolatry, the tractate includes extensive deliberations about what constitutes Jewish difference."
8   For some examples, see 1 Corinthians 8:4–6, 10:14 and 19. See also Grant, *Gods and the One God*, 45–54.
9   See Peter Schafter, *Jesus in the Talmud* (Princeton: Princeton University Press, 2009), 34–62, 95–130.
10 See Jacob Katz, *Between Jews and Gentiles* (Jerusalem: Bialik Press,1961); idem, *Exclusiveness and Tolerance* (New York: Behrman House, 1961); and Yaakov Elman, "Meiri and the Non-Jew: A Comparative Analysis," in *New Perceptive on Jewish-Christian Relations in Honor of David Berger*, ed. E. Carlebach and J. J. Schachter (Leiden: Brill, 2011), 265–296.

idolatry.[11] He does this by drawing from the biblical fusion of image worship and immorality to suggest that if a society is not immoral it cannot be idolatrous (since idolatry and immorality seem like two sides of the same coin in the Hebrew Bible) and thus since Christianity has created a moral society, it must not be idolatry.[12] But such views were not widely accepted in the Middle Ages and were only revived once Jews in modernity begin to question the medieval equation of Christianity with idolatry.[13] Meiri's view will become important for us when discussing Eliezer Schweid below. The Meirean model is underestimated in the discussion of modern Jewish understandings of idolatry. Goshen-Gottstein notes, "Meiri is, in my opinion, the single most important classical resource to be harnessed for a contemporary Jewish theology of religions, and the full import of his theology of religions has yet to be fully appreciated."[14]

As we reach the High Middle Ages, one finds the increasing popularity of the Maimonidean view of idolatry. From a radically conceptualized notion of monotheism, Maimonides views idolatry as being largely an error of representation.[15] According to this logic, since no other gods exist, thus any attempt to view the one God with any other god is simply a misrepresentation of the true God. Avishai Margalit and Moshe Halbertal call this Maimonidean move

---

11 Meiri raises two separate but arguably linked issues. First, the historicization of idolatry; and second, the relationship between idolatry and morality. Goshen-Gottstein proposes the following way of engaging these two questions in Meiri: "A key challenge in understanding Meiri, in cultivating his thought as a contemporary resource, and in applying his thought to new encounters, such as the encounter with Hinduism, is to understand the relation between the two components of Meiri's thought. What is the relation between the claim that contemporary religions are not idolatrous and their description as moral and law abiding? There are two ways of constructing the relationship between the two statements. The first is to consider them as interdependent. Accordingly, proof of morality is proof that a religion is not idolatrous, either because morality and religion are fully identified or because morality serves as an index to proper knowledge of God. The other way of considering these two statements is to consider them as complementary but independent of one another. If so, moral living might provide us with one component in light of which we might distinguish present-day religions from religions of old. But other criteria might equally apply, and the entire issue needs to be conceived in terms that are broader than whether a religion does or does not teach moral living. Let me begin by exploring the more common view that identifies morality with true religion." Goshen-Gottstein, *Same God, Other god*, 110.
12 See Goshen-Gottstein, *Same God, Other god*, 107–130.
13 Much of Meiri's work was only discovered in the Cairo Geniza in the twentieth century. Before that he was known mostly through being cited by other medieval authorities. See Moshe Halbertal, *Between Torah and Wisdom: Rabbi Menahem ha-Meiri and the Maimonidean Halakhists of Provence* (Jerusalem: Magnes Press, 2000) [Hebrew].
14 Goshen-Gottstein, *Same God, Other god*, 107.
15 See especially Leora Batnitzky, *Idolatry and Representation: The Philosophy of Franz Rosenzweig Reconsidered* (Princeton: Princeton University Press, 2000).

"idolatry as a category error."[16] "In Maimonides's view the purpose of the prohibition against idolatry was to ensure that the worship of God would be free from the possibility of the substitutive error where we see an absolute shift to the worship of one God, which is the crucial meaning of the prohibition of idolatry."[17] At the beginning of his Laws of Idolatry in his legal compendium *Mishneh Torah*, Maimonides treats the ancient belief in multiple gods as a logical misstep.[18]

Such approaches become further developed by modern Jewish thinkers, especially in the wake of the European Enlightenment. The rubrics of the Enlightenment were constructed from a Protestant reading of Christianity for which monotheism was central. Jewish philosophers from Moses Mendelssohn to Hermann Cohen, Leo Baeck, and Emmanuel Levinas asserted monotheism as the very ethical foundation of the Enlightenment, often also making such arguments to claim its ultimate debt to Judaism.[19] More generally, I think modern Jewish thinkers offer a combination of the Maimonidean model that views idolatry as a category error and Meiri's model (even though many did not know it) that idolatry can be deduced by the kind of society created by any religious tradition. The theological frame of monotheism—sometimes known as "ethical monotheism"—becomes the emblem of ethics among Jews and non-Jews alike.[20] Even as many modern Jews claim that Judaism provides a better example of "ethical monotheism" than Christianity, most acknowledge that Christianity, refracted through the Enlightenment, is indeed an example of "ethical monotheism."[21] In this context, the ethical, often described as humanism, is associated with monotheism, and the unethical, with idolatry.[22] Jews like

---

16 Avishai Margalit and Moshe Habertal, *Idolatry* (Cambridge, MA: Harvard University Press, 1988), 42–45, 108–136; and Goshen-Gottstein, *Same God, Other god*, 47–58.
17 Margalit and Halbertal, *Idolatry*, 4.
18 Maimonides, *Mishneh Torah*, Laws of Idolatry 1.
19 See, for example, in Frederick Beiser, *Hermann Cohen: An Intellectual Biography* (New York: Oxford University Press, 218), 4, 5.
20 See Ehud Benor, *Ethical Monotheism* (London: Routledge, 2017), 208. Benor views "ethical monotheism" as a motif that extends back into classical Judaism and is not only an iteration of Judaism's modernization.
21 This of course raises the complex question of the influence and role of Christianity on Nazism. See, for example, Susannah Heschel, *The Aryan Jesus: Christian Theologies and the Bible in Nazi Germany* (Princeton: Princeton University Press, 2010).
22 Here see Batnizky, *Idolatry and Representation*; Gideon Freudenthal, *No Religion without Idolatry: Mendelssohn's Jewish Enlightenment* (Notre Dame, IL: University of Notre Dame Press, 2012); and Robert Erlewine, *Monotheism and Tolerance: Recovering a Religion of Reason* (Bloomington, IN: Indiana University Press, 2010), Also see David Novak, "Emmanuel Levinas and Ethical Monotheism," in *Ethical Monotheism Pats and Present: Essays in Honor of Wendell Dietrich*, ed. T. Vial and M. Hadley (Providence, RI: Brown University Press, 2001), 240–258. What will become operative when we discuss Arthur Green below is that these

to complicate this binary in various ways to illustrate the fissures in Christianity that weaken its ethical monotheistic core. For example, in the words of Emil Fackenheim, "Jewish religious experience bears witness through the ages to the absoluteness of at least two distinctions—between God and man, and between the one true God and all the false gods."[23] The context of Fackenheim's quote is a challenge to G. W. F. Hegel whom he believed had undermined these categorical distinctions in his view that the genius of Christianity was precisely in overcoming the distinction between God and the human in the incarnation, which was the necessary overcoming of self and other to complete the project of religion making way for the fulfillment of philosophy. For Hegel, religion's universalization, and thus its fulfillment, are founded precisely on that theological move.

For the Jewish philosopher Samuel Hirsch, also challenging Hegel, the notion of human freedom is precisely the corner stone of "true religion" that was undermined by Adam refusing to take responsibility for his sin. For Hirsch the curtailing of any aspect of human freedom, either through the collapse of the human/divine distinction (incarnation) or the idea of the inevitability of sin (in doctrines like the original sin) is the beginning of slipping back into idolatry.[24] For Hirsch, contra Hegel, Christianity is not a complete religion but exists as an amalgam of truth and falsehood, the false being precisely what Hegel believed was its *raison d'etre*. To some degree, then, the medieval Jewish notion of Christianity as idolatry is revived, albeit with a new twist: for thinkers like Hirsch and Fackenheim, original sin and the diminishing of human autonomy that comes in its wake are Christianity's great errors, and it is Judaism, which keeps these categorical distinctions intact, that best enables "ethical monotheism" to flourish. In other words, for many modern Jewish thinkers who engage with this issue, the more Christianity exhibits "ethical monotheism," the more Jewish it is. In other words, modernity, invented by Christians, is best expressed through a modernized Judaism.

In what follows, I explore this dynamic in the thought of two contemporary Jewish thinkers, Eliezer Schweid and Arthur Green, and then offer my own

---

modern Jewish discussions of monotheism and its ethics and idolatry are often founded on the categorical distinction between God and the human and between God and the world.

23 See Fackenheim, "Moses and the Hegelians," in his *Encounters between Judaism and Modern Philosophy* (New York: Schocken Books, 1987), 85. A more sustained Jewish critique of Hegel can be found in Samuel Hirsch's *Die Religionsphilosophie der Juden* (Leipzig: Verlag von Heinrich Hunger, 1845). On Hirsch see Robert Erlewine, "Samuel Hirsch, Hegel, and the Legacy of Ethical Monotheism" (unpublished paper). I want to thank Professor Erlewine for sharing this with me before publication.

24 See Erlewine, "Samuel Hirsch, Hegel," 15. Cf. idem, "Resolving Contradictions: Samuel Hirsch and the Stakes of Modern Jewish Thought" (unpublished paper), 1.

view in the concluding section. Both Schweid and Green use the contrast of monotheism and idolatry (Schweid prefers the term אלילת, which, I submit, is *not avodah zarah*, and is perhaps best translated as "paganism," but may indeed constitute idolatry) as a means to conceptualize notions of Jewish society and theological correctness. In both cases, the criteria for monotheism, which each think is best expressed through Judaism combined with modernity, constructs an "other" deemed "idolatrous" that implicates various iterations of normative Judaism. Although the two do so with different aims and goals, they show how the contrast between monotheism and idolatry, through what one might call postmodern lenses, remains a productive practice for reflecting on Jewish communal norms and experiential practice. Even in postmodern contexts devoid of image-worship, the concept of "idolatry" remains a potent focus for thinking through the vicissitudes of Jewish experience, including attempts to understand the nature of the Jewish covenant and the internal and external "other" that continues to challenge Jewish normative belief and practice.

I argue that Schweid extends Meiri's notion of an ethical society and monotheism—Schweid calls it collectivist humanism—and thus any social theory or system that does not exhibit a collective spirit of responsibility and humanism toward the "other," is considered "pagan" or idolatrous. For Schweid, modernity exemplifies the fulfillment of monotheism to the extent that it combines both a look toward the past to cull its ethical foundations, and a look toward the future in cultivating secularism, so that it is bound to, yet not enslaved by, the past. Alternatively, Green adopts a reconstituted Maimonidean model of oneness that is now accessed through experience and not philosophical argumentation, thus wedding Maimonidean oneness with mysticism, which yields what he calls "mystical panentheism." This "mystical panentheism" is a kind of postmodern turn away from reason as defining truth. For Green, the postmodern is more indicative of the end of hierarchal religious identity. "The post-modern spirit needs to insists that the zero-sum game regarding religion is at an end. Religions acting in competition with one another bear responsibility for many of the most terrible acts of violence and bloodshed in human history."[25] For Green, this hierarchical view is viewed as an illustration of a fragmented (and this idolatrous) universe.

Thus I argue that understanding the use of the term "idolatry" in this postmodern context requires viewing it through the dual lenses of Maimonides and Meiri as the portal of experiencing oneness, and secularism, informed by tradition, as

---

25 Green, "Neo-Hasidism: A Judaism for Monists" (unpublished essay), 5. I want to thank Professor Green for sharing this with me before its publication.

the frame of constructing an ethical society. For Schweid, the Reformation and then democracy set the stage for monotheism that is then undermined through various political alternatives (Fascism, Communism, religious fundamentalism, free-market capitalism) that destroy the ethical principles. And for Green, the experience of radical oneness is the way to truly embrace the universal in ways that challenges any kind of particularism that is exclusionary, not necessarily *as* idolatry but as *susceptible* to it.

2. Eliezer Schweid

Eliezer Schweid's discussion of monotheism and idolatry is embedded in various studies dealing with his understanding of modernism, postmodernism, and globalization.[26] Modernity's view of history as tethered to the past will highlight postmodernity's radical break with the past juxtaposed to modernity's continuation with the past, and modernity's relationship to nature will introduce Schweid's critique of technology as facilitating the rise of the individual over nature as opposed to seeing oneself as part, and also caretaker, of nature. One reason for this is because once the human being no longer sees him/herself as the pinnacle of creation—being created "in the image of God"—a creature that stands in responsible relation to a higher creator, for Schweid a pinnacle of monotheism *and* ethics (or monotheism *as* ethics), nature simply becomes a tool to use for his/her benefit. Put otherwise, modern secularism for Schweid is inundated with a theological precept he calls monotheism without which secular humanism is impossible.

To illustrate this history/nature dichotomy, Schweid takes a long detour to discuss monotheism and idolatry (אלילות) as categories in both ancient and modern society that distinguish between civilizations that are primed for humanism verses those that are inclined toward anti-humanism. Schweid views monotheism and idolatry as civilizational categories rather than historical phenomena or theological dicta.[27] The monotheist for Schweid views the human

---

26 Eliezer Schweid, *Bikoret ha-Tarbut ha-Ḥiloni* (herafter, *Bikoret*) (Jerusalem: Magnes Press, 2009); idem, *Normos ha-Kiyum shel ha-Am ha-Yehudi be-Zeman ha-Ḥadash* (hereafter, *Normos*) (Tel Aviv: Hakibbutz Hameuchad, 2012); idem, *Ha-Ziyonut aharei ha-Ziyonut* (hereafter, *ZaZ*) (Jerusalem: Hassifria Haziyonit, 1996); and idem, "Humanism, Globalization, Postmodernism, and the Jewish People," originally published in *Massot Gordoiyuot Ḥadashit* (Tel Aviv: Hakibbutz Hameuchad, 2005).

27 The term Schweid uses is "אלילות," which is not quite polytheism. It is, rather, simply non-monotheism, the disbelief in a one creator God.

being as the pinnacle of creation and thus a creature who can conceptualize that which is beyond him- or herself and nature. It posits a God that is a sovereign above nature and also a God who "loves humanity."[28] The human thus stands in unique relation to that which transcends his/her world.

In addition, in Schweid's reading, here following David Hume, even as monotheism is a corrective to idolatry, idolatry remains embedded in all biblical religions (Judaism, Christianity and Islam) largely in the realm of folk religion. It is the Reformation that finally disentangles much of idolatry from scriptural monotheism and enables monotheism to express itself most fully in the form of idealistic humanism founded on the notion of all human beings created "in the image of God."[29] Thus, it is the Reformation that best prepares theology, including Judaism, for modernity. Humanistic secularism, often referred to in a religious/theological register as "ethical monotheism" becomes the great illustration of Schweid's belief that the secular is best articulated when it is an extension of the religious past. The value of the secular for Schweid is that it offers an iteration of monotheistic religion—constituted in its core belief in the sacrality of the human—without the idolatrous remnants of the ancient past that still remain in certain aspects of all traditional religion. Humanistic progress emerges from prophetic messianism and retains its aspirational goals. Here Schweid shares much with Reform Judaism although he takes issue with Reform's denationalized universalism and religious individualism (that is, its adaptation of Protestantism in separating religion from the secular) at the price of collective identity.[30] The national Jewish project of Zionism provides an important and, according to Schweid, the best test case for the implementation of Jewish monotheism actualized in a collective context. The combination of humanism and collective responsibility that stands at the center of Zionism as Schweid envisions it, allows for the flourishing of Judaism purified from its "polytheistic" folk elements. Much of Schweid's critique of postmodernism (including post-Zionism and globalization) is the way it undermines the Zionist project, emptying it of its humanistic and collectivist foundations.

Postmodernity for Schweid represents a slide back into a kind of idolatry in a number of ways. First, as Schweid understands it, postmodernity (here he speaks in broad strokes) adopts modernity's secularism but rejects its monotheistic

---

28 See *Bikoret*, 96–145, here 97.
29 *Bikoret*, 106–108.
30 *Bikoret*, 110, 111. On Reform, see "Interview," in *Eliezer Schweid: The Responsibility of Jewish Philosophy*, ed. Hava Tirosh Samuelson and Aaron Hughes (hereafter, *Responsibility*) (Leiden: Brill, 2013), 231, 232.

core of viewing the human as that creature who, as the "image of God," can conceptualize that which is beyond nature and, in unique relation to it, views him- or herself in the world as a responsible agent. That is, postmodernity (and here Fascism and Communism may serve as proto-forms of postmodernity for Schweid) embodies the secular void of the humanistic.

> These things bring us back to the discussion of secular postmodernity as an idolatrous worldview. It is certainly true that secularism [in general] is viewed as such from a religious perspective. The monotheistic worldview does not recognize human existence that is not subjugated to its creator as one who stands above it. On this logic, disbelief in a God who transcends nature and who is the source of nature and human reason that is bound to nature, from the monotheistic point of view, this is polytheism even if those who hold such views do not relate to the powers of nature as divine.[31]

Schweid stresses here how secular monotheism exists in its purest historical form in "ethical monotheism" or "idealistic humanism." He then compares it to secular postmodernity that he believes articulates a return to idolatry (that is, a move away from monotheism's "ethical" core) on the question of nature such that the human being and society are fully a part of nature and have no innate responsibility to it. This is one way for him to distinguish what he holds is the difference between the humanism and anti-humanism that separates modernity and postmodernity. Schweid notes that postmodernity does have a return to nature but this return is not to live *in* nature as much as *use it* for its owns needs. Thus technology becomes the dominant ideational framework for postmodern society.

To avoid confusion, it may be best to distinguish between postmodernism and postmodernity in Schweid's thinking. The birth of postmodernism in architectural theory, and later in art, literature, and philosophy is not what Schweid has in mind. Rather, he is talking about a series of societal, one might even say civilizational, shifts that indicate a collapse of the modern synthesis between humanism and collectivism that produced a "monotheistic matrix" of democracy and human rights. So when did all this postmodernity begin for Schweid? He views postmodernity more generally as a response to a series of geo-political

---

31 *Bikoret*, 128.

choices after World War II that contain military, political, economic, and technological components.

The first stage may have been the liberal defeat of Fascist and Communist/totalitarian collectivism that according to Schweid was anti-humanist in its secularism in large part because it severed any connection to the past and thus had no basis for an "ethical monotheism" upon which to build its new society. This part of Schweid's thinking views Fascism and Communism as iterations of a kind of modern idolatry. For Schweid, they serve as examples of modern idolatry in regard to their views on human domination and a rejection of any responsibility above the collective.[32] But their notion of the collective as the framework through which the individual identifies was in principle good, albeit in practice, evil (due in large part to its anti-humanism). Replacing the socialist dimension of collectivism (Schweid viewed socialism as Communism's positive side) with democracy and a free-market system, the West began a slow process of rejecting the very components of classical liberalism and humanism that had a socialist-like component of collective responsibility. In its place rose a free-market system whose primary purpose was to serve the individual through profit.[33] The severing of the individual from collective responsibility and the growth of chauvinistic individualism—for Schweid, an outgrowth of the free market—and the severing of humanism as the driving force of human flourishing results for Schweid in the loss of the secular humanism that drove the Enlightenment and constituted modern monotheism. The free market is not a solution to Fascism and Communism because its focus on profit simply substitutes radical individualism for the anti-humanistic collectivism of Fascism and Communism but does not offer an alternative version of collective responsibility and humanism. In the globalized free market as Schweid envisions it, everyone is out for themselves and the collective, here the corporation (and no longer the nation), only functions as it facilitates and proliferates profit. This is why Schweid thinks globalization is the death-knell of Zionism.[34]

---

32 *Bikoret*, 35; and *Responsibility*, 98, 99.
33 The "neo-liberal" (Schweid calls it "neo-capitalist") system is usually defined as part of Clinton's market-driven liberalism, or "third-way democrats" in opposition to the liberalism of FDR, LBJ, or the populism of people like Hubert Humphrey. In this sense the term is being deployed inaccurately but its use to distinguish between nineteenth-century humanistic liberalism and postwar, posthumanistic liberalism in the form of free-market capitalism is well taken.
34 An example would be the increasing number of Israelis now working for multinational corporations and drawing a salary from outside Israel, often having homes in Israel and outside. They are Israeli consumers but their allegiances are increasingly to the corporations that support them.

In addition, one religious manifestation of this postwar phenomenon is religious fundamentalism that also has a quasi-socialist ethos in regards to lifting up the poor in its community through charity, interest-free loans, and so forth. What it does not have is any stable sense of humanism in regards to global responsibility (that is, a responsibility to those who exist outside its orbit) nor a focus on democracy and freedom. Schweid's notion of religious fundamentalism is somewhat limited to the Israeli case and even there, underestimates the extent to which that community, the more it becomes integrated into the larger whole, begins to view itself as part, and not in opposition to, the secular society in which it lives.

But for Schweid, the deeply rooted theocratic elements in religious fundamentalism often repeat in some way the errors of Fascism and autocracy (and thus often exhibit similar traits), which are based on a religious myth as opposed to pure human power. The ability of these fundamentalisms to gain support, at least in Israel, is in part the result of space created by the turn away from a socialist ethos and the humanism it embodies and toward the free market. The increase in capital through the individualism of the free market resulted in a decrease in an ideological justification for collective existence (thus the rise of one form of secular post-Zionism). The ideological vacuum created by radical individualism generated by the focus on profit is occupied by religious fundamentalism, which, according to Schweid, contains the folk religion remnants of ancient idolatry not eradicated by modernity. The rejection of rationalism and the resurgence of myth for Schweid (re)produces idolatrous remnants of "primitive" religion that Hume discusses in his work. While such forms of religious maximalism may generate new and creative forms of religious meaning, they also produce a social structure that undermines the humanism implicit in Schweid's view of modernity, that is, collective responsibility and the sacrality of (all) humans.

The next error of postwar liberalism for Schweid was its adaptation of technology or scientism as a substitute for ideology. "The Marxist discipline also demanded abolition of philosophy (as ideology) and exchanged it for scientific praxis, while declaring the assumption that social existence determines consciousness, not the other way around."[35] Instead of reinstituting monotheistic humanism as the ideological foundation of the postwar west, Schweid claimed that the turn to American dominance, with its focus on manufacturing, production, and consumption as a social ethos, enabled technological progress

---

35   Schweid, *Responsibility*, 101; ZaZ, 15.

to become the very vehicle of human progress as opposed to a tool toward such progress. Places like Silicon Valley would be an illustration of Schweid's point.[36] The technological mindset is one that always looks forward without the need to look back. Here Schweid claims in some way that Communism's post-ideological program unwittingly won, except now technology does not serve the cultural revolution but serves the individual who seeks wealth and fortune.

From this brief survey we see how Schweid reinterpreted the categories of monotheism and idolatry, as he took them out of their biblical theological context and used them to describe the turns in Western notions of humanism, technology, free-market capitalism, and religious fundamentalism.[37] Monotheism becomes a civilizational model marked by humanism and collectivism; and contemporary idolatry is the rejection of one or both of modern monotheism's basic principles; humanism (viewing the sacrality of the human being) and collectivism, the belief in the individual's responsibility to the larger society in which it lives and the global community more generally. In Schweid we see an interesting adaptation of Meiri's model of idolatry as tied inextricably to an ethical society as a model to assess the value and sustainability of various forms of collective life.

In addition, the rejection of secularism in new forms of religious maximalism or fundamentalism for Schweid results, among other things, in the resurgence of idolatrous remnants embedded in folk religion that are now used to justify an anti-humanistic orientation toward society (a return to tribalism would be one example). Communism, Fascism, free-market capitalism, and religious fundamentalism for different yet overlapping reasons are all postmodern iterations of the undermining of modern monotheism in favor of a postmodern idolatrous alternative.

Schweid's assessment of idolatry is really a way for him to demarcate the categorical distinction between modernity (mature monotheism) and postmodernity (that contains idolatrous elements) as it applies to Zionism and the project of nationalism more generally. For Schweid, Zionism is a product of modernity in that it combines (1) a connection to the past, (2) a belief in humanism (the human as created "in the image of God"), and (3) a deep commitment to collective responsibility that may be centered around one ethnic group but also extends to the family of nations. In his view, ethnic nationalism can indeed be an

---

36 To cite an anecdote, a colleague recently told me that what she found so jarring about sitting in cafes in Palo Alto is that nobody was talking about the past, everyone was only talking about the future.
37 Schweid generally uses biblical as opposed to rabbinic motifs to sketch his views of modernity. See, for example, in Schweid, *The Foundation of the Bible as the Foundation of Jewish Culture*, trans. L. Levin (Boston: Academic Studies Press, 2009).

iteration of mature monotheism in spite of, or perhaps precisely, in its particularity. But only if that ethnic particularity views itself as responsible both inside and outside its own community.

Postmodernism, for Schweid embodied in Fascism, Communism, globalization, and American-style free-market capitalism, and also in the rise of religious fundamentalism, always lacks at least one component of his modern monotheistic paradigm, and thus his postmodernity embodies what he calls אלילות and what I am calling idolatry. In some cases, this manifests as worshipping the state (Fascism), in other cases the collective in opposition to the individual (Communism), and in other cases, the individual over the collective (free-market capitalism). Each case rubs against modernity and thus, for Schweid, threatens the future of Zionism.

One critique of Schweid is that he seems to want to return to a time that has long passed or, perhaps more strongly, a time that never really existed. Modernity had never quite cleansed itself of what he calls אלילות, or idolatry, and more pointedly, Zionism itself may not have ever quite embodied the evolved "monotheism" he suggests, even as it may have aspired to do so. For example, the ethnocentric turn in Israel today is not necessarily the product of "postmodernism" via the return of fundamentalist religion or communism but the hyper-nationalism of modernity itself, manifest in Israel through the Revisionist movement.[38] I would question whether Schweid's noble humanistic vision of the Zionist project, if it ever existed, can exist today for a variety of reasons, some internal and some external to the nation-state itself. As I see it, postmodernism, on Schweid's reading, does not bring something entirely new (or backslide to something old) but rather exposes a weakness in the modern project more generally; the weakness being that modernity's humanism always contained the "idolatrous" elements that Schweid claims arose with the social changes that produced postmodernism in the political rejection of classical liberalism. Gershom Scholem called this the mystical urge but one can call it idolatrous from the perspective of rationalism.[39]

Here I suggest the "post" of postmodernism points to an evolutionary and not revolutionary process. In this sense, postmodernism on Schweid's terms is the isolation and focus of certain aspects of modernity while relegating others

---

38 On the relationship between Revisionism and hyper-nationalism in Europe see Daniel Kupfert Heller, *Jabotinsky's Children: Polish Jews and the Rise of Right-Wing Zionism* (Princeton: Princeton University Press, 2017).

39 Schweid published a book-length critique of Scholem's historiography. See Schweid, *Judaism and Mysticism according to Gershom Scholem* (Atlanta: Scholars Press, 1985), esp. 133–168.

to an auxiliary role. Here then, postmodernity is not a radical break with modernity but a particular refraction of it, one that, in some cases, undermines certain aspects that were viewed as integral to the modern project. Along these lines, I prefer to view the erasure of the zero-sum attitude and absolute binary of idolatry and Israelite worship in the Hebrew Bible, beginning with the advent of *avodah zarah* in the rabbis, as a sign that religion and politics today must make peace with the idolatry that lurks within; it is always there and is constitutive of modernity itself. Its importance, I submit, is that there is something about the evocation of desire in idolatry that can be used to further the modern project. What I mean by "desire" is the materiality that seems emblematic to what we call idolatry, its sensuousness, its focus on the aesthetic and erotic, generates a sense of closeness and even intimacy that is arguably a desideratum of human flourishing. This can certainly be overdone and lead to negative consequences but in my view the occupational hazard should not lead us to excise that which can evoke such desire.

More to the point, that desire, where evoked through aesthetics or eros, holds a certain power that, if used cautiously and judiciously, can enhance, rather than detract from, our (monotheistic) religious and social lives. We can see that expressed in art, music, and other creative endeavors. In some cases, it emerges in romanticism, in other cases, revolutionary idealism. The revolutionary spirit contains components of idolatry as Schweid articulates it, and even if it fails, such movements often produce necessary change in the long run. Speaking about the revolutionary student movements in the 1960s, Hannah Arendt said, "The good things in history are usually of very short duration, but afterward have a decisive influence on what happens over long periods of time."[40]

I think Schweid understands the complexity of the idolatry-monotheism mix and therefore requires modernity's humanistic (and secular) tenor to enable his view of mature monotheism to come to fruition. He sees the danger of postmodernity in terms of its potential to undermine a sense of unity, continuity, and human responsibility that would undermine the humanism that enables religion to function as a force for the good. His Judaism is, in some sense, a religious secularism. The problem, in my view, is the attempt to excise idolatry completely, be it theologically or politically, fails to see how much it is embedded in the modern project itself. As opposed to Schweid's view that postmodernism is a negative force, a subversion of modernity's core principles, I think postmodernity can be best utilized as regulating, and not eradicating, idolatry. As the Bible

---

40 Hanna Arendt, "Interview with Albert Reif," Summer 1970, in her *The Last Interview and Other Conversations* (Brooklyn: Mellville House, 2013), 72.

commands us to destroy idolatry and the rabbis command us simply to avoid it, perhaps we can move to a level of regulation, or de-demonization, acknowledging the good idolatry can provide if not allowed to efface the moderating force of humanism. The force of Schweid's negation of postmodernity sets up a binary that I think potentially undermines his goal of human flourishing.

3. Arthur Green

Arthur Green has been engaged in what he calls a neo-Hasidic theological project for over half a century. In the last few decades, he published a trilogy that maps out the broad parameters of his theological thinking. The first installment was *Seek My Face: A Jewish Mystical Theology* (2003); the second was *EHYEH: A Kabbalah for Tomorrow*, also published in 2003, and the third was *Radical Judaism*, published in 2010. *Seek My Face* is written in a confessional style. Its structure is almost aphoristic, sometimes impressionistic, and it is seemingly meant more as inspirational reading than the presentation of a systematic theology. By itself it does not give its critical reader enough to extrapolate a theological system. But it does set the parameters of Green's theological project in a way that makes room for the two books that follow. *EHYEH* fills an important lacuna in *Seek My Face*: in his second book, Green challenges the reader with his rendering of the kabbalistic tradition (more implied than explicit in *Seek May Face*) and its radical interpretation according to his neo-Hasidic or New Age version of Kabbalah.[41] In *EHYEH* we find the building blocks of *Seek My Face*.

In *EHYEH* Green has much to say about the concept of oneness that filters through his entire theological project. The various names he uses for this concept—sometimes "mystical panentheism," sometimes "panentheism," and sometimes "religious humanism"—illustrate Green's grappling with a concept of oneness that is not fettered by the confines of classical monotheism, which, as we stated above, is intent on maintaining and policing the categorical distinctions between God and the human, and God and nature. While Green leans heavily on thinkers such as Moses Cordovero and early Hasidism, I argue below that his oneness theology is better understood as a kind of experiential (as opposed to

---

41 In general, Green does not ascribe to "New Age" religion and prefers "neo-Hasidic" as a better description of his thinking. I use New Age here in a colloquial sense to point to the shift toward "spirituality" and away from formal religion—the "spiritual but not religious" phenomenon—that marks the time, as well as much of the substance, of Green's approach. See, for example, Green, "A Neo-Hasidic Credo," in *A New Hasidism: Branches*, ed. A. Green and A. Evan Mayse (Lincoln, NB: Jewish Publication Society, 2019), 11–40.

philosophical) Maimonideanism that does not get caught up in the fragmented and multitudinous world of the *sefirot* (a point I will return to in my reflections).[42]

Green offers what I am calling a theology of radical oneness, the One that is not a unity apart from the world but the All that pervades both but is not contained by the world. In this sense, *Radical Judaism* represents the maturation of Green's theological project. It is here that his more impressionistic theology in *Seek My Face* is combined with his neo-Hasidic reading of Kabbalah in *EHYEH* to produce a programmatic worldview for a future Judaism. In addition, it is in *Radical Judaism* where Green fleshes out his oneness theology that also includes a new conceptualization of idolatry.[43]

Classical monotheism, from the rabbis to Maimonides and beyond (even in the more mythological monotheism of the Zohar, Lurianic Kabbalah, and Hasidism) maintained a tension between the omnipotence and omniscience of God and the world. Even figures such as the Safed kabbalist Moses Cordovero, who offered a kind of mystical panentheism, or Habad's acosmism, theologies that challenged the radical transcendence of Maimonides, maintained a strong sense of otherness, often described as *eyn sof*, in reference to God.[44] Maimonides's radical transcendence whereby God is a distant, explicable absence/presence was often challenged but never fully overturned, in part because that distance was crucial for monotheism's survival, not only theologically but politically as well.[45] The notion of divine election and the uniqueness of Israel is founded on the notion that God and the world are not unified, that distinctions exists between God's chosen and those not chosen. Divine election has a metaphysical, and paradoxical, foundation. All may be One but all is not equal.

42　Joseph Ben Shlomo discussed the term "panentheism" often used to describe Cordovero's theology although Ben Shlomo did not think the category was productive or useful. See Joseph Ben Shlomo, *The Mystical Theology of Moses Cordovero* (Jerusalem: Bialik Institute, 1986) [Hebrew].

43　For another brief engagement with Green's theology in this register, see Elliot Wolfson, *A Dream Interpreted within a Dream: Oneireopoiesis and the Prism of Imagination* (New York: Zone Books, 2011), note 34, 288–291.

44　It is significant to note that Elliot Wolfson stresses that in Buber's theology "*Ein Sof* is not impersonal, it is the absolute person, which must be marked by the pronoun *du*, the equivalent of *attah*. To be sure, absolute personhood cannot be reified, but it is a person nonetheless. . . ." Elliot Wolfson, "Theolatry and Making Present of the Nonrepresentable: Undoing (A)Theism in Eckhart and Buber," in *Martin Buber: His Intellectual and Scholarly Legacy*, ed. Sam Berrin Shonkoff (Leiden: Brill, 2018), 19. Here Green may have gone beyond Buber to depersonalize God in a way that comes closer to Maimonides.

45　On Maimonides radical transcendence in relationship to prayer, see Ehud Benor, *Worship of the Heart: A Study of Maimonides' Philosophy of Religion* (Albany, NY: SUNY Press, 1995).

The kabbalistic tradition brought God closer with its intricate cosmology (*torat ha-sefirot*) yet still maintained God was removed from material existence. Spinoza's pantheism collapsed God and the world and in so doing subverted any remnant of biblical monotheism, or divine election, even as some of his defenders claim that Spinoza was the most monotheistic of all.[46] Hasidism drew God even closer, into human experience and nature (Hasidism likes to point out that the numerical value of nature/*teva* is *Elohim*/God). But even in Hasidism, the transcendent component remains mostly intact and it is that sliver of "otherness" upon which classical monotheism hangs. The oneness and unity of God that plays a central role in classical monotheism, along with divine distance and categorical otherness, must contain a component whereby God and the world are categorically distinct. Idolatry along these lines is an act of misrepresenting that One, either through images or false conceptualizations that divide divine unity and then view those divisions as objects of worship.

Drawing from the mystical tradition but moving beyond it (or, on another reading, taking it to its logical conclusion) Green offers a "mystical panentheism" whereby oneness breaks through the classical monotheistic barriers that contained previous versions.

> By *mystical* panentheism I mean that this underlying oneness of being is accessible to human experience and reveals itself to humans—indeed, it reveals itself everywhere, always—as the deeper levels of the human mind become open to it. . . . The "radical otherness" of God is insisted upon by Western theology, is not an ontological otherness but an otherness of perspective. To open one's eyes to God is to see Being—the only being there is—in a radically different way. Such a unitive view of reality is *entirely other* (*ganz anderer*, in theological German) from the way we usually see things, yet it is the same reality that is being viewed.[47]

Mystical panentheism is an example of monotheistic iconoclasm in that it subverts the categorical distinction between God and all else that thinkers such as Emil Fackenheim and Samuel Hirsch argue is distinctive about Jewish monotheism in their critique of Hegel. Here Arthur Schopenhauer's comment captures

---

46 See Nancy Levene, *Spinoza's Revelation* (Cambridge: Cambridge University Press, 2004), 16–76.
47 Arthur Green, *Radical Judaism* (New Haven: Yale University Press, 2010), 18.

precisely this iconoclastic turn. "Theism . . . places the primary source of existence outside us, as an object. All mysticism . . . draw[s] this source gradually back into ourselves as the subject, and the adept at least recognizes with wonder and delight that he himself is it."[48] And yet arguably the "en" in panentheism protects Green from the charge of a post-monotheistic position. I remain skeptical that this holds, less in principle than in practice. As I have argued elsewhere, *eyn sof* in Lurianic Kabbalah functions largely as a placeholder, it has no intrinsic meaning, which may precisely be its function.[49]

What interests me more specifically about Green's mystical panentheism is the role idolatry could play in this schema when classical monotheism is challenged, or even undermined, by a radical theology of oneness. By moving outside the classical monotheistic paradigm, Green has presented an idea of the divine whose truth is expressed through a sense of oneness and unity of all creation.[50] The *mystical* component of this panentheism is based on Green's assertion that this oneness and unity can be *experienced* by human beings, constituting what Thomas Aquinas called *cognito des experimentiis*, and that this experience is one of unity, the realization of the radical connectedness of all of creation, perhaps manifest through nature, which is the disclosure of being. For Green this is the very apex of monotheism in its full disclosure through creation. Perhaps unlike Spinoza, who offered a philosophical and not experiential justification for pantheism, for Green, God is not identified with (or in some reading identical to) nature but *greater* than the sum of nature's parts, introducing divine excess, that element of oneness that extends beyond nature, beyond creation (the "en" of panentheism), and is disclosed in the *experience* of unity.

The experience of the divine for Green is not *of* nature but its underlying unity. "God is the underlying reality of being; peel off the surface or lift the veil of our divided and multifaceted reality and you will begin to peer through to the

---

48 Schopenhauer, *The World as Will and Representation*, 2 vols. (Cambridge: Cambridge University Press, 2014), 2:612, cited in Wolfson, "Theolatry and Making Present of the Nonrepresentable," 11.
49 See Shaul Magid, "The Word of God is No Word at All," in *Imagining the Jewish God*, ed. K. Koltun-Fromm and L. Kaplan (Lanham, MD: Lexington Books, 2016), 163–178; and idem, "God is Already Not One: The Postmonotheistic Turn in Contemporary Jewish Theology in America," *Ruach ha-Aretz* 1 (September 2012): 49–52 [Hebrew].
50 This aspect of Green's theology is quite close to Martin Buber's *Daniel: Dialogues on Realization*, trans. Maurice Friedman (New York: Holt, Rinehart and Winston, 1964). *Daniel* is an important transition for Buber from his earlier mystical approach in *Ecstatic Confessions* to his dialogical philosophy in *I and Thou*. See Paul Mendes-Flohr, *From Mysticism to Dialogue: Martin Buber's Transformation of German Social Thought* (Detroit: Wayne State University Press, 1989).

singularity of truth, the One that lies within and behind the many."[51] There is nothing particularly provocative about this assertion; versions of it can be found throughout the Jewish mystical tradition. Green's intervention comes in the way he conceptualizes the consequences of such a statement and the impact it has on classical monotheistic thinking and how that informs his understanding of idolatry.

Idolatry, as we have said, is the anti-monotheism created by monotheists; its parameters are determined by how monotheism is constructed. The basis of Green's monotheism in embedded in his notion of the mystery of divine excess. Green writes, "This glimpse of a monist or panentheistic worldview, one that sees God in all, the One manifest in each of the many, but the mystery ever beyond our grasp, lies deeply veiled within Judaism—and so too in Christianity and Islam—behind the mask of religious personalism, faith is a personified deity who created the world... rules over history, guides each person's fate, and promises redemption."[52] The "mystery ever beyond our grasp," is that which both unifies the world and also undermines the fragmentary nature of existence that produces, among other things, hierarchies of chosenness and exceptionalism. And here is where idolatry enters. It is worth quoting Green at some length.

> That first *mitzvah* is joined by a second, but one that is really only the reverse side of the first. "Worship nothing else." Beware of idols, of false gods in all their dimensions. Do not be led astray by venerating anything less than Y-H-V-H, the wholeness of being. The temptations range from "sticks and stones" as the Bible presents "idolatry" to the much more sophisticated distortions and limitations of truth that constitute most of religion, even in our own day. All of them lead us to turn away from the singular task of *sacred awareness without limits*. Each of them narrows our vision, keeps out part of the light. The Baal Shem Tov said it clearly and sharply, commenting on "lest you turn aside and worship other gods" (Deut. 11:16). "As soon as you turn aside", he said, "you are worshipping other gods".... Turn away from the whole and you are worshipping but a part, causing *perud*, fragmentation of reality, the beginning of all evil. This *mitzvah* is an admonition against

---

51 Green, *Radical Judaism*, 99.
52 Arthur Green, "Neo-Hasidism: A Judaism for Monists" (unpublished essay).

> false religion in the strongest sense. Any religion that makes exclusive claims and still plays on the field of "my god against your god" is by definition such an idolatry.[53]

Here Green engages the idolatry of the Second Commandment "no other gods," by his reading of the First Commandment, not simply "I am the Lord your God who took you out of Egypt," but rather, I am the One who set you free, the One that pervades everything, the One that is the excess beyond all that is. And so, "you shall have no other gods," is meant to convey that you shall never see, or worship, anything separate from that One, nor shall you conceive of that One as anything that is not present everywhere at all times. This *perud* or "fragmentation of reality" includes for Green, "[a]ny religion that makes exclusive claims," any religion that creates a hierarchy of us vs. them, even if it acknowledges that the God who chooses "us" is also the One beyond the fragments.

In Green's assessment, everything is susceptible to idolatry, even Judaism. "Might we have been fashioning revelation into an idol?"[54] Can Torah became an idol? In Green's thinking, the answer is "yes" if that Torah teaches anything except the oneness of being that infuses all creation, a oneness we can experience through the veil of our fragmentary world. Earlier teachings (in Kabbalah and Hasidism) that articulated similar sentiments lived within a solid monotheistic orbit that affirmed the various categorical distinctions made centuries earlier: between God and the world, between the universal and the particular, between Israel and the nations. In fact, they did so in chauvinistic ways. This is arguably the foundation upon which a normative rendering of the covenant precariously sits.

Green's neo-Hasidic rendering takes this new vision of the Second Commandment against idolatry—worship nothing aside from, and in opposition to, the One—and applies it in a way that undermines that very foundation.

> Here we need to go back to the universalism and vision with which we began. We need to go beyond our separate and divisive tales, back to the single great story that unites us all. The story of evolution, including the ongoing evolution of humanity, is bigger than all the distinctions between religions and their myths. . . . All of human worship belongs to the One. Any religion less open than that in its claims—whether under the

---

53   Green, *Radical Judaism*, 102, 103.
54   Ibid., 104.

> banner of "Judaism" or any other—is precisely "turning aside," lopping off of a certain part of human experience and taking it for the whole. That is idolatry, the worship of "other gods" meaning the taking of something less than the whole for God, which is the all-embracing One.[55]

Judaism is idolatry the extent to which it focuses on its exclusivity, and exceptionalism, certainly chauvinism, in relation to God. The extension of oneness as monotheism is that the distinction, or *havdalah*, that separates the Jews, and Judaism, from those who practice other religions, or no religion, slides easily into fragmentation of the oneness of being that produces *perud* and idolatry. In some real way Green seeks to supplant Mosaic religion with a revived Adamic religion. "I turn to the myth of the call to Adam precisely because that is a universal myth, one that will be inclusive of all humanity."[56] Sinai becomes the moment where the Jews answer "yes" to carry this message to the world, and to live it in a particular way but a way that does not exclude but embraces all others who seek that oneness. To the extent that it does not do that, Mosaism (the particular) loses its important Adamic (universal) roots. Put otherwise, the universal disappears into the recesses of the particular and eventually become effaced and nonfunctional. In some sense, Green might accede to Jan Assmann's transition away from the Mosaic distinction of "no other gods," to the more universalistic notion of "all gods are O/one." Assmann argues, "The idea that various nations basically worshipped the same deities under different names and in different forms eventually led to the belief in a 'Supreme Being.'"[57] Green might suggest that this idea of a Supreme Being, of oneness, then enables us to transition back from the particularism and exclusivity of "no other gods" to the universal "all gods are one," that is, all fragments are simply permutations of the oneness of being.

In such a metaphysical revision, what happens to the Jews, the recipients of the Sinai covenant, the people who carry this universalistic message? How can the Jew survive the transition to Green's universalistic call for unity and non-fragmentation? In short, I don't believe it can. That is, the fusion of the Jew and Israel as an exclusive biologically determined tribal category cannot bear the weight of this new approach.

---

55 Ibid., 105.
56 Ibid., 106.
57 Jan Assmann, *Of God and Gods: Israel, Egypt and the Rise of Monotheism* (Madison, WI: University of Wisconsin Press, 2008), 55. For a sustained critique of Assmann on these and other issues, see Mark Smith, *God in Translation: Cross-Cultural Recognition of Deities in the Biblical World* (Grand Rapids, MI: Eerdmans, 2008), esp. 243–274.

> Whom do we mean when we say "Israel"? The classic definition, those born into the Jewish people plus those who properly convert, is too simple, begging too many vexing questions. Is it all those who identify with this liberation from bondage? This seems too broad, for the story of Egypt has indeed become the property of all humanity? The fact is that there are many Israels. "Who is *my* Israel?" I ask myself. Who constitutes the community in whose midst I seek to share both my struggle for liberation and my joy in celebrating that freedom? *You* are indeed my Israel. You for whom I write, you whom I teach, you with whom I feel a deep kinship of shared human values and love of this Jewish language. Are you all Jews in the formal sense? I'm not much worried about that question. . . . Are you fellow-sojourners, non-Jews sympathetic to this theological language, or members of a newly defined "House of Israel"? Or does the ancient category of "Israel" make no sense anymore, in an age when we so urgently need to share our message with all humanity? Is it time to shed our tribal identity for the sake of our universal values? . . . Between these two groups, the historic Jewish people and the world community of seekers and strugglers, there lies a third, no less important community. We need to find a special place for those who revere and feel attached to the spiritual legacy of Israel without belonging to the historically defined Jewish people. Israel, "wrestler with God," is too big a name to belong to just a single people. . . .[58]

I offer this admittedly "strong reading" of Green with the assumption that his metaphysics informs his social critique. That is, his unwillingness to maintain the categorical distinctions of "Israel" as solely "the Jews" emerges from his theology of radical oneness and the dismembering of fragmentation. Here I believe Green makes the move that his predecessors do not make, could not make, the move that exhibits how his commitment of oneness and the prohibition of fragmentation (idolatry) cannot hold biological Israel intact. The biological Jew can exist, but he or she must share the name "Israel" with all those who seek oneness.[59] Just as God can be in the world but not be contained by it (Green's notion

---

58 Green, *Radical Judaism*, 139.
59 A similar non-metaphysical argument is made by Irving (Yitz) Greenberg in his *Between Heaven and Earth* (Philadelphia: Jewish Publication Society, 2004), 49–102. Greenberg

of divine excess) so too Israel can embody a people who struggle toward oneness (the Jews) but that struggle cannot be contained *in* Israel. It must extend beyond it just as God must extend beyond the world.

> Once we [biological Jews] recognize our essential message is a universal one, defining ourselves so narrowly as its exclusive bearers does not suffice. We *want* other to pick up the banner that proclaims all creatures sacred embodiments of the One, all humans the image of God. . . . No, I am not here announcing my apostasy or the rejection of my very own very deep commitment to the specific and ethnically defined heritage I received from my Eastern European Jewish grandparents. But I am pushing against the borders of my own community, and admitting (partly in sadness!) that it no longer suffices for me to limit my sense of spiritual fellowship to those who fall within the ethnic boundaries that history has given us.[60]

Elsewhere Green notes, "We [biological Israel/the Jews] are also part of a wide *yisra'el*—a term that literally refers to one who 'struggles with God' and celebrate that spiritual identity as well."[61] Green's pushing beyond the confines of ethnic identity is, in my view, an illustration of how monotheism as radical oneness seriously challenges the binaries foundational for biblical monotheism:

---

focuses specifically on Christianity. In addition, Greenberg's argument is openly pragmatic as a way to engage in inter-religious dialogue and pluralism and less theological, albeit he needs to alter the standard theological notion of divine election to make this work. Another salient example of this can be found in Hermann Cohen's *Religion of Reason* where Cohen's view of monotheism and true religion (for him, Judaism) is something in which non-Jews can take part. See, for example, discussed in Robert Erlewine, *Judaism and the West: From Hermann Cohen to Joseph Soloveitchik* (Bloomington, IN: Indiana University Press, 2016), 43. My reading of Green is that his theological move forces his new civilizational model, not simply as a way to engage the non-Jew in a respectful manner but to recalibrate Jewish notions of God and God's relationship to the world. I want to thank Alon Goshen-Gottstein for pointing out the Greenberg reference.

60 Green, *Radical Judaism*, 140, 141.
61 Green, "Neo-Hasidism: A Judaism for Monists," 7. This separation between "Israel" and "Jew" already exists n Philo of Alexandria. The following description of Philo's position by Michael Satlow sounds quite similar to Green. "Philo curiously distinguishes the communities of 'Israel' and the 'Jews'. The former he links to the experience indicated by his understanding of the term's etymology—Israel means 'one who sees God'. All who, following the model of the biblical Jacob, directly experience God qualify as members of Israel. The *Jews*, though, he sees as a social entity with no necessary equivalence with Israel." Michael Satlow, *Creating Judaism: History, Tradition, Practice* (New York: Columbia University Press, 2006), 101.

between God and the world (transcendence and immanence), between the universal and the particular, and between Jew and non-Jew. In each case, the two categories remain; transcendence is the excess of Green's "mystical panentheism." Differences can exist inside the orbit of the universal, and the biological Jew can remain, although she now shares the name Israel with fellow seekers and worshippers of oneness. But in each case the primary category gets subsumed in the secondary one. Classical theism stressing divine transcendence yields to the proximate intimacy of panentheism, the universal now becomes the operating system of the particular (and not the other way around), and Israel is no longer exclusively embodied in the Jew but describes non-Jewish fellow-travelers. Whether, for example, non-seeking Jews constitute Green's Israel is unclear, but I would venture to say no, they are part of a biologically determined covenanted community—the Jews—that has opted out of Green's new (post)monotheistic "Israel." They are "Jews" but not "Israel" because they are not oneness-seekers.[62] Alternatively, the Jew who rejects Green's theological revision and maintains the old models is, in fact, guilty of some sort of idolatry, not worshipping fragments but worshipping the One from the position of a fragmented universe expressed in Jewish exceptionalism and hierarchical particularity. The Jew as exclusively chosen, and the belief in radical transcendence where God and world are categorically different, yields a world of *perud* out of which new idolatry arises. While Green may disagree with this stark conclusion, I believe it filters through his rejection of theological "fragmentation" and, by extension, hierarchical religion.[63]

Here I would say that Green's notion of idolatry is not as severe as the Bible's and thus one must ask what he really means by idolatry. It means, as I understand it, one who still worships in a way that has been overcome through human evolution, an exercise in spiritual obsolescence. Thus, as I read it, idolatry for

---

62 Aharon Lichtenstein makes a similar distinction in his discussion of the status of the Jews who convert to Christianity. Such Jews maintain the name Israel (*shem yisra'el*) but no longer has the sanctity of Israel (*kedushat yisra'el*) because they have abrogated themselves from the Sinai covenant by adopting a supersessionist ideology whereby Christ overcomes Sinai. Green would be hard pressed to call a non-seeking Jew "Israel" even if the biological Jewishness remained intact. See Lichtenstein, "Brother Daniel and the Jewish Fraternity," *Judaism* 12, no. 3 (1964): 260–280, reprinted in his *Leaves of Faith*, vol. 3 (Jersey City, NJ: Ktav, 2004), 57–83.

63 Here I think the critical reviews of Green's *Radical Judaism* sensed something that may indeed be the case: that the extension of Green's theology takes us out of a classical monotheistic frame even as it tries to salvage it through panentheism. For my response to those critical reviews, see Shaul Magid, "(Re)Reading Jewish Radicalism: Reading Reviews of Arthur Green's *Radical Judaism*," *Zeek Magazine*, March 10, 2011, zeek.forward.com/articles/117106/.

Green is another version of Maimonides's "category error," simply functioning in a mistaken paradigm.[64] I am reading Green both systematically as well as linking his metaphysics to his social critique. Thus, Green's willingness to draw conclusions from a metaphysical revision that was already articulated numerous times before in the mystical tradition exhibits the extent to which the monotheistic framework of his time has changed such that this revision can now extend to the radical social consequences that earlier forms of monotheism prevented it from doing. As a result, idolatry is reconceived (as it always is) and ironically lands on the very foundations of normative Judaism. If for Green idolatry is that which serves, affirms, or founds, any fragment for the whole, and misconstrues the parts, or even the sum of the parts, to the whole, the Judaism that gave us monotheism is now relegated to its idolatrous fate, as Green notes earlier, even revelation can become an idol. It becomes an idol, on this reading, when it views religions hierarchically and exceptionally, whether through a theological rendering of God as other or through a politically rendering of Israel exclusively as a biologically determined people.

4. The Lurianic Alternative and the Necessity of Idolatry

One question that emerges from this exercise is how and whether "idolatry" is a useful category today to describe that which lies outside the orbit of one's understanding of a legitimate social system or set of beliefs and practices. The categories of ethics and theology, here framed as the Meiriean or Maimonidean paradigm, is exemplified in two contemporary Jewish thinkers who offer broad visions of monotheism and then use the category of idolatry to define that which lies outside it. Neither Schweid nor Green accede to the biblical paradigm of absolute intolerance for idolatry; that seems to have been abolished even in antiquity. And yet each one appears to develop their ideas more from biblical rather than rabbinic motifs and sources. Hence, each is really speaking about idolatry and not *avodah zarah*.[65] In addition, each assumes that idolatry is, to some degree, embedded in various forms of traditional religion that becomes excised through the evolutionary process of modernity whereby human progress sifts out idolatrous elements as it moves toward a more mature and developed

---

64 Admitted here I am to some extent reading Green through Zalman Schachter-Shalomi, who coined the term "paradigm shift" to describe his spiritual project. While Green avoids that terminology, I think it applies in this case.
65 The distinction between idolatry and *avodah zarah* is aptly discussed by Goshen-Gottstein in *Same God, Other god* discussed above.

notion of monotheism's humanism. Yet each one, in different ways, assumes idolatry continues to function as a way to draw borders between "in" and "out" to further ensure that the fruits of that progress remain operational. Below I offer a alternative model and weigh in on what I view may be the efficacy, and function, of the category of idolatry.

As I understand Green, the radical oneness of monotheism has its own serious drawbacks, politically and spiritually. Unity does not always, or even easily, translate into equality, and a belief in the sanctity of human life determined by the human as created "in the image of God," does not always translate into tolerance. As Jan Assmann has shown in his work, monotheism can also function in a violent manner to negate, sometimes violently, anything that does not cohere with its ostensible universalizing vision. We know, for example, that universalism while doing much good in the world, has been at times the banner of much death and destruction. Assmann's provocative thesis of the "Mosaic distinction," whether or not accurate in its totality and context, speaks to the occupational hazard of monotheism as a theological paradigm.[66] One might ask if Green's radical oneness theology, while certainly intended to bring peace and unity, opens itself to the critique of the totalizing nature of monotheism as Assmann explains it. This is certainly not an accusation and I am quite sure Green wants to avoid those consequences at all costs. I simply want to suggest that radical oneness has its own occupational hazards, theologically and politically, worth noting.

I would like to suggest an alternative paradigm to Green's mystical Maimonideanism of radical oneness. Green's theology emerges in large part from his reading of early Hasidism, which tempers the infinite fragmentary metaphysics of classical Kabbalah, specifically the Lurianic tradition, in favor of a notion of panentheism whereby the One that extends beyond creation is felt and experienced *in* creation.[67] Yet the Hasidic notion of *devekut* still functions inside the orbit of a deeply particularistic, even xenophobic, world. Once that traditional cloak is removed and the feeling (*devekut*) is translated into a metaphysics, that radical oneness demands total fidelity. Anything that turns away from that One, or views the experience of the fragments as the sum total of God, is for Green idolatry.

---

66 Mark Smith offers perhaps the best critique of Assmann. See Smith, *God in Translation*, esp. 243–274.
67 See, for example, Martin Buber, "Hasidism is no pantheism. It teaches the absolute transcendence of God, but as combined with his conditioned immanence." Martin Buber, *The Way of Man according to the Teachings of Hasidism* (Woodstock, VT: Jewish Lights, 2012), 6.

I prefer a more Lurianic-inflected approach of infinite fragmentation. In a Lurianic register, God is experienced through infinite divisibility. *Eyn sof* functions as a placeholder with no substance and thus no intrinsic meaning.[68] God as *eyn sof* is accepted as a truism but the kabbalists' experience of the divine in the world is not through it, but is rather through the infinite divisibility of the *sefirot* or *partzufim* (clusters of *sefirot*, or more literally, "divine faces") as the continually refracting divinity cascading through time and space.[69] Luria notes that the contemplative practices of prayer (*kavvanot ha-tefila*) change at every moment because the infinite refractions of divinity are constantly in motion.[70] The Lurianic tradition is the opposite of the quietude and harmony of oneness. It is, rather, the cacophonous disharmony of infinite refraction. This is one reason Luria claimed not to be able to write—his experience of constant change made the finality of writing impossible.

I am in full agreement with Green that the hierarchical notion of divine election, giving only Israel covenantal rights and promoting a Jewish exclusivity that too easily slides into chauvinism and worse, needs to be altered, and the best way to do so is through a revised metaphysics rather than social engineering. As I read him, Green does it by positing radical oneness and making all who strive for that oneness part of the larger "Israel," while retaining a biological community of "Jews." Another way is to posit a metaphysics of infinite divisibility, which enables multiple connections and prevents the stasis of the hierarchical structure, destabilizing the binary of Jew and gentile that stands at the center of normative Judaism.[71]

Idolatry for Green is denying the divine excess that bursts forth from that One. Idolatry for me is to suggest some stagnant or frozen hierarchical structure in the infinite divisibility of the divine. The lifeblood of the divine in the world is as a never-ending and always surprising cascade of fragmentary movement that is equally tangible and elusive; that is, like light, the favorite metaphor of the kabbalists, it appears and disappears without a trace (or leaving a trace!), only to appear once again. The notion of it all being rooted in the One is less important for me than its fleeting character and the experience of that in the circularity of

---

68 See my essays "The Word of God is No Word at All" and "God is Already Not One."
69 See Menachem Kallus, "The Theurgy of Prayer in the Lurianic Kabbalah" (PhD dissertation, The Hebrew University, Jerusalem, 2002), 161–197.
70 See Pinhas Giller, *Shalom Shar'abi and the Kabbalists of Beit El* (New York: Oxford University Press, 2008); and Kallus, "The Theurgy of Prayer in the Lurianic Kabbalah," 114–130.
71 On the construction of this binary and the "invention of the gentile," see Ishay Rosen-Zvi and Adi Ofir, *Goy: Israel's Other and the Birth of the Gentile* (New York: Oxford University Press, 2018).

time and the changing vicissitudes of space. Earlier Jewish mystics were wed to some unifying One in part because this was what they received, which itself may have been developed at a specific time to answer certain challenges to monotheism. Part of postmodernity is the liberation from that historically contingent oneness into a world of never-ending fragmentation. This is not to say that the One does not exist—Luria's *eyn sof* makes it clear that it does. The question is whether it should be the focus of one's attention. Here then, Luria may have been one of the progenitors of postmodernity while never reaching the state of deconstruction whereby a notion of the One would collapse.[72]

In addition, what I suggest is that this infinite divisibility should be combined with divine personhood, here following Buber, that God is the depiction of the Absolute Person. Just as a person can be seen and known but never fully revealed—in a psychoanalytic register, there will always remain something undisclosed in any individual, even to him/herself—so too God's unknowability is not in a divine excess of transcendence but precisely in God's fragmentary personhood. For me, then, idolatry would also be the depersonalization of God, what I see as a possible hazard of radical oneness that is manifest in the Maimonidean model discussed above. If the human is created in the image of God, with all that implies, then God must also exist in the image of the human. I develop this in my book *Hasidism Incarnate* arguing that indeed incarnational thinking is a motif that never fully leaves the Jewish mystical arena, and for good reason. One cannot deeply consider the humanness of the tree of *sefirot* as a cosmic template without envisioning a God who reflects the human in form.[73] Whether imaginal, as Elliot Wolfson argues, symbolic, or allegorical, the divine and the human seem inextricably intertwined.

This divine "humanity" is manifest, as infinite fragmentation; in some way the very opposite of oneness and unity. Thus, idolatry for me is also the denial of the human nature of the divine. This is not to say the human is God but rather that God, like the human, is infinitely divisible and it is the experience or elucidation of that infinite divisibility that makes for the authentic experience of God. Here I agree with Green that any religion that creates an absolute hierarchy, that is, divine election, can easily lead to chauvinism, which, for him and for me, is an expression of idolatry. Green claims this is so because of turning away from the

---

72   On this from a different vantage point, see Sanford Drob, *Kabbalah and Postmodernism: A Dialogue* (Bern: Peter Lang Inc, 2009).
73   See Shaul Magid, *Hasidism Incarnate: Hasidism and the Making of Modern Judaism* (Stanford: Stanford University Press, 2014). See also Elliot Wolfson, *Language, Eros, Being* (New York: Fordham University Press, 2008), 190–260.

One. I am suggesting it is so because such divisions fail to recognize the infinite fragmentation of God in all things. By turning away from the infinite expressions of God in creation and in the cosmos, we too easily fall victim to a totalizing narrative whereby the One God chooses one people to enact God's will. I think the Hasidic masters were sensitive to this but because they lived in such a closed orbit of monotheistic oneness and a social polarity that cultivated difference and exclusivity, determining their own special status (oneness), they could not pursue it further than merely gesturing toward God's presence in creation.

Along these lines, the Lurianic kabbalists, and not Maimonides, become the great monotheists in that their focus is never on *eyn sof* but rather the dizzying and infinite dividing of the cosmos as an organic pulsating manifestation of living divine fragmentation. In my view, the oneness of *eyn sof* cannot easily be a unifying force if it is, by its very nature, beyond the limits of our apprehension and experience. The function it provides is to prevent the infinite fragmentation of the world, the object of our experience, to become so diffuse as to lose any purported meaning. But the significance of that fragmentary experience is not that it is unified in some oneness, even though it may be so, but that the fragments are infinitely divisible. This is not a repudiation of kabbalistic metaphysics as much as a shift in emphasis in regard to where our attention should be focused. Idolatry is an attempt to stop that process by trying to see beyond it, or by ordering those fragments in ways that create hierarchies that, when translated into human encounters, can breed injustice and more. Here I can return to Schweid to state that humanism is indeed a necessary part of human flourishing and that humanism was a product in large part of modernity. The question for me is how to maintain that humanistic ethos in an infinitely fragmented reality that Lurianism, or postmodernism, suggests.

The periodic accusation of Kabbalah as potentially "idolatrous" is born from a Maimonidean perspective, one that, at least to some degree, Green adopts. On my reading, the depersonalizing nature of Maimonideanism is dangerous to the extent to which it creates a categorical separation between the human and divine that threatens the personhood of God and, by extension, the divine nature of the human.

More strongly stated, I would suggest that we add an additional paradigm to thinking about idolatry; that of Lurianism. Maimonides suggested a radical transcendence of the One that was philosophically proffered and defended. Meiri sought a more social-empirical rendering of idolatry by arguing that metaphysics may be less determinate of idolatry, in part because it is more diffuse, and opted for an ethical lens to determine whether a religion is or is not idolatrous. Green adds an experiential component to the Maimonidean paradigm and

Schweid extends Meiri's social model to posit first principles of modernity in relationship to humanism and/as monotheism. In Luria we find a metaphysics where infinitude is not presented as an undifferentiated One (in his language, *eyn sof*), about which little can be said. Rather, the Lurianic mind enters a world of infinite divisibility whereby the mystic engages, contemplates, and even experiences God through and not beyond that divisibility that is in constant motion without end. One nexus point between that understanding of existence and psychology, as has been noted by others, is the way the human psyche mirrors that infinite divisibility and thus the human mind becomes, so to speak, an exemplar of infinitude.[74]

What would constitute idolatry in such a model? First, as I stated above, stasis, the position that this cascade of infinitude somehow becomes ossified in ways that create unmovable hierarchies, whether in terms of revelation, or in terms of the a notion of chosenness. It is well-known that Jewish mystics have often argued for what Tamar Ross, reading Rav Kook, called "progressive revelations of a pre-existent ideal," an idea that innovation can be a new unfolding of revelation.[75] In Rav Kook's mind, this serves as a metaphysical justification for changing ideas in the infinite body of Torah. I would suggest that this can also serve as a model for the infinite possibility of Torah's manifestations. Denying that possibility, I submit, would constitute a form of idolatry. Second, the model of Lurianism I suggest posits that our focus should be more on the multitudinous divisibility of the divine as it presents itself in the cosmos and the world and less on the unity of *eyn sof* (about which cannot say anything), which serves as its origin. This would require ownership of the fleeting infinitude of the Lurianic model. That is, the kabbalist creates a topography of divine divisibility. This is precisely what we find in the *kavvanot* (contemplative practices) of Lurianic prayer, which hardly constitutes a quietist contemplation of the One. Quite the

---

74   See, for example Dvorah Bat-David Gamlieli, *Psychoanalysis and Kabbalah: The Masculine and Feminine in Lurianic Kabbalah* (Los Angeles: Cherub Press, 2006); Jonathan Garb, *Yearnings of the Soul: Psychological Thought in Modern Kabbalah* (Chicago: University of Chicago Press, 2015); Edward Hoffman, *The Way of Splendor: Jewish Mysticism and Modern Psychology* (Lanham, MD: Rowman and Littlefield, 2006), Z'ev ben Shimon Halevi, *Psychology and Kabbalah* (Nevada City, CA: Gateway Books, 1986); and Daniel Abrams, *Ten Psychoanalytic Aphorisms on the Kabbalah* (Los Angeles: Cherub Press, 2011).

75   See Tamar Ross, *Expanding the Palace of Torah* (Waltham: Brandeis University Press, 2004), 205, 206. The idea of "continuing revelation" extends back to the rabbinic "theology of the dual Torah" that legitimates the rabbinic project of legislation. Kook viewed it from a more mystical lens. On continuing revelation and the rabbis see, for example, Satlow, *Creating Judaism*, 122.

opposite, it is a detailed mapping of the cacophony of the ever-changing manifestations of divinity is its smallest and most complex fragments.[76]

This, of course, touches on questions of interpretive and legislative authority, that is, who gets to say what is or is not a viable manifestation of this unfolding infinitude. That is, if the cascading infinite takes myriad forms, what criteria are used to define the status of each manifestation? On this reading, how would the label "idolatry" relate to other religions from this particular Jewish perspective? What would be the criteria or limits in defining a religious tradition idolatrous given the infinite divisibility of divine light? Schweid offers socio-political criteria and Green suggests anything deviating from everything being unified in the One. I am suggesting it may be the ossification of divine hierarchies making one refraction superior to another. In all these cases, idolatry morphs into an attitude about one's understanding of divinity rather than a structural rendering of any iteration of that infinitude in a religious tradition.

Like any metaphysical system the Lurianic model has its hazards. One notable hazard is that this notion of infinite divisibility too easily becomes an instantiation of religious anarchy with no borders and no ability to create and police norms. Therefore, as opposed to the zero-sum tolerance for idolatry, or image worship, that we see in the Hebrew Bible, I suggest that this Lurianic notion of infinite divisibility has to be tempered by the "idolatrous" idea of containing divinity in order to make normative decisions necessary for a cohesive religious collective. That is, the precarious yet necessary move here is containing the divine from unraveling into anarchy. However, in the normalization of this infinite divisibility, that is, in creating religion from it, we should keep in mind that, in fact, the nature of the divine *is* anarchic. Tempering that anarchy, we should remain cognizant that such an exercise is a kind of "necessary idolatry" for the sake of coherence and normativity but not allow that containment, which is necessary, to become ossified in such a way that it is mistaken as the only legitimate iteration of the divine.[77] On this reading, the notion that divine truth exists exclusively in one iteration of the divine, only *here*, a view that easily slides into exclusivity, becomes itself a form of idolatry. This is what Green, paraphrasing the Kotzker *rebbe*, may have meant when he said "have we made revelation an idol?"

---

76 Here see Kallus, "The Theurgy of Prayer in the Lurianic Kabbalah"; and Giller, *Shalom Shar'abi and the Kabbalists of Beit El*.
77 The notion of "necessary idolatry" as an act of purification *from* idolatry has a history in Sabbateanism. See, for example, in Abraham Cardozo's letter to his brother Isaac on the subject of Sabbetai Zevi's apostasy. See R. Jacob Sasportas, *Zizat Novel Zvi*, I Tishby ed. (Jerusalem: Mosad Bialik, 1954), 289–297. An English translation can be found in *Sabbatean Heresy* Pawel Maciejko ed. and introduction (Waltham, MA: Brandeis University Press, 2017), 72.

CHAPTER 4

Jewish Feminist Liberation Theology and the Modern Criticism of Idols

Melissa Raphael

Jewish feminists have not used the criticism of idols as a stick with which to beat other religions. The criticism of idolatry has been regarded by liberal Jewish feminists, as it has been by other modern Jews, as the cognitive ground of prophetic praxis: of the drive for an intra and extra-Judaic social justice. But Jewish modernity has been a long time coming. Not since the biblical period has Jewish idol-breaking been an assault on material objects or those who revere them. And even then, the prophets' objections to idols seem to have owed as much to the worship of idols as a set of category mistakes or material occlusions of the spirit as defections to a foreign cult.

Centuries before Feuerbach and Marx, Maimonides recognized that the most powerful idols are not figures set up in places of worship, but customary erroneous ideas, mediated to the masses in ways that induce ignorance and forgetting.[1] Modern emancipationists have gone on to identify idolatry, religious and secular, as the medium of false consciousness. Oppression is ideological before it is material. Any serious bid for a redemption from one sort of captivity or another recognizes that idolatrous thought and language, as well as figurative images, give a dangerous artificial life to projections that inhabit and manipulate the imagination (Jewish imaginations no less than any others). Arguably, after Maimonides, and certainly after Marx, a primary function of Jewish idoloclasm

---

1   Maimonides, *Mishneh Torah*, Laws of Idolatry 1:2; Maimonides, *Guide of the Perplexed* 1:31. See, further, Moshe Halbertal and Avishai Margolit, *Idolatry*, trans. Naomi Goldblum (Cambridge, MA: Harvard University Press, 1992), 42–43, 116–117, 127–131.

has been the nullification of an ideology that enslaves the spirit to a set of false ideas perpetuated in the interests of a polity's own power.[2] The present essay rests on the principle that *avodah zarah* offers modernity a category of critical analysis that is the precondition of spiritual-political liberation. It petitions for the freedom of all that is alive to live.

The women's liberation movement, which began during the 1960s, theorized patriarchy as a primary colonization and alienation of the spirit and bodily energy of the Other as its actual or effective slave. Patriarchy, here, is a paradigmatically idolatrous world order that vacates and arrogates the human of its humanity, the divine of its divinity, and adulates inhuman powers. The normalization of this world order as natural and ordained is a primary moment of false consciousness. As Emma Goldman put it in 1910, women's emancipation would begin "neither in the polls nor in the courts," but with the liberation of women's minds from "internal tyrants." Goldman understood these tyrants as false ideas that acted as "jailers of the human spirit" whose ideological chains "cramp and bind" women's nature until their inner life is "empty and dead" and life rolls on in all its pathos and joy "without touching or gripping" their souls.[3] Feminism requires women to break the ideological chains of patriarchy for to be bound is to be in a condition of servitude; that is, vacated of one's full humanity.

I have recently argued that, in so far as it was a moment of idoloclasm, the women's liberation movement, in which non-Orthodox Jewish feminists played such an active and prominent role from the 1960s onwards,[4] was not, primarily, a struggle for equality of opportunity with men, for the status of honorary men. The women's liberation movement was, as I understand it, a criticism of culture rooted in the criticism of idols. Liberal feminism's struggle to end sexual discrimination was part of a larger and far more radical revolution against a

---

2 By "idoloclasm" I mean the breaking of false ideas that activate images of the human and divine that alienate their actual nature and agency. This little or never used word is not a synonym for "iconoclasm" but indicates that an icon and an idol are two different things. An idol is, by definition, a harmful image. An icon, however, is an image that, being translucent to some truth or good, wields no power in and of itself, and therefore should be cherished rather than smashed. While Judaism is broadly aniconic, the image of God, for example, renders the human face, at least, an icon.
3 Emma Goldman, "The Tragedy of Women's Emancipation," in Emma Goldman, ed., *Anarchism and Other Essays* (1910), 94–95, https://theanarchistlibrary.org/library/emma-goldman-anarchism-and-other-essays.pdf.
4 See Joyce Antler, *Jewish Radical Feminism: Voices from the Women's Liberation Movement* (New York: New York University Press, 2018).

cosmically grounded order in which the parameters of female being could be set by the ends of male being and becoming.[5]

The first moment of the women's revolution was to overturn the ontological, and then the material, conditions by which patriarchy took possession of the female bio-domestic labor that sustained its own project. Germaine Greer's 1970 *The Female Eunuch*, which was read as carefully by Jewish women as by any other, insisted that for women to seek mere equality with or sameness to men is a conservative goal. She argued instead, as all religious feminists were to do, that women first needed to be liberated into their full humanity.[6] Far from prescribing what women should be, the women's liberation movement sought to liberate women from the cultural constraints of their objectification or false image into the dimension of the protean, breathing, and free. The new woman was to be a woman who was, quite simply, fully human, fully herself, and therefore fully alive.

Criticism of Idols as the Basis of a Jewish and Christian Feminist Alliance

Secular women's liberationists have tended to regard religion as inherently conservative: as the sanctification of a patriarchal dispensation that has 'God on its side'. Religiously inclined women's liberationists' account of religion has been more nuanced. In particular, the religious feminist academy—Jewish and Christian—is habituated to a long history of *religious*, as well as secular, criticism of religion and can draw on the biblical redemptive thematic as the prophetic ground of social liberation. Feminist scholars of religion know it to be an engine of both oppression and liberation; both reactionary and progressive, depending on how, where and by whom it is practiced.

As such, the second-wave Jewish and Christian women's liberationists of the last three decades of the twentieth century were inspired by Latin American and Black liberation theology, which considered the God who ordained and policed

---

5   Melissa Raphael, *Religion, Feminism and Idoloclasm: Being and Becoming in the Women's Liberation Movement* (Abingdon, Oxon: Routledge, 2019), *passim* and esp. 15–33. Much of the current essay draws on this book and my previous articles such as "A Patrimony of Idols: Second-Wave Jewish and Christian Feminist Theology and the Criticism of Religion," *Sophia: International Journal of Philosophy and Tradition* 53 (2014): 241–259; and "Idoloclasm: The First Task of Second-Wave Liberal Jewish Feminism," *Melilah: Manchester Journal of Jewish Studies* 12 (2015): 110–121.

6   Germaine Greer, *The Female Eunuch* (London: Paladin Press, 1991 [1970]), 368–369.

socio-cosmic hierarchies to be a politically self-serving fiction of the white elite. While self-identified Jewish feminist theologians such as Susannah Heschel, Judith Plaskow, Rachel Adler (and later myself) have never been very numerous,[7] these women's intellectual and spiritual careers began on liberationist grounds that allowed them to enjoy collaborative conversations with Christian feminist theologians, as well as Jewish feminist philosophers, liturgists and hermeneuticists. Theirs was a modern conversation about the ideological alienation of power from the truth of power-with-others to power-over-the-Other.

As a modern Jewish critical turn, the second-wave Jewish feminist theological critique of idols was more characteristically liberal than Orthodox. While the criticism of idols is a defining moment of any variant of Judaism, right from the outset, when Blu Greenberg published her groundbreaking book *On Women and Judaism* in 1981, Modern Orthodox feminism (effectively the only type of self-identified Orthodox feminism) was an inherently conservative type of feminism with relatively weak ties to the women's liberation movement. If Modern Orthodox feminism sought to liberate women it was not from their domestic, familial and marital roles or, indeed, from traditional concepts of God, but by gaining them better access to study, prayer, divorce and other matters of direct relevance to observant women's lives.[8] Their activism was, and remains, that of an intra-halakhic negotiation with the tradition on its own (masculine) terms—not a break with tradition. There was no logical requirement to challenge traditional ideas about the feminine or God as false or idolatrous in order to make halakhic improvements to women's Jewish opportunities and standing.

It was the liberal wing of the Jewish feminist movement, which, together with Christian feminists, claimed that an exclusively masculine conception and dispensation of the cosmic/world order had mandated human male subjects, and the god called God created in their image, to rule over women and a feminized nature. Far from disappearing in modernity, patriarchal idolatry had intensified. Indeed, its hubristic self-idolization had actually *produced* secularization. A modern masculine elite had granted itself the economic, technocratic, and

---

7   See, further, Melissa Raphael, "Feminist Theology and the Jewish Tradition," in *The Oxford Handbook of Feminist Theology*, ed. Mary McClintock Fulkerson and Sheila Briggs (New York: Oxford University Press, 2012), 51–72; and idem, "The Impact of Gender on Jewish Feminist Thought: Exemplar: Jewish Feminist Theology," *Melilah: Manchester Journal of Jewish Studies* (2019): 30–34.

8   Not long after the publication of *On Women and Judaism* (Philadelphia: Jewish Publication Society, 1981), Blu Greenberg reaffirmed the essential domesticity of her feminism with the publication of *How to Run a Traditional Jewish Household* (New York: Simon and Schuster, 1983).

military power that replaced God's power over his creation. "Man" could now play God over women and all other "natural" objects in God's very absence.

Behind the many and various conference papers, anthologized essays, and books written by Christian and Jewish feminists during the last three decades of the twentieth century, lay a basic idoloclastic claim that ran as follows. Women, whether they are religiously observant or not, are held in a threefold captivity: to the self-idolizing patriarchal god called "Man," to the projection made in the image of his own will to power called "God," and to the idol of the feminine called "Woman." "Woman," here, is the result of "Man's" self-awarded power and authority from God to construct her as the biddable complement of men. The idols of God, "Man," and "Woman" are therefore a co-creative function of each other that together, under patriarchy, alienate women's being from its becoming.

Second-wave liberal Jewish and Christian feminists joined secular feminists such as Betty Friedan and Shulamith Firestone (both of whom were Jewish) in arguing that the purpose of women's idolization (well-understood by Ira Levin in his popular, and very Jewish, novel of 1975, *The Stepford Wives*) is to control women by supplanting their actuality as conscious, willing subjects with the false consciousness of a fantasized object obedient to the will of its creator. Such would contain and limit the risk of the natural (that is, the unruly feminine) "polluting" or otherwise disrupting the productivity of a given cultus. The idealization of a woman's maternal and domestic piety or, in a more secular environment, the adulation of her "good" figure and looks, would be the reward or crown of her self-effacing compliance with the requirements of the patriarchal order. In short, feminists understood an ideology of femininity as a patriarchal religio-political device by which to naturalize, socialize, and maintain power over women by molding their minds and bodies into conformity with its own standard ideal type. Differently inflected the world over, patriarchy produces local versions of the feminine same: the complementary object to the male subject.

Although Betty Friedan's 1963 *The Feminine Mystique* was the first major secular (if arguably Jewish) contribution to the feminist idoloclastic project, the earliest published feminist *theological* criticism of idols was not Jewish, but Catholic. Mary Daly's book *The Church and the Second Sex* was published in 1968, before Daly left the Catholic Church.[9] Between the close of the 1960s and the beginning of the 1980s, Daly was joined by other Catholic feminists such as Elizabeth Farians, Elizabeth Johnson, and Rosemary Ruether in arguing

---

9   These arguments appeared in a variety of texts from about 1968 with the publication of Mary Daly's 1968 *The Church and the Second Sex*, to the mid-1980s and included Rosemary Ruther's *Sexism and God-Talk* of 1983.

that a monosexual (masculine) monotheism cosmized the gender hierarchy and excluded, *a priori*, the feminine from the exercise of interventionary reason and morality as licensed by a masculine God's eternal perfections. In worshipping an omnipotent and omniscient God who made in men in his image—who was more "like" men than women—men were worshipping only themselves. Only by smashing those images that obstructed women's becoming in the image of God, would women be fully human. They also insisted that idolatry did not only demote women's humanity, it also cast the significance and truth of androcentric theology into question. Any patriarchal refusal to ever name God as "she" does not protect God but idolize "him."

These early and influential Catholic feminists' theological judgements of patriarchal theism as idolatrous informed and buttressed a Jewish feminist theological criticism of idols that was being formulated in the same academic and political American environment. Jewish feminists—first and principally Rachel Adler and Judith Plaskow (who studied Christian theology as a postgraduate at Yale, as I did as an undergraduate at Oxford)—joined Daly and other Christian feminists in reading scriptural and theological texts through a new feminist "hermeneutic of suspicion." The liberationist method of reading authoritative (or more precisely, authoritarian) texts "from below" suggested that the immediate allegiances of scripture and its hegemonic interpreters might be to ideological constructions that conferred power and authority on the status quo rather than on God.

Jewish Feminist Idoloclasm

The Hebrew Bible may have promised liberation from captivity to oppressors, whether actual or ideational, but, for women, the *way* that it criticized idols was not entirely helpful. The prophetic literature feminizes Israel's quasi-marital infidelity to God as "whoring" after false gods; as dishonoring God's name in ways analogous to adulterous wives who have betrayed and shamed their husbands. Ezekiel and Hosea, perhaps most notably, figured the divine punishment for Israel's faithless "harlotry" in grossly misogynistic, pornographically explicit images of female degradation. While it was expedient for the midrash to explain away Rachel's attachment to her family idols, the tradition did not exonerate the women who wove magical coverings for the image of Asherah (2 Kgs. 23:7), baked cakes for the Queen of Heaven (Jer. 7:16–20 and 44:17–19), and sat at the north gate of the first Temple, weeping in annual lamentation for the death of the Babylonian god Tammuz (Ezek. 8:14).

Of course, in contrast to biblical material that associates the sexual attraction or charm of the feminine with that of strange gods, there is also a midrashic tradition that applauds Jewish women's resistance to idolatry. It is worth noting that, according to the medieval midrash *Pirke de Rabbi Eliezer*, Israelite women refused to donate their gold jewellery to the making of the golden calf, though they had been glad to sacrifice it for the making of the Tabernacle. Women had been rewarded thereafter with a holiday from work at each New Moon (*Rosh Chodesh*). The Yemenite midrash (*Ki Tissa* 32:2) adds that this piety merited permission for all women other than Miriam, even Moses's 250-year-old mother, Yocheved, to enter the Land of Israel at a time when such was denied to men. Or again, the rabbinic literature tells the story of a widow named in *Lamentations Rabbah* as Miriam Bat Tanchum, who was glorified by God when, after the last and youngest of her seven sons, a three-year-old child, was beheaded by the Emperor Hadrian for refusing to bow down to Roman idols, she meritoriously threw herself from the roof.[10]

The rabbis differ in how and what they perceive as idols: whether, for example, they are real supernatural powers created by God but who have no dominion over Jews; whether they are rivals to God, or are merely formal vacancies to which the credulous are susceptible.[11] But whether or not Jewish women are more or less immune to the powerful hold of these than men is largely immaterial. If a Jew is one who, under the Second Commandment, is prohibited from making idols and worshipping them, then all Jews, male and female, are well-equipped to demystify the finite objects to which infinite powers have been attributed.[12] The Second Commandment warns that a culture that worships "Man's" power over the world he has created, rather God's in the world God-self has created, is a tyrannical, fraudulent one. It has arrogated divine power by hiding God's face/presence from the world and replacing it with an image of its own.

Jewish feminist activism was therefore broadly continuous with the modern Jewish relational philosophy that informed the praxis of Rabbi Abraham Joshua Heschel in his advocacy for peace and civil rights. Heschel understood prophetic Jewish praxis as that of the "iconoclast, challenging the apparently holy,

---

10 See, for example, BT *Gittin* 57b; *Lamentations Rabbah* 1:16; *Pesikta Rabbati* 43:4.
11 Rabbinic midrash on idols mocks them, for example, both because they impose form where there should be formlessness, and because they lack the quasi-corporeal capacities and consequences of God's power and agency. See Julia Watts Bresler, *Rabbinic Tales of Destruction: Gender, Sex, and Disability in the Ruins of Jerusalem* (New York: Oxford University Press, 2018), 122.
12 See Kenneth Seeskin, *No Other Gods: The Modern Struggle Against Idolatry* (West Orange, NJ: Behrman House, 1995), 20.

revered, and awesome. Beliefs cherished as certainties, institutions endowed with supreme sanctity, he [*sic*] exposes as scandalous pretensions."[13] It is no coincidence that his daughter Susannah went on to play an early and pivotal role in the development of Jewish feminism.

Initially at least, many of the Jewish women who brought the women's liberation movement into their communities were from liberal, modernizing Jewish denominations that were already, to varying degrees, open to the introduction of sexually egalitarian forms of Jewish observance. But feminist idoloclasm was not confined to liberal Judaism. Those who were drawn, for example, to the neo-Hasidic Jewish Renewal movement found that, under the progressive spiritual leadership of Rabbi Zalman Schachter-Shalomi, they could combine Orthodox spirituality and alternative, countercultural lifestyles in ways far more hospitable to feminist spiritual politics than a mainstream Orthodoxy inclined to criticize everyone's idols but its own.

Inevitably, one of the narrative centrepieces of Jewish women's liberationists' redemption of the world and God from patriarchal alienation was that of the Exodus: the redemption from slavery as enacted annually at Pesach. In 1975, Esther Broner, Marcia Freedman, and Naomi Nimrod held the first feminist *seder* in Haifa.[14] Theirs and other feminist *haggadot* were among the first of many trailblazing hermeneutical and midrashic experiments of the period. In these commentarial texts, women broke their silence. Their image came to life and interrupted a conversation between God and "Man" that had, for several millennia, prevented them from becoming the speaking subjects of their own experience.

It is not difficult to see how liberation from captivity to Pharaoh mapped onto the feminist liberation from captivity to patriarchy. The midrash on Ezek. 29:3 regards Pharaoh as the very paradigm of an idolater because he claims to be the creator and master of the world. He is the ruler of Egypt, here, not so much a country as a narrowed, blinkered, state of mind: one that is enslaved to the generic Pharaohs who license the privileged few to alienate the creative energies of the many. In the great urgency of the Exodus, Jewish feminist idoloclasm knew the inflated ego and hardened, spiritless heart of patriarchy as a carrier of death: a captivation of being from the freedom of becoming. The feminist claim that "woman" is a slave of a pharaonic world order is not a claim to be taken literally. Middle-class feminists may have borne an unequal share of a

---

13 Abraham Joshua Heschel, *The Prophets* (New York: Harper Perennial, 1962), 12.
14 They later published their liberationist version of the *seder* as Esther M. Broner and Naomi Nimrod, *The Women's Haggadah* (New York: Harper San Francisco, 1994 [1977]).

couple's responsibilities for childcare and routine domestic tasks, but even a lifetime of unpaid domestic and reproductive labor was emphatically not slavery as experienced by, say, black women in the antebellum period of the American South. Women's liberationists, including Jewish ones, were rather protesting the enslavement of women's consciousness to an ideology that variously forced them into compliance with a world order of objects created to serve the class and race interests of subject-masters.

Just a few years after the first feminist Seder, in 1979, the Jewish novelist and critic Cynthia Ozick made a significant move in the feminist-prophetic turn. Ozick pointed out that the Torah is scripture only insofar as it countermands the (patriarchal) ways of the world. She reminded Jewry that in "In giving the commandment against idolatry, Torah came face to face with a society in competition with the Creator" and turned away from it. It was therefore a scandal of "mammoth" and "terrifying" proportions that the Torah's own ethicality, or at least its mediation, has not extended to criticism of the dehumanization of women. Instead, it has sanctified a false idea of women as property or as non-juridical adults which had justified their effective exclusion from the learning, witness and (most time-bound) observances that lend the dignity of full Jewish personhood. This gaping critical omission, and the incalculable cultural and spiritual losses incurred by its ordination of discrimination against women's personhood, compelled Ozick to propose an Eleventh Commandment: "Thou shalt not lessen the humanity of women." This was a commandment proposed not only for the sake of women, but above all for the sake of the Torah itself.[15] With this new commandment she was, in effect, raising the consciousness of a halakhic order that congratulates itself on its leniencies and on having women's best interests at heart, to its own idolatry.

Ozick's feminist commandment is theologically and ethically congruent with the tradition. The Talmudic tractate *Avodah Zarah* ("Idolatry") assumes a set of shared Jewish ethical sensibilities that represent an implicit and explicit critique of the cultures in which idolatry has developed.[16] The rabbinic interpretation of the commandment to Jews not to follow "their" practices (Lev. 18:3 and its rabbinic midrashic interpretation in *Sifrah* 13:5) is not necessarily as xenophobic as it sounds. It is a rejection of the cultural habitus of idolaters, not of the nations as such. That is, Ozick rightly identifies rabbinic discourse on idolatry as more than a consideration of what images may or may not adorn the place

---

15　Cynthia Ozick, "Notes Toward Finding the Right Question," in *On Being a Jewish Feminist*, ed. Susannah Heschel (New York: Schocken Books, 1983 [1979]), 120–151, esp. 126, 144–150.
16　Halbertal and Margolit, *Idolatry*, 5.

of worship, but as a philosophical judgement on a given dispensation of power's moral, spiritual, and epistemological error. Interestingly, Ozick also did not spare liberal approaches to the feminist theology of the time. She considered any Jewish feminist reimagining of God as God/ess, Mother, or God-She to be no less idolatrous than any other imagining of God; such was, she thought, a regression to a paganism that Judaism existed to transcend.

In this latter criticism, Ozick seems not to have been acquainted with feminist theological disclaimers of the time. New/old feminine names for the divine were proposed by way of a corrective or provocation, not a substantive description. Idols were to be broken but not replaced. No feminist idoloclast claimed the epistemological wherewithal to discern true images of an essentially unknowable God from false ones.

Another of the first Jewish feminists who sought to liberate the divine and the human into the condition of what Hannah Arendt would have called "a who" from "a what," was Rachel Adler. The title of her now classic 1973 article "The Jew Who Wasn't There" criticized a femininity both over-fantasized and over-materialized by its association with the human needs and appetites for whose satisfaction it was required to labor. Adler announced that the time had come for patriarchy's female figure of clay to be liberated into life. "For too many centuries," wrote Adler, "the Jewish woman has been a golem, created by Jewish society. She cooked and bore and did her master's will, and when her tasks were done, the Divine Name was removed from her mouth. It is time for the golem to demand a soul."[17]

It was also, then, God's time to be God: a God whose will would be no more at his master's bidding than women. Judith Plaskow's book *Standing Again at Sinai*, published in 1990, laid the grounds of a Jewish feminist theology founded on the religious feminist conviction that "where a religious tradition makes the masculine body the normative bearer of the divine image of a God imagined in male language alone, and in ideas that cannot be 'tampered' with, its anthropology should be considered idolatrous."[18] Like Plaskow, the feminist biblical scholar Athalya Brenner also observed that "Man" creates god in his image, rather than God creates man in his. The irony, for Brenner, was that the Jewish God who demands that idols be broken is himself an idol. And it is an idol that

---

17 Rachel Adler, "The Jew Who Wasn't There: *Halakhah* and the Jewish Woman," in *On Being a Jewish Feminist*, ed. Susannah Heschel (New York: Schocken Books, 1983), 12–18, here 17.
18 Judith Plaskow, *Standing Again at Sinai: Judaism from a Feminist Perspective* (New York: Harper San Francisco, 1990), 147–148.

she could not finally break: "This is my heritage. I am stuck with it. I cannot and will not shake it off. And it hurts."[19]

But most Jewish feminism was also predicated on the conviction that its patrimony was polyphonic and permeable. A false image of the human or the divine cannot, in the end, contain either the living flesh or the spirit, the life through which the winds of divine *ruaḥ* blows. Some Jewish feminists breathed life back into the human and the divine by re-awakening the archetypally rebellious erotic power of Lilith, remodelled as the first and most defiantly radical of all Jewish feminists. (Plaskow's midrash had the outcast Lilith befriending, and joining forces with, Eve.)[20] Some, like the Jewish Renewal rabbis Lynn Gottlieb and Leah Novick, wanted to bring the Shekhinah, the immanence or quasi-maternal presence of the divine, back from her spiritual-political exile and into women's everyday lives by reading her rabbinic and mystical traditions against their patriarchal grain.[21]

Other Jewish feminists had little appetite for the polarities of either the idealized Shekhinah or the demonized Lilith. Preferring to avoid reintroducing what seemed to be spectral, ambiguous, neo-traditional images of the feminine into contemporary sexual politics, these Jewish feminists prioritized a demystification of female agency, equal in its religious operation, or at least not essentially different, to that of Jewish men.

But by the end of the twentieth century, the terms of Jewish feminist iconoclasm had, in any case, altered dramatically. By now, Jewish feminism was entering into its third wave. Those from the LGBTQ community were most emphatic in their conviction that gender itself stood in need of ideological liberation, not just women. Scholars such as Daniel Boyarin had taken note of gender-slippages and homoerotic elements in the rabbinic and mystical literature that obviated any fixed idea of masculinity to which femininity was the natural binary complement. Christian antisemitism and anti-Judaism had also long contributed to the destabilization of gender in Judaism by its contemptuous feminization of Jewish masculinity. But popular Ashkenazic Jewish culture had also subverted

---

19 Athalya Brenner, "The Hebrew God and His Female Complements," in *Feminism and Theology*, ed. J. Martin Soskice and D. Lipton (Oxford: Oxford University Press, 2003), 155–174, here 172.
20 Judith Plaskow, "The Coming of Lilith: Toward a Feminist Theology," in *The Coming of Lilith: Essays on Feminism, Judaism and Sexual Ethics*, ed. Judith Plaskow and Donna Berman (Boston: Beacon Press, 2005), 23–35. Barbara Koltuv's *The Book of Lilith* (York Beach, ME: Nicholas-Hays, 1986), was also typical of the Jewish feminist reclamation of the figure of Lilith in this period.
21 See, for example, Leah Novick, *On the Wings of the Shekhinah: Rediscovering Judaism's Divine Feminine* (Wheaton, IL: Quest Books, 2008).

that discourse and paid a back-handed compliment to the decidedly non-macho wit and brains of Jewish masculinity with affectionate humor. Gender, now thoroughly historicized, could be destabilized as a self-narrating fiction or performance rather suffered as a given, standing over and against the true self.

Similarly, the categorical and epistemological grounds for distinguishing true images of God from false ones had been all but lost. Modern Jewish theology operated with what traditionalists would consider an attenuated account of God, occasionally to the point of effective or practical atheism. Twentieth-century Jewish thought across most of the denominational spectrum could no longer accept the traditional account of God as the Lord of history and guarantor of justice, the sole and sufficient explanation for natural phenomena.[22] By the early years of the twenty-first century, a God-She would have seemed as overdetermined by anthropocentrism and anthropopathism as older accounts of God as Father and King.

Indicatively, Plaskow had had begun to disrupt the very idea of false ideas and wanted, instead, to use a fluid spectrum of non-gender binary, intra-gendered, and non-gendered images for God.[23] And by 2016, Plaskow had edged away from her lifelong modern commitment to ethical monotheism towards a vitalism which posits that all that exists does so for no extrinsic moral or historical purpose other than life itself.[24] That we can imagine a perfectly good and loving God does not entail that she, any more than he, exists.[25] Hers remained a criticism of idols of sorts in so far as God, if so the divine could still be named, was too dynamic and supra-personal an existential totality to be reified as a being at all. Yet the monistic nature of her theology also suggested that idolatry's category mistakes no longer really mattered.

---

22 Norman Solomon, "The Attenuation of God in Modern Jewish Thought," *Melilah: The Manchester Journal of Jewish Studies* 12 (2015): 97–109.
23 Judith Plaskow, "Dismantling the Gender Binary within Judaism: The Challenge of Transgender to Compulsory Heterosexuality," in *Heterosexism in Contemporary World Religion: Problem and Prospect*, ed. Marvin E. Ellison and Judith Plaskow (Cleveland, OH: Pilgrim Press, 2007), 13–36.
24 Plaskow, *Standing Again at Sinai*, 151–152; Carol Christ and Judith Plaskow, *Goddess and God in the World: Conversations in Embodied Theology* (Minneapolis, MN: Fortress Press, 2016), 127–128.
25 Christ and Plaskow, *Goddess and God in the World*, 173–174, 184–187.

A New Contribution to the Jewish Feminist Criticism of Idols

Pulling back from such positions, my 2019 study, *Religion, Feminism and Idoloclasm*, presented second-wave feminist idoloclasm as a founding religious and post-religious praxis of women's liberation that merits revisiting. In the Prologue to the book's exposition of the idolization of the feminine I offer a Jewish feminist theological reading of the second chapter of Genesis which suggests that it attributes the fashioning of the world's first idol to God. Here, in the carving and animation of woman from what, in Abrahamic culture, has been popularly understood as one of Adam's ribs, God is arguably the first to transgress against his own Second Commandment's proscription of the sculpting of three-dimensional full-body images of human beings.[26]

For in Genesis 2, woman is created *as* an image of woman, not *in* the image of God, as she was in Genesis 1. In Genesis 2, when God formed "man" (*adam*) from the dust of the earth (*adamah*), "man" has been regarded by most of its readers not as a hermaphrodite or as generic human "stuff," but as Adam, the name for a particular first man. And he begins his existence non-derivatively as the form of a "living being/soul." He is an incarnation of the very spirit of God as it blows through the earth (Gen. 2:7). By contrast, after a keyhole surgical procedure in which God removes what is popularly described as a "spare rib" from the man's insensible body, woman is quickly built or fashioned (*va-yiven*, in Gen. 2:22), into what the rabbis later imagine as a pyramid-like form that narrows towards a point at the top but which stands four-square on the ground (BT *Berakhot* 61a; BT *Eruvin* 18a; BT *Sanhedrin* 39a).

This formal woman-born-of-man is, as several feminist commentators have noted, set up as the first untruth: a primary "disavowal of the maternal debt."[27] And as a work of art that resembles a woman, she is, it seems to me, an appearance. Essentially two-dimensional, she can never fully "step forth" (*existere*) from herself. Moreover, she can never be the full subject of her own experience because in some senses she *is* him: bone of *his* bones and flesh of *his* flesh (Gen. 2:23).

The woman's existence is contingent. She exists only because, before her, the man was lonely (Gen. 2:18–20); because he needed to propagate so as not to

---

26 Raphael, *Religion, Feminism and Idoloclasm*, 1–7.
27 Elizabeth Grosz, *Sexual Subversions: Three French Feminists* (Sydney: Allen and Unwin, 1989), 120.

remain alone.²⁸ As R. Joseph Soloveitchik put it (uncritically), man must lose something of himself—his rib—to gain himself. She is the occasion of his human sociality. It is through her that he attains the *kavod* or dignity of a new rank: he is now *ish*—the man (Gen. 2:7).²⁹ He does not realize her as a woman. Whereas even the animals who have been created before her are "living creatures," woman is a prototype; the world's first domestic appliance, as it were. By this I mean that, here, woman's difference is more a construction that meets the prior specification of a need than does a creation proper.

Martin Buber famously united Genesis 1 and 2 with the phrase "In the beginning was the relation."³⁰ Yet Genesis 2 surely marks the beginning of the instrumental I/It binary: a male I being given a female It, or thing among things. Despite Buber and other Jewish commentators' best efforts to fuse Genesis 1 and 2 into a single continuous narrative, I suggest that attention to the ontological caesura between the two chapters should underpin a Jewish feminist bid for the human integrity of the feminine. It is only in Genesis 1 that woman enjoys the status of an original, non-fungible, non-replicable, presence or face of God as I AM: a becoming subject, not another custom-made object.

For there can be no refraction of the divine in a bone image or stand-in for a face.³¹ Whereas a man's creation from dust and ashes signals both the freedom of his life's becoming and the pathos of his finitude, the woman sculpted from bone is only a representation of a living agent. As such, she cannot die, but she also cannot live. She is non-existent.

In fact, Jewish tradition shares some of my unease. It did not escape rabbinical notice that the biblical account of the creation of a woman lacks any reference to the infusion of a soul. Among others, Rashi's and Maimonides's theology of marriage compelled them to translate *tzela* not as rib but "side." For Eve to have been nothing more than one of Adam's ribs would have been an offence not

---

28 As noted in *Pirke de Rabbi Eliezer* 12.
29 Joseph Soloveitchik, "The Lonely Man of Faith," *Tradition: A Journal of Orthodox Thought* 7 (1965): 5–67, here 22 ff. Compare Karl Barth's statement that a woman "marks the completion of his creation, it is not problematic but self-evident for her to be ordained for man in her whole existence." Karl Barth, *Church Dogmatics*, vol. 3, part 1: *The Doctrine of Creation* (Edinburgh: T. & T. Clark, 1958), 302–303.
30 Martin Buber, *I and Thou* (New York: Scribners, 1958), 18.
31 My debt to Levinas's essays "Reality and Its Shadow" and "The Prohibition against Representation and 'The Rights of Man'" will be evident. See, respectively, Emmanuel Levinas, *The Levinas Reader*, trans. and ed. by Seàn Hand (Oxford: Blackwell, 1989); and idem, *Alterity and Transcendence*, trans. Michael Smith (London: Athlone Press, 1999), 121–123, 128. It will also be evident that am not persuaded by his Talmudic reading "And God Created Woman" (1977) in *Nine Talmudic Readings*, trans. Annette Aronowicz (Bloomington, IN: Indiana University Press, 1990), 161–177.

only against her dignity, it would also, and perhaps more importantly to them, have dishonored her husband (in Hebrew, literally, her master). Ontologically, Eve had to be sufficiently cognate and complementary to Adam to enter into the union of marriage (BT *Yevamot* 62b).

A number of the rabbis, including Ralbag, interpreted Genesis 2 as a warrant for female subordination (though not, according to Abravanel, slavery). It is, after all, a fundamental principle of Western ontology that when one thing exists for the sake of another then it is inferior or subordinate to it. But even when the woman's role as *ezer k'negdo* is translated as not so much that of a "helper" as that of a (marital) "pillar of strength in times of trouble" or "opposite number," I remain unpersuaded that her construction as a prototype woman is much more than the first crime (of many) against the humanity of women.

The patriarchal anthropology of the story and its popular reception has done a fundamental injury to women's humanity that, variously institutionalized in the Abrahamic religions, has shaped the lives of most women on earth. The twentieth-century women's liberation movement charged patriarchy's ordination of the feminine as essentially ancillary to the masculine as an alienation of their being from their becoming. A modern Jewish understanding of the term *avodah zarah* is, or should be, that which does a (dis)service to the idolized: those human beings who are made foreign (*zarah*) to themselves and to God, in whose image they are made.

But there are grounds for hope. Genesis 1 surely criticizes—indeed, countermands—Genesis 2. In Genesis 1, God creates the male and the female in the perfect equality of God's own image. The possibility of idolization is radically obviated because God in God-self is a formless God. Whatever is made in the image of that God cannot be figured as an object of anyone's imagination. We are not, and cannot be, manmade.

With the Second Commandment having not so much proscribed images of the human as having reminded their makers that they must be produced and reproduced in ways that avoid or criticize idolatry, it seems clear that for all Jews, not just feminist Jews, images of persons must be stabilized in such a way that their idea can neither add to nor subtract from their finite reality. The biblical Second Commandment, crucially prefaced by the first, which proscribes the substitution of God by images of any other gods, sets the mysterious no-thingness of all being and becoming apart from harm; from being baked or hardened into an idol. Being will be and become what it will be and become. As made in the image of I AM and the I WILL BE, a woman's true, primordial, image, no more or less than a man's, is inalienable not least because, like any halakhically permitted image, it is unfinished or incomplete.[32] As such, a truly human image is a figure of the not-yet; an image of the restoration that is on its way: of the messianic. It is, after all, significant that God self-names as I am Who I Am or I Will Be Who I Will Be in the context of the Exodus narrative, of the going out from the narrowed space of ideological captivity into the open horizon of freedom. For it is the dynamic promise or futurity of an existence unbound from and by idols that makes God, God and the human, human.

---

32 See *Shulḥan Arukh*, Laws about Images and Forms 141; Steven Schwarzschild, "The Legal Foundations of Jewish Aesthetics," in *The Pursuit of the Ideal: Jewish Writings of Steven Schwarzschild*, ed. Menachem Kellner (New York: New York University Press, 1990), 109–116, here 114; Melissa Raphael, *Judaism and the Visual Image: A Jewish Theology of Art* (London and New York: Continuum, 2019), esp. 19–42; and idem, "The Creation of Beauty by Its Destruction: Idoloclasm in Modern and Contemporary Jewish Art," *Approaching Religion* 6 (2016): 14–22.

CHAPTER 5

Idolatry as Dehumanization

Rivon Krygier[1]

In an article published a few years ago, I defended sources supporting the idea that idolatry is neither what we believe it to be nor what is most often said about it.[2] For a long time, and even in today, idolatry has been decried as the most extreme form of blasphemy: one that undermines the dignity of the divine *either* by challenging God's hegemony by putting forth the belief that there exist other deities *or* by assigning to the Almighty some unworthy tangible form and then proceeding to worship that form as an image or statue forged by human hands. Following Maimonides (1138–1204), who set up this approach as a dogmatic doctrine on behalf of Judaism, idolatry is alleged to result from a *theological* aberration, a gross error in the understanding of the world order, which corrupts the mind and induces harmful conduct. However, while it is undeniable that idolatry may have been condemned in Jewish tradition in such terms, an in-depth analysis yields a more nuanced picture. And, indeed, this thesis leads us astray by putting the focus on *form* rather than *substance* when attempting to identify the perversity of idolatry. By dealing with the *object* of belief (the definition and representation of the divine), we have turned away from the *subject* of belief (the attitude of the faithful). And so have we focused overly on the symptom instead of the pathology itself.

Let me describe the background to the situation. Despite the efforts of various post-Maimonidean Jewish philosophers and exegetes to interpret the facts *metaphorically,* various sources—ranging from biblical texts to ones written in the late Middle Ages—speak freely about the existence of celestial powers other

---

1   Translated from French by Martin S. Cohen.
2   Rivon Krygier, "What Is Idolatry?" [French], *Pardes* 53 (2013): *The Disturbing Strangeness in Judaism*, 141–167; a shortened version is available in English: idem, "What Is Idolatry?", trans. Martin S. Cohen, *Zeramim* (2016), https://zeramim.org/conservative-judaism/822-2/, accessed May 2022.

than God. To be precise, these are generally described as angels or archangels, or even as protector princes or the constellations that govern nations, but sometimes they are *also* unambiguously called "gods" (*elohim*) or "divine offspring" (*bnei-elim*).[3] Nor do the texts in question insist that these entities are necessarily subordinate to the Creator like secondary cogs in some vast machine, and many suggest openly that God specifically intended that other ethnic groups or nations *legitimately* worship them.[4] Moreover, many biblical and rabbinical historians have shown that the biblical and rabbinical God is not as abstract, transcendent, or abstruse as many theologians have claimed. Different sources report divine manifestations that are not merely "created" phenomena such as clouds, columns of fire, voices, or sounds, nor mere "oracular visions" perceived in altered states of consciousness (as Maimonides argues systematically), but rather extensions of the divine entity, located temporarily (or sometimes durably) in concrete objects or even carnal bodies.[5] These phenomena were considered merely indicative of concentrated divine presence, even if, for modern people (including religious ones), all this may seem to be a matter of fantasy. The fact is that in many biblical and Talmudic sources, the distinction between angel and God is often blurry and almost always in flux, since many sources surreptitiously pass from the one concept to the other as if the difference between the two were to be more one of *degree* than of *nature* and the angel were best to be understood as a kind of divine *epiphany*. According to the striking midrashic

---

3   See, for example, Ps. 82. Most medieval exegetes have attempted to dispel the heterodox feel of this passage by interpreting the word *elohim* here not as designating secondary deities but as referencing human judges.

4   See Deut. 4:19 and 32:8–9. There is an ancient conception that a heavenly angel or prince presides over the destiny of each nation, of which there are seventy (or seventy-two). In the sources these angels are often referred to as "gods." Cf. Sirach 17:17, second century BCE; *Clementine Recognitions* (vol. 2, 42:3–8) and *Clementine Homilies* (18:4), second century CE; Jerusalem Targum on Deut. 32:8–9 and the Septuagint *ad loc*. The efficiency of astral worship is recognized by Spanish medieval rabbis such as Abraham Ibn Ezra or Nachmanides (in his commentary on Ex. 20:3). The kabbalist Shimon Lavi (Libya, sixteenth century) blames Maimonides for denying the idolatrous cult any effectiveness. This worship is not deemed repulsive because of its inanity but because it bypasses the higher will of God to which Israel is specifically committed (see his *Ketem Paz* [Djerba, 1940], fol. 159d; *Zohar* I, 64b). See also Alon Goshen-Gottstein, *Same God, Other god* (New York: Palgrave Macmillan, 2015), 59–80.

5   Cf. Alon Goshen-Gottstein, "The Body as Image of God," *Harvard Theological Review* 87, no. 2 (April 1994): 171–195; Yair Lorberbaum, *In God's Image, Myth, Theology and Law in Classical Judaism* (Cambridge: Cambridge University Press, 2015) based on his Hebrew original published by Schocken in 2004; Benjamin Sommer, *The Bodies of God and the World of Ancient Israel* (Cambridge: Cambridge University Press, 2009); Jean Costa, "The Body of God in Ancient Rabbinic Judaism, Problems of Interpretation," *Review of History of Religions* 227, no. 3 (2010): 283–316.

formula: "Wherever the angel appears, the *Shekhinah* (divine presence) appears" (*Exodus Rabbah* 32:9). Moreover, what should we say about the kabbalistic language that, speaking fully symbolically, never ceases to evoke the image of the expressive God as consisting of ten *sefirot* (that is, divine modalities or hypostases) laid out on high in anthropomorphic terms as male and female entities whose connective "channels" remain clear or become obstructed in response to human acts?

Certainly, despite this organic and dynamic conception of the divine, neither the kabbalists nor earlier biblical authors ever intended to reduce God's essence to the level of materiality, much less to corporeality affected by natural corruption such as that of the creatures that inhabit the earth. Nor was it ever anyone's wish to cast these divine manifestations as spirits or demons with erratic or capricious desires (whose independent existence is clearly affirmed in ancient rabbinic and kabbalistic sources). Nevertheless, there is in all this the idea that the Deity can self-invest to one degree or the other in the world—and thus self-manifest concretely, that is, by taking on various forms (for example, fire or light)[6] without ever severing the connection between the divine "thing" below and its ultimate and transcendent source. Such divinity is diffuse, present both here and there, in heaven and on earth, in one place but also, and at the same time, not anchored to any specific place, without these authors seeing in any of this the slightest contradiction. As Charles Mopsik brilliantly summarized it: "If God is everywhere, He is not everywhere the same, He is not everywhere Himself."[7]

An essential question therefore arises: if an abundance of divine entities or divine receptacles were truly to be perceived as exuding the pestilential smell of idolatry, why then does the Bible so often mention them? And why do the Jewish mystical circles incorporate all this imagery in their symbolic language so freely and self-consciously? In other words, what is it in idolatrous practice and ideology, other than the multiplicity of divine forms or expressions, that arouses such deep rejection?

Let us start from the understanding that the uniqueness of biblical monotheism lies in the fact that it is not *quantitative* but *qualitative*, that it is not so much belief in the existence of a single God as belief in a unique Creator who is the ultimate Ruler of the world and whom it is solely befitting to serve and worship. And so, rather than seeking to set out a set of dogmatic statements about God's essence and attributes, what Scripture exerts itself to do is to instigate *trust* in

---

6   For instance, in Num. 14:14; Deut. 24:17; Ps. 89:16.
7   Charles Mopsik, *The Great Texts of Kabbalah: The Rites Making God* [French] (Lagrasse: Verdier, 1993), 196.

God's redeeming power. And this notion, namely that divine governance (or providence) will lead to the establishment of justice in the world and bring salvation to its souls, is *conditioned* by obedience to divine will as expressed through the commandments of Torah. This principle is laid down from the first stages of Israel's liberation from the Egyptian yoke: "There God set them a law and a rule; there God put them to the test: if you listen carefully to the voice of the Lord your God and do what is right in His eyes, if you will listen to His commandments and keep all His laws, I will not bring upon you any of the diseases that I brought upon the Egyptians for I the Lord am your Healer" (Ex. 15: 25–26). And later: "And this will be our righteousness (merit) before the Lord, our God, to observe all these commandments as He has commanded us" (Deut. 6:25). To put it another way, to believe in God is essentially to recognize God's supreme authority and satisfy God's various demands or, to use the Mishnah's terminology: "to accept the yoke of divine sovereignty and God's commandments" (M *Berakhot* 2:2). Trust in God is thus identified with the loyalty shown by the faithful in embarking on the path prescribed by God as interpreted by the masters of tradition over the generations.

But allegiance to the ultimate God entails an ultimate ethic, a kind of constant effort to self-improve: "You shall be holy to Me, for I the Lord am holy, and I have set you apart from other peoples to be Mine" (Lev. 20:26). The Torah, in fact, in addition to the rule of justice and equity that constitutes the heart of its law,[8] requires a mastery of impulses, a regimen of pious conduct in the various areas of life as symbolized by obedience to the dietary laws (*kashrut*), by a general willingness to rein in one's sexual desires, by agreeing to a weekly retreat from labor on Sabbath, by accepting circumcision (*b'rit milah*), and so forth. The effort of *sublimation* or ideal holiness is profoundly linked with the singular bond that binds the supreme God to the people chosen as the herald of God's eternal message: "Have I not made heard it to you and said to you forever that you are to be My witnesses. Is there a god other than Me?" (Isa. 44:8). Therefore, the perversity of polytheists consists essentially of an attempt to break free from this elective condition and to free themselves from the "yoke" of the commandments. Idolatry is thus seen as the temptation to attach oneself to varied (and far more complacent) divine entities with which it could be possible to enter into a pact, to "do business" (so to speak) *with* them, to offer up various sacrifices to obtain in return precious blessings and indulgences *from* them, and thus to escape the difficult part of the covenant, namely the incessant tension

---

8   Cf. Gen. 18:19; Isa. 58.

towards the absolute, and the nagging guilt that failure to fully submit inevitably generates.

But what applies in the Jewish context, where idolatry is deemed synonymous with withdrawal from the unique covenant that binds God and Israel, also applies significantly and really to all nations. Indeed, according to the Talmudic tradition regarding Gen. 9:4–10, every human being—and, indeed, every nation—is bound by the duty to "fear God," that is to say, to revere God's desire for justice by obeying the seven so-called Noachide commandments.[9] Each people, by setting up courts and enacting legislation, defines its own normative laws, as well as its national spirituality. And with that thought we come to the cardinal point I wish to make: whether within the covenant of Israel or in the more universal framework conceived as "Noach's covenant," idolatry is deemed reprehensible when it aims to *instrumentalize* the divine, to assist the idolater in escaping the duties of conscience that rest upon every human being created in the image of God. Instead of "fearing God," the idolater tries to *domesticate* the gods, to tame them or coax them into compliance. In seeking to put them under house arrest, the idolater attempts to take control of celestial powers or earthly geniuses who might otherwise be hostile. Worship devoted to a host of protective gods or even to a partial or limited god is not so much an aberration as a manoeuvre. It is perversion to the extent that it is resignation. The sacred dimension is thus diverted from its "real" goal by placing it at the service of interests aimed at strengthening the power of the individual, the group, or the nation, and, under certain circumstances, ends up serving as a pretext for inhuman, violent, or humiliating conduct. More than a *dedivinization*, idolatry is *dehumanization*. Or, shall we say instead, it disfigures God in the same way it disfigures the human being created in God's image. This is the edifying idea behind this Talmudic rabbinical statement:

> Ben Azzai says of the verse "This is the book of Adam's lineage on the day God created man, when He made him in His likeness. Male and female created He them and blessed them, calling them by Adam's name" (Gen. 5:1) that it presents the single greatest principle of the Torah! Rabbi Akiba disagrees, opining instead that the verse that presents the greatest principle is "Love your

---

9   Cf. T *Avodah Zarah* 8:4; BT *Sanhedrin* 56a. For some rabbis such as Nachmanides or Yosef Albo, the duties of mind are imposed before God by reason alone, regardless of any revelation. See Moshe Halbertal, *On the Way of Truth* (Jerusalem: Hartman Institute, 2006), 285 [Hebrew].

neighbor as yourself" (Lev. 19:18) and that this is so because the result is that none can say: "Since I have been humiliated, may my neighbor also be humiliated; since I have been insulted, may he also be insulted." But Rabbi Tanḥuma (who attempted to reconcile these points of view) says: Whoever would do so, should know Whom he ultimately humiliates because: "God made man in His *likeness*" (Gen. 5:1; *Genesis Rabbah* 24:7).

If our analysis of what constitutes the quintessence of idolatry is correct, then the real issue that must concern the faithful monotheist is not the diversity or the multiplicity of divine forms, but what kind of behavior this fragmentation of the divine risks to bring in its wake. Two critical questions come right to the fore. Will such and such polythetistic belief or practice lead to the dehumanization of its followers or will it preserve or even promote ethical values? And to the extent that monotheism is the acceptance of the belief in a God who functions as the sovereign of all humanity and for all humanity, will this or that idolatrous act support or work against the effort to unify humanity around these universal values? Indeed, there is a set of opposing figures, one that comprises both ethically sensitive pagans and shameless monotheists, the consideration of which refocuses the problem entirely.

On the one hand, it can be seen that certain groups or peoples, while worshipping a local god, nevertheless express the "fear" in a unique and universal God to the extent that the ethical authority of that supreme being is recognized. The Bible gives many examples of this. One thinks, for example, of midwives who, because they "feared God," refused to carry out Pharaoh's command to put to death all Hebrew male newborns.[10] Another example is the pagan king of Nineveh who is depicted in the book of Jonah as ordering all his subjects to repent in light of the the prophetic message vouchsafed to him by Jonah. Certainly, idolatry in the Bible is often understood as capable of inducing profoundly immoral behavior. But this is not invariably the case. Indeed, the results of idolatrous worship vary dramatically in nature and degree from context to context and idolatry *per se* does not *ipso facto* lead to dissolute sexuality, to violent corruption (as in the case of Sodom and Gomorrah), or to human sacrifice. How else can we explain Abraham's confession to King Avimelekh of Gerar that

---

10 Unlike the Talmudic interpretation in BT *Sotah* 11b, Philo (25 BCE–50 CE), Josephus Flavius (37/38–100 CE), Abravanel (1437–1508), Shadal (Samuel David Luzzatto, 1800–1865), and Malbim (Meir Levush ben Yechiel Weiser, 1809–1879) consider that the midwives mentioned in Ex. 1:15 were Egyptian and not Hebrew.

he erroneously had supposed that there was no "fear of God" (meaning in this context moral decency) in Gerar, or Jacob's agreement to participate in an oath-taking ceremony in which Laban was surely going to swear by his own god?[11] For that matter, how are we to explain that Joseph married an Egyptian woman if Egypt, known for its predilection for polytheism and magic, was always deemed the embodiment *par excellence* of idolatrous perversion?[12] And how can it have been that General Naaman of Aram was able to obtain the permission of the prophet Elisha to continue to worship the god Rimon despite his clear recognition of the sovereignty of the God of Israel after he, Naaman, was cured of his leprosy?[13] Moreover, we must also notice that the prophets never harangue other people for their beliefs or worship practices, but rather solely for their *moral* corruption.[14] In fact, it was only when the *tannaim* were called upon to determine the status of the *ger toshav* (as non-Jewish residents of Israel under Jewish jurisdiction were called) in light of the Noachide laws that they determined that idolatry was henceforth to be deemed a capital crime for non-Jews as well as Jews.[15] This development was probably abetted by the disarray caused by the destruction of the Temple, but also by the new developments in rabbinic eschatology the destruction brought in its woeful wake, developments according to which one of the signs of the end of days would be the expansion of the prohibition of idolatry to include the world's non-Jewish citizens.

On the other hand, it is easy to find followers of monotheism in all religious contexts who engage in conduct that instrumentalizes the divine and who embrace misguided practices and beliefs that lead away from this universal ideal and the humanization of its members.[16] This is the indictment of the prophet Malachi against his people, who compares their beliefs unfavorably to the attitudes of at least some pagans: "I do not take pleasure in you, says the Lord of hosts, and offerings from you shall I not accept. For, from where

---

11 Abraham: Gen. 20:9–11; Jacob: Gen. 31:53.
12 For its part, the Talmud declares that "six measures of sorcery descended to earth, of which nine found their home in Egypt" (BT *Kiddushin* 49b).
13 2 Kgs. 5:18–19.
14 Cf. David Novak, *The Image of the Non-Jew in Judaism* (Toronto: Edwin Mellen Press, 1983), 108–115, where the author offers numerous examples, including many gleaned from the long harangue of Amos against the gentile nations and city states of Damascus, Gaza, Tyre, Edom, Ammon, and Moab (Am. 1:3ff.).
15 Cf. ibid., 108. *Tannaim* is the general name for the rabbinic masters of the first two centuries of the Common Era.
16 See, for example, Isa. 58 or the criticism of the prophet Elisha towards his servant Gehazi in 2 Kgs. 5:25–27. The misbehavior of Israel in many traditional sources is considered as "profanation of the name of God."

the sun rises to where it sets, My name is honored among the nations, and in every place are incense and pure oblation offered to My name; for My name is honored among the nations, said the Lord of hosts" (Mal. 1:10–11). Nor is it uncommon for monotheism itself to be taken as a kind of license for its faithful adherents to rely upon as they oppress or even eradicate other human groups, arguing that the convictions or norms of those other groups do not conform to the religious beliefs they advocate. The religious rules they claim to be divine, carved in marble like a frozen statue, are conceived as a written law that lacks any adaptive oral interpretation, a law essentially indifferent to the way human societies grow naturally to embrace equity and fairness. Religion, in this view, has nothing to do with the common sense, with moral conscience. The suffering of innocents has no resonance with such pious people. To summarize, there are forms of polytheism that aim, despite the plurality of gods they embrace, to promote the humanization of people[17] and which even retain the belief in a God of all and for all, while within monotheistic religions we find ample evidence of chauvinism, supremacism, and violent segregation. One ends up wondering whether, given the level of *dehumanization* it so often fosters, monotheism—at least in its fundamentalist version—does not constitute the most perverse expression of idolatry that exists in our day in that it corrupts the ideal it theoretically exists to foster. More than monotheism, such religion deserves the name of monolatry: the worship of only one idol instead of the universal God.

We still have one final point to consider, the sensitive question that asks how Jewish people should relate to the plurality and corporeality of the divine manifestations to which other peoples or communities are commited. Firstly, they should do so by realizing that within Judaism itself various conceptions of God can and do coexist without violating the spiritual impulse of the people towards belief in one God, and by accepting that such pluralism surely deserves to be extended to other religious groups possessed of other spiritual or philosophical convictions, insofar as their ethics respond to the standards of human dignity. Secondly, they should do so by remembering that the purpose of Judaism is not to homogenize humanity by imposing the covenant of Israel on all nations, but rather to "sanctify the name of God" through acts of justice and benevolence and thus to encourage the nations of the world to commit themselves to

---

17 It is worth noting that many pagan philosophers of antiquity wrote ethics treaties, which influenced significantly Jewish thinkers in the Middle Age. For a famous example, Maimonides was clearly borrowing ideas from Aristotle's *Nicomachean Ethics* when he composed his famous *Shemonah Perakim*.

the Supreme God by seeking out the light of God's face as refracted through their own prisms. The God of the Bible is the "God of all flesh" (Jer. 32:27). All human beings shall one day be called to gather around God in the fullness of their diversity, as the prophet Micah dared to imagine. Reproducing the vision of Isa. 2:2–4 in which the nations are seen gathering in the Lord's house, the prophet adds a staggering new element:

> In the days to come, the mount of the Lord's House shall stand firm above the mountains; and it shall tower above the hills. The peoples shall gaze on it with joy, and the many nations shall go and shall say: "Come, let us go up to the mount of the Lord, to the House of the God of Jacob; that He may instruct us in His ways, and that we may walk in His paths." For instruction shall come forth from Zion, the word of the Lord from Jerusalem. Thus, He will judge among the many peoples, and arbitrate for the multitude of nations, however distant; and they shall beat their swords into plowshares and their spears into pruning hooks. Nation shall not take up sword against nation; they shall never again know war, but every man shall sit under his grapevine or fig tree with no one to disturb him. For it was the Lord of hosts who spoke. *Though all the peoples walk each in the names of its gods, we shall walk in the name of the Lord our God forever and ever.* (Mic. 4:1–5)

Micah does not see an irreducible divide in the fact that peoples advance under the banner of their gods, while Israel moves forward by maintaining fidelity to the one God! Such a vision can only be realized, however, through the medium of profound transformation both in the relationship between the nations themselves and in Israel's relationship to the nations. By seeing in Israelite faith the original monotheism, the nations will acknowledge the sovereignty of God; Israel, by seeing the nations and their diverse spiritualities no longer as symbols of unrepentant idolatry but as real partners in the promotion of human dignity, and thus of the one God, will do the same. In that way, we can appreciate the *programmatic* definition that the most famous Jewish exegete, Rashi (1040–1205), gave to monotheism in his commentary on the verse, which, more than any other, constitutes the daily declaration of allegiance to God and the confession of faith: "Hear O Israel, the Lord is our God, the Lord is One" (Deut. 6:4):

> The Lord who is our God for the time being, not the One of the pagan nations, will one day be the One Lord [of all], as said the prophet Zephaniah (3:9): "For then I will transform the language of nations into a clear language by which they will all supplicate the name of the Lord." In that way shall be fulfilled the word of the prophet Zachariah, who proclaimed (14:9): "On that day shall the Lord be One and His Name One." (Rashi on Deut. 6:4)

The unity of God envisioned here is not a theological definition built around the unitary conception. Nor is the divine unity which Israel first witnessed described as a relationship with God intended to remain solely part of Israelite culture. Monotheism is not an accomplished fact, therefore, but a project to be pursued and shared not by converting other peoples to the Jewish way of life or to Jewish doctrine, but by trying to unify humanity around the same God, around the God identified as the guarantor of fundamental universal values.

CHAPTER 6

Contemporary Idolatry and a Path to Freedom

Eilon Shamir

a. Introduction: The Idolatrous Climate in Current Culture

Recently, I went with my thirteen-year-old son to see the movie *Avengers: Endgame*, which is one of the best blockbuster movies ever. Like five of the ten top grossing movies,[1] it is a mythology of gods and superheroes who fight each other. While sitting there, watching gods wrestling, I contemplated the reason such mythologies are so popular today. Why are they much more popular than biblical stories? Why do their heroes seem so cool, funny, and vital whereas biblical stories seem deductive, serious, pious, and old-fashioned?

It is part of a wider phenomenon of a strong idolatrous tendency today. There are numerous television series and books in the same vein. Our culture is full of idolatrous terms, such as "American Idol," "movie stars," "music stars," and so forth. I believe it is an indication of an unconscious, or semi-conscious tendency for idolatry that prevails in our culture.

In this paper I will examine this phenomenon from the perspective of late capitalism. I will focus on some of its psychological aspects: Why does it emerge in the culture of late capitalism? How does it differ from the biblical belief in God? What are the psychic sources for these idolatrous tendencies? I will examine them from a "biblical" standpoint and present the way I understand them. However, I do not wish to follow the judgmental condemnation of the Bible, I will examine them from my own standpoint of belief in God, which is influenced by the heritage of the Bible and its understanding of idolatry. Yet I do not

---

1   As of 2020, these movies are: *Black Panther*; *Avengers: Endgame*; *Avengers: Infinity War*; Marvel's *The Avengers*; *Avengers: Age of Ultron*. See "Box Office Mojo," https://www.boxofficemojo.com/chart/ww_top_lifetime_gross/?area=XWW&ref_=bo_cso_ac.

wish to follow the judgmental condemnation of the Bible, but to examine the contemporary idolatry from a compassionate point of view. From this perspective, I will try to point at a direction of liberation from the misery of idolization, toward self-integration and growth.

b. A Metaphoric Realm of Idolization

Idolatrous language is usually light, funny, and exaggerated: it is not serious or committed to an exact meaning. For example, Leo Messi, the soccer player, is described as "the god of football," "god amongst men." These titles are accepted enthusiastically by millions of fans all over the world. Messi belongs to a long list of former idols, like the basketball player Michael Jordan, the Beatles, and many others who were idols in their time. Where does this idolatrous tendency come from? Of course, it is part of a modern structure of media with its gigantic spotlights, which tend to focus our attention on media stars. But this is only a partial explanation. One should ask what psychic mechanism leads to such admiration: the orientation of the media reflects our feelings, hopes, and beliefs, and the use of idolatrous language teaches us something about ourselves, about our culture. I believe we truly need those heroes; we need to worship them because they tell an important story about our own lives.

It is true that this use of the language is illusive. We seldom consider ourselves as "pagans," like the ancient Greeks. The location of the new pantheon is not on the Olympus but in the illusive and metaphorical realm of language. The new gods hide in our minds and wishes. They thrive in the semi-acknowledged stratum of language; they reside on the borderline between signifier and signified.

One can claim that the metaphoric field should not be taken so seriously. But I believe that there is no clear distinction between metaphor and reality: humans are beings who are endowed with significance, and metaphor is an important tool in doing so; metaphor has an intermediary role between the object and the significance attributed to it. The metaphor is both part of the object as well as the subject, the inner world of the signifier. Thus, for example, the expressions "media idols" or "media stars" can be perceived as light and unbinding: indeed, when such expressions are sporadic, no conclusions can be inferred from them regarding an entire culture. However, when used intensively by broadcasters, reporters, and audiences, metaphors turn into expressions of something real and palpable. When a rich repetitive system of metaphors carrying its own inner logic accumulates, it can be used to decode the manner in which culture perceives itself. This is why we should take metaphors of idolatry seriously.

c. Belief in God as an Outside Perspective

In order to understand idolatry, we need a punctum, a cultural Archimedean point, which allows an outside perspective. For me, such an outside point is the biblical belief in God, the way I understand it.

The Bible does not begin with idolatry: it does not tell us about Tiamat, the goddess of waters, or any other God beside Elohim. God is the one who created everything. This notion is deliberate, as if to say that the simple and "natural" structure of the world—and human mind—is the one that God created. The base, the essential foundation of the soul is not that of idolatry but that of believing in one god. Of course, it contradicts not only our anthropologic knowledge, but the underground level of biblical text itself, which reveals struggle against idolatrous mythology.[2] But there is no explicit sign for an idolatrous layer. According to Genesis, God is behind reality as a whole. God is the essence, the "Being" itself: the deity's name is YHWH, the one who constitutes reality. Humans have the capacity to relate to God because we are created in God's image. As I understand it, the Bible invites us not merely to *believe* in God but to *be* with God: to relate to reality as a whole. Relations like this can be described as "living-with-God," something as Noah did: "And Noah walked with God."[3] A. D. Gordon called it *havayah*: life in and with reality, with being itself.[4] Being with God derives from being present. Thus, *being present* has a religious aspect, which is *living in and with reality as a whole, which means God*.[5] When we live in this way, we are *present*: we have a connection to reality as a whole, and thus manifest our likeness to God, the creator of all. We say, without words, "here I am," *hineni*, as Abraham or Samuel did.[6] We relate to reality as a whole because potentially we ourselves are whole. There is a correlative connection[7]

---

2   Umberto Cassuto, *A Commentary on the book of Genesis, From Adam to Noah Translated from the Hebrew by Israel Abrahams*, vol. 1 (Jerusalem: Magnes Press and Hebrew University Press, 1961–1960), 1–47.
3   Gen. 6:9. All quotations are from KJV.
4   The interpretation to the verse is mine, following Gordon. See: Aaron David Gordon, *Selected Essays by Aaron David Gordon* (New York: Arno Press, 1973), 187. According to Gordon, a sick consciousness blocks *havayah*, whereas a healthy one enables it, and the ability to be present. See: Eilon Shamir, *For the Sake of Life: The Art of Living According to Aaron David Gordon* (Tel Aviv: Hakibbutz Hameuchad, 2018), 31–63.
5   The usual English translation of the word *havayah* as "life experience" fails to capture this religious aspect.
6   Gen. 22:1; 1 Sam. 3:4–8 (Adam failed to do so when God asked him "Where art thou?"—*eykha?*—Gen. 3:9).
7   See Hermann Cohen, *Religion of Reason: Out of the Sources of Judaism*, trans. Simon Kaplan (Atlanta, GA: Scholars Press, 1995). Though Cohen considered reason as the element of

between the way we relate to reality or to God, and the way we relate to our own souls: when we achieve inner integration, we can live as a whole and in *being*. Likewise, when we truly live with the one God of the being, we achieve inner integration: we are then in God's image, not only potentially but actually.

The Bible begins with the one God because it wants to tell us that basically, in our nature, we have that layer of inner integration; living with the one God is our inner nature, and not an intellectual dogma. It is a simple existence, despite complexities that may develop later in our souls. Yet it is not simple to be simple. That is why, when Abraham believes in God, God "counted it to him for righteousness."[8] It also explains why the struggle against the tendency towards idolatry plays a major role in the Bible.

d. What Is Idolatry?

I understand idolatry as a worship of mediators, a notion I borrowed from Maimonides (although I am not committed to his philosophy as a whole).[9] Such mediators are but part of the whole, and never the divine force above or within the united reality. Therefore, idolatry is the *worship of partial elements of reality that mediate between man and God*. Idolatry doesn't necessarily mean multiple gods. It can be manifested in worship of one element, namely henotheism; such partial elements can be the sun, the sea, and so on.

Ancient Greeks, for example, idolized such forces, worshipped them, attributed qualities like power and even independent will to them. They worshipped them because of the immeasurable might and influence these forces were believed to have upon their life. Today as well, people are overwhelmed by such forces: when things turn for the worse many of us tend to believe it's a punishment for sins; when they turn for the better it's because someone is pleased by a certain deed. Such belief arranges reality in a fathomable order. Paganism is a complex of rituals, temples and shrines, priesthood and knowledge based on these beliefs.

---

correlation between God and human beings, I follow Gordon, who suggested that presence, as a connection between ḥavayah and consciousness, is the base for the correlative connection.

8   Gen. 15:6.
9   "The essential principle in the percepts concerning idolatry is that we are not to worship anything created—neither angel, sphere, star. . . ." Maimonides, *Mishneh Torah*, Book of Knowledge, trans. Moses Hyamson (Jerusalem: Boys Town, 1962), 67a.

From a psychological perspective, there is a correlation between the believers and their beliefs, parallel to the correlation mentioned above between god and man. Greek idol-worshippers attributed divine forces to multiple elements of nature, and therefore had a multi-faceted image of reality. An ancient Greek could worship Zeus, the father of gods, yet worship Aphrodite too; worshippers had various focuses of intent in their world, and gods were personifications of the multitude dimensions in their souls. The multitude focuses in reality is a projection of the internal soul outward and from the external reality inward. It created a multifaceted picture that was comprised of many different elements. These elements were not submitted to a harsh hierarchy. It can be seen clearly in the instance of the Greeks' worship of the gods Apollo and Dionysus, discussed by Nietzsche.[10] In the Greek pantheon these two gods represented two opposing elements: Apollo represented truth, sublime ideals, beauty, and purity along with discipline and virtue. Dionysus, in contrast, represented the passionate, exuberant, chaotic facet. The sublime facet and the impulsive facet are both aspects of man's life: the "external" world, and internal world of the soul. Greek idol-worshippers could attend the temple of Apollo in Delphi, and later participate in ecstatic rituals dedicated to Dionysus without offending the fundamental dogma of their belief of plurality. That is because gods were perceived as partial elements of a plural reality.

This is the origin of the link between idolatry and moral relativism: Greek gods were not conceived as moral. They had impulses, and were driven by passions and whimsical caprices. They could sin, murder, steal, and commit adultery; above all, they were gods of power, not justice. This is why Plato wanted to forbid recounting tales of the gods' wrongdoings to the young man who may think "... that in doing the utmost wrong he would do nothing to surprise anybody ... but would only be following the example of the first and greatest of gods."[11]

e. A Source for Idolatrous Belief

As presented above, the Bible perceives people as endowed with *tzelem elohim* (the likeness of God), namely a capacity for integration and unity of the soul. It raises the question where the tendency for idolization comes from. The story

---

10 Friedrich Nietzsche, *The Birth of Tragedy*, trans. Ronald Speirs (Cambridge: Cambridge University Press, 1999), 6–46.
11 Plato, *The Republic of Plato*, trans. Paul Shorey (Cambridge, MA: Harvard University Press, 1982), 179–181 (book 2, 377–378).

of Noah offers an explanation. It is the same Noah that once "walked with God" in unity of his soul and his belief. But after the flood he was changed: apparently, he was not able to contain the trauma, and became addicted to alcohol. Because of the biblical attempt to undermine the category of idolization he is not described as idolatrous. Yet, his addiction displays an idolatrous tendency. *Addiction is a form of idolatry*, because idolatry means attributing to a partial element of reality more than its natural value, endowing it with more than its natural "place" or weight. Notice: this element by itself is not bad or evil. The sun or the oceans are but elements in God's good creation. The problem is not in the essence of the element, but with the value we attribute to it. For example, wine is good: "And wine that maketh glad the heart of man."[12] Wine becomes bad when it gains excessive value. Noah attributed too much value, *too much weight* to alcohol, wished for more than it could fulfill. Alcohol ceased to be just a good glass of red wine, drunk when evening falls while sitting on the porch, enjoying the growth of the world. It is now the answer to the pain inside, to fears; to life itself, which becomes too heavy to bear. Alcohol bears a promise of self-confidence, self-assurance, happiness. It turns into a mediator between Noah and reality, life, being; not yet a formal idol, not yet accompanied by ceremonies in a temple, it reflects an idolatrous tendency. It is as if the fabric of reality becomes distorted: the aura around the idea of alcohol is no longer calm, flexible, with appropriate proportions to reality around it. Like cancer, it is a partial element that grows wild and unruly. It has now acquired a heavier weight in the soul of the worshipper. And the more significance it is given, the more it controls the life of the addict, or the unconscious idol-worshipper. Unlike God of reality as a whole, who is leading the world to goodness and the soul to integrity, the idol consumes its worshipper's soul. Its "interest" is not in the well-being of its worshipper, but in dominating and growing ever stronger and bigger. True: it promises the worshipper some benefits, which are gratifying in a certain way: alcohol does make life seem more bearable under its influence. But it doesn't reward with self-confidence, self-assurance, and happiness, which are the true needs of the alcoholic. This is because it is merely a partial element, and not the God of reality in its entirety, of the soul as a whole.

---

12 Ps. 104:15.

f. Roots of Idolatry in Modern Culture

In Jewish tradition there are sages who have talked about the weakening of the urge for paganism.[13] Yet there are other opinions. Maimonides, for example, thought that the idolatrous tendency is inherent to human consciousness.[14] I believe this is the reason why a Jew should say at least twice a day "Shema Israel": "Hear, O Israel: The Lord our God, the Lord is One." *Not many.* The tendency for idolization is integral to the human soul; therefore, one should always strive for integration and freedom in the belief in God.

I believe the tendency to idolize has grown strong today. True, we are not "pagan" in the full sense of the term. We have a secular culture, therefore we don't have temples or shrines or pagan priesthoods.[15] Yet we are experiencing a split of the I, a disintegration of the self that is an outcome of an idolatrous inclination. We can observe this inclination already in early modern time, in the writings of Niccolò Machiavelli. Machiavelli endeavored to espouse a (pre-Platonic) pagan moral creed instead of the Christian one. The soul is no longer submitted to "the whole." The role of rationality is not to direct man in a wholistic way, but to achieve fame, manliness, and heroism. Machiavellistic rationalism leads to egotistic action directed at effective achievement of goals.[16] This feature is also present in the libertinism of the Marquis De Sade. De Sade (1740–1814) embraced the idea of man's pursuit of Happiness. He perceived happiness as an outcome of pleasure, and, according to him, suffering of others induced pleasure. Thus, one was permitted to torture others,[17] or more accurately: *I* was permitted to torture others. The center was the I, which was not integrated as a "whole" but subject to impulses. This feature reached its apex in the creed of Friedrich Nietzsche. Nietzsche's attempt was to shatter "the old temple," to demolish the old Judeo-Christian God. Let us acknowledge, he claimed, that we no longer believe in God. "God is dead, and all we have is God's shadow." Man was imprisoned by the submission to God: "In the moral epoch of humanity, people sacrifice to their

---

13 BT *Yoma* 69.
14 Maimonides, *Mishneh Torah*, Book of Knowledge, 67a–68a. Note: I do not follow his emphasis on materialistic realization of God in his concept of idolization.
15 One can claim, for example, that shopping malls are the new temples, where advertisers are the new priests, and so forth. But such a claim cannot cross the limits of metaphor mentioned above.
16 See Niccolò Machiavelli, *The Prince*, trans. William J. Connell (Boston: Bedford and St. Martin's Press, 1995); Isaiah Berlin, *Against the Current* (London: Hogarth Press, 1979), 39–65.
17 Donatien Alphonse François (Marquis) De Sade, *Justine or The Misfortune of Virtue* (Olympia Press, 1956).

god the strongest instincts they possess, their 'nature.'"[18] Christianity weakened the self. Nietzsche yearned for heroism, laughter, boldness. He wanted a free man, which would break down religious chains and grow to be an *Übermensch*, an I that is God in itself. Again: this imagined ideal I was not integrated. It had a free will but was devoid of a center to its soul.

There were, of course, those who did not approve of modern idolatrous tendencies. Heinrich Heine, for example, warned in 1835 against German philosophers of nature who had revived paganism in Germany and would unleash the German militarism and violence.[19] Salomon Formstecher, basing his theory on Schelling, described (in 1841) Judaism as a religion of the spirit in contrast to the pagan religions of nature.[20] Several modern Jewish thinkers struggled against idolatry, each one with his particular definition. For instance, Rabbi Samson Raphael Hirsch identified idolatry with modern centralism of the self, and later so did Yeshayahu Leibowitz. Erich Fromm, following Marx, described tendencies for idolization in capitalist culture, and identified them with alienation.[21]

Yet, despite these warnings, the tendency for idolization did not disappear. Nietzsche's thought had an enormous influence upon postmodern philosophy, such as that of Jean F. Lyotard. Lyotard invites us: "Let's Be Pagans."[22]

18　Friedrich Nietzsche, *Beyond Good and Evil*, trans. Adrian del Caro (Stanford, CA: Stanford University Press, 2014), 54–55.
19　Heinrich Heine, *On the History of Religion and Philosophy in Germany*, trans. H. Pollack-Milgate (Cambridge University Press 2007), 42–117. I believe this work of Heine had a profound influence on Nietzsche, who was one of the "philosophers of nature" Heine warned against.
20　Eliezer Schweid, *A History of Modern Jewish Religious Philosophy* (Tel Aviv: Am Oved, 2002), 41–50 [Hebrew].
21　Erich Fromm, *You Shall Be as Gods: A Radical Interpretation of the Old Testament and its Tradition* (Greenwich, CT: Fawcett Publications, 1966), 17–51, and in many other places. On Fromm's concept of idolatry see Svante Lundgren, *Fight against Idols: Erich Fromm on Religion, Judaism and the Bible* (Frankfurt am Main: Peter Lang, 2012), 136–142; and Ronen Pinkas, "Correlation and Orientation: Erich Fromm's Position on Religion in Light of Hermann Cohen and Franz Rosenzweig," Da'at 85 (2018): VII–XXXVI. In this paper I follow Fromm's ideas, such as his criticism of capitalist culture. Yet I differ in some aspects: for example, I object to Fromm's emphasis on rationality and humanist morality (and a vague concept of God), whereas I suggest a more religious concept. Fromm identifies idolization with alienation and by that tends to abstraction, while I understand it in a more concrete and simple way. In addition, Fromm suggests a third category of non-idolatrous secularity, whereas I, from a late capitalist perspective, go back to the Old Testament dichotomy between idolization and the belief in the one God.
22　Jean-François Lyotard, *Let Us Be Pagans* (discussion between Lyotard and F. L. Thebaud, Tel Aviv, 1996), in his *The Postmodern Condition* (Tel Aviv: Hakibbutz Hameuchad, 1999), 79–119 [Hebrew].

He suggests nurturing a "heteronymous idol-worshipper," who surrenders to social cultural traditions. This idol-worshipper moves at will between narrative-planes and morals, without having to choose between them:

> Paganism means accepting the possibility that we have several games, each of them interesting only as long as it is interesting to make moves within it. "Making moves" means developing schemes and freeing the imagination. If you ask me why I pass from one to another—my answer is that it does not concern me overmuch. If compelled to name the "reason," let's call it *will*. . . . If we are pagans it does not stem from preferring one game over the other, but because we have at our disposal several kinds of games. There are games not invented yet, which we may invent while creating new game rules, and it is all most interesting: something like imagination or will—I am not exactly sure—may evolve.[23]

Lyotard invites us to a postmodern celebration in which there is no integration of the soul. We can play as we like, be what we like. The outer reality and the inner reality—the self—is a kaleidoscope of fragments. Everything is light, like soap bubbles drifting on a slightly windy afternoon. It seems like a vision of freedom. The new pagans' will is free to do whatever they want. According to this, we are now celebrating the realization of Nietzsche's vision of a self that follows its own free will. We do what we want, we eat what we want, and we buy what we want, as long as we can afford it. Actually, we don't need Lyotard's approval: this is the cultural logic of late capitalism. The will is most dominant in our culture, but unlike Nietzsche's vision, it is not powerful and authentic. It is not the center of the soul. It tends to disintegrate, as in Lyotard's description. The I "chooses," but is actually subject to many powerful economic-cultural manipulations. We are impacted by numerous culture-agents such as advertisements or movies. We are solicited to do what we want, though the demands are contradictory. "Eat whatever you want! Fast-food or gourmet!" And on the other hand: "You are fat! You should look like the skinny models on the fashion channels!" "Follow our latest diet!" Buy this and buy that. "Purchase! Consume! Now!"[24] There is

---

23 Ibid., 106.
24 See discussion of the Dionysian and Platonic aspects of today's culture: Camille Paglia, *Sexual Personae: Art and Decadence from Nefertiti to Emily Dickinson* (New York: Vintage Books, 1990), 40–100.

no real contradiction, as long as we keep on consuming. Thus, in consumerist culture, Nietzsche's vision of *Übermensch* is reduced to the subjection of the will to the conducts of the market. Lyotard's version of paganism is a mockery version of the Nietzschean concept of authentic will.

The tendency to idolize grows from the inner structure of the self. But the common picture today is of a weak self, whose inner structure is fragile, with a weak will and a liquid center. We are invited to do what we want, but we are confused. We want this and this and that, but actually we don't know what we want. The weak I is full of fears and anxieties. Instead of self-assurance, which creates a strong will, instead of the creativity and inner motivation Nietzsche strove for, the self is addicted to compensations and approvals from others. That may be the reason for the popular wish "to be famous," "to be shown on TV." I'll gain self-esteem if only I get enough applause. And I'll need it over and over again, the more the better. Because the truth is: I'm insecure, I'm afraid.

g. Idolatry in Capitalist Culture

Unlike ancient Greeks, we do not believe in forces of nature. In late capitalism the real powers are not those of nature, which is weak and succumb to our unmerciful hands, but the powers of human society and culture. This is because in late capitalism people experience isolation of the self, which is subject to powers beyond its reach. These are the powers that control the reality of competition and survival, and are built on our beliefs. These powers reveal themselves by explicit values: money, health, beauty, sex, technology, and so forth. Of course, attributing value to something doesn't necessarily mean idolization. The subtle question is whether it develops into worship.

Let's take, for example, the old subject of idolization of money.[25] Money is a social mechanism, a means that enables us to get what we want. We can buy material things such as food, clothing, dwelling, and also more abstract objects

---

25 Idolization of money was pointed out time and again. For example: Jesus, "No one can serve two masters. . . . You cannot serve both God and money" (Mat. 6:24, NIV). At the end of the eighteenth century, Rebbe Nachman of Breslev described a pagan society worshipping the god of money: Rebbe Nachman of Breslev, "The Story of the Master of Prayer," in *Rabbi Nachman's Stories*, tr. A. Kaplan (New York: Braslev Research Institute, 2015), 282–279; Moshe Hess, "On Capital," in his *General Writings* (Jerusalem: Hasifriyah Hazionit, 1956), 70–95 [Hebrew]. Karl Marx wrote that "The riddle of the money fetish is therefore the riddle of the commodity fetish, now become visible and dazzling to our eyes." Karl Marx, *Capital*, vol. 1 (London: Penguin Classics, 1990), 187.

such as education, and so forth. With money one can purchase sex, technology, science, beauty, and other desires, which can be translated into materialistic values. Therefore, money is a mediating means between men and their will: it helps the realization of material needs and social aspirations. Bear in mind: money is not "evil." Money is but an element in the good world God created. When I buy a tomato at the grocery store, money is just that: a mediator between me and the thing I want, which enables me to have a good salad. Worshipping money occurs when money becomes a goal rather than a means, when I believe it may solve my inner problems. When my real need is, for example, self-esteem, and I chase money in order to gain it from others. This is the psychological stage when we attribute *too much weight* to money; when it becomes a promise for self-confidence, self-assurance, happiness, as alcohol was for Noah. In this way, we try to avoid our inner problems, and seek answers elsewhere. We prefer to pursue the shadow outside than to confront ourselves, our inner weaknesses and fears. In that way money becomes an idol, which is presumed to supply such needs. Yes, it may provide material and social benefits. Yet, it cannot and will not answer our deep needs.

The connection with capitalist culture is clear: consumption culture is based on the belief that money and objects whose value can be expressed with money are the answer to our wishes, our needs, our wills. And the will is not static. It can be shaped and manipulated so we want more than we have. We will always want more, because we believe these objects will fulfill our inner needs. Thus, the more we buy the more we add fuel to the engine of late capitalist economy.

Yet, we remain dissatisfied, because we don't find answers to our anxieties, to the void in our heart. The will, the center of the self, becomes disintegrated. We become confused. We don't know what we really want anymore. We chase shadows in order to escape our confusion, our inner doubts, and our fears, but we don't find answers, so we continue compensating by chasing, more and more.

This is how the "god of money" enslaves us. And since it is only the reflection of our ill will, it's better to say: this is how we enslave ourselves. However, money is but one of the major idols today. There are others, such as beauty, technology,[26] and so on. Actually, anything we value can become a subject of our idolization. In the idolization process it acquires more than a plain social or cultural value. The tissue around it thickens, grows beyond its natural proportion. The fabric surrounding it becomes twisted, rigid, the cancerous tissue dislodges from a "whole."

---

26 See Hava Tirosh-Samuelson, "Transhumanism as a Secularist Faith," *Zygon Journal of Religion & Science* 47, no. 4 (2012): 710–134.

I believe this is the case with Donald Trump's environment policy. Something in his beliefs and personality prevents him from reacting to the enormous ecological crisis we have caused. Something twists the tissue of reality around him. Is it his narcissism? Is it his belief in the logic of capitalism and money, in which "an invisible hand" would fulfill the best interest of society? Either way it demonstrates how such beliefs and disintegration of the Self can disconnect a person (leader of billions) from the "whole," from the constant creation of God. Note: this is not a conscious idolization. One can go to church, synagogue, or mosque and still worship money, beauty, and so forth. Syncretism is always an option,[27] and religion does not provide all the answers.[28]

h. Nurturing an Alternative

We need an alternative. We need to find a way to relate again to the world as a whole, to God. And I believe the most important issue is that of the self, the sick I, and the main question is how to nurture it into a positive direction.

There is always an option of judgmental condemnation. Some people today (including myself fifteen years ago) denounce idolatry as a sin, a disgrace, and shame.[29] Such an approach derives from a subconscious assumption that it's the problem of others, not mine. The tendency to idolize, the weaknesses, and the fears belong to others who are inferior to me. They are weak, shallow, hedonistic, materialistic, and I am righteous, pure, and pious. I have answers. This can lead to anger and frustration, because I am the one who "knows" the truth, closed within a Gnostic perspective.

I didn't realize fifteen years ago that revealing and condemning idolatrous inclinations does not necessarily bring liberation. I understand now that accusing others enabled me to conceal my own fears, my own addictions from myself. And in that sense it delayed the process of growth and liberation.

---

27 Erich Fromm explains: "If, for instance, a man worships power while professing a religion of love, the religion of power is his secret religion, while his so-called official religion, for example Christianity, is only an ideology." Erich Fromm, *Psychoanalysis and Religion* (New Haven: Yale University Press, 1950), 35–37.
28 See Abraham J. Heschel, "The Spirit of Jewish Education," *Jewish Education* 24, no. 2 (1953): 14–15.
29 Eilon Shamir, "Idolatry and the Potential of Renewed Covenant in Israeli Society Today" (first prize winner for original philosophic essay), in *What will Be?*, ed. Tamar Landau (Tel Aviv: Tel Aviv University Press, 2004), 9–40.

This is usually what happens with ideologies. We tend to rely on them because they provide confidence and aspire to strengthen us. They make us feel self-assured. We know the way. We have God's key in our pocket. The problem is not ours but others'. Ideologies provide a false confidence that enables us to hide our real problems. But the sin of idolatry always lieth at the door. The path to freedom is that of constant growth. We cannot "catch" God, not even within religion itself: one can attend synagogue regularly and still worship money, power, and so forth. Underneath halakhic observance one can idolize other gods, such as tradition or halakhah itself. The problem begins when religion becomes an ideology; when it neglects the constant effort of *avodat ha-midot*, of an inner growth. At that point it doesn't address the problem, but becomes part of it.

Instead of condemning our fears and weaknesses we can approach them with compassion. When I take a closer look, I may realize that those fears are not extraneous to me, I have my own tendencies for idolization within me. Perhaps they are somewhat different than those of others, but why should I judge other people? You cannot force fears out: there is no point in intimidating fears, because they will grow still deeper and mightier. Rather, I can accept them, accept myself with them. This is who I am: weak in certain aspects.

I'll give an example. Sometime ago I escorted my young son, who was seven years old, to an amusement park. Despite my fear of heights I climbed into the Ferris wheel with him. The moment the wheel started turning I was overwhelmed with anxiety. I tried to cling fiercely to my seat, paralyzed with fear, my eyes closed tightly. Meanwhile my son was happy, free . . . and supportive: he accepted my anxiety with no "helpful" suggestions. The wheel turned, stopping high in the sky, and I was sitting there, eyes closed, paralyzed. Now, at this point I could have appealed to a false idol, for example, to the idol of masculinity and manhood. This idol could have commanded: open your eyes, you fool! Are you a baby? Look at you, a former officer in Golani . . . be brave! Be manly! . . . Had I listened to such idols, I would have tried to present a façade of bravery, repressing my fears and weaknesses.

Being able to step aside away from this automatic tendency is a turning point in which one can deal with idolization. It demands training of the soul, as yoga does for the body. I've been practicing it for years now, using a method called "conscious thinking," developed by Yemima Avital.[30] Thus I am trained to step aside from these automatic tendencies, and deal with my fears differently. Instead of listening to urges of masculinity and ego, I observed: here I am. That's

---

30   Tsippi Kauffman, "The Yemima Method as a Contemporary-Hasidic-Female Movement," *Modern Judaism* 32, no. 2 (2012): 195–215.

who I am, afraid, weak. There is no point in condemnations or rational persuasions. The frightened child within me will not understand anyhow. I shouldn't be embarrassed or feel ashamed. This fear is part of me. I accepted my fear and myself with it.

Something calmed down and I thought: what may happen if I open one eye for a second, just a peep? So I did, immediately shutting it back. Then again. And now two eyes. For just a flicker. Then both eyes. And then something opened inside. I sat there, watching the beautiful landscape around me. Such a broad view . . . so much space . . . so much inner space. A verse echoed in my mind: "מִן־הַמֵּצַר קָרָאתִי יָּהּ עָנָנִי בַמֶּרְחָב יָהּ." "From a suppressed space, out of distress I called upon the Lord; the Lord answered out of a wide, vast space."[31]

I am sharing this because I think this is a more fruitful path than criticism and condemnations. If I encounter . . . no, *when* I encounter such fear, which can easily lead to an unwitting idolization, there is no point in accusations and guilt. I don't condemn myself when I seek popularity or fame in order to fortify myself, to ease a fear of nullity . . . if I try to derive assurance from other people . . .

I accept myself with my fears. But I try not to idolize, and even if I do, I observe it with acceptance and compassion. That doesn't mean I am going to be an idol worshipper. On the contrary, it means I accept myself with my shortcomings, even though I understand those weaknesses are not in my favor. I accept, and let God do the rest. In this way, time and time again, I am helped by God, in the process of growing and liberation from fears. The propensity to idolize is always there. Hopefully, during a lifetime, I'll experience constant growth, but it's an ongoing process of dealing with fears and proclivity towards idols. I'm not free yet, so the only way is to accept myself the way I am. This is how God created me. Therefore, I shouldn't escape to ideologies and righteousness; instead, I should try to meet these shortcomings, not with rage and accusation, but with compassion, with *naḥas-ruaḥ*, with tranquility and calmness.[32]

This way of dealing with idolatry enables us to focus not on criticism, as in a direct struggle against idolatry, but on a positive direction. Between "depart from evil" to "and do good" (Ps. 34:14) the emphasis is on the latter. As

---

31 Ps. 118:5. This verse is very difficult to translate, because there are several layers in the words מיצר and מרחב in Hebrew. In KJV: "I called on the Lord in distress; The Lord answered me *and set me* in a broad place."

32 Like in the prayer of Rabbi Elimelech from Lizhensk: "Let not hatred arise from one to another. Strengthen us that we might love You more for You know well how our intention is that it all should bring You pleasure and joy, for this is the root of our intention." See Zalman Schachter-Shalomi and Elimelekh Weisblum of Lizhensk, "Rabbi Elimelekh of Lizhensk's Prayer to be Able to Pray," July 24, 2017, https://opensiddur.org/prayers/praxes/davvening.

A. D. Gordon said: "Nothing will change unless we understand the simple fact: instead of fighting darkness we should increase the light."[33] The energies of such endeavor are those of creation and growth, and through these I become a part of the divine growth around and within me.

i. Reconstruction of the Self

The issues discussed here concern the inner structure of the self. I see two alternatives: one is the structure of the self and the ego that is based on fears. As I tried to show above, this is the structure that breeds idolization; the other alternative is a self that is not based on ego. Of course, there are fears (which are the base of ego), but instead of running away from them, this kind of self is prepared to confront them, to recognize and deal with them. A different self emerges from the ongoing process of growth-out-of-dealing-with-fears. It's a self that has self-confidence and self-assurance; a self that has strong inner will, and thus is not enslaved by addictions and idols; a self that understands that one is not the center of the world, because the world has a center, which is God, and the soul has a center, which is the likeness of God. This is a lifelong enterprise of growth, on and on, in this garden of God, the world we live in. The reward is enormous. It is living. It is being. It is a constant self-construction and self-integration. The reward is freedom from miserable slavery.

The process of growth may begin at any time. It can begin right now. We don't have to wait for any mega scale mechanisms to change. We don't have to change media, or technology, or structures of world economy. We can begin with ourselves. With nurturing the alternative self, which derives from life-with-God, like that of Noah. And I believe that this can also bring a change in society, politics, and culture.

j. A Jewish Way of Life

The self is not enough, since it is not enclosed within itself like an island. Every man is a piece of the continent, a part of the main, of the culture we inherit. I as a Jew have a heritage of struggle against idolatry. It's the culture that brought the world the gospel about the one God of the universe, the one God of the soul.

---

33 A. D. Gordon, *The Nation and the Labor* (Tel Aviv: Hasifriya Hazionit, 1957), 304 [Hebrew].

The Bible is a testimony of generations upon generations who experienced revelation and relationship with God: a constant effort to maintain the covenant. Judaism is a very rich heritage, a culture that contains treasures of wisdom and human experience, and I am a link in this chain and obliged to it.

Yet my role is not passive. I am obligated towards creativity in this process: "In every generation a person must regard himself as though he personally had gone out of Egypt."[34] In every generation, a person must free himself from an outdated perspective. Time and again we should identify current idols, and seek a personal way of living-with-God. The Ba'al Shem Tov asked, why do we say in our prayer "the God of Abraham, the God of Isaac, and the God of Jacob," instead of "the God of Abraham, Isaac, and Jacob"? He answered that each of the fathers had to seek God by himself.[35] Every generation is tasked with its own enterprise of seeking God. So am I. Living in late capitalist culture, for instance, challenges me in a way unknown to my ancestors. I need to change tradition in order to be able to maintain the main course of living-with-God and getting free from idolatry.

k. Conclusion

Idolatry, as I perceive it, is the inclination to worship partial elements of reality, in contrast to the belief in one God. And because of the correlative nature of belief, it creates multiple orientations of the soul, whereas living-with-God creates inner integration. The tendency to idolize springs from our weaknesses and fears, and therefore it is an immanent part of human being. However, postmodern shift of contemporary capitalist culture seems to foster this tendency: we witness strong and semi-explicit idolatrous currents, which thrive in our culture. The reason for it may be the weakness of the postmodern self. Postmodern individuals live in a competitive, alienated, and atomistic society. We tend to be isolated, and we are left alone to deal with our fears and weaknesses. We are inclined to idolize entities such as money, beauty, and so on, because it enables us to escape our inner world, our pains and demons; in the short term these idols "reward" us. But the price is high: we neglect our inner soul, and cannot attain self-integration. This is how these idols enslave us, and nullify growth and self-liberation. And there is a lot of misery in this slavery.

---

34 M *Pesaḥim* 10:5.
35 Martin Buber, *The Hidden Light* (Tel Aviv and Jerusalem: Shocken, 2005), 63 [Hebrew].

The path toward liberation cannot be that of ideology—not even a religious ideology. Cultural and social climate are important, but the main path is that of *avodat ha-midot*, a process of an ongoing self-education. Yet, this must not develop out of judgmental condemnation: there is no point in fueling our fears. The road toward salvation is that of self-acceptance; instead of resisting, we should accept our fears, our shortcomings, and tendencies to idolize. It is a process in which God usually has much more patience than we do. And it leads to growth and ongoing strengthening of the self. We don't know what will happen in the future; perhaps the capitalist culture is more fragile than it appears now, considering the enormous ecological crisis we are marching towards. But there is always an alternative, a path to liberation: "In that day a man shall cast his idols..." (Isa. 2:20).

# CHAPTER 7

The Idolatry of Humankind

Jonathan Wittenberg

Introduction

A person taking a selfie is an iconic image of our times. People take selfies to show the sites they're visiting, the view behind them, the company they're keeping, the food they're eating, a new item of clothing (should I buy this?), a fresh haircut, or simply today's good or bad mood. There's nothing intrinsically wrong with selfies. Posted in seconds, they are an ultra-convenient way of keeping in touch with friends, family, and, as the name suggests, with oneself. Selfies are at worst harmless and at best good fun.

Yet, the preoccupation with our own image is also symbolic of a disturbing concern. In a whole range of ways, we have accepted and embraced a way of life in which it is overwhelmingly ourselves, our own interests, and our self-image that we serve. Put bluntly, today, individually, collectively, as societies but most dangerously as a species, we are at risk of allowing our entire Western civilization to become a cult of idolatry of self, into which we have so long, so subtly, and so persistently been seduced that we struggle even to recognize it as such. Thus, in practice, we often mistake the First Commandment as if it read not "I am the Lord your God, but "I," that is, "Me, and what I need and want," "am the Lord and master of the world." Maimonides understands idolatry as a descent from the service of the God of all creation into the adulation of its significant parts, the sun, the moon and the mountains, to the point where they become the ultimate objects of worship and the God who made them is forgotten (*Mishneh Torah*, Laws of Idolatry 1:1–2). The portion of creation we are in danger of worshipping in this manner today is our own self, separated not only from our divine source, but from the sanctity of all other God-given life. The ultimate price of such an anthropocentric and self-serving attitude may be the destruction of creation itself.

In his powerful and humbling lecture, *The Concept of God after Auschwitz*, delivered in Marburg, the very university where Heidegger, an unrepentant Nazi sympathizer, had previously held the chair of philosophy, Hans Jonas spoke of his "myth" in which he imagined the deity voluntarily withdrawing from the world in order to allow space for creation to evolve of its own accord. At the apogee of this long and slow process over many aeons, humankind arrives on the scene:

> the thrust of evolution, carried by its own momentum, passes the threshold where innocence ceases and an entirely new criterion of success and failure takes hold of the divine stake. . . . To the promise and risk of this agency the divine cause, revealed at last, henceforth finds itself committed; and its issue trembles in the balance. The image of God, haltingly begun by the universe, for so long worked upon—and left undecided—in the wide and then narrowing spirals of pre-human life, passes into man's precarious trust, to be completed, saved, or spoiled by what he will do to himself and the world.[1]

This is not far different from the midrashic picture of the angels attempting to prevent God from creating the one being with free will able both to fulfil God's service more fully than any other, yet with a sufficiently querulous spirit and enough independent power to be capable of upsetting and destroying the entire divine enterprise: the human being. Perhaps the angels were right; free will is a dangerous gift.

It could be argued that it was ever thus, that all idolatry amounts to the worship of self and power. Yet, a number of relatively recent economic and cultural developments have brought us to the current crisis, this moment of severe existential danger in which the misplaced role of self has brought not only our own species but all life on earth to the edge of disaster. While it would be possible to describe these processes with scarcely any reference to God other than as an outdated notion, which people once used to credit, I would argue that the significance of God, the awareness of the sacred in all life, and the service of God through showing compassion towards all living beings are absolutely central to a resolution of humankind's most pressing concern, the future of life on earth.

---

1 Hans Jonas, "The Concept of God after Auschwitz," in his *Morality and Mortality, A Search for God after Auschwitz*, ed. Lawrence Vogel (Evanston, IL: Northwestern University Press, 1999), 135–136.

I would therefore describe idolatry in relation to its place and definition in the Ten Commandments. Following immediately after the First Commandment, the recognition of the sovereignty of God, the prohibition of idolatry is its necessary and essential complement. No alternative, false gods must occlude the awareness of God; they must not come *al panai*, before Me, thus constituting a barrier that renders God invisible, just as a larger, nearer object may prevent us from seeing something further away (Ex. 20:3). This is not, of course, to suggest that God actually is more distant, only that it is easier for us humans to see physical than it is to perceive metaphysical realities. Hence the "idols and images" to which the subsequent verse goes on to refer need not necessarily be Canaanite or any other deities; rather they represent any object, objective, or goal that intervenes between ourselves and the service of God. The familiar midrash on the verse "*Torah tzivah lanu Moshe*" ("Moses commanded us the Torah," Deut. 33:4) notes that since the numerical value of the word *Torah* adds up only to 611, there must be two other commandments, which Moses did not transmit. These, the midrash teaches, were the first and the second of the Ten Commandments, "I am the Lord your God" and "You shall have no other gods before me": they were heard directly by the entire people at Sinai *mi-pi ha-Gevurah*, from the mouth of the Almighty (Rabbi Simlai in BT *Makkot* 24a). This highlights both the unique status and the inextricable connection between these two key commands.

It is tempting, in the manner of Hasidic creative misreading, to translate the opening words of the Second Commandment *lo ta'aseh lekha* as "don't make your self" into an idol, though this would of course be grammatically inaccurate, since the object "you" is indirect, in the dative rather than the accusative case. But it would not be unfaithful to the meaning of the verse, which is that we must not turn any icon or image into an object of worship and few images are more important to us than those we have of our own self.

I will divide this essay into three short sections: the importance we attach to autonomy and status at the individual, personal level; the criteria by which we measure success as nations; and the absolute right to power we ascribe to ourselves as a species, the anthropocentric exceptionalism of our own kind from the mutual interdependence of all life. While these concerns may be considered as separate and distinct, I will argue that each leads almost inevitably to the others and that a change in attitude in any one necessitates a transformation in our understanding of all. Indeed, it is precisely in this awareness of the interconnectedness of all life that *teshuvah*, our return to God, and the deepening of *da'at*, the awareness of the presence of God throughout creation, are to be sought.

In writing this essay I am motivated not by a need to criticize and condemn; I am after all a participant in the way of life and its wrongs that I intend to outline. Nor do I see this civilization as entirely misguided; it is rather a matter of degree, a rebalancing of the relationship between ourselves, our communities, our environment, and our God. Rather, I am writing out of shame and, above all, out of fear. Judaism requires us to teach God's commandments diligently to our children. There is no greater way of failing future generations than by bequeathing them a dying world in which the remnants of humanity and whatever other species still remain in existence battle for the ability to survive. We therefore urgently need to change our collective ways and, while this involves amending many wrongs, at the heart of the matter lies a profound imbalance in the way we regard ourselves in relation to the rest of creation and God—what I have called the idolatry of our own kind.

1. The Individual

Judaism traditionally regards each person as a member of a group, part of a community bound together by shared responsibilities and obligations to God, each other, the poor, the stranger and the refugee. This group connection is twofold. First, it is the contemporary link to our *re'a*, our neighbor whom we are commanded to love, or at least, as Hillel famously put it, not to treat in a manner we ourselves would not want to be treated (BT *Shabbat* 31a). Samson Raphael Hirsch, who lived through the granting of broadly equal rights to Jews in Germany in 1871, understood the command to love one's neighbor as oneself as the duty to seek the same rights and opportunities for others as we desire for ourselves (see his commentary to Lev. 19:18). As such, the love of one's neighbor is the foundation of any just society, binding its members together in the pursuit, and defense, of equality for all.

At the same time, the connection is also historical. For Jews, it is the link to the Jewish people across the generations, for whose fate and faithfulness we are, during the course of our short lifetime, answerable before God and history. Although each individual is unique and important before God, and although we are each personally responsible for our conduct, the significance of our life is traditionally understood not just in terms of personal achievement, but within the context of the collective identity and fortunes of which, whether we like it or not, we are part. It is a telling indication that the virtues most often mentioned in epigraphs on tombstones are generosity, loving-kindness, and service to the community.

The ultimate goal of each individual, every community, and the Jewish people as a whole is redemption. Like the horizon to a weary traveller, it never seems to get nearer, yet it never ceases to define life's purpose. Not personal success, not wealth, not triumph over others, but participating in the creation of an harmonious world in which each person, nation and species has its rightful place and interacts peacefully with others—this remains the eternal objective.

Today, however, we tend to see ourselves first and foremost as individuals. Most of us consider the decision to join a faith community as a matter of choice. Consciously or unconsciously, we want good reasons for any infraction of our personal autonomy. *Kefiah datit*, having religion forced upon us by the institutions that purport to represent it, or the curtailment of civic freedoms by a fascist or proto-fascist state, are rightly regarded in free and open societies as unacceptable forms of totalitarian control. We take as self-evident many rights and freedoms for which earlier generations fought hard: freedoms of conscience, speech, movement, and sexual orientation, as well as gender equality and freedom from bullying, abuse, and coercive control. In this context, without necessarily having recourse to physical violence, the power of the group can, and often still does, constitute a blunt and almost inescapable form of oppression. Most of us would agree that free societies have travelled a complex and arduous path towards vast achievements on behalf of their individual members.

But there are also dangers. Placing the individual self and his or her rights and liberties at the center, and also often as the pinnacle, of all values risks leading to the erosion of commitment to community, with the concomitant loneliness and isolation this entails for many. The "right" to expect from society can quickly come to dominate the importance of contributing to it. The desire for personal achievement then trumps the importance of service of others. Activity becomes valued not by its intrinsic worth or its impact on humanity or nature as a whole, but by what we can get out of it for ourselves. We demand goods and opportunities, which the world cannot afford to offer everyone on an equal basis. We expect to have what we want when we want it and to go where we want in the timespan and by the mode of transport we choose. The only limitation is the financial means at our disposal. But most of us in developed countries have little idea of who really pays for the privileged way of life we have widely come to regard as ours by right. Even when tempered by concern for and devotion to others and high levels of altruism, we often take it as given that our goals legitimately focus largely on ourselves and our immediate family as individuals: personal success, wealth and pleasure.

At some point on the scale, as the balance tips from committing ourselves to our responsibilities towards demanding our rights, and from serving others to the advancement of our own self, that very self becomes deified, *de facto*, if not *de jure*. It is liable to become what Paul Tillich terms our "ultimate concern"; it is what we worship in practice, if not in stated belief. It is the primary organizing focus not just of our daily life but of our mind, the motivating ideology that governs our life.[2]

While accepting not just our human nature by encouraging us to rejoice in our heritage, but also the fact that we are only human and have legitimate expectations for food, clothing, companionship, and leisure, Judaism constantly sets before us the ultimate task of serving God. We are all *metzuvim*, subject to the commandments, and the purpose of life is defined not by the satisfaction of our own wants alone, but by our resolute commitment to higher goals. Dedication solely to our needs and desires, including even self-fulfilment, if it does not also comprise care and concern for others as directed by the Torah and developed in the long tradition of Jewish law and ethics, is also a form of self-worship as opposed to the service of God. The Torah calls on us to be aware that we are in the presence of God in all we do, including the most earthly, quotidian tasks of farming, business, eating, and relating to those around us. It requires all our conduct to be consistent with the ultimate goal of affirming the sovereignty of the divine. It is no accident that the biblical term *avodah* holds in the span of its meaning both daily work and the service of God in the heart.

2. Societies and Nation-States

The individual dangers of self-worship are mirrored, if not amplified, in the way states widely regard themselves and their achievements. Growth constitutes the almost universal criterion by which the success of nations is assessed. (Bhutan is apparently the only country that claims to measure its achievements in terms of collective happiness.) Such growth is invariably quantified in economic, and not moral, social, cultural, or spiritual terms. It is broadly true that in wealthy countries with expanding economies there is more for everyone, including the poor. But were the prophets of the Hebrew Bible living today, they would surely demand to know who in each country was actually benefitting from its "growth" and to what extent; as well as who, within it and beyond it, was paying the true price for this attainment. They would wander the streets of our cities and count the numbers of homeless people sleeping in doorways; they would go down in

---

2   Paul Tillich, *Dynamic of Faith* (New York: Perennial Classics, 2001), chapter 1, part 1.

person to our borders and demand to know why destitute refugees seeking safe haven from persecution were being turned away and why, if they did manage to enter, they were so often threatened with deportation. They would walk the fields and forests and demand to know the causes of semi-silent, virtually insect-free springs and summers. They would question fiercely the impact of economic growth without concomitant spiritual development on the heart and soul of humanity: was it making us more compassionate, more dedicated to the wellbeing of others, more awake to the presence of God?

Isaiah's description of what God requires of us, given prime time by the rabbis who determined that it was to be read on Yom Kippur morning, offers a very different account of collective achievement: "It is to share your bread with the hungry, to take the wretched poor into your home; when you see the naked, to clothe them, and not to hide yourself from your own flesh" (Isa. 58:7). That is what he understood God to want from society. Instead, while social and cultural achievements are by no means ignored in most countries, what states chiefly worship is power, economic potential, military might, global influence, and the creation of wealth that is rarely equally shared.

Precisely this danger lies at the core of the brief discussion of kingship in Deuteronomy. The Torah insists that the king must not possess too many horses, that is, see military prowess as his primary goal since horses were at that time beasts of war; not take too many wives; and not gather too much gold and silver. He was not to forget his ultimate purpose as sovereign by luxuriating in the status and privileges of power. Instead, he was to write a copy of the Torah "and read in it every day of his life, in order that he should learn to fear the Lord his God" and keep the precepts of the Torah (Deut. 17:19).

The apotheosis of the true role of human kingship and government is that of Pharaoh in Egypt. The rabbis chose Ezekiel 29 as the prophetic reading to accompany the Torah portion *Va'era*, which contains the first seven of the ten plagues God sends to chasten the unrepentant tyrant. In it, Pharaoh is made to declare: "The river [Nile] is mine and I made it" (Ezek. 29:3). Rashi's explanation is telling:

> "The river is mine": I don't need the *elyonim*, the higher beings, because I have my river and it fulfils all my needs.
> "I made it": By my might and through my wisdom I increased my greatness and my power.

These words have an uncomfortably contemporary ring. Pharaoh, the Torah's central anti-god, reveals an attitude disturbingly similar to that of modern humankind. We decry the hard-heartedness, selfishness, and blind bigotry of Pharaoh as the very epitome of tyranny and slavery, yet, even as we condemn them, we commit some of the very sins that underlie his conduct. We implicitly share the attitudes Rashi ascribes to him: I'm self-reliant; I have no need of a higher being; I know how to get what I want from my world and I do so by means of my own inventiveness, skill, and power.

Instead, the Torah, and the prophetic writings arguably even more so, have at their heart a vision of a just society governed by the pursuit of social justice (though today we would and should challenge the acceptance of the inequitable status of men and women and the tolerance of any form of slavery). The goal of nations is therefore to foster societies in which the presence of God can reside.

Abraham Joshua Heschel, who declared that it was above all the passion of the prophets that compelled him to leave a private life of scholarship and enter the public domain, decried the platitude that "God is at home in the world." God is not at home in our societies, he insisted; our task is to transform them so that God can indeed dwell among us.[3]

Naomi Klein, never afraid to be outspoken in the name of what she rightly sees as the most urgent item on the agenda of humanity itself, does not blame capitalism *in toto* for bringing us to this pass, but rather "deregulated capitalism."[4] This is the attitude that places economic gain over all other considerations, including exploitation of workforces, the degradation not only of forests, meadowlands, and rivers, but of the very elements of earth, air, and water themselves, and the untold and untellable suffering and death of animals both as a result of human consumption and the destruction of their habitats. It is difficult not to regard this as a crime against humanity, nature, and, indeed, God. For "the earth is the Lord's and the fullness thereof," and, as the Talmud states, whoever takes what is God's without due acknowledgement has committed *me'ilah*, the sin of misappropriating the sacred (BT *Berakhot* 35a).

Me'ilah is the unintentional misuse for secular purposes of what pertains to God's service. It is a painfully apt description of how we have treated the earth in the name of national and corporate self-interest. *Me'ilah* is by definition inadvertent, something done because of a lack of awareness of the context of the object misused and without conscious intention to do wrong. It is therefore clearly

---

3 Abraham Joshua Heschel, "The Reasons for My Involvement in the Peace Movement," in his *Moral Grandeur and Spiritual Audacity*, ed. Susannah Heschel (New York: The Noonday Press, Farrar Straus and Giroux, 1996), 224.
4 Naomi Klein, *This Changes Everything: Capitalism versus the Climate* (London: Penguin, 2015), 18ff.

distinct from idolatry. Yet, there is an insidious connection: the misconduct we drift into gradually leads us to forget essential values. This was not our objective at the outset but, by losing sight of our goals, we end up unable to recognize the sacred nature of what we have bent to our own use. The insidious loss of recognition creates a barrier between ourselves and God, all the more dangerous because we are unaware of it.

Democracy, widely regarded as the best form of national government so far developed by humanity, has the advantage that its leaders are forced to listen to the will and concerns of their electorates. But it has the resultant disadvantage that those leaders are usually wedded to pleasing the people by offering short-term economic benefits for the sake of reelection, at the cost of implementing strategic long-term policies for the good of generations not yet born. In today's age of renewed populism, with its seductive appeal to the mood of the moment, this shortcoming is especially acute. In contrast, Torah can be seen as a cross-party, transgenerational foundational document of ultimate and enduring values, supreme among which is the deepening of the consciousness of the presence of God so that we act in harmony with it.

If we are to solve, or at least work towards resolving, humankind's most pressing problems, we need to do so internationally, with a universal vision such as inspired Isaiah when he looked forward to the time when "They shall not hurt nor destroy in all my holy mountain, for the earth shall be full of knowledge of the Lord as the waters cover the sea" (Isa. 11:9). The "holy mountain" is surely not one specific location but a metaphor for the entire world.

The uses of the word *de'ah*, knowledge, is key. While it is employed frequently in the Tanakh to describe intimate human relations ("and the man *knew* his wife," Gen. 4:1), it refers no less often to the close, intuitive connection between a person and God, as, for example, in Jeremiah's exhortation that "It is in this that a person should take pride: in knowing and being aware of me" (*haskel ve-yado'a otti*, Jer. 9:23). It is notable that in the daily prayer for insight and understanding, *da'at*, knowledge, is not described as having any practical objective such as gaining a grasp of a particular science or skill. Rather, the blessing should be taken as a plea for awareness itself; that is, for consciousness of God and the sacred in all we do. The early Hasidic teacher Rebbe Menachem Nachum of Chernobyl wrote in depth about *galut ha-da'at*, "the exile of knowledge," the absence of such awareness and its resultant dangers.[5] Contemporary Western civilization urgently needs the counterbalance of greater consciousness of

---

5   Menachem Nachum of Chernobyl, *Me'or Einayim*, see especially his commentary to *Va'era*.

the sacred in all life, to redress the overwhelming dominance of knowledge as power, as the accrual and analysis of data for the sake of control. Otherwise, we will continue to set our own desire for mastery above a humble and harmonious relationship with the sanctity of God's creation. This change in attitude requires substantive rethinking not just as individuals but as nations about how we relate to our home, a reconsideration of our "economics," our *oikos nomos*, the ethics and rules of how we understand our connection with our land, our planet, and our God.

3. Nature

As a species, we have taken our presumed supremacy over and consequent exploitation of the rest of nature to the point where there is finally, possibly too late, a desperate recognition that unless we instigate rapid and radical change we will destroy the whole of creation and, like Samson, perish with it in the ruins. By regarding ourselves as distinct from and superior to the rest of nature and by arrogating to ourselves the unlimited right to use it as we will, we have too often commodified and monetized other forms of life, including the soil, rivers, seas, and the animals and minerals they contain. We have reached the point where broad expanses of land are rendered sterile tracts of dust, animals are becoming extinct at a terrifying rate, and large human populations are likely to be forced to seek refuge in other, generally unwelcoming territories. As Zen Roshi Susan Murphy writes, the problem with the notion that "all of human well-being depends upon indefinite expansion of the market is that the price of this indefinite expansion turns out to be the forfeiture of climatic conditions hospitable to our species. And of course not only to *our* species."[6] Perhaps the pain so many of us are now experiencing at the realisation of what we have done and continue to do to nature itself is a sign of profound residual moral health.

Taken together, the primacy of individualism, the overwhelming focus on material growth, and the unquestioning belief in the supremacy of humankind over the rest of creation constitute a critically dangerous form of idolatry. We displace the centrality of serving God and God's creation as we focus solely on the service of ourselves and our own interests.

---

6   Susan Murphy, "The Koan of the Earth," in *Spiritual Ecology: The Cry of the Earth*, ed. Llewellyn Vaughan-Lee (Point Reyes, CA: The Golden Sufi Center, 2013), 110.

As already indicated, this concern might be less acute were it not that it correlates with the most urgent and extensive crisis of our time: the abuse of the world. In declaring that "The earth and its fullness are the Lord's" (Ps. 24:1), the Psalmist expresses the attitude that underlies the entire Hebrew Bible and rabbinic thinking: we live in a place that is not ours to possess and destroy. We are, at best, stewards of creation, entrusted to care for and preserve God's world. The earth is our home, but we do not own the freehold; we are ultimately only sojourners, temporary tenants, passers-through. We are answerable to God and the rest of creation for how we use "our common home," as Pope Francis aptly subtitled his remarkable encyclical *Laudato Si*. Yet we have so thoroughly subjugated nature that the very earth, air, and water are threatened with death from the toxins we put into them to increase their yield and enable a way of living that constitutes the betrayal of all other forms of life. Disturbingly, geographers agree that we have now entered the Anthropocene age, in which, whether we like it or not, humankind is the driver of the forces of nature, a challenge for which most of us are neither economically, morally, nor spiritually prepared.

It is often alleged, though, that the Hebrew Bible itself endorses the very anthropocentric understanding of the world that has given rise to the attitudes and behaviors I am critiquing. Indeed, this approach could be understood as deriving from the biblical story of creation in which God created humans to "fill the earth and conquer it," to "rule over the fish of the sea, the birds of the air and all the animals that traverse the land" (Gen. 1:28). This, it has been argued, implies that human beings have the right to act *in loco Dei*, with unlimited power to exploit the rest of creation to their own advantage.

Yet, numerous passages in the Bible itself, let alone in rabbinic thought, make it clear that such a view is a profound misunderstanding of the text's intention. Thus, as has often been noted, in the very next chapter of Genesis God "takes the man and places him in the Garden of Eden, to work it and keep it" (*l'ovdah uleshomrah*, Gen. 2:15). In other words, if the garden represents the world, we may derive benefit from it by working it, but we remain responsible for preserving it and everything living within it.

Yet, this verse too has been subject to misreading as a further, if less aggressive, justification for an exploitative attitude to the rest of nature. The simple form of the verb "work" is taken as if it were the causative "make to work," leading to the view that we are entitled by divine sanction to make the earth work for us. As Norman Lamm rightly explains: "Man is not only an *oved*, a worker and fabricator, he is also a *shomer*, a trustee who, according to the halakhah, is obligated to keep the world whole for its true Owner, and is responsible to return it in no worse condition than he found it."[7] Indeed, the verb *l'ovdah* indicates the very opposite connotation of subjugation: it signifies service, including and especially religious service. It is the word most frequently used across the Hebrew Bible for serving God through the observance of the commandments, the performance of the temple rites, and, more intimately, the worship of the heart, prayer. As Ellen Davis astutely notes, "the wider usage of the verb suggests that it is legitimate also to view the human task as *working for* the garden, serving its needs. Even the connotation of worship (cautiously implied) may inform our understanding." With equal acuity, she notes that the subsequent verb, *le-shomrah*, generally translated as "to keep it," also has a deeper range of meanings:

> ... to acquire wisdom by observation of the workings of the world (Ps. 107:43; Isa. 42:20), to abide by moral guidelines or the dictates of justice (Hos. 12:7; Isa. 56:1) or even the rhythms of nature (Jer. 8:7), and ... to observe the ordinances of God.... So it may be that the human is charged to "keep" the garden and at the same time to "observe" it, to learn from it and respect the limits that pertain to it....[8]

Thus, our very relationship with the land itself, and with nature, is intended to be one of attentive respect and reverence.

The Torah will subsequently develop this view in the context of the sabbatical year in which the land must rest, not because it is good for people to take a year off, or because the soil needs to recover for one season out of seven if it is to produce an adequate yield, but because *li ha-aretz*, "the earth is mine" (Lev. 25:23). The earth belongs to God and has an intrinsic relationship with God on its own terms. As Samson Raphael Hirsch notes (though the concession is somewhat qualified), "The earth and its creatures may have other relationships, of which we are ignorant, in which they serve their own purpose" (see his commentary to Gen. 1:26). In the beautiful *Perek Shirah*, the Chapter of Song, each and every tree, crop, insect, bird, and animal, even the very elements themselves, have their own unique melody with which they offer praise to God. Each morning we too bless "The One who spoke and the world came into being, who has mercy on the earth, and compassion for all creatures."

---

7   Norman Lamm, "Ecology in Jewish Law and Theology," in *Torah of the Earth*, ed. Arthur Waskow (Woodstock, VT: Jewish Lights Publishing, 2000), 126.
8   Ellen F. Davis, *Scripture, Culture and Agriculture* (New York: Cambridge University Press, 2014), 30.

Thus, the perspective of the Hebrew Bible is far from the overwhelmingly anthropocentric and utilitarian view of nature, which predominates in current Western culture and which is now at this late hour being challenged by a host of environmental movements. Rather, it is the Biblical antihero, Pharaoh, who regards himself and his minions in such a vain and arrogant manner. The encounter between God and Pharaoh in Exodus is structured to show Pharaoh in opposition to God, and Moses and Aaron set against his advisors and magicians. Alongside no doubt a large proportion of the Egyptian population, the innocent victim of this epic battle is, as in every war, the land, its animals, trees, crops, insects, amphibians, and the very water of the Nile itself. Eventually, even his own councillors turn on Pharaoh: "Haven't you yet realized that Egypt is ruined?" (Ex. 10:7). But their challenge comes too late; Pharaoh is incapable of changing his mind. He is the prototype of the many dictators who, while proclaiming that they will make their country great, lead it and their own people to ruin. Pharaoh lacks the vision and the humility to appreciate that it is in its very interconnectivity that the sanctity and safety of all life, including that of his own country, lies. It is precisely by setting himself apart from and regarding himself as lord over not only his resident aliens but also his own people, livestock, and crops, and by insisting that it is "my river and I made it," that he ensures his and their destruction.

Not only the overall attitude of the Bible but a number of particular commandments focus specifically on respect for creation. These include the requirement to allow the land to rest on the sabbatical year out of respect for its relationship with God; the *mitzvah* of leaving the corners of the fields, fallen stalks, forgotten sheaves, and overlooked fruits for the poor; the expansion of the law of *bal tashḥit*, "you shall not destroy," beyond its limited context in the Torah to encompass any and all forms of needless destruction; and the concern for *tza'ar ba'alei ḥaim*, the suffering of animals, understood in the Talmud as a *de-oraita*, Torah-enjoined, commandment. Sadly, these are rarely taken seriously enough, neither within the Jewish world nor in our surrounding culture, nor are they sufficiently far-reaching to constitute a robust protection of the natural world with its as yet uncounted wealth of species, and to form an adequate defense against the encroachment of consumer culture.

A deeper perspective is urgently needed, a whole-hearted return to reverence and awareness. In *Mishneh Torah*, Laws of the Foundations of the Torah 2:2, Maimonides understands the love of God and the fear of God almost as moves in a dance. The love of God entails taking a step forward into the world, in the desire to pursue knowledge and understanding, motivated by respect and wonder. Smitten at once by *yirah*, awe, one steps back in humility and shame before the grandeur of creation. Though such feelings are experienced towards God and not specifically God's works, nevertheless, it is the response induced by the impact of the world around us, which leads to this awareness of God. God as God truly is remains inscrutable; yet we can discover God's glory through the majesty of God's works.

But it is the mystical tradition in Judaism that opens us most deeply to the awareness of God's presence within nature. Isaiah overheard the angels singing that "The whole earth is full of God's glory," which the Zohar understood as meaning that there is literally "no place void of God," summoning us to perceive and experience the sacred within all life (Isa. 6:3; Tikkunei Zohar 122b). The Maggid of Mezerich taught that the words of the daily *shaharit* service, "*mal'ah ha-aretz kinyanekha*," imply not only that the entire world belongs to God but that everything within it can become a *kinyan*, a way of acquiring awareness of, and relationship with, God.

Just as there is a need to balance our ability to analyze the processes of nature scientifically and materially with a restored sense of magic and mystery, so there is an urgent need to rebalance our capacity to control the natural world with a renewed alertness to its sanctity and beauty. There may be no task as urgent for all humanity as the re-evaluation of how we perceive nature, so as to decommodify and resacralize our attitude to the rest of creation.

4. Where does this take us?

If we implicitly misread the First Commandment as "'I' am the Lord God," perhaps we should commit a similar error with regard to the Second Commandment as well. Instead of understanding "*Lo ta'aseh lekha phesel ve-khol temunah*" as "Don't make for yourself an idol or any image," we should (mis)take it as saying "Don't make of yourself an idol," "Don't idolize yourself or your self-image" (Ex. 20:2–4). Don't allow your own self to be *al panai*, a barrier to your awareness of God. Don't look at the world and see only what you want to extract from it for yourself. See God; see the sacred in all things.

We need to change both our consciousness and our conduct. This was expressed decades ago with characteristic conciseness and precision by Albert Einstein:

> A human being is part of the whole called by us "the universe", a part limited in time and space. We experience ourselves, our thoughts and feelings, as something separate from the rest—a

kind of optical illusion of our consciousness. This delusion is a kind of prison for us, restricting us to our personal desires and affection for a few persons nearest to us. Our task must be to free ourselves from this prison by widening our circle of understanding and compassion to embrace all living creatures and the whole of Nature in its beauty.[9]

The years since his death have made this change of attitude even more urgent. Though he did not consider himself a believer, he had a profound sense of wonder, which some would describe as an intuitive awareness of the presence, if not of God, then of the sacred, within and throughout the universe.

The greatest danger of the absence of the centrality of God in the structure, disciplines, and consciousness of societies and individuals does not, in my view, lie solely in the widespread decline in many places of traditional religious life. Rather, it is the accompanying loss of *yirat shamayim*, fear of heaven, which I find most profoundly disturbing. At the core of *yirat shamayim* is the understanding that we are accountable before one who knows. Thus, for example, the commandment not to curse the deaf or place a stumbling block in the path of the blind, is followed by the reminder *ve-yaretah me-Elohekha*, "you shall fear your God." Rashi explains this to mean that although we may think that there are no witnesses, since the deaf can't hear and the blind can't see, there remains the One who sees and knows (Lev. 19:14 and Rashi ad. loc.). This is especially relevant in an "I can get away with it" culture, which sadly includes some of the world's most powerful leaders. The rabbis regarded the fear of punishment as a lower form of *yirat shamayim*. Yet it is important in itself and shouldn't be spurned as a purely negative response. Fear of the consequences may today be the key driver in the critical process of cutting carbon and methane emissions and trying to halt the extinction of hundreds of thousands of species.

Yet, it is the higher meaning of *yirat shamayim* that is of the greatest spiritual significance: the sense of awe and wonder, respect and reverence before all living things as they embody, in different material and spiritual forms, the breath of the one God who gives life to all. This is the heart and soul of all spirituality. As Anatoly Sharansky wrote in a remarkable letter to his mother from Chistopol prison, it is both rooted in and engenders a profound humility: "In the course of time, one begins to understand that fear of God is a result of an inner stirring brought about by the lofty Divine vision, by a feeling of submission and respect

---

9   Quoted by Jules Cashford in *Spiritual Ecology: The Cry of the Earth*, ed. Llewellyn Vaughan-Lee (Point Reyes, CA: The Golden Sufi Center, 2013), 182.

for God's essence...."¹⁰ In this sense, *yirat shamayim* calls on us to treat life with constant attentive awareness and care, because we are entrusted to interact on a daily basis with what is sacred and infinitely precious, with what lies within our power to honor and bless, yet also to damage, wound and kill. That is why, out of all the lengthy confessional prayers of Yom Kippur it is one single word that troubles me most and leaves me with an unshakeable sense of guilt: *bagadnu*, "we have betrayed." I am ashamed at my participation in the betrayal of creation, and thus of God, who is present in all living being.

In this context, a kabbalistic description of sin, *kotzetz bi-netiyot*, "cutting off the shoots," feels closely relevant. As we come to understand more fully the essential interdependence of all life, the image of existence as a tree, a single organism through which all being is interconnected, seems not only a profound metaphor but also a plain description of the literal truth. To harm any form of life through wilful cruelty, contemptuous neglect or persistent but avoidable ignorance is to damage all of life in its complex totality and commit a profound wrong against the God of all existence.

The threat today derives not only from the many other twigs and branches we may have snapped, but from the breaking off of our own selves from the tree of life by imagining that we are not a dependent part of it, receiving from it and giving back to it, but its owners and possessors. We have recast ourselves not only as independent but also at the centre of and in control of creation. As a result, we are now in the terrifying position of endangering its very survival, like some form of alien predator preying on existence itself.

The true objective of the first two of the Ten Commandments is the deepening of the awareness of God and the sacred in all life. Perhaps this is what was meant by Rabbi Simlai in his insight referred to earlier on the verse *Torah tzivah lanu Moshe*, that Moses transmitted to us 611 or the 613 commandments, but that "I am the Lord your God" and "You shall have no other gods before Me" were heard by the entire Jewish people directly from the mouth of God. I have always understood this comment as an appeal to the present rather than an observation about what happened at Sinai in the past. Are we attentive to the voice of God as it calls out to us with a resonance so much deeper than speech that it is readily possible not to hear it at all? The midrash describes the call to hear as reaching us unmediated, *mi-pi ha-Gevurah*, directly from "the mouth of [God's] power." It is a power that, though absent nowhere, is latent everywhere.

---

10   Martin Gilbert, *Shcharansky: Hero of Our Time* (Harmondsworth: Penguin, 1987), 402.

With an astuteness characteristic of midrash, the *Pesikta de-Rav Kahana* notes that the phrase in Psalm 29, "The voice of God is *be-koakh* [with power]," is pronounced without a definite article, not as "His [that is, God's] power," but as "its power." This opens up the question: "the power of whom?" God's voice, the midrash answers, is attuned to the different powers and capacities of living beings, so that each of us hears it according to the measure of our ability. As the Psalmist declares, that voice is present in the cedar forests and the birth-pangs of the wild deer, in fire and over the waters. But if we persistently put ourselves and our own personal, economic, and national interests in the way, we will be unable to perceive, let alone heed, God's voice as it calls to us from all of creation (*Pesikta de-Rav Kahana* 12:25). We therefore need to deepen our *da'at*, our attunement to the presence of God.

Severed from the God of all life, we may appear independent, strong, and authoritative. Endowed with intelligence, imagination, and creativity, we may have the ability to dominate the world though a form of anthropocentric economic and spiritual colonialism. But in the vast scale of time this will prove a short-lived enterprise. Like all forms of idolatry, it will ultimately implode, leaving in its wake the destruction of nature, unjust societies at war with each other, and individual seekers in search of a deeper sustenance not found in the legacy of such a civilization. In the words of Abraham Joshua Heschel, we need to restore "the mutual allegiance" of God and humankind, and work towards the time when "the world will be full of the knowledge of God as the waters cover the sea" (Isa. 11:9).[11]

---

11 Abraham Joshua Heschel, *Quest for God: Studies in Prayer and Symbolism* (New York: The Crossroads Publishing Company, 1987), 12.

CHAPTER 8

"We Live as Did the Ancients": Reflections on the Ambiguous Role of Idolatry in Contemporary Jewish Thought

Arnold Eisen

Several of the most significant ways in which contemporary Jewish religious thought engages with and is challenged by idolatry and *avodah zarah* were captured with remarkable prescience by the great sociologist Max Weber just over a century ago in an essay often seen as his personal credo. Addressing an audience at the University of Munich amidst the continuing ravages of the First World War, Weber wondered in "Science as a Vocation" whether any sort of ultimate meaning could be found in a "rationalized" and "disenchanted" world. *Wissenschaft* was particularly unsuited to the search for such meaning, in his view. "Science, this specifically irreligious power," could uncover the facts that guide decisions of value but could not itself determine what was right or good. The reason that Weber cited for that unbridgeable divide bears directly on the subject of *avodah zarah*: "The various value-spheres of the world stand in irreconcilable conflict with each other.... If one proceeds from pure experience, one arrives at polytheism."[1]

---

1   Max Weber, "Science as a Vocation," in *From Max Weber: Essays in Sociology*, ed. H. H. Gerth and C. Wright Mills (New York: Oxford University Press, 1969), 139, 142, 147. For a concise discussion of the terms "idolatry," *avodah zarah*, and "polytheism," see Moshe Halbertal and

The claim is striking: like the Deuteronomic books of the Bible and the writings attributed to Israel's classical prophets (sources that he knew well and highly valued[2]), Weber believed that monotheistic faith was somehow essential to the moral compass of humanity, while recognizing that adherence to such faith, in his day as in earlier eras, was difficult to achieve and maintain. Belief and trust in a single deity was undermined, first of all, by the fact that many different gods were worshipped in the world. If one takes "gods" and "worship" in a figurative and not only a literal sense, as religious thinkers in our own day commonly do, the prevalence of polytheism is still more pronounced. Weber's scholarship on religion identified five elements of monotheism, as opposed to idolatry, that continue to prove especially relevant and challenging in the twenty-first century.

(1) The God of monotheism, unlike pagan deities, is *universal rather than local, distant rather than near-at-hand, and more abstract than concrete*. Weber saw a direct connection between Deuteronomy's "rationalization" of Israelite religion and the centuries-long process that had rationalized every area of modern life. Ancient and medieval believers had to contend with misplaced allegiance to many gods, but modern believers, thanks to "disenchantment" and secularization, were more and more left with faith in no gods. And yet, Weber argued, it was precisely the "irreligious" character of our scientific culture that made the conflict among value spheres, the "gods" of the day, "irreconcilable."

(2) The God of the Bible and the rabbis *rules supreme over history*, demonstrating both power and presence by periodic interventions in human affairs. God repeatedly punishes Israel and other nations for transgressions against the divine will and rewards them for faithful obedience. The regime of reward and punishment extends to individuals as well, in this world or the next. No theological question has dominated Jewish thought of the past half-century nearly as much as "God's Presence in History" (the title of an influential book by theologian Emil Fackenheim). The question at issue is whether God has somehow been involved in the two most significant events in recent Jewish history: the Holocaust and the creation of the State of Israel. It is widely agreed that belief in many gods, no gods, or One God Who was *not* "Lord of History" would not have posed a comparable challenge to faith.

Avishai Margalit, *Idolatry*, trans. Naomi Goldblum (Cambridge, MA: Harvard University Press, 1992), 1–8.

2   Max Weber, *Ancient Judaism*, trans. H. H. Gerth and Don Martindale (New York: Free Press, 1952).

(3) *It is forbidden to make visual images of the biblical God and impossible to adequately imagine "Him."* The prophets, followed by the rabbis, defined idolatry not only as worship of other (and therefore false) gods, but as errant, image-laden worship of the One true God. Moshe Halbertal and Avishai Margalit note correctly that Jewish (and other religious) sources have distinguished between (forbidden) pictorial representation of God, and (permitted) linguistic representation.[3] In contemporary Jewish theology—especially but not only in feminist thought—linguistic imagery and pronouns are at issue, and, if gendered male, are pronounced idolatrous. Whether any sort of God possessing personal attributes can legitimately be worshipped or conceived is hotly debated.

(4) Religion, ancient or modern, is never without a *political dimension*. Idolatrous faiths without apology make worship of the tribe, city or state explicit; monotheistic faiths, and Judaism in particular, evince obvious tension in this regard. God is believed to be the Lord of all humanity, yet stands in special relation to one people, and perhaps to one faith. "We live as did the ancients," Weber wrote provocatively, "when their world was not yet disenchanted of its gods and demons.... [Today, as before,] everybody sacrifice[s] to the gods of his city."[4] Weber's audience must have felt the tension keenly as the World War raged among the Christian nations of Europe. A version of that same tension has taken on new salience in Jewish thought in recent decades, thanks to the religious significance ascribed by Jews to the State of Israel, on the one hand, and American Jewry's commitment to ethnic and religious pluralism on the other. If one broadens the notion of the "political" (as Weber did) to signify, first, the ways in which *avodah zarah* serves to mark off Jews from other peoples, and, secondly, the degree to which Jewish belief and observance are shaped by consideration of what the surrounding Gentile state and cultures will approve or tolerate (that is, what is politic for the Jewish minority)—then the salience of the "political dimension" in Judaism is greater still.

(5) Finally, as we have seen, Weber suggested that the worship of many gods—or no god—carries deleterious *moral implications and consequences*. In his view, these included a moral relativism that he himself, lacking religious faith, seemed to endorse, albeit reluctantly. Moral decline or danger is perhaps the dominant theme of contemporary Jewish thought concerning idolatry. *Avodah zarah* is rarely taken to mean worship of God in ways other

---

3   Halbertal and Margalit, *Idolatry*, 37–66.
4   Weber, "Science as a Vocation," 148.

than "ours." Nor is the term deployed (outside the Haredi world, at least) to critique conceptions of God that posit multiple divinities (the Christian trinity, say, or the Buddhist pantheon). Idolatry, rather, signifies immoral behavior above all else: the direction of "ultimate concern" to causes, activities or persons who are less than ultimate, including, preeminently, the self.

My aim in this essay is to analyze and evaluate how the theme of idolatry plays out in important and representative essays in contemporary Jewish thought, particularly in North America. We will find that recent use of *avodah zarah*, implicit and explicit, has enriched and complicated Jewish faith; that marking the difference between Jews or Judaism and other faiths and faith communities via claims of *avodah zarah*, while rarely central to Jewish thought in recent decades, has rarely been absent altogether; and that in discussions of morality and politics the concept of idolatry has remained indispensable. Weber concluded "Science as a Vocation" with Isaiah's parable of the watchman—a passage that I shall read, and endorse, as an ironic plea for monotheistic faith in a faithless, or polytheistic, time.

1. One God, Creator of the Universe

The Torah, the Deuteronomic history books, and the writings of the biblical prophets are replete with expressions of divine frustration—later amplified by the rabbis—at Israelite failure to worship YHWH, or "Him" alone, despite ample evidence of "His" beneficence and power. Idolatry poses challenges to Israelite monotheism so persistent that one wonders if they are perhaps inherent in that faith. The problem is in part that Israel's God demands to be worshipped to the exclusion of other deities, and to be worshipped at only one central shrine—requirements that scholars have long connected to the distancing of God from local features of the natural world such as hills, trees and springs. Israel's God of Covenant dwells in heaven and "comes down" to earth for particular purposes. YHWH is the Creator of Nature rather than part of it; transcendent rather than immanent, or, if both, far more the former than the latter.[5] While Jews in the rabbinic period seem not to have been personally tempted as their ancestors were by the paganism all around them, texts from the period express wonderment

---

5   Stephen A. Geller, "The Sack of Shechem: The Use of Typology in Biblical Covenant Religion," *Prooftexts* 10, no. 1 (1990): 1–15.

that God had permitted the idolatrous Roman empire to exercise dominion over much of the world.

The most powerful nations of the contemporary world are, of course, not pagan—which perhaps explains why *avodah zarah* does not much figure in contemporary Jewish (or Christian) writing in America about the relation of God to nature. Gods of the earth pose no immediate threat to monotheism, even as concern about the future of the natural world takes on new importance at this moment of COVID pandemic, environmental destruction and global warming. Even theologians who reject the notion of a transcendent deity Who acts on the world from outside it tend to stress that they are not pantheists but panentheists who discern underlying unity in the workings of divinity.[6] Mordecai Kaplan maintained nearly a century ago that his God—a Force or set of forces rather than a personal Being—was not "natural" or "supernatural," but "trans-natural."[7] Bradley Artson makes a similar argument in his more recent statement of Jewish process theology.[8] I am not persuaded by these arguments, which seek to ascribe purpose (or at least direction) to divinity even as they deny God personality, will, or consciousness. Then again, I am reminded of Max Weber's humbling observation that "every consistent rationalism" at some point resembles long division: it leaves a remainder and does not "come out even with nothing left over."[9] Theology is no exception.

Scientific developments since Darwin and Einstein offer a serious challenge to any theology that attempts to construct a view of reality that includes both a God Who reigns supreme over nature and history and scientific belief in eons of evolution and a universe composed of "dark matter," "black holes," and galaxies that number in the billions. Few contemporary Jewish thinkers even make that attempt, silenced perhaps by inability to speak credibly about the latest scientific theories. It is more common to regard science and faith as separate domains ("facts" versus "values," in Weberian terms). A select few seek to harmonize mystical imaginings of God with some of the more esoteric theories of

---

6   Arthur Green, *Radical Judaism: Rethinking God and Tradition*, Franz Rosenzweig Lecture Series (New Haven and London: Yale University Press, 2010), 16–27.
7   Mordecai M. Kaplan, *The Meaning of God in Modern Jewish Religion*. (New York: Reconstructionist Press, 1962); Mordecai M. Kaplan, *Judaism without Supernaturalism; the Only Alternative to Orthodoxy and Secularism*, 1st ed. (New York: Reconstructionist Press, 1958).
8   Bradley Shavit Artson, *God of Becoming and Relationship: The Dynamic Nature of Process Theology* (Woodstock, VT: Jewish Lights Publishing, 2013).
9   Max Weber, "The Social Psychology of the World Religions," in *From Max Weber: Essays in Sociology*, ed. H. H. Gerth and C. Wright Mills (New York: Oxford University Press, 1969), 281.

contemporary physics.[10] One might have thought that *avodah zarah* would perhaps have reentered the stage at this theological moment, as it were inverting Deuteronomy's logic of one temple for the one people of the one God. If the cosmos hosts many more than three dimensions, untold trillions of stars, and multiple universes; if there are life-forms in existence that human beings cannot begin to know or imagine—why should humanity not conceive of a *plurality* of gods, and worship them in an *infinite variety* of modes?

That option, which I too would not recommend, has not been pursued as yet to my knowledge by Jewish thinkers, perhaps because sacrifice of God's universal attributes at this point in time would run contrary to the scientific search for a unified field theory that accounts for all of reality as well as to salient facts of contemporary life such as globalization of trade, mass media, jet travel, and instantaneous communication. These and other taken-for-granted realities—heightened by the threats posed to all life on earth by pandemic and global warming—have increased consciousness that all human beings belong to a single species and are endangered as never before by the harm we have done to the planet we share. With human beings united by the need to defend the human species against common enemies, Jews are unlikely to be attracted to a God of narrower purview than the entirety of the earth and all the vastness of the heavens. A God less all-inclusive than the diverse human beings that God created in God's image would likewise be unable to undergird precious notions of humanity, human rights, human dignity, and the like—all values fundamental to the world's major civilizations.

Jewish theology will surely adapt in coming decades to the challenge posed by twenty-first-century science, as it has to previous challenges, but in the meantime it seems to be widely assumed that science and faith are completely separate domains (a claim that I find unconvincing, but to which I see no viable alternative given our present state of knowledge). It is no less widely asserted that sacred Jewish texts such as the opening chapter of Genesis impose special responsibility on human beings created in God's image to serve as faithful stewards of God's creation (a claim with which I agree wholeheartedly).

Judaism has always sought to have the benefits of particularity as well as universality in its God, Who has long been called not only Elohim, a generic name for divinity, but also by the personal name YHWH. I suspect that today, too, this divine duality helps to stave off the need for more than one god and serves to counter the slide that Weber charted from a universal and transcendent God to

---

10 Cf. Daniel C. Matt, *God & the Big Bang: Discovering Harmony between Science & Spirituality* (Woodstock, VT: Jewish Lights Publishing, 1996).

a deity so irrelevant that faith gives way to atheism or disinterest. Contemporary Jews are thankfully heirs to a tradition that conceives God to have infinite attributes, only a relative few of which are known to human beings. Knowledge of God comes via a combination of reason, revelation, tradition and experience. God's attributes include a kind of personhood as well as concern for justice and lovingkindness. The fact that the One God possesses so many attributes obviates the need to find these attributes in multiple gods. I doubt that a religious perspective any more universal—or any less—will win widespread adherence among Jews today. It would certainly not win mine.

2. The "Free God of History"

Half a century ago and more, Martin Buber approvingly contrasted the "free God of history" to "the fettered deity of natural things," thereby pointing to a second obstacle to belief in Judaism's God: the tendency of history not to work out the way the prophets had said it should and would.[11] The problem, of course, endures in every age, but it has remained particularly salient in ours, thanks to the awful events of mid-twentieth-century history that caused Buber to note that "the true word [of prophecy] is almost powerless. . . . God does not corroborate it. . . . God will speak to [the people] only in the language of history" and history more often than not "makes it burdensome for the believer and light for the unbeliever." As a result, "His revelation is nothing but a different form of hiding His face."[12] Buber's use of present tense is striking; recent Jewish history compelled him to repeatedly address the problem he named "the eclipse of God."[13] Concern with the matter has not abated in the decades since he wrote.

The question of God's role in history, and particularly in the eventful history of the Children of Israel, has not surprisingly been the subject of a veritable outpouring of Jewish theology in the past fifty years, provoked by both the two major events of twentieth-century Jewish history: the Holocaust and the creation of the State of Israel. A key distinction often made between Judaism and paganism has in this matter worked both for and against the tradition that it is

---

11 Martin Buber, *The Prophetic Faith*, trans. Carlyle Witton-Davies (New York: Harper & Row, 1949), 81.
12 Ibid., 176–177.
13 Martin Buber, *Eclipse of God: Studies in the Relation between Religion and Philosophy* (New York: Harper & Row, 1952). For a heartfelt meditation by Buber on the issue of God's role in or absence from history, see, for example, Martin Buber, *For the Sake of Heaven*, trans. Ludwig Lewisohn (Philadelphia: Jewish Publication Society of America, 1945).

invoked to justify. Jewish thinkers can and do claim, quite plausibly in my view, that Israel's God—Sovereign of the Universe—directs or supervises world history in a way that local deities, members of a pantheon of gods, could not possibly do. The latter are limited in scope and power not only by other gods, but by the fact that they exist immanently: *in* the world rather than *above and outside* it. But belief in the One Lord of History gives rise to hopes or expectations of salvific divine action that in many (most?) cases, and quite inevitably, are disappointed. Faith in God's providence is thereby undermined. I remember a noted theologian who confessed to me one day that he had arrived at faith in God on rational grounds and had lost that faith irretrievably soon after when he confronted the awful facts of the Holocaust. He is surely not alone in this.

Fackenheim, who did not lose faith in God, was reluctantly forced by the Holocaust to question the core rabbinic belief that God is present in history. Perhaps, he suggested, Jews should no longer recite the passage in the Passover Haggadah that affirms that "in every generation You have saved us from their [the enemy's] hand."[14] Fackenheim could not abide the belief held by some Jews, most notably the Satmar Rebbe, that God was very much present in history during Hitler's reign and had allowed the Nazis to kill Jews as punishment for collective Jewish sin. Rabbi Joseph Soloveitchik, likewise rejecting that position, concluded that God's inaction to save Jews from the Nazi onslaught was incomprehensible—a case of *hester panim*, the "hiding of God's countenance." But God's presence was soon revealed once more, Soloveitchik wrote: when the United Nations voted for the partition of Palestine in 1947 and when the emergent State of Israel prevailed on the battlefield against its enemies.[15] Rabbi Abraham Joshua Heschel, responding to these same events, declared unequivocally in his book, *Israel: An Echo of Eternity*, that "God's will does not dominate the affairs of men."[16] He, too, opted to invoke the "hiding of the divine countenance" as a placeholder for explanation that is lacking. Only theologian Richard Rubenstein took the position that "after Auschwitz" Jews should give up belief in a God who is Lord of History. The Jewish people, having recently returned to the Land of Israel, should work toward "resurrection of the divinities of Israel's

---

14   Emil L. Fackenheim, *God's Presence in History: Jewish Affirmations and Philosophical Reflections* (New York: Harper & Row, 1970), 32.
15   Joseph Dov Soloveitchik, *Listen—My Beloved Knocks*, ed. Jeffrey R. Woolf, trans. David Z. Gordon (Jersey City: KTAV, 2006).
16   Abraham Joshua Heschel, *Israel: An Echo of Eternity* (New York: Farrar, Straus & Giroux, 1969), 130–131.

earth." The "gods of earth" may be "the very real and very potent expressions of the inner vitality of contemporary Israel."[17]

Rubenstein denied the charges of atheism and blasphemy that some critics leveled against him, even as he embraced a form of worship that he knew had long been considered *avodah zarah*. His argument for renewed paganism has as little appeal to me (or to most other Jewish thinkers of this generation) as the belief that God permitted, encouraged, or instigated the Nazi slaughter of Jews as punishment for sin. Nor am I persuaded that the "hiding of God's countenance" can reliably be said to begin and end at defined moments of history, as judged by outcomes that conform to or conflict with Jewish hopes or expectations. Heschel's position seems to me far wiser: "The presence of God in history is never conceived to mean His penetration of history. God's will does not dominate the affairs of men."[18] Elsewhere Heschel declared succinctly that "none of us pretends to be God's accountant," keeping track of divine attendance at, or absence from, history.[19] Jewish theology on this matter cannot in my view "come out even." God's countenance is hidden, God's light is eclipsed, God's presence in history is obscured.

It is striking that Heschel's declaration about God's role in history was made into a book written in the immediate aftermath of the Six Day War—an event that launched a religiously inspired political movement in Israel that claimed divine sanction, or even a divine command, for Jewish settlement in the territories that had just been conquered. Many Israeli Jews, but few American Jews outside the Orthodox world, saw messianic significance in the events of the day; a small number of Israelis went so far to exclaim that the Land of Israel took precedence over the people of Israel and the Torah of Israel—a position laden with overtones of paganism. Conversely, American Jews have for nearly a century been committed to a doctrine of religious pluralism that is not nearly as influential in Israel. Heschel's view was much more congenial to the latter. "Our imperishable homeland is in God's time," he wrote pointedly in his one book about Israel. "We enter God's time through the gate of sacred deeds... The great sacred deed for us today is to build the Land of Israel."[20] This is the view to which

---

17   Richard L. Rubenstein, *After Auschwitz: Radical Theology and Contemporary Judaism* (Indianapolis: Bobbs-Merrill, 1973), 142.
18   Heschel, *Israel*, 131.
19   Abraham Joshua Heschel, "No Religion Is an Island," in his *Moral Grandeur and Spiritual Audacity: Essays*, ed. Susannah Heschel, 1st ed. (New York: Farrar, Straus & Giroux, 1996), 246.
20   Heschel, *Israel*, 127–128. It is striking that Buber, Heschel, and Soloveitchik, along with other thinkers of that time, remain live presences in the contemporary Jewish thought in the West. Few theologians have entered the scene in recent decades to challenge or supplant them.

I subscribe. Jewish thinkers in the past few decades have not to my knowledge ventured answers to the question of God's role in history in addition to those summarized here.

3. Imaging and Imagining God

It is a commonplace of Jewish thought, now as in previous eras, that human beings must not make visual images of God, and cannot conceive or imagine God adequately; this limitation of the One true God, as opposed to pagan deities, is a mark of God's uniqueness and power. Gods of whom sculpted images can be made; whose biographies and workings are familiar to human believers; and whose responsiveness to proper ritual approach can be counted upon as reliably as magic—are by definition false. Scholars of the Bible note that ancient Israelite writings, at least those preserved in the biblical canon, show little interest in understanding the beliefs actually held by pagan worshippers, as opposed to the practices in which they engaged—a pattern that has largely held firm for Jewish religious thinkers down to the present day.[21]

Claims about the essential character of God's invisibility have always been popular among philosophers, for whom reason is transparently superior to imagination or emotion as a path to truth. Not surprisingly, we often encounter this claim in the works of modern Jewish thinkers who wish to argue the superiority of Judaism as a "religion of reason" over other religious traditions, or the superiority of rational over irrational elements within Jewish tradition.[22] The contrast between monotheism and paganism, to the disparagement of the latter, is made systematically throughout Franz Rosenzweig's masterwork, *The Star of Redemption*.[23] Heschel wrote that Jews were forbidden to worship images of God because human beings are themselves (that is, *bear upon themselves*) the

---

21 Yehezkel Kaufmann famously maintained that "the biblical writers seem ignorant of the world of mythology that described the lives and actions of these living gods.... Israel was no longer aware of the real nature of paganism.... What the Bible calls idolatry is just that: the worship of images, fetishes, nothing more." Moshe Greenberg, "Kaufmann on the Bible: An Appreciation (1964)," in Moshe Greenberg, *Studies in the Bible and Jewish Thought* (Philadelphia: Jewish Publication Society, 1995), 180. See also Greenberg's "additional note" on the contrasting views of other biblical scholars (ibid., 188).

22 Hermann Cohen, *Religion of Reason out of the Sources of Judaism*, trans. Simon Kaplan (Atlanta: Scholars Press, 1995).

23 Franz Rosenzweig, *The Star of Redemption*, trans. William W. Hallo (Notre Dame: Notre Dame Press, 1985).

image of God.[24] Despite his spirited defense of the prophets' use of anthropomorphic language to describe God, Heschel insisted that God inhabits a realm that is "ineffable," meaning, beyond accurate verbal description, let alone visual or plastic imagery.[25]

That claim is crucial to feminist theologians, who argue that even verbal imagery is problematic when it describes God exclusively in male terms or uses exclusively masculine pronouns. Rita Gross, in a perceptive and representative piece on "Female God Language in a Jewish Context," suggested that the debate over what images and pronouns should be used to describe God has given new meaning to idolatry, "usually an empty category in contemporary religious discourse." She noted that employment of exclusively male "God language," despite recognition that God is genderless, focuses the mind on metaphor rather than on the reality to which metaphor points—and that, she observed, is the very meaning of idolatry. Where some feminists have recommended abandoning the notion of God altogether, and others have urged that ascriptions of personality to God be dropped in the interest of avoiding the pronoun problem, Gross insisted that Judaism is "theistic through and through." Jewish tradition holds that "the absolute can be imaged as a person entering into relationships of love and responsibility with human beings," a conviction that Gross did not want to sacrifice. Anthropomorphic imagery should be retained, but it must not be exclusively male, lest it serve to legitimate patriarchy.[26]

Catherine Keller, in a more recent essay that reflects on a half-century of feminist writing about the issue, suggests that feminists may have "pumped a few decades of life force into the God question," just when other theologians "had deemed God good and dead." She worries that, "no matter how much we adjust and supplement and deconstruct and reconstruct God, He will remain pretty

---

24 Abraham Joshua Heschel, "Religion and Race," in his *The Insecurity of Freedom: Essays on Human Existence* (New York: Farrar, Strauss & Giroux, 1967), 95.
25 Abraham Joshua Heschel, *Man Is Not Alone: A Philosophy of Religion* (New York: Harper & Row, 1951), 3–23.
26 Rita Gross, "Female God Language in a Jewish Context," in *Womanspirit Rising: A Feminist Reader in Religion*, ed. Carol P. Christ and Judith Plaskow (New York: HarperCollins, 1992), 167–173. See also Marcia Falk, "Notes on Composing New Blessings toward a Feminist-Jewish Reconstruction of Prayer," *Journal of Feminist Studies in Religion* 3, no. 1 (1987): 39–53; Cynthia Ozick, "Notes toward Finding the Right Question," in *On Being a Jewish Feminist: A Reader*, ed. Susannah Heschel (New York: Schocken Books, 1983), 129–151; Judith Plaskow, "The Right Question Is Theological," in *On Being a Jewish Feminist: A Reader*, ed. Susannah Heschel (New York: Schocken Books, 1983), 223–233. For a perceptive discussion of the distinction between "linguistic and pictorial representations" of God, see Halbertal and Magralit, *Idolatry*, 52–66. They note (ibid., 21) that in order to speak of idolatry, a personal anthropomorphic God is required.

much a he." Even the God conceived by feminists, having remained personal, is not sufficiently other. "He gets frozen in his high but still literally He-ness."[27] I have heard it said (but cannot trace the source) that Jews worship "a relatively genderless male deity." This seems an accurate description of some theologians, who are not comfortable with gendered pronouns but continue to use them for the reasons set forth by Gross and Keller.

Jewish theology, feminist or not, insists on the paradoxical claim that the only God who can save us in any sense of the word, physical or spiritual; the only one who can truly *be* God, is the One Whom human beings cannot see, image, or adequately imagine. Idolatry by contrast is patently "based upon a lie that everyone knows to be a lie," writes philosopher and theologian David Novak.[28] However, he and other Jewish thinkers maintain that the abstract "God of the philosophers" is not the God of history and covenant to Whom most modern Jewish thinkers (including Novak) remain committed. Heschel declared categorically that philosophy will not lead one to the living God.[29] Buber went so far as to accuse philosophical believers of idolatry if they "replace him by the image of images, the idea, [and thus] remove themselves and remove the rest of us furthest from him.... A God who is not a living personality is an idol."[30]

Contemporary theologians, as we have seen, face an additional problem: disbelief in gods who can be seen tends to carry over to disbelief in the One God, Who cannot be seen. Weber, heir to an Enlightenment tradition of skepticism about the truth of religion, took the ubiquity of religious belief of some sort over the course of history and culture, and the continuities between modern and ancient forms of religion, as evidence that the critique of any religions may well apply to all. Social scientific theories of religion tend to "explain" or "explain away" all religions, monotheistic or pagan, modern or ancient, without exception.[31]

Jewish thinkers, in order to defend their faith against such attack, have had to argue that some religions are more valid than others—monotheism is superior to idolatry—while conceding that some aspects of Jewish belief and practice too require significant adjustment. "Folk religion" by definition

---

27 Catherine Keller, "Returning God: The Gift of Feminist Theology," in *Feminism, Sexuality, and the Return of Religion*, ed. John D. Caputo and Linda Alcoff, Indiana Series in the Philosophy of Religion (Bloomington: Indiana University Press, 2011), 58, 66.
28 David Novak, *Zionism and Judaism: A New Theory* (New York: Cambridge University Press, 2015), 107.
29 Heschel, *Man Is Not Alone*, 51–56.
30 Buber, *Eclipse of God*, 50, 52.
31 Max Weber, *The Sociology of Religion* (Boston: Beacon Press, 1993).

aims to serve the needs of the masses; elites or "virtuosos" will generally think about matters differently. The dilemma is obvious: the more that personality is ascribed to God, the more God seems to resemble pagan deities. (Heschel was roundly criticized for his notion of divine "pathos.") But the less personality God displays, and the more abstractly God is conceived, the more faith is subject to the claim of religious skeptics that science has rendered God irrelevant and/or illusory.

I suspect that Jewish thinkers in recent decades have faced an additional challenge from idolatry. They have learned from personal experience what art historian David Freedberg called "The Power of Images."[32] Almost all have visited churches that feature statuary and paintings depicting Father, Son, Holy Spirit, and Mary in graphic detail. Many have noted the role played by such images in eliciting or facilitating reverence. Acquaintance with Hinduism and Buddhism—and visits to shrines and temples of those religions—is more widespread than ever before. One does not hear Jewish thinkers suggesting that Judaism should relax its prohibition on visual and plastic imagery, and I certainly would not do so. But I confess that, observing the "power of images" to move worshippers in Christian churches or Hindu temples, I have sometimes felt what religious studies scholar Lee Yearley terms "spiritual regret."[33] One is aware that members of other faith communities seem to have access to experiences, and perhaps to a measure of truth, that one will never attain. I am a Jew who worships this God and not another, in this set of ways and not others. That is all the more reason to learn from practitioners in other traditions, and test the limits of similarity and difference. Study of other religions also stimulates attention to the occasions on which Jews invest physical objects with holiness: bowing before or kissing the Torah as it is paraded around the synagogue, for example, or standing while it is raised, "dressed" or "undressed." These and other acts and gestures of love and deference heighten the Jewish worshipper's sense, even in the absence of visual or plastic imagery, that the God of all the earth is with us, right here, at this very moment.

---

32 David Freedberg, *The Power of Images: Studies in the History and Theory of Response* (Chicago: University of Chicago Press, 1989).
33 Lee H. Yearley, *Mencius and Aquinas: Theories of Virtue and Conceptions of Courage* (Boulder, CO: NetLibrary, Inc., 1999), 1–23.

4. "Not by Might, Not by Power"

The distinction between false faith and true, *avodah zarah* and Judaism, is further complicated today, as Weber's credo essay suggested it would be, by the ties that bind Jewish thought about the God of all the world to Jews' particular political loyalties, interests and conflicts.

It is telling that Spinoza called the work that is generally held to mark the preamble to the corpus of modern Jewish thought, "A Theological-Political Treatise." Moses Mendelssohn subtitled his "Jerusalem," the first major response to Spinoza's Tractatus (albeit after a gap of more than a century), "On Religious Power and Judaism." Both works, and many others since, highlighted the political dimension of virtually all Jewish theology in the modern period. On the one hand, Jewish thinkers have sought to differentiate Judaism from other faiths, including other monotheistic faiths—a task made more necessary in recent years, and more difficult, by the plurality of worldviews to which Jews are exposed and the thinkers' commitment to religious pluralism. Contemporary Jewish thinkers cannot and do not follow the rabbis of old and argue that every faith foreign to Judaism (*avodah zarah* in the literal sense) is idolatrous (*avodah zarah* as the term is usually understood). On the other hand, Jewish thinkers now more than ever have to offer their readers cogent reasons for choosing Judaism as opposed to other religions or subscribing to no religion in particular, or none at all—options that are increasingly popular in twenty-first-century North America.

What is more, arguments for Judaism, to be successful, must be couched in terms that suit the majority culture in which most Jews have been raised, rather than in language specific to Jewish tradition, of which many American Jews know very little. The case for Judaism must also contend with the fact—also political in nature—that large numbers of American Jews will not adopt or consider practices or beliefs that they fear would render them more distinctive than they wish to be in the eyes of the surrounding Gentile culture, society, and state—or more distinctive than Gentiles are willing to tolerate without loss of privileges and acceptance that Jews seek or value. Christianity sets the terms of discourse and the limits for legitimate religious difference.[34] Monotheism falls within those limits. Idolatry does not.

Kaplan wrote almost a century ago that Jewish belief and practice in the modern world would necessarily vary depending on whether Judaism functions as a

---

34 Arnold M. Eisen, *Rethinking Modern Judaism: Ritual, Commandment, Community* (Chicago: University of Chicago Press, 1998), 107–134.

"subordinate," "coordinate" or "dominant" culture in a given state or society. In America, as in France, Judaism would play the "subordinate" role in the hyphenated identity of Jews. (Only in Palestine could Judaism come to be "dominant," in his view.)[35] Jews could secure their distinctiveness, in his view, only by developing a "civilization" that encompassed far more than religion alone: communal institutions, rituals, arts, and cultural forms—including religion, for those so inclined. This civilization would have to prove attractive enough to compete successfully with the reality of religions diversity and the blandishments of assimilation.[36] The model of hyphenated identity that Kaplan urged has since been accepted in some form by thinkers of every Jewish denomination in America except the Ultra-Orthodox—a development that presumes a positive relationship between Judaism and the religion of the majority (which in America, and the West as a whole, means one or another form of Christianity).

The great majority of Jews in the West take that relationship for granted—and as a result cannot accept the vision of non-Jews as "idolatrous," or even as profoundly *other*. They could not have accepted (and would likely not have been offered) full participation in countries that worshipped a different God, let alone many gods; their enthusiastic advocacy of the so-called "Judeo-Christian ethic" and, more recently, of the notion that a common heritage shared by the three "Abrahamic religions," testifies to the importance of Jewish belief in a common monotheistic faith. Their neighbors' way of serving God could be "foreign" (*zar*) to Jews without being in any way illegitimate, let alone idolatrous. Jewish thinkers and communal leaders, particularly in America, have striven to join Judaism as full partner to the majority faith. They did so in part by distinguishing Christianity (and, more recently, other religions as well) from *avodah zarah*, at the same time as they have continued to distinguish Jewish forms of worship favorably from all others. It is hard to gauge just how much of Jewish religious thought is motivated or shaped by desire to unite Jews more closely to Gentile neighbors at the same time as one seeks to maintain Jews' distinction from those neighbors. My guess would be that the role played by this desire remains significant.

Was Franz Rosenzweig's theory of the "dual covenant" binding Judaism and Christianity, a concept that awarded world-historical significance to these two religions, and only them, meant to secure Jews a place in Germany, an

---

35   Mordecai M. Kaplan, *Judaism as a Civilization: Toward a Reconstruction of American-Jewish Life* (Philadelphia: Jewish Publication Society, 2010), 215–216.
36   Arnold M. Eisen, *The Chosen People in America: A Study in Jewish Religious Ideology*, The Modern Jewish Experience (Bloomington: Indiana University Press, 1983).

overwhelmingly Christian nation?[37] Was Heschel's dictum that Judaism sanctifies time and not space a strategy meant to chart a theological path for Jews who wished to play a full part in America but in other ways remain apart from America?[38] Heschel's alliance with Martin Luther King and his prominent role in leading religious opposition to the War in Vietnam, however controversial, arguably cemented relationships between Jews and like-minded Christians and underlined the potency of the "Judeo-Christian ethic." So did his equation of racism with idolatry. "What is an idol? Any god who is mine but not yours, any god concerned with me but not with you, is an idol."

Exactly: The survival and thriving of Judaism in the diaspora is based on the theological presumption that Jews and Christians (but not idolaters) worship the same God, albeit through differing practices and beliefs; that what they share is more basic, and far more important, than where they differ. Heschel spelled out that conviction in his 1965 address at Union Theological Seminary, entitled "No Religion Is an Island." I do not doubt that he fully believed that Judaism and Christianity "must acknowledge indebtedness to one another,"[39] just as Rosenzweig believed that Judaism is the fire that burns at the core of the Star of Redemption, and Christianity the rays that bring light of that fire to the nations.[40] But we should not underestimate the importance of these convictions for the very possibility of Jewish coexistence with Gentiles.

I suspect that historical memory also played a role in the Jewish embrace of Christianity in contemporary America and the two religions' shared condemnation of idolatry. The United States had within living memory fought against or contended with totalitarian adversaries whose leaders claimed near-divine status among their peoples. Hitler, Stalin, and Mao had been joined in this practice by lesser tyrants of similar bent. The wartime Chancellor of JTS, Rabbi Louis Finkelstein, annually summoned philosophers, scientists, and theologians of diverse views to join in common defense of American democracy. American Jewish leaders today usually draw the line of legitimacy in a way that includes Islam but places "Islamic extremism" beyond the pale, along with idolatry. One knows that God is the Lord of all humanity, but nonetheless prays regularly that

---

37 See Mara H. Benjamin, *Rosenzweig's Bible: Reinventing Scripture for Jewish Modernity* (Cambridge: Cambridge University Press, 2009).
38 This point is expressed most famously in Heschel notion of the Sabbath as a "palace in time." See Abraham Joshua Heschel, *The Sabbath: Its Meaning for Modern Man* (New York: Farrar, Straus and Young, 1951).
39 Heschel, "No Religion Is an Island," 233–302. The quotation can be found ibid., 243.
40 Rosenzweig, *The Star of Redemption*, 298–303, 336–337.

God will favor some of God's creatures, those on our side, over others—further evidence that the tie between religion and politics remains inseverable.

All these presumptions have been notably strained in recent years in the United States by the widely recognized polarization of politics that reached its climax in the Trump presidency and the still-contested 2020 election that unseated him. Divisions within America—and inside the Jewish community in America—are arguably now as great as, or greater than, divisions between Americans, or Jews, and others; indeed, the question of how strictly one should police internal and external borders has become paramount. Issues on which there once had been, or would have been, moral consensus are now politicized and subject to vitriolic dispute. The notion of idolatry has taken on renewed importance as a result—a development to which I will return in the conclusion to this essay.

5. "I have set before you good and evil"

Heschel's equation of racism with idolatry points to the final major role that *avodah zarah* plays in contemporary Jewish thought: the conviction – once more echoing the prophets and the rabbis of old—that worship of other gods is both cause and effect of immorality. Abuse of power, social injustice, violence, sexual impropriety, and excessive regard for the self are commonly cited as examples of idol-worship. As biblical prophets warned about idolaters who passed their children through the fire in service to the god Moloch—and rabbinic sages routinely associated Roman paganism with violent cruelty and sexual license—so contemporary preachers and religious thinkers, Jewish and non-Jewish, sermonize against immoral behavior and urge their congregations, in God's name, to live up to a higher ethical standard. True religion stands on one side of a gaping moral divide, and idolatry on the other.

"What do we mean by 'idolatry?'" asks theologian Arthur Green in a not-untypical discussion of the subject. What could the term signify "at a time when calves ... are not venerated in our society?" "Are there idols and idolatries against which we together can stand up today?" The latter question is followed immediately by criticism of Donald Trump; the former elicits the avowal that "there are plenty of easy targets for designation as idolatry in our day," including worship of money and material wealth; the cult of eternal youth; the deification of sports figures and Hollywood celebrities; the quest for success; and the "degree of subtle idolatry that can exist within our own religious lives." The State of Israel is worshipped this way by some Jews, Green writes. Even God, as the

Zohar reminds us, can be an idol.[41] An informal sample of recent rabbinic sermons shows the term "idolatry" being invoked to condemn materialism, a gun fetish, belief that only your own point of view can be correct, "making children our religion," idolizing pop culture celebrities, and worship of science, class, race, or nation.[42]

I have cited Green's work in particular because I so much admire it; because his use of the notion of idolatry is typical; and because I believe the underlying source of his and similar remarks about idolatry is Paul Tillich's influential conviction that true faith should be understood as "ultimate concern," or "concern about the truly ultimate," while idolatrous faith is the treatment of non-ultimate individuals or concerns ("preliminary, finite realities") as if they were ultimate.[43] Green's comments about idolatry are not central to the volume in which they appear—and that is also typical of the way *avodah zarah* figures in contemporary Jewish thought. One can say without exaggeration that, by and large, idolatry plays far more of a *moral* than a *religious* role in contemporary Jewish thought. It is assumed or even argued that Judaism is not the only valid (or "true") religion. It is also assumed that all monotheistic faiths are superior to any form of idolatrous worship. The latter assumption too requires and receives no argument—except on moral grounds.

It would of course be difficult to demonstrate that idolatry is cause or effect of immoral behavior. There seems to me no way to test the claim that monotheistic individuals and societies are more ethical than idol-worshippers, or to verify the larger claim that religious individuals or societies of any sort are more ethical (or less!) than non-believing and non-observant individuals or societies.

---

41 Arthur Green, *Judaism for the World: Reflections on God, Life, and Love* (New Haven: Yale University Press, 2020), 88–89, 131.

42 See, for examples, Elliot Cosgrove, "The Intersection of Philosophy and Mitzvot," in *Walking with Mitzvot*, ed. Bradley Shavit Artson and Patricia Fenton (Los Angeles: Ziegler School of Rabbinic Studies, 2011), 80–83, https://www.aju.edu/sites/default/files/sites/default/default/docs/Walking%20With%20God/Walking%20With%20Mitzvot/10%20-%20WALKING_WITH_MITZVOT_%5BUNIT_9%5D.pdf; Elliot Cosgrove, "A House Divided," accessed October 29, 2021, http://blog.peaceworks.net/2015/09/a-house-divided-by-rabbi-elliot-cosgrove/; Stuart Weinblatt, "Britney Spears and the Threat of Idolatry in Our Time," September 23, 2006, https://images.shulcloud.com/13746/uploads/uploaded_files/Rabbi/HH_Sermons/2006/Britney%20Spears%20and%20the%20Threat%20of%20Idolatry%20in%20Our%20Time%20RH%20092306.pdf; Menachem Creditor and Eileen Soffer, "Channeling The Power of Faith to End Gun Violence," *The Forward*, July 18, 2016, https://forward.com/scribe/345327/channeling-the-power-of-faith-to-end-gun-violence/; Jonathan Sacks, "Without God We Tend to Start Worshipping Ourselves," *The Office of Rabbi Sacks* (blog), February 23, 2013, https://rabbisacks.org/credo-real-community-means-sharing-a-world-of-meaning/.

43 Paul Tillich, *Dynamics of Faith* (New York: Harper & Row, 1958), 1–12.

How would one show that aggregate human morality has declined over the past century as the process of secularization has advanced? Were the aggressive energies of fascist and communist regimes loosed by the loss of belief in divine judgment in this world or the next? Perhaps—but Islamic terrorists do not lack such belief, indeed see themselves as the instruments of God's judgment here on earth. Would an avowedly idolatrous culture be more violent, more sexually obsessed and licentious, more materialist, than contemporary America, the majority of whose citizens profess to be Christians? All these cases would be difficult to make.

However, I would speculate, without any claim to empirical evidence, that there is something in the modern self so ably analyzed by Charles Taylor that—as Leo Strauss famously claimed—wants to keep God at a safe distance so as to pursue the projects of world-mastery and self-direction undisturbed by any higher authority.[44] (Tillich called this tendency idolatrous: "The human mind, as Calvin has said, is a continuously working factory of idols."[45]) This is Soloveitchik's "Adam I" of mastery and majesty, a legitimate and God-given aspect of humanity—illegitimately working unrestrained by "Adam II" commitments of love and covenant;[46] Buber's "I–It" of use and control leaving no room for "I–Thou" relationships of presence.[47] "Moderately affiliated" American Jews interviewed in the late 1990s about their Jewish identities and commitments repeatedly proclaimed, even without being asked, that no one had the right to tell them what to do or think. Not only did they have the right to decide such matters as "sovereign selves," they asserted, but it would be wrong *not* to decide for themselves, wrong to observe any ritual or entertain any belief that they did not find meaningful at that moment.[48]

It would not be too much of a stretch to call the extreme form of this attitude idolatry of the self. Anthropologist Erving Goffman argued cogently that in today's world human beings enact rituals of "deference" and "demeanor" that were once performed to honor the gods or God, and are now directed at one another or themselves. Goffman cited gestures of "obeisance, submission and

---

44 Charles Taylor, *Sources of the Self: The Making of the Modern Identity* (Cambridge: Harvard University Press, 1989); Leo Strauss, "Preface," in his *Spinoza's Critique of Religion* (Chicago: University of Chicago Press, 1997), 1–31.
45 Tillich, *Dynamics of Faith*, 97.
46 Joseph Dov Soloveitchik, *The Lonely Man of Faith* (New York: Doubleday, 1992).
47 Martin Buber, *I and Thou*, trans. Walter Kaufmann (New York: Charles Scribner's Sons, 1970).
48 Steven Martin Cohen and Arnold M. Eisen, *The Jew Within: Self, Family, and Community in America* (Bloomington: Indiana University Press, 2000), 13–42.

propitiation"; keeping a distance and avoiding eye contact; and "presentation" rituals such as "salutations, invitation, compliments, and minor services." These and similar acts of "tribute" demonstrate that "the self is in part a ceremonial thing, a sacred object which must be treated with proper ritual care and in turn must be presented in a proper light to others."[49]

One could argue with justice that human beings have always acted this way to some extent, and that these rituals of the modern self—like those performed in the presence of God, or God's appointed representatives—derive from rituals performed at court in the presence of royalty. "Goffman seems intuitively correct, however, in maintaining that 'the person in our urban secular world is allotted a kind of sacredness' that is not simply a survival of premodern religiosity but a function of the self's enhanced modern status. In this case, it is because 'many gods have been done away with' that 'the individual himself stubbornly remains a deity of considerable importance.'"[50]

Speculating further, I would suggest that two very different motives drive idolatry of the modern self, sometimes simultaneously. On the one hand, God is pushed off to the side of modern consciousness because the self has become God in its own eyes. Religious skeptics since Feuerbach have argued that the gods are projections of human traits onto otherwise non-existent supernatural entities. Today's non-believers take divine attributes upon themselves, convinced that there are as many gods as there are human beings who confidently assert, as they do, their own divine status and assume total and rightful responsibility for their world.

At the other end of this same spectrum, we find human beings so despairing of their own worth in an impersonal, bureaucratized, out-of-control world, spinning in an out-of-the-way corner of a minor galaxy of an infinite universe, that they cannot believe that any God that actually existed would take notice of them. This is the fallen world of Kafka's grim parable, *The Castle*. The villagers regard K's hope for direct contact with the Lord of the Castle as hopelessly naïve and patently arrogant. At best one can glimpse the lower officials who serve the Count, when these personages deign to visit the village. Messengers of dubious status bring words of ambiguous content from above. Divine beings seem to number in the thousands, if they exist, and do not matter very much; human beings sadly place credence and hope in a clerical bureaucracy that has

---

49 Erving Goffman, "The Nature of Deference and Demeanor," in his *Interaction Ritual: Essays on Face-to-Face Behavior* (New York: Pantheon Books, 1982), 58, 72, 77, 91.
50 Eisen, *Rethinking Modern Judaism*, 102.

no relation to the distant Lord of the castle and no interest in saving them even if they could.[51]

In one vision, human beings are too large to care about God; in the other they are in their own eyes too small for God to care about. Lesser gods in greater numbers would perhaps be more approachable, if less powerful. They might be less demanding, and—in their own diversity—perhaps more tolerant of diverse human behavior.

Conclusion: "Return, Come"

What, then, does idolatry mean to Jews of faith today? How does it figure, how *should* it figure, in contemporary belief and practice? And what do the five meanings or usages of idolatry identified by Weber a century ago, as they have played out in Jewish thought in recent decades, portend for the roles that idolatry will play in Judaism going forward?

Let's begin by stipulating one role that idolatry has often played in the course of Jewish history but does *not* have currently, and is unlikely to have in the near future, outside of ultra-Orthodoxy: drawing a clear line between authentic and inauthentic faith communities on other than moral grounds. As we have seen, that distinction is difficult to make in a world in which adherents to a particular faith (Judaism, for example) are acutely aware that other highly respected individuals, including close friends and family members, belong to other faiths. The latter cannot be discredited prima facie as idolatrous. Whether Weber was correct in averring that many gods are worshipped in the contemporary world, or, on the contrary, only one God is being worshipped under many names in many ways, as the prophet Malachi had predicted long ago,[52] is not one that Jewish religious leaders tend to ask. I am not sure of the answer, frankly, and like Goshen-Gottstein, I do not know how one could determine that gods worshipped under different names are, or are not, the same God. Nor am I sure that I need to decide.[53] This once-prominent issue of *avodah zarah* is currently off the table.

---

51   Franz Kafka, *The Castle: A New Translation, Based on the Restored Text*, trans. Mark Harman (New York: Schocken Books, 1998).
52   Mal. 1:11: "For from where the sun rises to where it sets, My name is honored among the nations, and everywhere incense and pure oblation are offered to My name; for My name is honored among the nations—said the LORD of Hosts."
53   Alon Goshen-Gottstein, *Same God, Other god: Judaism, Hinduism, and the Problem of Idolatry* (New York: Palgrave Macmillan, 2015), 21.

I suspect that, if pressed on the matter, contemporary rabbis would agree with Buber's assertion in *I and Thou* that the gods are one, almost by definition. "... All names of God remain hallowed—because they have been used not only to speak of God but also to speak to him.... Whoever goes forth to his You with his whole being and carries to it all the being of the world, finds him whom one cannot seek."[54] Heschel seems to have believed that all mystical experience of God is the same, no matter the faith or community in which it takes place, or the beliefs and practices to which those experiences give rise.[55] I suspect that this belief too is widespread among Jews today, though I am not sure the various aspects of religious life can be so rigidly distinguished from one another, and doubt that religious experience is entirely independent of biography and culture. My reading of contemporary Jewish thought leads me to guess that theologians and "average" believers alike—knowingly or unknowingly, explicitly or inchoately—develop rough criteria for determining whether someone else is worshipping the same God as they are. My personal criteria—never formulated until now, and stated here in summary form—would overlap with all three of the thinkers mentioned above in some, but not all, respects. They evince intimate connection to the five areas of engagement with idolatry that Weber identified:

(1) the God in question must be Lord of all the world rather than one god among many, and cannot be the god of one nation or land only;
(2) God must have an integral connection to being, and be (or become) in a way that grounds all being, and is somehow greater than non-being;
(3) in this sense, God stands "above" nature and is not merely part of nature even when infusing nature and glimpsed through it; God therefore cannot be adequately imaged or conceived;
(4) justice and compassion must be among God's attributes, as affirmed in the pronouncement attributed to YHWH in the Book of Exodus,[56] so that when human beings perform acts of justice and compassion, we can be sure we are standing with God, and have reasonable confidence that we are performing God's will;
(5) in ways that are beyond human understanding, God must care about the world and enter into relations with human beings, but must not be conjurable by magical formulas or ritual routines. God's will is never to be

---

54 Buber, *I and Thou*, 123, 127.
55 Heschel, "No Religion Is an Island"; Arnold M. Eisen, "Abraham Joshua Heschel and the Challenge of Religious Pluralism," *Modern Judaism* 29, no. 1 (2009): 4–15.
56 Ex. 34:6–7.

identified with inner human voices or desires of the self. (I assume that the balance between God's immanence and transcendence will always be a matter of legitimate debate among believers. I lean strongly to the transcendent, yet personalist side of these debates—God is both YHWH and Elohim—a stance that in my view is lent support by both Jewish tradition and personal experience, and is by no means ruled out by reason.)

The fact that *avodah zarah* is not a useful designation for faiths other than Judaism does not mean that the concept of idolatry no longer plays an important role among Jews in the contemporary world. Nor does it mean, in my view, that faithful Jews do not need, now as ever, to contest morally idolatrous beliefs, avoid idolatrous ritual practices, and—most important—guard against the consequences of idolatry in the moral and political realms. Jews are commanded to choosing the good along with life and blessing. Idolatry, as numerous rabbis and thinkers have argued, takes its adherents in the opposite direction. I shall for heuristic reasons try to summarize briefly how and why I too believe that is the case in terms of the five meanings, or usages, of idolatry that Weber identified. It will be clear at once that—as is famously the case with Weberian "ideal types"—the five do not function isolated from one another but rather interact in complex ways.

If God is not essentially One but many, the notion of humanity as essentially one in all its diversity is likewise undermined, and with it indispensable notions of human rights, human dignity, and human obligation. God's Oneness and status as "Master of the Universe" similarly seems necessary for human beings to hold onto existential confidence, in the face of increasing knowledge about how utterly marginal we and the planet we inhabit are in the universe, that nature is ultimately constituted as order rather than chaos; that purpose rather than randomness governs the cosmos. Jewish texts since the Book of Job have subverted the attempt to draw too simple a correspondence between the cosmic and human orders, but they have insisted nonetheless that nature's apparent indifference to the collective and individual well-being of humanity is not the only or the final word to be said about God's intentions for us. *Idolatry stands as explicit or implicit foil or threat to these core elements of faith*—a function that is no less important because it is generally not articulated explicitly.

Similar reasons impel rejection of belief in *multiple gods who struggle with one another on earthly battlefields*, as in Greek and other mythologies, even if such a view would perhaps make it easier to explain the recurring human propensity to mutual slaughter in wars and attempted genocides. (We must conclude that Weber, if taken literally on this point, was wrong.) Rejection of the claim that the

One God sets the course of human or Jewish history, and therefore directed, condoned or instigated the Holocaust and was responsible for the rebirth of Jewish sovereignty in the Land of Israel, has led in all too many cases to banishing God from history altogether and denying God any providential role, however indirect. Rubenstein's preference for "gods of the soil"—the most pointed contrast to that view of providential history—is understandable but unfortunate; Jewish thinkers should not act as if God's presence in history were all or nothing, thereby ignoring personal testimonies to God's role in assisting individual acts of courage, wisdom, selflessness and love. I find great theological acumen in the old joke about the Jew who rejects rescues by lifeboats, helicopters, and submarines that would have saved him from drowning, but then berates God when he gets to heaven for not saving him miraculously. (In the phase of the COVID pandemic still upon us in America as I write, we hear about individuals who tragically die waiting for God to save them from the disease and who do not believe that the doctors and scientists who tried to vaccinate them operate with divine blessing or assistance.) Once again, idolatry stands in the background of current religious thought rather than the foreground, but its role remains significant.

Feminist thought about the pronouns and *imagery used to name and describe God* remains a vibrant source of theological insight and debate today, heightened by recent demands that our image of God accommodate the reality of transgendered human beings as well as those who reject "gender binaries." I do not think that the use of male pronouns exclusively when addressing God or thinking about God, in keeping with biblical and rabbinic precedent, is tantamount to idolatry, as some feminist theologians have maintained. Neither, however, is that exclusive usage advisable or correct; it lends legitimacy to continued male dominance and privilege. What is more, it makes thought about God in personal terms, hard enough today given the challenges that we have noted, even harder than it would otherwise be. Male pronouns cannot possibly prove adequate to infinitely complex divine reality. One could perhaps make the case, though I would not do so, that visual imagery is no more powerful or determinative of thought than linguistic imagery, and therefore that Jews should be free to paint and sculpt God as they see fit, just as they are free to deploy virtually unbounded linguistic imagery. One can imagine controlled experiments designed to see what new experiences of God or forms of worship develop from the creation of, or focus upon, these visual images. Jews might be more open to such experiment were it not for justified fear that it would blur the distinctiveness of Jews and Judaism. That to me is sufficient reason *not* to undertake the experiment; there is of course much wisdom, too, in the age-old fear that worshippers will confuse images of God with actual attributes of the

God they worship, and confuse their ability to make images with their ability to conjure God at will. It remains true, I think, that "the power of images" is greater than that of words on a screen or printed page. The practice of bowing to images, *avodah zarah* in the most literal and concrete sense, may lead to *avodah zarah* in the other sense: worshipping gods other than God. For both reasons, it marks out territory that Jews will not and should not explore.

Grainy black-and-white footage of rallies at which hundreds of thousands swore allegiance and paid obeisance to Hitler or pledged loyalty to Mao drive home the wisdom of Judaism's instruction that God alone is to be worshipped, and not human beings, especially when the latter claim divine authority, status, or prerogatives.[57] The demagogues who are the objects of such worship (the world has spawned many over the last century) generally do so in the name of nations that likewise claim divine favor and historical destiny greater than that enjoyed by all other nations. *Politics is doubly idolatrous* in these cases—but, as we have seen, it is more common than not, even for believers in the One God, to ask for special favor and believe, on the basis of sacred texts and history, that they merit that favor. This widespread conviction, taken one step farther, can lead a particular faith community to the belief that God cares *only* about their group, can be depended on to fight for them against all enemies, guarantees eternal life to them alone, and so forth. The ancient and common association of gods with particular cities, tribes, clans or households is of course what led Weber to assert that religion is inherently political, and what led Jewish thinkers such as Heschel to argue that serving the "gods of the city"—any god "who cares about me but not about you"—constitutes idol-worship.

The extreme degree of political polarization in the United States in recent years, a development that seems to some observers the most serious threat to national cohesion since the Civil War, has given renewed credence to several traditional Jewish claims about the nature of idolatry. The first is *the importance to states and societies of telling the truth*. (Recall Novak's assertion that idolatry is a lie.) It struck me, hearing members of the previous administration cast doubt on the value or truth-telling again and again, and then brazenly lie about the results of the election of 2020, that being forced to worship idols is among the very worst in the litany of curses set forth near the end of the Book of Deuteronomy *because it requires a lie* that unmoors the person forced to do it from reality. You know that X is the case, but the ruling power says it is not the case, some

---

57 I suspect that Fackenheim speaks for the great majority of contemporary Jewry when he calls Nazism "the supreme and unsurpassable modern idolatry." See Fackenheim, *God's Presence in History*, 102, n. 40.

respected leaders agree, and hundreds of thousands—tens of millions in the present case, actually, including many Jewish and Christian believers in God—signify their assent. Should one not bow to the prevailing sentiment, "cast truth to the ground,"[58] and make peace with the lie? *Obedience to the charismatic leader at the cost of independent, rational judgment* is the second aspect of the current situation that brought to mind biblical and rabbinic images of idolatry. The riot at the Capitol building, in which a mob aroused by its leader attacked police officers and threatened to kill elected members of Congress, has since been defended by many of those same representatives, joined by tens of millions of others, as lawful protest against a perceived injustice (election fraud). Where one side sees reality—the news footage is incontrovertible—the other side sees "fake news," partisan political slur, and so on.

Is this how Jews felt in Rome, I wonder, when they alone maintained that there is One God, and everyone else—buoyed by enthusiastic stadium crowds—held that this stance was unpatriotic, self-serving, elitist, exclusivist, and merely an excuse not to work on the Sabbath? In the current climate, there is no moral issue that is not regarded by one side or the other as political, and therefore subject to polarized debate—not even the need to minimize loss of life in the pandemic.

Weber justly feared that precisely here, at the point where political choices bear profound moral consequences, is where the fact that many gods figuratively hold sway rather than One, would have it greatest impact on the stability of the social worlds and the meaning of individual existence. The term idolatry is most often deployed by contemporary Jewish thinkers to denounce excessive concern with wealth, power, sexual prowess and other less than "ultimate concerns." But Weber knew, from the inside as it were (he saw it happening in Germany in the final days of World War I and afterwards) that idolatry had a still more insidious hold on modern minds and souls: the inability to say with total conviction that some things, any things, are Right and others Wrong, Good rather than Evil, True rather than False. One cannot obey the command that obligates faithful Jews to choose good, choose blessing and choose life if one cannot say what is and is not right.

*****

---

58 *Genesis Rabbah* 8:5.

Weber concluded "Science as a Vocation" with a surprising quotation from the Book of Isaiah, in which the prophet warns the people of Israel not to rely on the "watchman" in order to know what the future will bring. "The morning cometh, and also the night." They should therefore not "inquire" but "return, come."[59] Remarkably, Weber then cautioned that "the people to whom this was said has enquired and tarried for more than two millennia, and we are shaken when we realize its fate.... We shall act differently. We shall set to work and meet the 'demands of the day'.... This, however, is plain and simple, if each finds and obeys the demon who holds the fibers of his very life."[60]

One can easily understand why Weber pleaded with his German audience in 1917 not to "tarry for new prophets and saviors." They needed to take immediate steps to safeguard and shape the future of their country. He recognized that religious believers in an age of advancing rationalization and "disenchantment" faced an additional set of unprecedented challenges to their faith—a predicament that contemporary Jews share, a century later, at another moment of significant challenge. Contrary to the final line of Weber's essay (in my eyes, the most mysterious in the essay), the task of confronting the challenges that Jews face today is the very opposite of "plain and simple." No demon—and no angel or prophet—exists to point the way. It would indeed be a mistake to wait on the sidelines of faith (or remain safely inside religion's existing guidelines) until the difficulties disappear or it becomes clear how to resolve them. It would be utterly counterintuitive to change nothing in Jewish belief or practice in the face of the most rapid technological change humanity has ever undergone, exacerbated by the effects of global climate change. To change everything in Judaism, on those same grounds, would be equally foolish. What is one to do? How should Jews "set to work and meet the demands of the day" in matters of faith, politics, climate change and so much else?

Weber, of course, was in no position to answer that question, certainly not within the bounds of a scientific vocation that in his view demanded the separation of facts from values. But the fact that he ended the essay as he did, with an explicit statement of values—citing the prophet Isaiah, and reminding his audience of the urgent need to meet, rather than shirk, the moral demands of the day—offers helpful guidance to religious leaders whose vocation demands that they not only "inquire" but "return, come." Reflection about *avodah zarah*, I believe, will prove helpful in clarifying in new ways which of the lines that distinguish Judaism from other faiths need to be redrawn, and which should be

---

59 Isa. 21:12.
60 Weber, "Science as a Vocation," 156.

erased or reinforced. This work will be particularly important because today, far more than at previous moments of transformation, *contested* reason and *multiple* strands of traditions will offer guidance, supplemented by *diverse* personal religious experiences and the wisdom of *traditions other than Judaism* no longer discounted because they are "other." One hopes that the tension among these sources of authority will itself serve as an important guidepost to action rather than a cause of endless waiting and inquiry. Getting things right will likely remain beyond reach. Meeting the day's demands, even partially, will be achievement enough.

CHAPTER 9

The Dynamism of Idolatry

Haviva Pedaya

Idolatry—Definitions and Manifestations

I will start with my basic argument regarding idolatry: the definition of the term changes with each generation, since the very concept of divinity never remains static. Just as in every generation, each person must regard themselves as though they actually left Egypt, in every generation one must define the foreignness of the period, if only because the concept of God and divinity becomes refined, clarified, and distilled—or blurred—in each and every period. Every new reading of the Torah, whether consciously or unconsciously, whether out of perceived resistance to the zeitgeist or awareness of "going with the flow," is at the same time a new reading of divinity that is embedded in a worldview. Idolatry must always include something close, even very close, to the concept of God, and at the same time far from it—so far that the *Sitra Aḥra*[1] lurks there in the sense of the other, distorted side of things. The corrupting of self and society, of another nation, of the world—all originate with the forgetting of God, and are, therefore, also types of idolatry.

Thus, there is both a chronological and an eternal existential element to idolatry. Moreover, gathering all the dimensions together along the synchronic and diachronic axes leads us eventually to another statement, which is that idolatry is the entirety of places where man betrays the concept of divinity, while actually performing "service," doing something that is "foreign" to the very existence of God in this world, to the very moral position to which a person of religion and morality is committed—he does that which must not be done, let alone in God's name. In other words, God's service is in fact a kind of covenant between man and God, the violation of which is idolatry.

---

1 This is the kabbalistic designation for the dark, evil, other side, used here by association.

Thinking of idolatry in our time requires a fundamental, dramatic and poignant definition thereof. The Hebrew term for idolatry, *avodah zarah*, is made up of two words: service or worship, and foreign, meaning an identity that is different or set apart from a given group or community, or the sacred itself, or the defined discipline associated with sanctity. The Bible offers several indications to a potential definition of foreignness. The first major context is the following: "but a stranger shall not eat thereof, because they are holy" (Ex. 29:33), and in the Targum, "but a secular man shall not eat." This is one of the first references to the term "secular." This first and ancient definition of secularity as a one-for-one translation for foreignness or strangeness is fascinating: whoever has no faith, whoever is a stranger to the worship or the holy place, cannot draw near. This is a primary and important definition, because we are talking of the biblical world, which not only precedes modern secularity, but also conveys a different vein than that of the Mishnaic world. As a later, modern concept, secularity (*ḥiloniut*) would also arise from the rabbinic terminology of *ḥol* (profanity) and *ḥulin* (mundaneness), not as the opposite of that which has been marked as pure and holy, but rather as a "neutral" situation that is not related to lack of faith in God or refusal to follow the commandments. There are also instances of the word *ḥol* or the adjective *ḥiloni* (secular) that are much closer to the sense of "neutral,"[2] and should not be associated with foreignness—these are the instances in the Tannaic language, which perhaps suggest the gap between the conceptions of holiness and worship in the biblical and rabbinical worlds, respectively, moving from foreignness to neutrality. In this case, the early transition from the Bible to the Mishna, when charted in rough lines, would be from *ḥilul* ("desecration" or "profanation," where there are only two options—holy or impure—or, alternatively, a caste member or non-member) to *ḥilun* ("secularization," which offers a third, neutral option).

Let us consider another biblical instance, with reference to the paschal sacrifice: "And even when a stranger shall sojourn with thee . . . he shall be as one that is born in the land. For no uncircumcised person shall eat thereof" (Ex. 12:48). What is the concept of strangeness, whether in the sense of foreignness or the more abstract sense of oddity? When the Psalmist says, "I have become a stranger

---

2   Consider the Tannaitic category of *ḥulin*, animals slaughtered for ordinary, non-ritual consumption, spelled out in tractate *Ḥulin*, and contrast with the ritual sacrifice described in tractate *Zevachim*. The neutral category of *ḥulin* forms the basis for the halakhic term of *ḥulin al taharat ha-kodesh*, meaning that the owner decides for himself to treat his *ḥulin* food similarly to *kodesh* or sacred food for the purposes of purity laws.

unto my brethren, an alien unto my mother's children" (Ps. 69:9), "stranger" almost converges on "strange" in the sense of "different" and "separate."

Another trajectory related to the concept of idolatry, which is Tannaic, as mentioned, may be found by tracing the biblical term "strange fire" (*esh zarah*). We are told that Nadab and Abihu, the priests who were Aaron's sons, died after offering "strange fire before the Lord, which He commanded them not" (Lev 10:1).[3] In that context, strangeness is derived strictly from the fact that this is the thing regarding which they have not been commanded. That is all. There is discipline and there are rules of worship when approaching the sacred. Respect for this discipline accounts for the story of David and Uzzah: when the latter sees that the oxen have shaken the Ark of God, he takes hold of it to prevent it from falling, whereby "God smote him there for his error" (2 Sam. 6:6–7). This definition brings us back to idolatry as a function of closeness and strangeness. It is like the definition of a caste, or the rules of profanity and purity as discussed by Mary Douglas, for instance, or the pariah as discussed by Max Weber, a universal symbol of exclusion.[4] What starts out as neutral assumes a negative valence that views the other as negative and reprehensible.

In its more advanced definition in the Mishna and Talmud, *avodah zarah* requires praxis, and is therefore dissimilar to *esh zarah*, that which overwhelms one out of ecstatic enthusiasm, and is perhaps one of the spiritual origins of the four who entered the orchard (*pardes*).[5] The two come together, eventually, in rabbinic literature, by means of the use of the same adjective, *zarah*, strange or foreign. It is extended to refer to the very worship of anything that is not the Israelite God. Thus, should readers try to follow the rationale of the Mishna, and subsequently the Gemara, regarding idolatry, they would immediately find themselves delving into the minutest details of a shared socioeconomic life, into the heart of a question that would seem at first to be completely tangential—how to avoid gestures involving objects and money from serving indirectly as the worship of a foreign divinity.

The rabbis differentiated between the destructions of the First and Second Temples, arguing that the former was due, among other things, to idolatry, and

---

3   See further Num. 3:4 and 26:61.
4   Mary Douglas, *Purity and Danger: An Analysis of the Concepts of Pollution and Taboo* (London: Routledge, 2002); Max Weber, *The Sociology of Religion* (Boston: Beacon Press, 1963 [1920]).
5   Space limitations prevent me from reviewing the literature on the *pardes*, from Shcholem to Urbach through Halperin, Goshen-Gottstein, and Nurit Be'er. I suggest that invasive curiosity expressed in the forbidden gaze functions in the rabbinic world in a manner akin to *esh zara* in the biblical one.

the latter to wanton hatred.[6] It is also said that the evil inclination of idolatry was eliminated in the days of the Second Temple (BT *Yoma* 69b). This reflects their hindsight view of a world gone by. The rabbis may have tried to point to a transition from idolatry in the sense of worshipping other deities to its redefinition as an instrument for casting blame on others, used in the struggle to appropriate the Jewish God waged among the various contemporary currents and sects within Judaism. This is probably a historical perspective: was it Hellenism—with the hedonism and atheism inherent thereto—which eliminated the worshipping of the Baal, Tammuz, and Ashtoreth? What this suggests, then, is that the definition of idolatry is always relative, always contemporary, always dependent on the context of "legitimate worship." This applies for example to the defunct worship of gods of wood and stone.

Similarly, we can see that at first, the discourse on Buddhism was very much different from what it is today. The first European travelers and thinkers and priests did not understand Buddha's ideas when discussing Buddhism, as their first impression was of Buddhists worshipping wooden and gilded deities; only subsequently did they come to appreciate that this was an abstract concept, and then explained that this was the representation of a human being. Some priests, upon appreciating the Buddhist emphasis on the concept of emptiness, came to consider Buddhism the first atheist religion.[7]

The ancient concept of idolatry does not originally represent the norm of God's explicit name, the tetragrammaton, without an image, formulated by Maimonides in *The Guide of the Perplexed* as well as in *Mishneh Torah*— leading to a well-known polemic with the Rabad, which I will not expound here.[8] Rather, it mainly represents the prohibition of "making" a deity with a shape and image, and worshipping it, based on the concept of "for you have not seen any image."[9] Thus, the concept of idolatry is gradually constructed to eventually

---

6   "Due to what reason was the First Temple destroyed? . . . Due to . . . three matters . . .: idol worship, forbidden sexual relations, and bloodshed. . . . However, considering that the people during the Second Temple period were engaged in Torah study, observance of *mitzvot*, and acts of kindness . . ., why was the Second Temple destroyed? It wad destroyed due to . . . wanton hatred. . . . This comes to teach you that the sin of wanton hatred is equivalent to the three severe transgressions: idol worship, forbidden sexual relations, and bloodshed" (BT *Yoma* 9b).

7   See Donald S. Lopez Jr., *From Stone to Flesh: A Short History of the Buddha* (Chicago: Chicago University Press, 2013).

8   Rambam and Rabad to Maimonides, *Mishneh Torah*, Laws of Repentance 3:7.

9   See Haviva Pedaya, *Vision and Speech: Models of Revelatory Experience in Jewish Mysticism* (Los Angeles: Cherub Press, 2002) [Hebrew]. In the first two chapters of that book I discuss the conceptual and verbal images Judaism theoretically allows with regard to God and His environment—images kept in the mind alone.

contain the abstract God, He who has no shape or image, He who is worshipped by the people of Israel. It may be that already in this tension inherent in the proximity to the holy, expressed in human activities directed at a God that cannot be visualized or conceptualized, lies the future category of secularity.

Throughout the Middle Ages, Jews lived with idolatry, with foreign worship, with Christians, and with Muslims. Led by the great philosophers, the gradual transformation in the conceptualization of divinity occurred simultaneously in all three monotheistic religions. These included Avicenna, Maimonides, Nachmanides, and Meister Eckhart. The more advanced insights on God's image or its absence were often associated with the upper classes, with theologians making efforts to eliminate idolatrous beliefs from among the masses of their coreligionists.

Thus, a struggle ensues over the conception of the abstractness of God as a criterion for true monotheism that begins to be shared by the three religions, and the struggle against idolatry as waged in various arenas along the synchronous socio-religious axis, that is, the way each religion defines itself with reference to the other religions' self-definitions, and along the hierarchic-class axis, meaning the tension between philosophers and often also kabbalists and the masses. It is therefore clear, as stated above, that the definition of idolatry changes with the generations, not least because the concept of divinity is dynamic. Just as in every generation each person must regard themselves as though they actually left Egypt, in every generation one must define the strangeness or otherness of one's period anew.

I will now add to this opening argument the following one: since the relation to God Himself cuts across several circles of being on the human level, this implies that idolatry as well—always arguably inseparable from the concept of God—cuts across these four circles or levels: the individual, communal and social, political, and relating to the world-creation. In each there is a concept of betraying God, sacrilege, and the ways foreignness violates the concepts of truth, purity, beauty, the good, and the moral.

On the *individual*, psychological and moral level, of the person within himself, Hasidism admonished: "There shall be no strange God within you," suggesting that one can serve God outwardly, while in fact serving his own passions, pride, and hubris, or any other emotion.[10] The rabbis had already said that he who is angry is akin to an idol worshipper,[11] and similar things were said of the proud,

---

10 See, for example, R. Yakov Yosef of Polnoye, *Ketonet Pasim*, Balak, s.v. *ve-ze she-amar Shema*; R. Chayim of Teschernotiz, *Be'er Mayim Chayim*, Vayechi.
11 BT *Shabat* 105b; Maimonides, *Mishneh Torah*, Laws of Deot 2:3.

to the point that "he and I cannot inhabit the same world."[12] This moralist perspective is further developed by the great Hasidic thinkers to form a crystallized structure that deals in detail with the definition of *kelipat nogah*, which I compared in my book *Kabbalah and Psychoanalysis* to the false and mendacious self discussed by Winnicott,[13] thus further clarifying the relation between one's foreignness to oneself and to God.[14] One who worships God out of the motivations of vanity, power over others, or pride in one's knowledge, is a stranger to both.

On the *communal and social* level, exploitation of other group members as objects of one's passions by means of one's religious authority serve simultaneously to victimize the other, using the conscious or unconscious argument that the wrong doing is only a function of the individual's desires run wild, while in fact the social order itself is not, in and of itself, derived from the very act of standing before God.[15] This is a second type of idolatry, unfortunately common nowadays among cult leaders who subject members to sexual abuse and make illegitimate use of their messianic beliefs.[16]

Earlier, I wrote that every profound contemporary discussion of idolatry requires a dramatic and precise answer to the question, what is this day that stands before us, what is our era? After referring in brief to the Middle Ages, I can now take a huge step and engage with modernism and postmodernism to arrive in our times, because I consider these times to be a blend of modern and postmodern configurations that coincide, if not coexist.

On the *political level*, modernism's idolatry is nationalism. The huge tension between the real God and the other God who seeks to infiltrate, so to speak, into the real definition of divinity and through it to eliminate religion from within leads us to seek idolatry in something that is very close to religion and uses its language. This is because idolatry must contain something that is both near and far. Accordingly, I believe that in modernity this is nationalism—the element

---

12 See BT *Sotah* 4a–5b.
13 D. W. Winnicott, "Ego Distortion in Terms of True and False Self" [1960], in his *The Maturational Process and the Facilitating Environment: Studies in the Theory of Emotional Development* (New York: International UP Inc., 1965), 140–152.
14 Haviva Pedaya, *Kabbalah and Psychoanalysis: An Internal Journey in the Footsteps of Jewish Mysticism* (Tel Aviv: Miskal, 2015), 24–27 and 72–99 [Hebrew].
15 Yitzhak Rosenblum recently conducted a study on the view of perpetrators in the Jewish ultra-Orthodox world that sin, even against one's fellow man, is a sin only before God rather than before another. See in brief in Aharon Rabinovich, "Halakha instead of Morality: How do Sexual Predators in Haredi Society Justify Their Deeds," *Haaretz*, June 1, 2021 [Hebrew], https://www.haaretz.co.il/news/education/.premium.HIGHLIGHT-MAGAZINE-1.9948314.
16 Eli Shai, *Messiah Incest: New and Uncensored History of the Sexual Element in Jewish Mystical Messianism* (St. Louis: Dunaway Books, 2002).

that shapes and unites identities, which can infiltrate religion and exploit and even eliminate all its concepts—primarily the strictly religious, but also the mystical and even secular. Nation-state worship can lead to a series of actions that are incommensurate with the religious vision. Nationalism is the idolatrous handicap of modernity.

In making this claim, I am not suggesting that nationalism is fundamentally wrong. Both God's service and idolatry require a constant inquiry into motives and inhibitions. To apply a term coined by Rabbi Isaac Luria (the Ari): *birur nitzotzot* (elevation or sifting of sparks). The wheat must be separated from the chaff. The why and wherefore must be understood. Nationalism that goes astray and steers too far from its origin and context takes over religious terminology and empties it from within. The danger is that in the shadow of the state and politics, and with the parallel atrophying of innovative religious teachings, young seekers who are in need of passion and renewal might be led to confuse the ongoing need for innovation and rejuvenation with the ease and availability of an experience of renewal, as it is made available through collective identity and the desire for spatial (territorial) expansion, out of an identity collective and a passion for expansion in physical or in identity space.

This is a complex or deceptive form of secularization, akin to the extension of religion itself, or the other way around—a religious movement that is nothing but secularization. Let me reiterate that I do not reject nationalism per se, I only reject is as a substitute, as a palliative, or as an element that tops the hierarchy of a set of beliefs, identities and practices. This is how we arrive at a most fundamental conventional application of the discourse of idolatry: in the case of Judaism and Israeliness, oppositions that argue over the status of Zionism. Just as it is common to speak of and consider it as the sanctification of God and the foreshadowing of the redemption, it is also common to hear that it is idolatrous.[17]

The truth, I believe, lies not in the final verdict regarding Zionism, but in the final verdict regarding the relations between religion and mysticism and nationalism. Religion need not translate itself into national terminology, neither as a state nor as an empire. In all of today's modernist enclaves in the world we see religions that turn homicidal in the name of nationalism. This is true of ISIS and the dream of a new Islamic Caliphate.[18] It is also true of China, originally

---

17 I'm referring here of course to the known tension between the view of Rabbi Kook and that of the Rabbi of Satmar. See Haviva Pedaya, "Eretz: Apocalypses of End and Apocalypses of Beginning," in *The Land of Israel in Twentieth-Century Jewish Thought*, ed. Aviezer Ravitzky (Jerusalem: Yad Ben Zvi, 2004), 560–623 [Hebrew].
18 Haviva Pedaya, "ISIS on the Grass," *Haaretz*, November 26, 2015 [Hebrew], https://www.haaretz.co.il/opinions/.premium-1.2785579.

an ancient civilization with strong religious foundations, which has undergone intensive cultural erasure under modernism, and today, despite communist and atheist configurations, now persecutes its Muslims out of a sense of nationalist rootedness, to the point of detaining them in concentration camps and engaging in genocidal practices.[19] It is indeed difficult for young or emerging states or for rising powers to give up on this religion-nationalism nexus, the fruit of the medieval heritage and the cataclysms wrought by European, and also Christian colonialism in the world entire.

Idolatry—Modern and Postmodern

As the rabbis have said, Whoever is greater than the other, his *yetzer,* evil inclination, is greater as well (BT *Sukkah* 52a). Does this mean that each person has a *yetzer ha-ra* equal to his *yetzer ha-tov* (good inclination), or that when the person develops, both develop with him as well? I think it does not necessarily mean "evil" in the sense of committing all manner of sins. Rather, it refers to the evil inclination that is close to the self; which is "me" and "not me" at the same time. This echoes taking pride or becoming vain, under the influence of this thing or another.[20]

If we adopt the principle that *yetzer ha-ra* grows in parallel with the development of *yetzer ha-tov*, then in the context of idolatry, the paraphrase will be that the more the concept of divinity develops, the more *avodah zarah* grows with it. Thus, in a reality where ascribing physical form to divinity is seen as idolatry, then a statue is the form of idolatry. In the present-day reality of imagination-based media, idolatry would be located there.

Similarly, precisely because nationalism and religion are factors that once constituted collective identity, today, with secularization having entered the fray, we cannot allow ourselves to let them be tightly bound with the concept of religion without first seeking conceptual order and clarity. In fact, we are talking about such a bind here. So, in talking of nationalism and idolatry we must rethink their relationship. In its own way, the strong anti-Zionist position of the Hassidic Rebbe of Munkacs drives the point home.[21] In referring to Satan as the *ba'al*

---

19 "China Guilty of Genocide, Crimes against Humanity against Uyghurs, Watchdog Finds," *NBC News*, December 10, 2021, https://www.nbcnews.com/news/china/china-guilty-genocide-crimes-humanity-uyghurs-watchdog-finds-rcna8157.
20 This echoes the meaning of *kelipat nogah* as suggested above.
21 See Aviezer Ravitzky, *Messianism, Zionism and Jewish Religious Radicalism* (Chicago: Chicago University Press, 1996).

davar, literally—the owner of the thing, he points out how idolatry emerges clinging to a thing, to an object rather than the essence. In the anti-Zionist view, the *ba'al davar* rushes to any place where he conspires to cause the people of Israel to fail. And then in the end, when arriving in the Land of Israel, the Zionist land, he is seen standing first on the beach. This is a joke designed to mock the Zionist project.

Note that I do not claim that Zionism is idolatry. Rather, nationalism itself can become idolatry. However, national identity could become a form of idolatry and to lead to the kind of negative nationalism, read—chauvinism, that could be equated with idolatry. Spiritual Zionism must find ways of keeping this tendency of political Zionism at bay. This requires restatement under today's circumstances.

Nationalism has been the number one problem of modernism. The post-colonial, postmodernist age has seemingly pushed it aside, or at least blatant European and American colonialism has ceased. Conversely, in the developing world—in Asia, Africa, and the Middle East, it is never absent. In Israel/Palestine it remains a problem, since Israel has participated in both modernism and postmodernism to a higher extent than other Western countries, given that it has achieved statehood only in 1948, and has been subjected to colonialist processes until that time. It was only after the Holocaust and the end of the British Mandate that it entered processes of nationalism, while the relations between state and religion had not been properly worked out.

Thus, Israel is in a very tight bind, which requires some kind of solution, some regulation, no matter if you are a conservative or a liberal. I believe that once you are a religious person, you must realize that from a religious or mystical standpoint, it is impossible for the relationship to be based on subordination or statelessness of a collective of second-class citizens, at best. I of course do not share the aspiration for total secularization of the entire country. It is precisely from a religious and mystical perspective that I state the case that people must be allowed to hold on to their identity.

A new position on this nationality would accept the fact that collectives have shared identities, but when it comes to territorial conflicts between nations, the solution would strive for the middle road between a realistic political settlement and the perspective of a collective with a religious or mystical identity, realizing that we cannot hold everything in our hands. It is a kind of cleansing from the dross that comes from idolatry; it is a kind of soft messianism that holds on to future hopes without violating individual or collective rights in the name of an eschatological vision.

This claim, whereby nationalism is the idolatry of modernity, could have more easily been made, however, in the pre-COVID era. The pandemic has forced nationalist processes back into the global arena. I must refine my argument, therefore: the fact that idolatry grows with the times does not mean that all the past forms of idolatry cannot be contained, or that we might not stumble back to them. I do not mean to say that COVID-19 has led exclusively to regressive processes, but it has set in motion a deceptive process of simultaneous acceleration and retreat on several levels.[22]

At this point in the discussion, since our postmodern age is deeply entwined with modernism, we need to ask ourselves, what should be the new interpretation of *avodah zarah*, and its opposite, *avodah tehorah*? Let us take the well-known verse "and Moses drew near unto the thick darkness where God was" (Ex. 20:21). There are many beautiful interpretations for this verse, that the "thick darkness" is in fact the darkness of revelation, the cloud of unknowing, or that it represents the relations between the invisible God and the visible one. Perhaps another way of interpreting that "darkness" is to define it as veils and opaqueness of the imaginary, the obstacles, inhibitions and thorns surrounding the rose. They are the things that need to be pruned, as captured in the expression *zamir aritzim*.[23] I consider the cloud here as an illusory veil, clouding the distinction between true and false, suggesting that purification from the imaginary is in order, leading to the understanding that it is precisely the modern world that on the one hand seeks a world without borders, and at the same time an expansion of frontiers, that requires boundaries as well. The boundaries of modernism should have arisen from the restriction of the concept of progress and the concept of truth as exclusive to a single supreme race or high culture. Modernism is characterized by several beliefs, all of which as a single whole were among the main causes leading—despite the Enlightenment—to colonialism, and at its most extreme to Nazism. What these beliefs share is the conception of the one, of the absolute truth, and of progress, the view of the Other (however defined) as inferior (mentally, socially, and religiously), and the granting of license to oneself to eradicate the Other in the name of backwardness or primitiveness, resulting in one half of the world dispossessing the other.

---

22 See Haviva Pedaya, "The Siren Test of the Four Horsemen: On Postmodern Ethics and Pandemics," Havivapedaya.com, April 8, 2020, https://web.archive.org/web/20210128080004/ https://www.havivapedaya.com/post/the-siren-test-of-the-four-horsemen. A deeper analysis is beyond the present scope.

23 "The branch of the terrible ones shall be brought low" (Isa. 25:5).

Liberation from the dichotomy of universalism and particular identity would seem to be the key to liberation from the idolatry of modernity. What of the idolatry of postmodernism? In the postmodern world, and particularly over the past twenty years, idolatry is clearly carried on the wings of the media. I do not wish to come across as someone who preaches avoidance of the internet. Nevertheless, this virtual world, devoid of boundaries, is in fact the world where white noise is constantly being produced, a very high space of images shrouded by a thick cloud, which in fact not only prevents the possibility of enlightenment almost completely, as this is certainly not an aspiration of those browsing the web of endless imaginary desires. This makes it impossible to fulfill a process of spiritual development, or to live a modest community life. On the global level, this makes it hard to uphold the existence of the world and to follow the command enunciated in the midrash: "Pay attention that you do not corrupt and destroy My world" (*Ecclesiastes Rabbah* 7:13). This brings us back to Isaiah: "In that day a man shall case his idols of silver, and his idols of gold, which they made each one for himself to worship" (Isa. 2:20); "in the day of the great slaughter, when the towers fall" (Isa. 30:25). Media processes narrow and almost eliminate the distance between the real and the symbolic. Applications such as Tinder—one of the markers of the accelerated postmodern, post-COVID age—not only end the possibility of love and contribute to treating others like objects, but obstruct the access to faith, miracle, creation and redemption, as conservative as it may sound. Idolatry is not only our stance vis-à-vis the Other, significant, great God, but also its derivative, our stance vis-à-vis the human Other.

Idolatry's Fourfold Expression

This brings us back to some of the thorniest of our existential questions. A person who wishes to live an idolatry-less life encounters it in the various circles by which he is surrounded. Let us review these and delve more deeply into idolatry's fourfold expression.

The first idolatry is the worship of self rather than God—doing things for my ego, as opposed to "There shall no strange god be in thee" (Ps. 81:9), whereby things lose their meaning or importance. Rather, one must do things for their own sake, which is not as an extension of one's ego or out of the hope for reward of the fear of punishment.[24]

---

24 I read this rabbinic saying in the context of the Bhagavad Gita and its emphasis on not to do things hoping for the fruits of action or inaction.

Individual idolatry is the worship of the ego. Many pietistic books tackle this dimension of the spiritual life. Many of these books have, in fact, brought into Judaism a message that comes from the Sufi realm, where similar concerns are explored. The concern for self-worship finds a later expression in Hasidism, where we find an attack on rabbinic scholarly society as potentially leading to self-worship. From rabbinic literature we recognize how pride is also an expression of idolatry. Pride for the performance of worship turns it into idolatry. Even true intention for the sake of God, the true God, does not eliminate the idolatrous dimension that is introduced through pride. Indeed, such a mixture of motivations and spiritual realities is what that mixed spiritual reality that kabbalists refer to as *kelipat nogah* is about.[25] Still on the level of the individual is that expression of idolatry wherein a leader ends up serving his desires, be they in the form of sex, money, or power. He sins, he causes others to sin and, as the rabbis teach, he loses his share in the world to come.

The second idolatry is the trampling of social morality in pursuit of power, money, etc. This can go as far as sexual abuse, as often discovered after the fact in the Catholic Church as well as among rabbis here in Israel.[26] This requires that individuals split their own minds: here I'm acting morally, but when I'm going to work or to a government office, there it is legitimate to lie, and so on. It is not legitimate in any context—that is the second idolatry. Everything revolves around it. Many Nazis were certainly good family men, while activating the bureaucratic mechanism of the concentration camps. Many people today are involved in financial fraud, to take a less extreme example, are wonderful fathers and husbands.

The third idolatry is the confluence of religion and state, or nationalism. Moving to the level of *state*, we come to the idolatry of nationalism. Here we take note of remarkable superpowers that have brought some of the finest cultural gifts to the world. Yet, as the case of present-day China suggests, nationalistic concerns corrupt the testimony and contribution of beauty, by practices such as the genocide currently practiced in relation to Muslim minorities. Similarly, China destroyed the Tibetan nation and culture. It is this concern for the harmful spiritual impact of nationalism, tantamount to idolatry, that leads to concrete political consequences, when we consider Israel's reality. This is why Israel must reach a political settlement with the Palestinians. It cannot afford to remain trapped

---

25 For more on that, see Pedaya, *Kabbalah and Psychoanalysis*.
26 For a recent example, see Sylvie Corbet, "French Report: 330,000 Children Victims of Church Sex Abuse," *AP*, https://apnews.com/article/europe-france-child-abuse-sexual-abuse-by-clergy-religion-ab5da1ff10f905b1c338a6f3427a1c66.

in the religion-nationalism bind, while an entire people of different nationality and religion live within its borders in a state of statelessness. I do not accept the view of the Satmar Rebbe, cited above, according to which Zionism is idolatry. Nevertheless any religion is in danger of turning idolatrous once it is wed with nationalism. Throughout the Middle Ages, once they were no longer a minority, Christians uprooted others, converted them by force, or simply murdered them. Missionary work undertaken under such circumstances is worthless—it is idolatry of the first degree. To take one blatant example: in the colonial age, the missionaries did not always followed the path of religion. Those who followed the Spanish conquerors took part in annihilating the Native Americans.

The fourth idolatry is the destruction of the environment to the point of threatening our very survival on Earth in the name of insatiable corporate greed. We are here on this Earth to obey God's commandment, not to destroy the world. The corrupting of self, of society, of the national or racial Other, of the world entire—all are due to the abandonment of God, and are therefore types of idolatry. Having discussed the self, society, and the world, idolatry moves on to ever-widening circles. Namely, here is the juncture between idolatry along the chronological, historical-developmental axis and that along the eternal existential axis "that belongs to every person in every generation." Accordingly, when we think of idolatry on the *global* level, we must consider the way various civilizations have treated the Earth as an object of exploitation and looting is also a form of idolatry. The appropriate response is the call that must issue from religious leaders to protect earth from humanity, for the sake of humanity. Any support by religious institutions for capitalist corporations or their use of power to empower themselves, while failing to protect the Earth, is yet another type of idolatry.

Idolatry can give vent to various drives. As described above, these four categories of idolatry originate in personal interest—the desire to have things, to call them mine, to take all I deserve. This is in fact one type of idolatry. Another type, which similarly comes to expression in multiple circles, is born not of the assertive will or desire, but of the mistaken or misplaced imagination. One—individual or collective—has self-regard that is too high. One lives in the imaginary regarding oneself. This is the false self, *kelipah,* that I discuss in my abovementioned book. Such people may operate within the sphere of religious law, while in fact, due to the imaginary, they are able to inspire their followers to do all manner of things, whether related to power or sexuality or both, out of illusory promises for redemption. This is idolatry par excellence, the guru's idolatry. Everyone who wants to be a mentor must be free of it. The psychological prototype for this type of idolatry is the psychopathic gurus who present themselves to society as the servants of God whereas in fact they serve their own passions, such that all laws extend from them, and valid and invalid are derived from their moods and desires. The same charismatic personality structure that is also typical of saints and people of virtue can serve as a veil or cloud for psychopaths that take religious command, regrettably. Israeli society is currently undergoing a process of identifying and publicly exposing such gurus, some of whom come from ultra-Orthodox society.

The idolatry of the imagination, if we may call it that, applies not only to the individual and communal levels just discussed. It also applies to the collective level and indeed informs mistaken self-perception, which in turn impacts both the modern and the postmodern expressions of idolatry. This has become especially prominent with reference to the idolatry of the imagination that finds expression in media. The media themselves may be corrupted by religious leaders, whether inciting today for religious war on Temple Mount, or for converting Native Americans in the colonial age. The media are also implicated in the discussion of the *imaginary* and its relation to idolatry. As an illustration, we have witnessed the rise of ISIS with its pretentions for building a new empire, with Facebook and other platforms facilitating the spreading of its murderous messages. In the digital era, a symbol is no longer abstract, it is an icon, an image spread everywhere at lightning speed. This can lead to a rapid escalation of violence in several areas simultaneously, even at the scale of a war, as extremists on both sides are well aware of the messages of the other side. The clash is particularly intense, because each side ascribes to itself the status of a collective icon. Thus, a complete cult of photos and icons has developed around the Temple Mount, accelerated in the age when the icon is the message.[27]

---

27 On the use of Islamic sermons to enflame emotions regarding the condition of Haram al-Sharif (Temple Mount) under Jewish occupation see Yitzhak Reiter, "The Third in Holiness, the First in Politics: Al-Haram al-Sharif in Muslim Eyes," in *The Sovereignty of God and Man: Holiness and Political Centrality on Temple Mount* (Jerusalem: Jerusalem Institute for Israel Studies, 2001), 155 [Hebrew]; Nadav Shragai, *The "Al-Aksa Is in Danger" Libel: The History of a Lie* (Jerusalem: Jerusalem Center for Public Affairs, 2012), 21–23. See also Haviva Pedaya's Hebrew articles in *Haaretz*: "Mass Psychosis between Temple Mount and Facebook," October 22, 2015, https://www.haaretz.co.il/opinions/1.2758202; "Israel Ignores the Writing on the Wall," October 29, 2015, https://www.haaretz.co.il/opinions/.premium-1.2764125.

Encounter across Religions

My definition of idolatry also has consequences for relations with other religions. Recognizing where the core of idolatry lies can free certain dimensions in relations between religions. It can open up a space of commonality and allow for positive influence. Idolatry would not be the very contact with another religion, but rather the domain described above, as distinct from more pure religious concerns, where believers of different religions could find common ground.

Thus, there can be similarity in praxis across religions. For example, both Muslims and Jews would sit or kneel while praying, bow down in a certain way, and so forth. This means that people felt that the praxis of their worship is located in the neighboring religion. For instance, Rabbi Abraham, son of Maimonides, considered kneeling something that was lost to Judaism.[28] Accordingly, I would claim that there is a certain boundary up to which bodily praxis and gestures can be shared across religions, providing enrichment and illumination to the other. Along with the notion of an abstract God, common to different religions, comes greater ease in religious borrowing. Jewish Sufism, a movement that lasted for several hundred years, headed by none other than Maimonides's son, Abraham, is proof for this. Thus, along with theoretical or theological influence, we also encounter some degree of practical influence. God is worshipped through the heart, not only the mind, making expressions of the service of the heart transferable from one religion to another. Such transfer is free from the charge of idolatry.

Not only practical forms of worship and performance have migrated from one religion to the other. Abstract forms of worship have also made similar migration. Thus, mysticism has adopted abstract concepts of divinity, because the working tool in mysticism is not the external ritual of physical actions or sacrifices, but is much more about the hearts and minds. Such worship is seen as capable of migrating and being copied from one religion to the other. This point is of great relevance today. It actually represent the overturning of the pyramid, in relation to earlier periods. In previous eras, it was the practical that readily migrated, leading to the borrowing of magical practices across religions. Today, by contrast the first thing that migrates across religions is abstract meditative practice. Consequently, even meditative practices that may have originated in Hindu or Buddhist religious context are absorbed and not considered truly

---

28 See the material collected and discussed by Mordechai Akiva Friedman, "Controversy for Heaven's Sake: Readings in the Prayer Polemic of R. Abraham Son of Maimonides and Members of His Generation," *Teuda* 10 (1996): 245–298 [Hebrew].

foreign. This, of course, invites us to further reflection as to where exactly the boundary between religions lies. Is it in naming God? Is it in the description of the person of God? Or is it in the stories and mythologies associated with God?

In any event, to the degree that the concern not to betray God by worshipping another deity lies at the core of idolatry, we must revisit this concern. It is not in openness to another religion that one necessarily betrays God. Rather, it is in the all too frequent reality that while worshipping God one, in fact, does something that is foreign to the very existence of God in the world, to the very moral stand a religious person is committed to. Betrayal is when one does things that must not be done, certainly not in God's name. I believe this is the most significant definition of idolatry in our times, and perhaps this has always been the core. This, again, finds expression on multiple levels. On the individual level it involves self-worship rather than God's worship. On the social level, it finds expression when a person who is a leader, a clergyman, rapes children, or when a tyrant uses his power or vision or messianism or prophetic talents to manipulate his followers and abuse them. To me, these are instances of idolatry par excellence. Herein lies the paradox: idolatry resides at the heart of religion. It is always right next to the rabbi, priest or imam, perhaps even more than next to the common man: "whoever is greater than the other, his evil inclination is likewise greater."

I would like to conclude with a constructive reflection that draws on idolatry and how it is understood and that paves the way to greater understanding between religions. I refer to the tension between negative theology or apophatic theology and religion as commonly practiced. This may also be expressed as the tension between *being* and the *nothingness* as attributes of God, or, alternatively, the tension between the religions of the East and the shamanist religions and the religions of the West, primarily the Judeo-Christian aspiration to conceptualize the abstract. This tension is active in all the Religions of the Book since it has been established by Avicenna, among others, followed by Maimonides and the kabbalists and Meister Eckhart, and it is also central to phenomenological comparisons of the Orient and Occident.[29] This allows us to consider similarities and differences between all religions in a way that can isolate and distinguish the meaning of idolatry from its traditional meaning of worshipping another deity. This also allows us to refine its suggested meaning as a way of violating

---

29 See my critical discussion of Rudolf Otto's conceptions of holiness in his book *Mysticism East and West* in Haviva Pedaya, "Revelations of Dread: The Dual Face of God and Split Consciousness: The Metaphysical Other and the Social Other: A Century to Rudolf Otto's *Das Heilige*," in *Theopoetics: Collected Essays*, ed. Avi Elqayam and Shlomy Mualem (Tel-Aviv: Idra Publishing, 2020), 159–194 [Hebrew].

the covenant with God. Awareness shared by all religions of the existence of the abstract God, that meta-divinity, so to speak, that lies beyond the narrative God associated with each particular religion, will purify the human spiritual existence without detracting anything from the narrative God and the obligations, stories, teachings, and commandments specific to each religion. This is how I envision universal harmony, and that is my goal. My definition of idolatry opens up the possibility of turning towards that higher dimension of divinity, common to all religions.

Let us consider the contribution of this negative theology to the tension, described above, between the conceptual and theoretical aspect of idolatry and its practices. On the theoretical level, we may discuss whether God has an image. Obviously, this question also has a practical aspect, assuming one is interested in creating a statue of God. From the point of view of Judaism and Islam, however, and certainly for Avicenna, this question can also have a purely theoretical aspect, which is not to think about God using positive adjectives. These are tensions that exist within religion on the theoretical level of the divinity, and that in turn impact how idolatry is understood. This more internal, spiritual, or theological challenge of idolatry points to a common ground in the struggle against idolatry, which can provide a ground for unity across religions. Needless to say, this must be distinguished from the more practical level of idolatry, that involves specific prohibitions.

Freeing idolatry from its purely outward or objective concerns also allows us to return to the axes along which idolatry is approached within the religion. This brings us, once again, to the tension between the two axes of idolatry, between the elites of philosophy and mysticism or between them and the masses. In this sense, the mystics and theoreticians of all religions are closer to each other than are the simpletons in all religions. That is, each, on the axis that runs *within* his people and his group, has a concept of idolatry that is stricter than that espoused by the masses of his coreligionists. Thus, paradoxically, mystics or leaders of various religions are closer in their supposedly more advanced or esoteric views to each other than to the masses. This is a phenomenon as old as the Middle Ages, when Maimonides could find himself closer to al-Farabi than to the Rabad.

One of the finest achievements of the monotheist religions, thanks to the push by Avicenna with his apophatic theology, and by Maimonides—who in turn influenced Meister Eckhart, on the one hand—and by the Kabbalah, on the other, is the tension between negative and positive theology. This translates not only into the tension between fullness and emptiness, but also to the psychological and psychoanalytic tension between the minimal and narrative self.

This tension between the negative and positive attributes also allows us to move along the East-West axis. It also enables us to find the common denominator of all religions in the negative attributes, in the divinity that is beyond all attributes, and thus also beyond the narrative of any individual religion. The main encounter that enables interreligious dialogue is the recognition of the abstract God, the counterpart of the minimal self that precedes any narrative articulated by the narrative self, which is also the object of the positive attributes. This encounter can take place on common moral grounds, but also on grounds of ecstasy, poetry, and so on. The coming together of these two factors—the ability to simultaneously hold the minimal and narrative together—is also a counterweight to idolatry.

This also translates into the different levels of idolatry described above. In the same way that God can be objectivized, leading to idolatry on the theological or religious plane, so self-worship is a form of objectivizing the self, making it the object of worship. The dangers of nationalism similarly emerge from objectification and absolutization of group identity, profiling the particular narrative at the expense of the broader foundational reality that recognizes a broader unity that makes room for self and other. And misplaced boundaries of self and other, grounded in false understanding of the self in relation to the absolute are also the source of corrupting social norms and the abuse of power in its various manifestations.

What all this suggests is that the battle against idolatry is a developmental process. It requires growth of the person beyond selfish desires that lead to self-worship. It requires a higher sense of self and other on the personal, communal and national level. We now realize the question of proper boundaries and the location of self in relation to others applies equally to the form of idolatry that threatens our common life on earth. And all these are grounded in the foundational challenge to grow in understanding of God, finding the balance between the various approaches to God, the minimal and the narrative. This balance in approaching God holds the key to addressing a range of social, political, and existential problems, all of which are grounds for contemporary idolatry as well as arenas for manifesting the true knowledge and recognition of God.

We opened with the recognition that idolatry is the flip side of proper knowledge of God, and as such is dynamic, taking on different expressions in different generations. We are now in a better position to affirm what it means today to call "on the name of the Lord, the everlasting God" (Gen. 21:33). Precisely at a time when the inclination for idol worship seems to have disappeared, I find it ubiquitous. It corrupts the real by climate disasters. It corrupts love and faith due to its control of the imaginary. And it corrupts the symbolic, the religious and metaphysical, by harnessing them to narrow interests, be they nationalist politics on the global sphere or coercive sexuality on the personal level, as embodied in the corrupt guru. Yet, as much as ubiquity of idolatry is a problem, it is also an invitation. Recognizing how prevalent idolatry is amounts to an invitation to growth of self, community, state and humanity, in the direction of higher self, recognition of the otherness of the other, and ultimately—the fuller knowledge of God.

CHAPTER 10

On Petrification

Michael Marmur

Definitions

Definitions are petrifications, attempts to trap complexity. Definitions of idolatry often sacrifice nuance on the strange altar of clarity. This risk notwithstanding, formulae offered by modern thinkers designed to capture the essence of idolatry shed light on different aspects of what is a phenomenon as significant and prevalent as it is elusive.

A tantalizing comment concludes the study of idolatry authored by Moshe Halbertal and Avishai Margalit. Noting the many and varied ways in which the term has been employed in Jewish discourse, a number of which are analysed in their book, they remark that "the category of the strange, or the wrong god, unleashed by the monotheists, proved itself to be powerful and complex. . . . It is this complexity that gave an astonishing fluidity to 'idolatry,' a category that is supposed to be the firmest and strictest of all."[1] Idolatry is indeed a fluid concept in Jewish culture, and it changes almost beyond recognition through time and between contexts. So broad is the range of beliefs and behaviors to which the term idolatry has been applied, its meaning has been stretched almost to its limit. The idol is perceived as being "out there" in the perverse rituals and practices of the Other, "in here" in the misconceptions and superstitions of believers; it is portrayed as the scourge of godlessness and as a surfeit of gods. It represents unbridled power and epitomizes impotence.[2]

---

1 Moshe Halbertal and Avishai Margalit, *Idolatry* (Cambridge, MA: Harvard University Press, 1992), 250.
2 For a sense of the range of possible understandings of idolatry from the biblical period onwards, see also José Faur, "The Biblical Ideal of Idolatry," *Jewish Quarterly Review* 69 (1978): 1–15; and David Novak, "The Law of Idolatry," in *The Image of the Non-Jew in Judaism:*

Halbertal and Margalit highlight a striking irony about idolatry. Ostensibly concerned with that which is all too solid, mired in fixity, it has been understood in fluid and changing ways. It is tempting to ask if there is any meaningful use for the term beyond the relational. Beliefs and practices I abhor are idolatrous, but is there something essential to this determination? Joan-Pau Rubiés has argued that developments in theological, ethnographic and historical discourse in the early modern period in Europe "eventually destroyed the concept of idolatry."[3] Oona Eisenstadt has noted that many argue that the term "is outdated and intolerant and that we ought to abandon its use."[4] While neither of them recommend announcing the demise of the concept, they each express the sense that old formulations need to be revised, and the complexity of the task acknowledged.

Naomi Janowitz asks whether an abstract definition of idolatry is indeed possible. Her analysis includes a perceptive and provocative assertion:

> Every religion has some objects that are understood to represent divinity formally; that is, every group interprets some signs as being iconic forms of representation. Religious texts may attempt to regiment these modes of representation by establishing whose interpretation is most authentic, but it is in fact impossible to fix the meaning of a symbol unless it is dead. On this understanding, idolatry is the claim that other people have the wrong way of interpreting their images, which is by definition, an impossible case to make.[5]

These words inspire a degree of caution in undertaking a description, let alone a definition of idolatry. Janowitz is right in my view when she suggests that any definition has to be read in its context, and such was ever the case. Depictions

---

The Idea of the Noahide Law, ed. Matthew Lagrone (Liverpool: Liverpool University Press, 2011): 65–96.

3   Joan-Pau Rubiés, "Theology, Ethnography and the Historicization of Idolatry," *Journal of the History of Ideas* 67, no. 4 (2006): 574. The article offers a reading of Voltaire's attack on the concept of idolatry, rather than a philosophical dismantling of that concept.

4   Oona Eisenstadt, "The Impossibility of the Prohibition of Images: Idolatry in Adorno, Levinas, and Schoenberg," in *Judaism, Liberalism, and Political Theology*, ed. Randi Rashkover and Martin Kavka (Bloomington: Indiana University Press, 2014), 289. In her excellent article she effectively demonstrates the shortcomings of such a position. Her reading of Schoenberg's opera, and by extension of the incident of the golden calf, is a profound contribution to the contemporary literature on that ancient episode and on the phenomenon of idolatry.

5   Naomi Janowitz, "Good Jews Don't: Historical and Philosophical Constructions of Idolatry," *History of Religions* 47, nos. 2–3 (2007–2008): 251.

of idolatry may be read as portraits of the iconoclasts who set them up, even if only to knock them down. With these warnings in mind, I want to highlight a number of readings of idolatry. Most of these readings are offered by twentieth-century Jews. My own understanding of idolatry owes something to each of the ideas presented by these thinkers. In the thought of each I identify a strand contributing to a picture of idolatry understood as a tendency rather than simply an attribute, more a verb than a noun—to petrify, to turn to stone.

Set in Stone, But Not Made of Stone

A tradition with a compelling image at its heart is to be found in the Talmud of the Land of Israel. It offers a remarkable reading of the drama of revelation and disappointment described in the Book of Exodus. This midrash both underscores and yet undermines the biblical account:

> Rabbi Samuel bar Nachman in the name of Rabbi Yochanan said: the length of the Tablets was six handbreadths and its width was three handbreadths. Moses held two handbreadths and the Holy One of Blessing held two and the there was a gap of two handbreadths between them. After Israel did "that deed," the Holy One of Blessing wanted to take the Tablets from Moses's hands. Moses's hands prevailed and he grabbed them from him. Rabbi Yochanan in the name of Rabbi Yose bar Abaye said to him: the Tablets wanted to float up to the skies and Moses attempted to grab them. It was taught in the name of Rabbi Nehemiah: the writing itself floated up. Rabbi Ezra in the name of Rabbi Judah the son of Rabbi Simon: the Tablets were forty *se'ah* in weight [one *se'ah* is equivalent of nearly two gallons] and the writing bore the weight. After the writing had floated away the Tablets were too heavy for Moses. They fell and broke.[6]

Three episodes in the Sinai story are linked here. First, the physical proportions of the tablets of the covenant are described. The episode of the golden calf is referenced, and then these two events are linked in the description of a struggle of kind resulting in the breaking of the tablets. The moment of revelation at Sinai is portrayed as one of transmission, handing off from one domain to the other.

---

6   PT *Ta'aniyot* 4:8, 68c. See also *Exodus Rabbah* 28:1; and *Tanḥuma Ekev* 11.

Consider the dimensions of the tablets of the law. Three equal thirds are described. While the hands of God, if such a thing could only be said, hold two handbreadths, and at the other end Moses, representative of all mortals, holds two, there is a kind of buffer zone in the middle, unoccupied by either power. As a contemporary Jewish reader of this ancient image, I cannot help but think of Rosenzweig's tripartite distinction between God, humanity, and the world, radically incommensurable yet inextricably connected.

The delicate balance between these three components can easily be broken—when Moses overreaches, when God despairs, when the letters depart the tablets and the stone is too heavy for Moses to carry. The sublime moment of revelation can be perverted in an instant. When the tablets of the law no longer bear within in them the latent energy created in the tension of revelation, in the tension between God, humanity, and the world, then the conditions for idolatry pertain. Idolatry happens when you think you are holding on to the Torah but all you have in hand is stone.

The midrashic concern with the physical substance of the tablets of the law can be read as a discussion of the essence of law itself. In the language of the midrash, the law without its spirit becomes an unwieldy and inanimate object. Precepts are set in stone, but (so the midrash implies) they should not become things of stone.

Fixing an Image of God: Batnitzky, Rosenzweig, Leibowitz, Wolfson, and Mendelssohn

Leora Batnitzky's analysis of idolatry in the thought of Franz Rosenzweig is rich in insights that reach beyond the immediate object of her investigation. In the first part of the work she offers a convincing parallel between Maimonides and Hermann Cohen on one side of a debate, and Judah Halevi and Rosenzweig on the other. In brief, her claim is that "[f]or Cohen and Maimonides, idolatry is the worship of the wrong God. Since the true God cannot be represented, any representation of God is necessarily a representation of the wrong god."[7] Rosenzweig, in contrast, is not scandalized by a plurality of images of the divine, so long as none of them is given an ultimate and unchanging status. "Rosenzweig argues that images can authentically represent God. But to fixate on and worship any one image is idolatry. *Idolatry comes from the way in which an image is*

---

7   Leora Batnitzky, *Idolatry and Representation: The Philosophy of Franz Rosenzweig Reconsidered* (Princeton, NJ: Princeton University Press, 2000), 20.

worshipped and not from the thing itself. Idolatry is the fixing of an image of God, which, Rosenzweig argues, is a denial of divine freedom."[8]

Ever since biblical times, various and sometimes contradictory claims about the sin of idolatry have been discernible.[9] In a sense, rationalistic and mystical approaches can be seen as exemplifying two understanding of the essence of idolatry. According to the former worldview, it is the very creation of images to represent that which is beyond and devoid of all images that is the heart of the sin. Not so the kabbalists, many of whom not only tolerated but themselves generated elaborate imagery. To read the *Idrah Rabbah*, for example, the Great Assembly section of the Zohar, is to encounter descriptions that in the rationalist camp can only be seen as an outrage.[10]

In a characteristically sharp and clear essay designed to outline the essence of idolatry, Yeshayahu Leibowitz makes in passing the claim that "mysticism ... is another name for idolatry."[11] From his explanation it is clear that for Leibowitz the core assumptions of the Kabbalah are but another version of a familiar phenomenon:

> In classical idolatry the gods belong to the natural world; in the covert idolatry of Christianity, God takes the form of man. In the Kabbalah, the worlds are made up of, or at least thoroughly imbued with, spheres and configurations that are aspects of the divine. . . .[12]

I am not convinced by this sweeping condemnation of the realm of the esoteric. Leibowitz's critique can be read as part of a long tradition of idol-smashers and angry prophets. But the Kabbalah in its various manifestations taps into traditions no less venerable or persistent. In his analysis of the idolatrous impulse in Kabbalah, Elliot Wolfson has uncovered many of the paradoxes and ironies that surround this question. For example, "it is precisely the injunction against iconic figuration of God that unleashed such a powerful visual imagination on the part of kabbalists in their effort to chart the contours of the divine body. There

---

8   Ibid., 23.
9   See Faur, "The Biblical Ideal of Idolatry." See also Halbertal and Margalit, *Idolatry*, esp. 180–213.
10 This material has recently been explicated in a remarkable way in Melila Hellner-Eshed, *The Seekers of the Face* (Rishon Lezion: Yediot Achronot and Hemed, 2017) [Hebrew].
11 Yeshayahu Leibowitz, "Idolatry," in *Contemporary Jewish Religious Thought*, ed. Arthur A. Cohen and Paul Mendes-Flohr (New York: Charles Scribner's Sons, 1987), 447.
12 Ibid.

are, however, occasional indications that kabbalists behind the composition of Zohar themselves were aware that they were pushing the limit of theological discourse to the point of brushing up against the limits of idolatry."[13]

This seems to be a more nuanced and fruitful approach, even though there is something about the stringency and clarity of Leibowitz's position that many find attractive. If we are to heed Janowitz's warning not to claim that we know others better than they know themselves, we need to acknowledge that faithful and committed Jews have understood the ban on idolatry in very different ways. And besides, to excise the Kabbalah and related literatures from Jewish discourse about God is to pay too high a price, since they greatly enrich the discourse.

The Zohar (III.279b), for example, includes a fascinating distinction between stone and stone. The material is presumably the same, but there is stone that is used to break the *tzelem*, the image with divine pretentions. This refers to Nebuchadnezzar's dream, which Daniel recounts and interprets in the second chapter of the Book of Daniel. According to the *ra'aya mehemna*, the faithful shepherd, this is the stone of God's name, and it is activated by speech. It is, as it were, in a molten state, full of creative potential. The other kind of stone is identified with the "figured stone" of Lev. 26:1. It is devoid of wisdom or dynamism. Rather than place all stone out of bounds, this mystical tradition promotes discernment and distinction. It promotes creativity at the risk of confusion.

Leora Batnitzky demonstrates that the ages-old debate between rationalist and mystical voices continues down to the greatest figures of twentieth-century Jewish thought in the West, and presumably will continue well beyond. Her formulation according to which idolatry is the fixing of an image of God is important. It places the emphasis not on the objects of stone (and silver and gold) but on the process by which the fluid is turned to stone. Her reading of the Rosenzweig-Halevi side of the argument is significant, and it acts as a useful corrective to the urge, represented both by Maimonides and by modernism, to place such voices beyond the pale of religious conformity. At the dawn of modernity, we find a fascinating example of thinking about idolatry in terms of

---

13 Elliot R. Wolfson, "Iconicity of the Text: Reification of Torah and the Idolatrous Impulse of Zoharic Kabbalah," *Jewish Studies Quarterly* 11, no. 3 (2004): 232. I want to mention a remarkable responsum by Rabbi Isaac ben Sheshet (Spain, fourteenth century). In responsum 157 he mentions the fact that some in the philosophical school regard the prayer of the kabbalists to be as idolatrous as that of the Christians. He proceeds to tell of a conversation with a well-respected friend from among the kabbalists, who explained that the individual *sefirot* were not prayed to as separate divinities, but rather they allow the worshipper to focus their prayers on the appropriate aspect of God. What is striking in the responsum is that this debate between the rationalists and the mystics could be conducted without the need for wholesale disqualification.

fluidity and paralysis. Until recently the theories of the origin of idolatry offered by Moses Mendelssohn in *Jerusalem* have been largely ignored or disdained. In an important feat of reclamation, Gideon Freudenthal has returned to this stone, rejected by most builders and interpreters, and proposed that it be seen as one of the foundations of Mendelssohn's entire project.[14]

In his *Jerusalem*, Mendelssohn hypothesizes that "the need for written symbols was the first cause of idolatry."[15] His suggestion is based on the notion that the ḥartumim (mentioned in Exodus 7–9 and elsewhere in the Hebrew Bible) are to be seen as those agents of written language who facilitate its perversion into idolatry. Mendelssohn sees the letters of the alphabet as removed only slightly from coarse animal iconography.

This linkage of the written word with the idolatrous impulse is presented in *Jerusalem* in order to provide an explanation for the particular value of the ceremonial law:

> We have seen how difficult it is to preserve abstract religious concepts by the use of permanent symbols. Images and hieroglyphics lead to superstition and idolatry, while alphabetic script makes man too speculative—it displays and interprets the symbolic meaning of things and their relationship far too superficially, spares us the effort of penetrating and searching the material, and creates too wide a gap between doctrine and life. To correct these defects, the lawgiver [Moses] gave the *ceremonial laws* to this nation.[16]

Ceremonies in Mendelssohn's view have the virtue of avoiding fixed status, and therefore demonstrate greater immunity to the risks of corruption and manipulation so characteristic of idolatry. A number of objections to this position come to mind, but for my current purposes Mendelssohn's intuition, based on extensive reading of the scholarship of his day, is a source of fascination.

---

14 Gideon Freudenthal, *No Religion without Idolatry—Mendelssohn's Jewish Enlightenment* (Notre Dame: University of Notre Dame Press, 2012). A different reading is offered in Elias Sacks, *Moses Mendelssohn's Living Script—Philosophy, Practice, History, Judaism* (Bloomington: Indiana University Press, 2017), esp. 31 and 176. See also Batnitzky, *Idolatry and Representation*, 33–40.

15 Moses Mendelssohn, *Jerusalem and Other Jewish Writings*, ed. Alfred Jospe (New York: Schocken, 1969 [1783]), 85.

16 Ibid., 90.

Is written language the source of idolatry or a guarantee that it can be overcome? And do the "living script" of rituals and ceremonies offer an escape from the lure of idolatry or do they and the accoutrements that go along with them not provide a lure yet more seductive? In my emerging definition of idolatry as a form of petrification, a paralysis, the dangers and opportunities inherent in both the written word and the ritual deed are to be highlighted. Where either has turned to stone, the idol lurks.

The Act of Replacement: Cynthia Ozick

Both in her fiction and in her other writing, Cynthia Ozick has long been preoccupied with the theme of idolatry in general, and with the Second Commandment in particular.[17] In an article about Harold Bloom, she states succinctly what an idol is not, or at least the old definitions to which it cannot be reduced: "An idol is obviously not only a little wooden graven image standing in the mud. Nor is the idol merely a false idea."[18] In that essay and elsewhere Ozick grapples with the essence of the idol. Her working definition is very wide-ranging:

> there is always the easy, the sweet, the beckoning, the lenient, the interesting lure of the Instead Of: the wood of the tree instead of God, the rapture-bringing horizon instead of God, the work of art instead of God, the passion for history instead of God, philosophy and the history of philosophy instead of God, the state instead of God, the order of the universe instead of God, the prophet instead of God. There is no Instead Of. There is only the Creator. God is alone.[19]

---

17 See Daniela Fargione, "Cynthia Ozick: A Jewish Woman Writer and Her Many Paradoxes," *Studi e ricerche. Quaderni delDipartimento di Scienze del linguaggio e letterature moderne e comparate dell'Università di Torino* 3 (2008): 149–169; Elaine M. Kauvar, "The Dread of Moloch: Idolatry as Metaphor in Cynthia Ozick's Fiction," *Studies in American Jewish Literature (1981–)* 6 (1987): 111–128; Victor Strandberg, *Greek Mind/Jewish Soul: The Conflicted Art of Cynthia Ozick* (Madison: University of Wisconsin Press, 1994); Deborah Heiligman Weiner, "Cynthia Ozick, Pagan vs Jew (1966–1976)," *Studies in American Jewish Literature (1981–)* 3 (1983): 179–193.
18 Cynthia Ozick, "Judaism & Harold Bloom," *Commentary* 67 (1979): 47.
19 This appears in a 1975 essay "The Riddle of the Ordinary" and has subsequently been quoted in anthologies and elsewhere. It is quoted here from Strandberg, *Greek Mind/Jewish Soul*, 23.

Ozick's mention of the passion of history as a replacement of God may be surprising, but in a 1972 essay she confessed to falling prey herself to this particular idolatrous tendency. "What grips me is not God, but something else. I am in thrall to the history of the Jews. It is the history of the Jews that seizes me ultimately, and with the obligation of *kavannah*. History is my master, and I its servant...."[20]

In Ozick's reading, then, the tendency to idolatry reaches well beyond material objects of strange ritual, and even beyond the strange gods usually cited—Mammon, Thanatos, the ego. For here, it is any version of the Instead Of, worthy, superficial, or downright pernicious. God can turn the heart of stone into a heart of flesh—all else will lead ultimately to a thickening of the arteries.

Ozick's bracing definition, while different in tone from Leibowitz, shares with his approach a kind of iconoclastic zeal. The risk of idolatry is ever present, and constant vigilance is demanded. If the idols were confined to houses of worship, it would be easy to avoid or counter them. But in this formulation the yeast of idolatry is bound to begin to foment in every nook and cranny.

Her account of idolatry raises an echo from an ancient source. Rabbinic literature compares a number of reprehensible activities to *avodah zarah*, but one of the more perplexing statements in this mode is to be found, among other places, in BT *Sanhedrin* 92a: "Whoever alters his voice—it is as if he has performed *avodah zarah*." While this statement is usually interpreted to mean that duplicity in negotiation, pretentiousness, or changeability are to be regarded negatively, Ozick's interpretation of idolatry suggests to me a different interpretation of the rabbinic teaching. Whoever replaces the Voice—not by masking their own voice but by offering an Instead Of for the unmediated Divine speech—that person is, as it were, an idolater.

This reading of the Talmudic dictum runs against the grain of its literal meaning, and as stated here, it is my own suggestion. But the notion that this teaching is connected to the idea of replacing the centrality of God is not new. Rabbi Isaiah Horowitz, author of the *Sh'nei Luḥot ha-Berit*, asks why the Talmud insists on a link between changing one's words and *avodah zarah*. Citing the notion that deception is alien to the divine essence, he explains that a liar replaces the God of truth with an alternative deity.[21] To change one's own words in an act of deceit is, in Ozick's terminology, another case of Instead Of.

---

20   Cynthia Ozick, "Four Questions of the Rabbis," *Reconstructionist*, February 18, 1972, 23.
21   *Sh'nei Luḥot ha-Berit*, Shoftim, Torah Or, 2.

The Self as Idol: Barfield, Fromm, Fackenheim, and Seeskin

Erich Fromm offers a bracing internally focused reading of the essence of idolatry. He claims that "the history of mankind up to the present time is primarily the history of idol worship, from the primitive idols of clay and wood to the modern idols of the state, the leader, production and consumption—sanctified by the blessing of an idolized God."[22] Ever the psychologist, he claims that "[t]he idol is the alienated form of man's experience of himself."[23] Connecting the biblical concept of idolatry to the Hegelian-Marxian notion of alienation, he declares that "[i]dolatry is the worship of the alienated, limited qualities of man."[24] This frozen and partial image of the self is in essence dead, unlike the living God. "By identifying himself with a partial aspect of himself, man limits himself to this aspect; he loses his totality as a human being and ceases to grow."[25]

This notion of idolatry as self-worship is not a modern invention. BT *Shabbat* 105b offers a reading of Ps. 81:10: "There shall not be a strange god within you, and you shall not bow down to a foreign god." "What is the strange god that is within a person's body? Say that it is the evil inclination." We see here a bold expansion of the notion of idolatry from the graven images of foreign tribes to every expression of the evil inclination within the heart of every person, including the most blameless and righteous. It is telling that the Talmud brings this teaching in support of the surprising opinion according to which any expression of anger is to be likened to *avodah zarah*. When the red mist of rage descends, when I fall prey to the dictates of one aspect of my personality, the strange god within holds sway.

In a retelling of aspects of the Eden story redolent with Islamic influence, the entry of the evil inclination in the form of a demonic force into the human heart is recounted. In one version the provenance of which is uncertain,[26] Adam is so

---

22 Erich Fromm, *You Shall Be as Gods—A Radical Interpretation of the Old Testament and its Tradition* (New York: Holt, Rinehart & Winston, 1966), 43.
23 Ibid., 44.
24 Ibid., 44, unnumbered endnote under *.
25 Ibid., 44.
26 This text appears in Louis Ginzberg, "Beno Shel Samael," *Hagoren* 9 (1913): 38–41 (and was later reprinted in a collection of Ginzberg's articles). It is summarized in Louis Ginzberg, *Legends of the Jews* (Philadelphia: Jewish Publication Society, 1968 [1913]), 154–155. The Islamic origins of and parallels to this tradition are discussed in Zohar Hadromi-Allouche, "The Death and Life of the Devil's Son: A Literary Analysis of a Neglected Tradition," *Studia Islamica* 107, no. 2 (2012): 157–183. For a discussion of midrashic parallels, see Ryan S. Dulkin, "The Devil Within: A Rabbinic Traditions-History of the Samael Story in *Pirke de-Rabbi Eliezer*," *Jewish Studies Quarterly* 21, no. 2 (2014): 153–175.

perplexed by the relentless crying of a baby (not his own, but in fact a manifestation of Samael whom Eve has been asked to look after) that he kills the child, and when even that fails to silence the screams, cooks and eats it. In a dark inversion of the Genesis account, Adam offers this forbidden food to Eve, and the two of them ingest the gruesome stew. So as to make the point abundantly clear, this obscure midrash has the voice of the baby call out from the human heart, saying to Samael: you may leave now, since I am ensconced in their hearts and will never be dislodged. Our original progenitors take to heart a demonic force, a hardness of heart, and it is stuck inside for eternity, a metaphysical heartburn, a spiritual dyspepsia. To worship the strange god within is to come up against that strange god, lodged inside forever.

This is a mythic version of Fromm's socio-psychological description, in which the person loses their humanity and ceases to grow. It expresses an inner enslavement and paralysis. An internalized demon prevents growth, and ensures that we are locked in to patterns of behavior, to bad habits of the heart. In this iteration of idolatry, the strange god within ensures that we remain short-circuited, incapable of growth, morally stunted. Such an internalized reading of idolatry links it to contemporary ills. Self-harm, addiction, *anomie*—all these may be read as worship of the strange god blocking the heart from within. The original sin of ingestion is punished by perpetual moral indigestion.

This motif of the idol as a form of congestive heart failure resonates with an expression found in the fourteenth chapter of Ezekiel and echoed in the Damascus document. The *gilulim* are to be found on or in the heart.[27] This term for idolatrous practice, *gilulim*, is found predominantly in the prophecy of Ezekiel, and its etymology has been the subject of much speculation. Is it related to the physical form of the idols, or might it be a scatological reference designed to express ultimate disdain for these practices? Whatever the historical explanation may be, and despite the fact that the heart is less the seat of emotions and more the seat of the intellect in ancient Jewish imagery, this expression can be applied to Fromm's understanding of idolatry. A circular, self-referential obstruction has entered the heart, and it results in an alienated narcissism, a worship of the partial self.

"For Fromm, idolatry is connected to narcissism (man worshipping himself), alienation (the dependence of man on outside powers), and necrophilia (the worship of dead things and destruction). For him, the fight against idolatry is a

---

27 Discussed in Johan Lust, "Idols? גלולים and ΕΙΔΩΛΑ in Ezekiel," in *Florilegium Lovaniense*, ed. H. Ausloos, B. Lemmelijn, and M. Vervenne (Leuven: Uitgeverij Peeters, 2008), 317–333, especially 323–324.

fight for man's freedom and for a sane society."[28] His approach, then, straddles the psychological and the social, the personal and the political. In my striving for a working definition of idolatry, something of this approach will be invoked. In the 1950s Owen Barfield outlined a remarkable theory of the evolution of consciousness in which a certain notion of idolatry played a central part.[29] Barfield's approach is in fact profoundly Christological. He charts a process in human development in which what he calls "original participation" is eroded, and the possibility for "final participation" emerges. Science brings about the emergence of "alpha-thinking," in which attention is paid to phenomena themselves. This can be understood as a cause of the weakening of participation, that state in which individuals experience the outside world as alive and conscious. He arrives at his discussion of idolatry in the course of his description of the evolution of human consciousness in general. The process he describes is one replete with evolutionary promise and yet fraught with spiritual danger. Our ancestors identified passionately with phenomena in the world. Our "progress" is predicated on our capacity to remove ourselves from this original participation, but such an act of removal raises the specter of alienation, a modern scourge.

Barfield regards the Second Commandment as "perhaps the *unlikeliest* thing that ever happened. As far as we know, in every other nation at that time there prevailed unquestioned the participating consciousness which apprehends the phenomena as representations and naturally expresses itself in making images. For the Jews, henceforth, any dealings with those nations were strictly forbidden."[30] In his view, science both reflects and hastens the decline of participation. Now we are positioned as the observer of phenomena in the world. In Barfield's lexicon, our increasing preoccupation with these phenomena "involves experiencing them, non-representationally, as objects in their own right, existing independently of human consciousness. This latter experience, in its extreme form, I have called *idolatry*."[31]

Idolatry so understood has brought many blessings to humanity, not least the advances of science. Barfield looks forward to the time in which "what will be chiefly be remembered about the scientific revolution will be the way in which it

---

28 Ronen Pinkas, "Correlation and Orientation: Erich Fromm's Position on Religion in Light of Hermann Cohen and Franz Rosenzweig," *Da'at* 85 (2018): XXV.
29 Owen Barfield, *Saving the Appearances—A Study in Idolatry* (New York: Harcourt Brace Jovanovich, 1965 [1957]).
30 Ibid., 109.
31 Ibid., 142.

scoured the appearance clean of the last traces of spirit, freeing us *from* original, and *for* final participation."³²

Barfield seems to posit two kinds of idolatry in the world. The first is to be found in an unthinking participation with nature, a participation liable to yield all manner of myths, fantasies, and images. Barfield sees this as fundamentally pagan, and perhaps incidentally idolatrous. The second, more potent, is to be found in that act of distancing the human observer from the detached processes of nature. If the true God is challenged in the age of participation, God is more potently challenged in this second development, comparable to what Charles Taylor has called "disenchantment." Taylor offers an acute description of God's changing fate as this major plotline in the drama of modernity unfolds:

> Once disenchantment has befallen the world, the sense that God is an indispensable source for our spiritual and moral life migrates. From being the guarantor that good will triumph, or at least hold its own, in a world of spirits and meaningful forces, he becomes (1) the essential organizer of that ordering power through which we disenchant the world, and turn it to our purposes. At the very origin of our being, spiritual and material, he (2) commands our allegiance and worship, a worship which is now purer through being disintricated from the enchanted world.
>
> But . . . the very notion that God has purposes for us beyond fulfilling his plan in the world, equated with our good, begins to fade. Worship shrinks to carrying out God's goals (= our goals) in the world. So element (2) becomes weaker and weaker.³³

In this reading of the dawn of the secular world, God is both purified and yet weakened through the process of disenchantment. To reference Fackenheim's distinction between the ancient and modern varieties of idolatry, we might say that the defeat of the former sets the stage for the rise of the latter.

Barfield defines idolatry as "the effective tendency to abstract the sense-content from the whole representation and seek that for its own sake, transmuting the admired image into a desired object."³⁴ I notice a striking similarity with Fromm's formulation, framed as it is in psychological terms. For Fromm, it is

---

32 Ibid., 185.
33 Charles Taylor, *A Secular Age* (Cambridge, MA: Belknap Press, 2007), 233.
34 Barfield, *Saving the Appearances*, 111.

an aspect of the self that becomes dislodged from its appropriate place as part of the whole and then fetishized. Something similar is described in Barfield's theory. When we remove the sense-content from the whole representation, we make an idol of the world around us. There would appear to be ample evidence for this kind of idolatry, in which things of flesh, which live in full participation, are turned to stone.

Emil Fackenheim offers a strong distinction between the ancient and modern varieties of idolatry:

> The ancient idol is not a finite object that distinguishes itself from the divine Infinity even as it points to it. The idol is itself divine. The idolatrous projection of infinite feeling upon the finite object is such as to produce not a symbolic but rather a *literal* and hence *total* identification of finiteness and infinitude.[35]

Fackenheim distinguished between this ancient prototype and its modern successor. While the latter gave external expression to "the strange god within,"[36] its modern mutation remains within, in the dimension of metaphor. In his view, there are two versions of the modern strain of idolatry: "elevation of the finite individual or collective self" and "degradation of the infinite aspect of selfhood to a false finitude."[37] In this way Fackenheim wishes to suggest that American confidence in immunity from the virus of Nazism is misplaced. Even if jackbooted oppressors may not march in Central Park, another insidious form of modern idolatry may take hold, and must be resisted.

Fackenheim's formulations are linked both to Fromm's and Heschel's. All three of them lived through the tumult of the twentieth century in which both varieties of the idolatry he names were rampant—the identification of the finite political entity or racial group with infinite power and privilege; and the deification of the self, or an aspect of the self. As he concludes his analysis of idolatry as a modern possibility, Fackenheim makes a passing comment concerning the

---

35 Emil L. Fackenheim, *Encounters between Judaism and Modern Philosophy—A Preface to Future Jewish Thought* (Philadelphia: Jewish Publication Society, 1973), 189. For discussions of Fackenheim's reading of idolatry, see Batnitzky, *Idolatry and Representation*, 229–230; Laurie McRobert, "Emil L. Fackenheim and Radical Evil—Transcendent, Unsurpassable, Absolute," *Journal of the American Academy of Religion* 57, no. 2 (1989): 325–340; Richard L. Rubenstein, "Emil Fackenheim's Radical Monotheism," *Soundings* 57, no. 2 (1974): 236–251.
36 Fackenheim, *Encounters between Judaism and Modern Philosophy*, 197. He is referring here without citation to BT *Shabbat* 105b.
37 Fackenheim, *Encounters between Judaism and Modern Philosophy*, 196.

specific role of Judaism: "Opposition to the idolatries of the present age is not confined to Jewish faith of to religious faith as a whole. Yet it remains true that within Judaism such opposition can achieve its full significance only in the context of a covenant with a jealous God."[38]

Fackenheim is convinced that any attempt to rob the struggle against idolatry of its religious dimension is evidence of the strength of the adversary. Our modern temptation is to relativize and secularize, to turn God into a wholly metaphorized "God," but Fackenheim is sure that this temptation has to be overcome. Just as it is idolatrous to elevate the state or the party or hatred of the other to an ultimate level, so is it an insidious modern form of idolatry to demote the transcendent God of commandment into a domesticated deity offering no more than a reflection of ourselves.

These three disparate modern thinkers all offer readings of idolatry that relate it to the modern self, the sovereign self. From Fromm's perspective, idolatry means worship of the alienated, limited qualities of the self. Barfield suggests that the distancing from the natural world, which is a necessary corollary to the process of modernity, leads to a new form of idolatry. And Fackenheim, too, sees in the contemporary human situation the breeding ground for a new strain of an age-old virus: the identification of finiteness with infinitude. Within the modern human heart, such a misidentification yields fearsome results.

Kenneth Seeskin, a professor of Jewish Philosophy at Northwestern, also reads idolatry as a mutation of the self. He understands it to be a form of narcissism. He argues that by rendering the divine in physical form, by imagining gods who behave and respond as we do, "in bowing to an image of god, we are really bowing to our own image."[39] He develops this insight into a call for universalism:

> At its core, idolatry is a form of flattery, and this fact explains its appeal to the human psyche, its appeal throughout history, and its appeal today. It is comforting to think that God looks like you rather than your enemies, that God inhabits your territory and stands for your ideas.
>
> Rather than to glorify our biases or convictions, the purpose of monotheistic religion is to do the opposite: induce a feeling of awe and humility in the presence of One infinitely greater than us. Monotheism therefore demands that when we enter the Holy

---

38   Ibid., 197.
39   Kenneth Seeskin, *No Other Gods: The Modern Struggle against Idolatry* (Springfield, NJ: Behrman House, 1995), 33–34.

of Holies, we take a critical attitude toward human accomplishments, seeing them as neither ultimate nor irreplaceable.

... At a minimal level, to think like a monotheist is to give up any form of cultural or religious chauvinism.[40]

Any God Not Yours: Heschel, Novak, and the Critique of Racism

Seeskin's statement displays a confidence in the salutary qualities of monotheism that is not necessarily vindicated by observing the behaviors and theologies of avowed believers. Even in theoretical terms, the tension between particularist claims and universalist aspirations is more complex than his formula allows.

It was certainly not always the case that positing an ontological difference between the true believer and the outlier was regarded as negative, let alone idolatrous. Rabbi David Solomon Eibeschutz (1755–1813) offered a reading of idolatry from within a quite different world of discourse:

> From the time of Adam's sin, good and evil have been commingled. In Israel the good represents the overwhelming majority, and the evil a negligible minority. It is also the case that even though Israel is at the root of the positive human qualities, it is inevitable that within the Israelite man some traces of the power of the evil qualities will be found, because of the confusion of good and evil [from the time of Adam]....
>
> ... every evil quality is called idolatry, as our sages say [BT *Shabbat* 105a]: who is the strange god who dwells within the human body? It is the evil inclination. And it is necessary to uproot that evil quality completely from the heart. If all Israel will do so then the nation whose spirit is nourished by that bad quality will be diminished, and it will be completely worked out. And to the extent that any of the bad quality remains in Israel, then to that degree will be great or small, for Israel has the power to defeat that other nation insofar as it overcomes that evil quality within itself.[41]

40　Ibid., 37.
41　David Solomon Eibeschutz, *Arvei Naḥal* (Warsaw, 1905), Lekh Lekha [668], 28a. The translation is mine.

According to this worldview, it is not that opposition to idolatry necessarily obviates the possibility of chauvinism. Rather, the epic struggle of the people Israel against the powers of evil within is understood as a part of their struggle against the enemies who surround them. Eibeschutz does not suggest that the Jews take up arms against the peoples who surround them, but rather he proposes that the war against idolatry, understood in a broad sense as resistance to the evil inclination, is in parallel a war against all the other nations. Seeskin tells us that you cannot oppose the idols and hold with chauvinism. Eibeschutz assures us that to resist the idols is to undermine all nations other than our own.

It is not difficult to imagine a rejoinder to this position offered from a liberal perspective, decrying both its metaphysical assumptions and practical implications. Such a response would display the usual shortcomings of anachronism, "blaming" the thinker for living at a different time and in a different cultural and religious milieu. In any case, it is worth trying to avoid a banal dynamic according to which one is either a chauvinist or a universalist. "Liberal theologians now hear themselves summoned to recapture a compelling particularism without sacrificing the gains of the universalization of Judaism."[42]

Abraham Joshua Heschel can hardly be described as a rootless liberal. Indeed, the political engagement of his later years was profoundly embedded in his reading of Jewish sources.[43] Heschel's understanding of idolatry shows a sensitive twentieth-century Jewish reader employs this category in a theopolitical context.

Like the other chapters in Abraham Joshua Heschel's *God in Search of Man*, chapter 42 is short. Atypically, however, it is not accompanied by copious endnotes referring the reader to sources from within and beyond Jewish tradition. Rather, it offers a clear statement of what Heschel takes to be the essence of Judaism.[44] The first of the chapter's three subsections is entitled "The Meaning of Spirit," followed by "The Spirit of Judaism" (also the title of the chapter as a whole) and "The Art of Surpassing Civilization." These four and a half pages offer a response to the question: What term best sums up the singular nature of Judaism? It was a question that Heschel was to continue to ask in public lectures and other settings over the course of decades.

---

42 Eugene B. Borowitz, "The Autonomous Jewish Self," *Modern Judaism* 4, no. 1 (1984): 43.
43 I have discussed Heschel's sources and their significance in Michael Marmur, *Abraham Joshua Heschel and the Sources of Wonder* (Toronto: University of Toronto Press, 2016).
44 Abraham Joshua Heschel, *God in Search of Man* (New York: Farrar, Straus & Cudahy, 1955), 414–419. Two of the endnotes in that chapter refer to Heschel himself, and the third to a section from Maimonides's *Mishneh Torah* with which Heschel chooses to conclude the chapter.

Heschel responds thus: "Perhaps Sabbath is the idea that expresses what is most characteristic of Judaism."[45] Continuing from his 1951 work of that name, Heschel makes the case for the central significance of the Sabbath. For our present discussion, most striking is the theme of the first of the chapter's subsections: idolatry. The implicit teaching of the chapter is that the Sabbath epitomizes an alternative to idolatry.

Heschel asserts that within all of us there is "a perpetual temptation to worship the imposing: to make an idol of things dear to us. It is easy to adore the illustrious, and hard to see through the masquerade of the ostentatious."[46] He lauds Amos of Tekoa for his capacity to stay immune to the lure of the superficial, and to identify the moral depravation lurking behind the splendid exterior.

He goes on to offer a definition of idolatry that does not imply that the problem lies "out there" with the false practices of the "other." Rather, the impulse to idolatry is widely prevalent and ever present:

> We must not regard any human institution of object as being an end in itself. Man's achievements in this world are but attempts, and a temple that comes to mean more than a reminder of the living God is an abomination.
>
> What is an idol? A thing, a force, a person, a group, an institution or an ideal, regarded as supreme. God alone is supreme.
>
> The prophet abhors idolatry. He refuses to regard the instrumental as final, the temporal as ultimate. We must worship neither mankind nor nature, neither ideas nor ideals.[47]

Heschel is not usually compared with his contemporary Yeshayahu Leibowitz, but in this discourse a parallel does present itself. In his brief article on idolatry Leibowitz avers, as he often did, that no intrinsic holiness adheres to things of this world beyond the fulfillment of God's command, and that therefore attempts to impute intrinsic holiness is idolatrous. For Leibowitz "[t]he most dangerous use of all of the term *holiness* is in the phrase 'the holiness of the people of Israel'." Only by recalling the medieval teaching that holiness lies in fulfillment of the commandments may this notion be saved from "transformation

---

45 Ibid., 417. In a 1948 essay he excoriated those journalists who were so seduced by the aesthetic appeal of the 1937 Nazi rally in Nuremberg that they failed to identify the toxic implications. See Abraham Joshua Heschel, *Moral Grandeur and Spiritual Audacity*, ed. Susannah Heschel (New York: Farrar, Straus & Giroux, 1996), 58–59.
46 Heschel, *God in Search of Man*, 414.
47 Ibid., 415.

into an object of idol worship."⁴⁸ Divided on so many issues, the two men share the belief that any institution or object, even if it is intrinsically worthy, bears within it the potential for idolatrous perversion.

It is likely that Heschel's political formulation owes something to Paul Tillich's definition of idolatry as "the elevation of a preliminary concern to ultimacy. Something essentially conditioned is taken as unconditional, something essentially partial is boosted into universality, and something essentially finite is given infinite significance (the best example is the contemporary ideology of religious nationalism)."⁴⁹ For Heschel, the origins of this understanding of what he calls "'The Idolatry of Might' lie in the teachings of the Hebrew prophets, who denounce 'the guilty men, whose own might is their god' (Hab. 1:11)."⁵⁰

In a lecture on "Religion and Race" in 1963 he offered a more trenchant definition, one that went beyond his earlier somewhat abstracted notion of the human elevated to the status of the divine: "What is an idol? *Any god who is mine but not yours,* any god concerned with me but not you, *is an idol.*"⁵¹ Here Heschel has identified institutionalized racism as a specific form of his more general understanding of idolatry. In this formulation Heschel is placing any version of a supremacist or supersessionist worldview firmly beyond the pale of religious legitimacy. This is a more provocative definition of idolatry, one designed to rob religious racists of any hope of justification. While a decade earlier he had limited himself to the generality that an idol is that which is promoted to divine status, now he is making a bolder claim: if you are worshipping a God who is concerned with you and not with everyone else, you are worshipping no God.

David Novak reads this 1963 essay not as a shrill liberal screed, but rather as a rejection of both Jewish liberalism and Jewish traditionalism. "One can read and reread the lines of that powerful essay and see Heschel's theology skillfully grounding his politics."⁵² How, then, are we to understand the statement, so far from much of Hasidic thinking about Israel and the nations, that any God mine and not yours is an idol? There is rhetoric and pathos at work here, to be sure, but also theological bedrock. The only image of God to be accepted in

---

48 Leibowitz, "Idolatry," 449.
49 Paul Tillich, *Systematic Theology* (Chicago: The University of Chicago Press, 1951), vol. 1, 13. This formulation is reviewed critically in Fackenheim, *Encounters between Judaism and Modern Philosophy*, 182–184.
50 Abraham Joshua Heschel, *The Prophets* (Philadelphia: Jewish Publication Society, 1962), 159.
51 Abraham Joshua Heschel, *The Insecurity of Freedom* (New York: Farrar, Straus & Giroux, 1966), 86. This lecture was given in 1963.
52 David Novak, "The Theopolitics of Abraham Joshua Heschel," *Modern Judaism* 29, no. 1 (2009): 107.

our iconic tradition is that of the human being. To understand that, but to fall short of ascribing a divine dimension to *all* humanity, that should now be read as idolatry. Enraged at the sight of racial discrimination wrapped in the cloak of religious respectability, Heschel pronounces this to be the polar opposite of what religion strives to be.

Tellingly, Novak mentions idolatry in his penetrating analysis of Heschel's theopolitics. He writes:

> The human quest for God would be futile, and could even involve idolatry, if humans did not believe that the God whom they desire to intimately know already desires them and knows them. Human desire without the prior experience of being loved often becomes the desire not to know God but to be God, and to be a God who only loves himself. This God is not the God of Abraham, Isaac or Jacob.[53]

Heschel's strategy was not to claim that Judaism "as refracted through the generations" (to cite the title of his great work on rabbinic Judaism) all leads to the march at Selma with Dr. King. It was sufficient for him to argue that Judaism is multivocal, and that in his view, the current eon calls for this interpretation. He believed that each generation necessitates a new understanding of perennial truths. It was this conviction that moral intuition had to be employed in each generation that led him to aver that "[i]n this aeon diversity of religions is the will of God."[54] Heschel believed that this aspect of truth had come to be generally understood only in recent years, but its provenance was not Western faddishness, but rather the same voice of God that animated those who came before. He held that the most resonant expression of a living Judaism includes the attempt to discern what is demanded today, what is the will of God at this hour.

To spout racial theories from the standpoint of religious Judaism,[55] as some in Israel and elsewhere are doing in the twenty-first century, is to meet the criteria set out in this paper for idolatry—it is self-aggrandizement and self-flattery. It involves petrifying a dynamic process, making Torah into an inanimate object.

---

53   Ibid., 112.
54   Heschel, *The Insecurity of Freedom*, 14.
55   Rather than cite particular unsavory examples, the reader is referred to a site in which evidence of such views is preserved: "Yair Nehorai: Ha-Mahapekha Ha-Shlishit," Facebook.com, https://www.facebook.com/yairnehorai1/.

It is not that any focus on the Jewish people and Jewish particularism is to be condemned as idolatrous. In fact, such a claim is a familiar anti-Semitic canard. My claim is different. It is that while I cannot define idolatry, I think I know it when I see it. When a petrified reading of the tradition gives rise to narcissism and bigotry, when the sin of anachronism is committed, then idolatry may not be far behind.

In his fifteenth-century commentary on Zach. 13, Isaac Abravanel quoted a phrase from the liturgy in describing his dream of a Jerusalem purged of strange worship: "the idols shall surely be cut off." His words were not idolatrous when he wrote them, even if they make uncomfortable reading for contemporary students.

Where, then, is the idolatry? In 2015, the Church of Multiplication of Loaves and Fishes was burned and vandalized. The attackers left a message sprayed on a wall, quoting a famous passage from the liturgy: "the idols shall surely be cut off." Here some of the themes we have surveyed, among them rage, replacement, self-aggrandizement, and anachronism, all make an appearance. These young Jews, apparently motivated by the belief that they were furthering the interests of Judaism, were in fact performing desecration through petrification.

CHAPTER 11

The Idolatry of the Written Word

Paul Mendes-Flohr

Idolatry comes in many and varied guises. Common to all its expressions is an attitudinal sensibility,[1] whereby given social and cultural phenomena are venerated as endowed with intrinsic, absolute value. So understood idolatry abounds even in the Age of Reason. Heeding the call of Descartes—endorsed by Spinoza and Leibniz—to give precedence to epistemology, the theory of knowledge and perceiving reality, continental philosophy unyieldingly questioned inherited theological and metaphysical claims to truth. As a consequence, "the Christian system of God-created values corresponding to a God-created soul in man," was displaced by the "self-consciously individual" who seeks to know "the external world through the self and the self through the external world," hence "the self became the Godlike creator of the world."[2] Friedrich Nietzsche gave this unabashed "idolatrous" sense of the self, rhapsodic affirmation: "The I will be pronounced holy when man has transcended himself, and recognized that he is God, the creator of his own values."[3]

As outrageous as such a defiantly idolatrous pronouncement might be, the Protestant theologian Karl Barth held it was inherent in the very logic of the

---

[1] On the concept of "attitudinal sensibility" is an evaluative experience that represents its object as having a property independent of the phenomenal impression of that experience. As opposed to perceptual sensibilities, attitudinal sensibilities are culturally inflected and not only physiologically conditioned. On the concept of "attitudinal sensibility," see Emily Brady and Jerome Levinson, eds., *Aesthetic Concepts. Essays after Sibley* (Oxford: Clarendon Press, 2001), 76f.

[2] Robert Langbaum, *The Mysteries of Identity. A Theme in Modern Literature* (Chicago: The University of Chicago Press, 1977), 6.

[3] Friedrich Nietzsche, *Thus Spoke Zarathustra*, trans. Walter Kaufmann (New York: Viking Press, 1966), 59–60.

anthropocentric turn of modern philosophy and culture. "In all the busy concern with concrete things [of the world] is always a revolt against God. For in it we assist at the birth of 'No-God,' at the making of idols."[4] Echoing Barth's appeal not to lose sight of the biblical God as Wholly Other, as utterly distinct from humanity, Yeshayahu Leibowitz endorses Maimonides's aphoristic theology and his understanding of *avodah zarah* as mental acts that negate the foundational principles of Judaism,[5] and extends this definition as the indictment of idolatry to contemporary Jewry. The "sin of the calf" (Ex. 32:2), he insists, need not "necessarily have to be of gold. It can be of stone; it can be a place, a country or even a people, or even an idea (for example, messianic redemption), or a particular personality."[6] The anthropocentric usurpation of God's transcendence entails a retreat from the biblical God who judges our deeds. One is perforce no longer accountable before a transcendent tribunal, which also issues a caveat that all that is created by human activity and judgment courts the danger of false worship.[7] Beholden to a transcendent personal God, we are beckoned to epistemological and axiological humility—to decenter our egos and thus to resist the idolatrous thrust of a culture that promotes and honors self-promoting ambition. "O mortal, what is good. And what does the Lord require of you? To act justly and to love mercy and to walk humbly with your God" (Mic. 6:8).

Two centuries before Leibowitz, Moses Mendelssohn (1724–1783) discerned idolatrous implications of the humanistic celebration of the written word, which since the invention of the printing press, gained an unprecedented cultural status, especially as embellished with the veneer of humanistic learning celebrated by the Enlightenment as the imperial road to truth. Challenged to defend his dual loyalty to his ancestral faith and the rational precepts of the Enlightenment, Moses Mendelssohn penned his duly famous *Jerusalem* (1783).[8] Explaining that Jewish religious observance allows for unfettered intellectual freedom, he referred to the traditional Jewish reading practice of communal Torah study—*talmud Torah*—as promoting a cognitive orientation that fosters a critical, rational discourse that is at the heart of the Enlightenment project. Noting that study

---

4   Karl Barth, *Epistle to the Romans*, trans. Edwyn C. Hopkins (New York: Oxford University Press, 1968), 50.
5   Maimonides, *Guide of the Perplexed* 3:8.
6   Yeshayahu Leibowitz, "Idolatry," in *Contemporary Jewish Religious Thought. Concepts, Movements, and Beliefs*, ed. Arthur A. Cohen and P. Mendes-Flohr (New York: Charles Scribner's Sons, 1986), 448.
7   See fn. 16, below, and the sentence in the body of the essay to which it refers.
8   Moses Mendelssohn, *Jerusalem, or On Religious Power and Judaism*, trans. Allan Arkush, intro. and comm. Alexander Altmann (Hanover, NH, and London: University Press of New England for Brandeis University Press, 1983).

of the Torah and its commentaries is integral to Jewish communal worship, he presented it as a means to resist the "idolatry" of the word, anticipating the postmodern critique of Western logocentrism (and its hubristic failure to recognize the epistemological limits of rational thought and language).⁹ *Talmud Torah* is conducted as a symposium in which members of the community—be they learned or not—read together given sacred texts, freely debating their meaning. (Since *talmud Torah* is often conducted in conjunction with the liturgical prayer of the community, the synagogue may also offer a place for a *bet midrash*, a house of learning, either in a separate room adjacent to or even situated in the same space in which the worship service takes place; hence, the synagogue in Yiddish is often referred to simply as a *shul*, a school.)

The standard layout of the texts that are studied—with the focus text in the middle of the page, surrounded by two or more commentaries from different authors, schools of thought, and disparate historical periods—encourages questioning and even disagreement. While the cognitive ambit of *talmud Torah* is synchronic (focusing on the trans-temporal cognitive structure of Torah teachings that touch upon ontological questions about the nature and meaning of being), its hermeneutic axis is uniquely diachronic (attentive to the teachings' historical development and, therefore, interpreted contextually and thus our ethical and religious responsibilities in the here-and-now). It thus moves along a dialectical pendulum, swaying back-and-forth between ontology and ethos, contemplation on the eternal truths of Torah to one's quotidian responsibilities to God and to one's fellow human beings. Accordingly, Mendelssohn noted, *talmud Torah* complements the "ceremonial law"—the *mitzvot*—as "a kind of living script, rousing the mind and heart, full of meaning, never ceasing to inspire contemplation and to provide the occasion and opportunity for oral instruction."¹⁰ As an ever renewed communal dialogue about the meaning and normative imperatives of God's word, *talmud Torah* resists hermeneutic closure, and thereby serves as a prophylactic against the idolatry of the written word.

---

9   In his critique of the Western logocentrism and its celebration of the written word, Jacques Derrida argues that there are no *fixed meanings* present in the text, despite any appearance to the contrary. Rather, the apparent identities (that is, literal meanings) present in a text also depend for their existence on something outside themselves, something that is absent and different from themselves (they depend on a procedure Derrida calls *différance*). Preceding Derrida by two centuries, Mendelssohn made a similar argument. By implication, he would also concur with Derrida, that the meanings in a text constantly shift both in relation to the subject who works with the text, and in relation to the cultural and social world in which the text is immersed.

10 Mendelssohn, *Jerusalem*, 102f.

The traditional Jewish reading practice was, alas, threatened by the invention of the printing press in the late fifteenth century, because:

> ... the diffusion of writings and books which, through the invention of the printing press, has been infinitely multiplied in our days, has entirely transformed man. The great upheaval in the whole system of human knowledge and convictions, which it has produced, indeed, had on the one hand advantageous consequences for the improvement of mankind, for which we cannot thank the beneficent Providence enough. However, like every good, which can come to man here below, it has also had, incidentally, many evil consequences, which are to be attributed partly to its abuse, and partly also to the necessary condition of human nature.[11]

The sociological consequences of the burgeoning of printed books—within two decades of Johannes Gutenberg's invention in c. 1449, twenty million volumes were in print—were far-reaching. For Jews the ever-increasing availability of printed books served to shift the site of knowledge from the synagogue to the privacy of one's home, thus undermining the bonds of community forged by *talmud Torah* as a communal activity. Far more significantly, it transformed the very nature of knowledge:

> We teach and instruct one another only through writings; we learn to know nature and man only from writings. We work and relax, edify and amuse ourselves through excessive writing. The preacher does not converse with his congregation; he reads or declaims to it a written treatise. The professor reads his written lectures from the lectern. Everything is dead letter; the spirit of living conversation has vanished. We express our love and anger in letters, quarrel and become reconciled in letters; all our personal relations are by correspondence; and when we get together, we know of no other entertainment than playing or reading aloud. Hence, it has come to pass that man has almost lost his value for his fellow man.[12]

---

11   Ibid., 119.
12   Ibid. The advent of the printed books—whereas previously the written word was only available in manuscripts—led to a radical change in reading culture, which Mendelssohn

The published author has eclipsed the reverence formally paid to the traditional Torah sage (*talmid ḥakham*), whose wisdom was shared by oral instruction and conversational exchange:

> Intercourse with the wise man is not sought, for we find his wisdom in writings. All we do is encourage him to write, in case we should believe he has not yet published enough. Hoary age has lost its venerability, for the beardless youth [*sic*] knows more from books than the old man knows from experience. Whether he understood correctly or incorrectly does not matter; it is enough that he knows it, bears it upon his lips....[13]

The epistemological consequence of the printed word and its elevated cultural status, Mendelssohn contended, engenders an idolatrous conception of knowledge.

> We have seen how difficult it is to preserve the abstract ideas of religion among men by means of permanent signs. Images and hieroglyphics lead to superstition and idolatry, and our alphabetical script makes man too speculative. It displays the symbolic knowledge of things and their relations too openly on the surface; it spares us the effort of penetrating and searching, and creates too wide a division between doctrine and life.[14]

Mendelssohn's affirmation of the "orality" of traditional Jewish learning thus had two distinctive but complementary vectors: hermeneutic and sociological. The former eschews closure; the latter—communal, dialogical reading practice—serves to sustain the bonds of community, culturally and socially.

Mendelssohn, accordingly, bemoaned that the intimate bond between Jewish ritual practice (the performance of the *mitzvot*) and Jewish learning (*talmud*

---

lamented because one no longer need to gather with his or her fellow or community to read and study. The resulting fragmentation of the community entailed a reconfiguration of reading culture—whereby one reads alone and perhaps discusses what one reads with a select few, such as fellow academics. The digitalization of the written word, replacing for many the printed book, might not only lead to a reconfiguration of reading culture but also give further salience of preferential communities and their attendant hierarchies and principles of inclusion and exclusion. Such criteria of community would undermine the egalitarian and universal inclusion of Talmud Torah as understood by Mendelssohn.

13 Ibid., 121.
14 Ibid.

Torah) had been severed, both of which in tandem were to "induce" the pious Jew "to engage in reflection." For each of the "prescribed actions" of Torah are "closely related to the speculative knowledge of religion and the teachings of morality, and was the occasion for a person in search of truth to reflect on these sacred matters or to seek instruction from wise men [to lead them in *talmud Torah*]." To be sure, the life of *mitzvot* and Jewish learning may very well "lead to idolatry through abuse or misunderstanding." But they also have an "advantage over" the printed word "of not isolating man, of not making him to be a solitary creature, poring over writings and books. They impel him rather to social intercourse, to imitation, and to oral, living instruction."

Communal learning—socially inclusive of all the members of the community, peddlers and professors alike, and thus transcending the sociologically stratified character of contemporary intellectual life—renders the learning community an ethical fraternity. It thus challenges the radical individualism of post-Enlightenment modernity and its veneration of individual expression as an absolute value (not to speak of social status). Wrenched from primordial communities by the challenging call of the Enlightenment as intoned by Kant—*sapere aude*, to dare to think for yourself, guided by reason alone, the denizens of the modern world find themselves "solitary beings," adrift, homeless in the world. "One can," as Martin Buber noted, "stretch out one's hands to one's image or reflection in a mirror, but not one's real self."[15] But "human existence touches upon [the absoluteness of life] only by virtue of its dialogical character, for in spite of his uniqueness man can never find it when he plunges into the depth of his life, a being that is whole in itself and as such touches upon the absolute." Thus, "man can become whole not in virtue of a relation to himself but only in virtue of a relation to another self. This other self may be just as limited and conditioned as he is; in being together the unlimited and unconditioned is experienced." In an impassioned plea to return to commentarial, dialogical community, the literary critic George Steiner speaks of this experience as a "necessary possibility," of being "God haunted," subject to the "blackmail of transcendence," accountable to a higher order than the human self.[16] Indeed, without positing the very "possibility" of God's existence, as the as the inimitable Portuguese

---

15 Martin Buber, *Between Man and Man*, trans. Ronald Gregor Smith, intro. Maurice Friedman (New York: Macmillan, 1965), 167.
16 George Steiner, *In Bluebard's Castle. Some Notes towards the Redemption of Culture* (New Haven: Yale University Press, 1971), 44.

writer Fernando Pessoa observed, "even doubt is impossible, even their skepticism will lack the strength to question."[17]

Whereas Steiner's hermeneutic community would be a virtual community instantiated by a dialogue with fellow Jewish literati past and present, Franz Rosenzweig would also embark on an "off-modern" journey toward retrieving Talmud Torah. He envisioned the communal reading of classical Jewish texts as a bulwark against the idolatrous intellectual vanities of the Age of Reason,[18] which has also been aptly cast as an Age of Uncertainty, having lost a firm ontological and metaphysical orientation.[19]

Having passed through the purgatory of anthropocentric humanistic education, Rosenzweig's journey back to the commentarial community of *talmud Torah*, however, would perforce, as he put it, be a "groping" quest to find a firm footing in the tradition, for along the way he could not but honor the questions engendered by the critical reflexes of reason acquired in the passage to modernity. In doing so he would embark on what the late Svetlana Boym (1959–2015) called the "off-modern" pursuit. Without retreating to premodern structures of Judaism, she adumbrated a strategy for tapping "unexplored potentials" of the modern project inscribed in lingering, dormant legacies that have not been utterly expunged. Pushed to the "side-alleys" at the margins of modernity's narratives of progress, the spiritual potential of these discarded cultural codes are to be recovered and revalorized. In Boym's own words, "the adverb off confuses our sense of direction; it makes us explore side-shadows and back-alleys rather than the straight road of progress; it allows us to take a detour from the deterministic narrative of twentieth-century history. Off-modernism offered a critique of both the modern fascination with newness and no less modern reinvention of tradition. In the off-modern tradition, reflection and longing, estrangement and affection go together."[20]

---

17 Fernando Pessoa, *The Book of Disquiet*, ed. and trans. Richard Zenith (New York: Penguin Books, 2003), 230.
18 See Rosenzweig's letter to Friedrich Meinecke, in which he explains why he declined an academic career, whose questions and "aestheticism" no longer strike him as relevant to his and other's existential concerns. Nahum N. Glatzer and Paul Mendes-Flohr, eds., *Franz Rosenzweig. His Life and Thought*, 3rd ed. (Indianapolis: Hackett Publishing Co. 1998), 92f.
19 Cf. "The common element in modern pluralism is [the] awareness of the markers of certainty and of a continuous search for them, which conscious of the impossibility to attain certainty." Claude Lefort, *Democracy and Political Theory* (Cambridge: MIT Press, 1989), cited in G. Delanty, "An Interview with S. N. Eisenstadt: Pluralism and the Multiple Forms of Modernity," *European Journal of Social Theory* 7 (2004): 391.
20 Svetlana Boym, *The Future of Nostalgia* (New York: Basic Books, 2001), xvi–xvii.

Halting at the baptismal font, where he was to enter the Christian covenant, Rosenzweig suddenly decided to remain a Jew. But he would "grope" his way back to Judaism through the "back-alley" of *talmud Torah*, a lingering remnant of traditional Jewish spirituality, which he perchance came across through the person of a charismatic Orthodox rabbi.[21] Inspired by the early morning Talmud study sessions at this rabbi's Frankfurt synagogue, Rosenzweig resolved to revalorize *talmud Torah*—for himself and his fellow "enlightened" German Jews, who like himself were "alienated" from the tradition.[22] His envisioned renewal of the wellsprings of Jewish spiritual life was primed by a realization that the academic culture sponsored by the Enlightenment had inexorably led to a spiritual *cul-de-sac*, a miasmic relativism with no sure footing in ontological certainties. Forfeiting a prestigious university appointment, he founded in August 1920 in Frankfurt, Germany, a *Bet Midrash (Freies Jüdisches Lehrhaus)*.[23] At his *Lehrhaus*, Jews would gather to *learn* as a communal activity of a shared reading of sacred texts as opposed to the individual *study* of texts. In his inaugural address opening the first semester of the *Lehrhaus*, Rosenzweig underlined this distinction: "Learning—there are by now, I should say, very few among you unable to catch the curious note the word sounds, even today, when it is used in a Jewish context. It is to a book, the Book, that we owe our survival. . . . The learning of this book became an affair of the people, filling the bounds of Jewish life, completely. . . ."[24] Alas, with "one blow" the traditional mode of Jewish learning came to end. For in the wake of the Emancipation, Jews left the ghetto to expand their intellectual horizons. What was new, however, was "not so much the collapse of the outer barriers; even previously, while the ghetto had certainly sheltered the Jew, it had not shut him off. He moved beyond its bounds [intellectually], and what the ghetto gave him was only peace, a home, a home for his spirit. . . . The new feature is that the wanderer no longer returns [home to the ghetto] at dusk."

---

21 The Hungarian-born Orthodox rabbi Nehemiah Nobel (1871–1922) drew a small band of devoted young university-educated Jews to his early morning *talmud Torah*. Inspired by Rabbi Nobel's traditional learning and deeply felt piety, they spearheaded a renaissance of Jewish spiritual life in post-World War I Germany. See Rachel Heuberger, *Rabbi Nehemiah Nobel: Die jüdische Renaissance in Frankfurt am Main* (Frankfurt a/M: Societäts-Verlag, 2009).

22 In an obituary for Rabbi Nobel who died suddenly at the age of fifty, Rosenzweig attested to the singular impact he exercised on his *teshuvah*. See Franz Rosenzweig, "Der Denker: Nachruf auf Anton Nehemiah Nobel," in his *Der Mensch und sein Werk. Gesammelte Schriften*, vol. 3 (The Hague: Martinus Nijhoff, 1984), 667–669.

23 See fn. 17, above.

24 Franz Rosenzweig, "On Jewish Learning," in *Franz Rosenzweig. His Life and Thought*, ed. Nahum N. Glatzer and Paul Mendes-Flohr, 3rd ed. (Indianapolis: Hackett Publishing, 1998), 228f.

The Jew now "finds his spiritual and intellectual home outside the Jewish world. The old style of learning is helpless before this spiritual emigration."[25] What is, therefore, required is new form of Jewish learning:

> "Learning"—the old form of maintaining the relationship between life and the Book—has failed. Has it really? No, only in the old form. For down at heel as we are, we should not be a sign and a wonder among the peoples, we should not be the eternal people, if our very illness did not beget its own cure.... We draw new strength from the very circumstances that seemed to deal the deathblow to "learning," from the desertion of our scholars to realms of the alien knowledge..., from the transformation of our erstwhile *talmide hakhamim* into the instructors and professors at modern European universities.[26]

Rosenzweig's *Lehrhaus*—*bet midrash*—would revive Jewish learning by welcoming Jewish university professors but not as professors, but rather simply as Jews. Indeed, the *Lehrhaus* welcomed all Jews who find their spiritual and intellectual home beyond the gates of the ghetto and Jewish tradition, to engage in Jewish learning—and to do so without jettisoning the knowledge they have acquired in the cognitive and axiological universe inaugurated with the Enlightenment universe; on the contrary, they will bring that knowledge—its insights, judgments, concerns, questions—to bear on their encounter with traditional Jewish texts. The new "learning" will perforce not start from:

> the Torah and [lead] into life, but the other way round: from life, from the world that knows nothing of the Law [*Lehre*], or pretends to know nothing, back to the Torah. That is the sign of the time. It is the sign of the time because it is the mark of the men of the time. There is no one today who is not alienated, or who does not contain within himself some small fraction of alienation [from Judaism].... we all know that in being Jews we must *not* give up anything, not to renounce anything, but lead everything back to Judaism. From the periphery back to the center; from the outside, in.[27]

---

25 Ibid., 229.
26 Ibid., 230.
27 Ibid.

Accordingly, the adjective "free" in the name of Rosenzweig's "House of Study" designated its new mode of Jewish learning: All questions and perspectives brought from the "periphery" of the Jewish world would be freely entertained in a dialogical encounter with traditional Jewish texts. (Registration in the courses of the *Lehrhaus* was actually not free of charge, but, indeed, rather expensive, for Rosenzweig felt a costly tuition would ensure a serious learning commitment, and not be construed as mere intellectual entertainment as was generally the character of institutes of adult education.)

What is crucial is that one who is "groping one's way home" seeks to participate in a dialogue with the sacred texts of the traditional Jewish library. Agreement or endorsement of the views expressed in these writings is not the objective. As Rosenzweig wrote to Martin Buber, "The very fact that you engage me in debate over the issue of observance is what is crucial. We would be parting ways with one another only if you were to feel it necessary for you being a Jew to say yes or no."[28] As a spiritual descendant of Jacob the Patriarch, a Jew is to wrestle with the text, and God—an unyielding struggle constituting the kerygmatic ground of Israel's spiritual patrimony. As such, the struggle resists the idolatry not only of the word, but also—and perhaps most significantly—questions all doctrinal, set conceptions of Jewish faith and practice. After all, as Rosenzweig insisted, "God created the world, not religion."[29] Informing this disarming *obiter dictum* is a caveat alerting us—as Leibowitz unwaveringly had—to the all-too-human folly of rendering religious affiliation idolatrous fixations, construing faith as religious patriotism, subjugating faith to the dictates of the politics of identity.

The deictic persistence of communally engaged Talmud Torah is uniquely open to the existential and metaphysical uncertainties of the post-traditional Jew, spurred by an endless, ever faltering quest to comprehend the meaning of our lives marked by the ultimate signature of our finitude, our inevitable death and of those whom we love. *Talmud Torah* is thus preeminently a "spiritual exercise," much in the sense which Pierre Hadot understands to have been the original impulse of ancient philosophy: "To know oneself *qua* non-sage: that is, not as a *sophos*, but as a *philo-sophos*, someone *on the way toward wisdom*."[30] This quest, as Socrates taught, can only be truly pursued in real conversation

---

28 Franz Rosenzweig to Martin Buber, letter dated July 16, 1924, in *The Letters of Martin Buber. A Life of Dialogue*, ed. Nahum N. Glatzer and Paul Mendes-Flohr (New York: Schocken Books, 1991), 318.
29 Franz Rosenzweig, "Das neue Denken," in his *Kleinere Schriften*, ed. Edith Rosenzweig (Berlin: Schocken Verlag, 1937).
30 Pierre Hadot, *Philosophy as a Way of Life: Spiritual Exercises from Socrates to Foucault*, ed. Arnold Davidson, trans. Michael Chase (New York: Blackwell, 1995), 91.

and not through written texts and lectures. "Only he who is capable of a genuine encounter with the other is capable of an authentic encounter with himself, and the converse is equally true.... From this perspective, every spiritual exercise is a dialogue, insofar as it is an exercise of authentic presence, to oneself and to others."[31]

Albeit in a new key, post-traditional *talmud Torah* is consistent with the pristine "spiritual exercise" of Israel's primal struggle to comprehend the divine Word in the dialogical presence of others, whom we hence acknowledge are like ourselves "frail and contradictory."[32] But *talmud Torah* casts existential questions as ontological *theologumena* bearing on the ultimate meaning and significance of human being, or, more precisely, of *being* human.

Talmud Torah as the font of divinely disclosed truth (ontology) thus not only resists the regnant ontological nihilism of Western modernity, but also insists that the celebrated cultural diversity need not be construed as ipso facto antithetical to a universal conception of the human. Existentially, each of us is bound to unique experiences that determine our life's journey, whose itinerary unfolds in diverse cultural communities in which one is embedded by the contingencies of birth and circumstance; ontologically, irrespective of existential contingencies, our very being is marked by the same stamp of existential destiny and ultimate concerns. These concerns are said to render all men and women from time immemorial, regardless of the cultural and religious idiom they may draw upon to give voice to those concerns, *homo religiosus*. These fundamentally religious or ontological concerns are registered in the universality of the quest for truth and justice.[33] One may thus acknowledge the spiritual universe of other faith communities not as academic or anthropological voyeurs, but rather as representations of a shared humanity.

An appreciation of the universality of this quest should ennoble Jewry to eschew the allure of an idolatrous self-adulation as uniquely blessed and the attendant ethical scandal of a supercilious indifference to the other.

---

31 Ibid.
32 Buber, *Between Man and Man*, 168.
33 Kwame Anthony Appiah, *The Ethics of Identity* (Princeton: Princeton University Press, 2005), 250. In his comparative study of societies "past and present," the sociologist S. N. Eisenstadt identifies "a sense of transcendence" as a hermeneutic "cipher" warranting their comparison as expressions of our shared humanity. "The sense of transcendence" is "inextricably related to the intrinsic symbolic and reflexive nature of humankind, in its capacity to reach beyond material, visible layers of the mundane and given." Cited in Ilana F. Silber, "Deciphering Transcendence and the Open Code of Modernity: S. N. Eisenstadt's Comparative Hermeneutics of Civilizations," *Journal of Classical Sociology* 11, no. 3 (2011): 273.

CHAPTER 12

The Concept of Idolatry in Current Times

Hanoch Ben-Pazi

The concept of idolatry, which has accompanied Jewish thought since biblical times, can arouse feelings of discomfort in the hearts of those living in the contemporary period. Ostensibly, this notion gives expression to the violent and problematic side of monotheism and religious faith, which tends to regard other religions as unworthy of respect.[1] It is a notion that challenges the very possibility of all interreligious discourse. The halakhic discourse that employs this concept goes even further, evincing an increasingly extreme discourse regarding the possibility of contact among religions. This can perhaps be translated into the concrete halakhic question regarding whether a devout Jew can enter a church, visit Buddhist temples, or visit temples belonging to the Hindu pantheon.

Should the Bible or biblical monotheism be understood as one of the formative fundamental elements of violent religious culture? How should we relate to the disturbing calls that appear in the Bible for extremist action by the devout in their contact with other religions which they regard as idolatry? At least in the context of the Western religions, we can advance this weighty argument with regard to one fundamental element of the religious faith: a willingness to struggle for the religion, sometimes to the point of a willingness to sacrifice one's life in the name of his or her faith. However, this struggle is also translated as the denial of other religions and therefore results in acts of repudiation of the faiths

---

1   On religion and violence see, for example, Mieke Bal, *Anti-Covenant: Counter-Reading Women's Lives in the Hebrew Bible* (London: A&C Black, 1989), 13–19; G. L. Jones, "Sacred Violence: The Dark Side of God," *Journal of Beliefs and Values* 20 (1999): 184–199; Yehuda Liebes, "Of God's Love and Jealousy," *Azure* 39 (2010): 84–106; Adi Ophir, *Divine Violence: Two Essays on God and Disaster* (Jerusalem: The Van Leer Jerusalem Institute and Tel Aviv: Hakkibutz Hameuchad, 2013) [Hebrew].

of others.² This repudiation may be based on error and falsity on the part of the other religion and idol worship in the sense that it is untrue, "for all the gods of the nations are idols," says the Psalmist, leaving truth and honesty as the domain of one faith alone. This repudiation may also be a manifestation of the struggle between the gods and is actually an ongoing part of religious war and the broad pantheon of faiths struggling against one another, perhaps with justification.

This article does not seek to trace the history of the Jewish religion's prohibition of idolatry, as expressed in the formative prohibitions in the books of Exodus and Deuteronomy, the biblical prophets' articulation of the prohibition of idolatry, and the way in which the Talmudic and the medieval halakhic discourse broadens but at times also limits the prohibition's applicability.³ Rather, it attempts to understand the concept of idolatry by means of a philosophical inquiry, with the aim of proposing a possible religious typology that passes the test of ethicality.

General Directions of Thought on Idolatry

I break down modern Jewish thought's discussion of idolatry into four aspects: consciousness-related, psychological, spiritual, and ethical. In other words, we can attempt to identify the fundamental elements of different positions found within Jewish thought on idolatry not as formalistic positions but rather as an ideological or ethical ones. In this way, we can refrain from proposing a legal position that rules out certain practices of "idolatry" or "prohibited worship" and instead propose an observation of the deep meaning of the movements that requires different depths of inquiry in order to understand the meaning of idolatry or acts that are referred to as such. We can even characterize it as deep movements of struggle against idolatry: the struggle for "religious consciousness," the struggle for "religious authenticity," the struggle for "religious sanctity," and the struggle for "religious ethicality." I regard all of these elements as part of one project of major importance that enables us to rethink the notion of idolatry: the concept of sanctity (*kedusha*)—proximity and distance, refinement and risk.

---

2   See Hanoch Ben-Pazi, "The 'War against Midian' Narrative in the Book of Numbers: The Bible's Prototype for Religious Wars and Violence," *Education and Its Context* 39 (2017): 71–95.
3   For a systematic and organized review of this subject, see Moshe Halbertal and Avishai Margalit, *Idolatry*, trans. Naomi Goldblum (Cambridge, MA: Harvard University Press, 1994).

The Consciousness-Related Aspect

To present the consciousness-related aspect of idolatry here, I make use of a number of important essays, all of which, to some extent, play a role in the ongoing discussion regarding idolatry that was presented by Maimonides. This allows us to think about the act of contending with idolatry as the major act of monotheistic faith: relating to God through "negative theology."

This is an attempt to propose not only that the biblical Jewish faith evolved under specific historical conditions as an ongoing struggle against "paganism" and "idolatry," but also that *this* has been the dynamic, permanent, and frequent meaning of the struggle against idol worship: the construction of a worthy monotheism. In my view, this is one of the most interesting directions for the philosophical construction of the meaning of "idolatry" as an endless project. The extended process that is the intention of the Torah and Judaism is an ongoing process of refining and purifying faith that is carried out through the performance of an infinite consciousness-based act of removal. Ostensibly, the deep meaning of religious faith is coming to know divinity in its infinite and imperceptible sense. This, however, is not a one-time act of faith versus faith, but rather the ongoing engagement in a boundless consciousness-based struggle against all actualizing and reductive concepts of divinity.[4]

This approach is of course simply ongoing philosophical development of Maimonides's position regarding idolatry, and the place of his halakhic and religious position in the context of the doctrine of the recognition of, and faith in, God, which he presents in *The Guide of the Perplexed*. According to this approach, the project of negative theology is not a linguistic game regarding what can and cannot be said about God, but rather an ongoing consciousness-based project in which all negative consciousness can be translated into positive consciousness. For this reason, it is also necessary to continue repudiating the refined faith in order to continue refining it.

Hannah Kasher proposes an analysis of this concept in Maimonides's thinking in her book *Heretics in Maimonides' Teaching*. Clearly, the most important application of negative theology is the systematic examination of the possibilities of idolatrous faith. In her book, Kasher proposes undertaking a mirror reading of

---

[4] In his collection of writings *The Religion of Israel*, Yehezkel Kaufmann clarifies this argument as the best historical way of reading the religion of Israel as it emerges from the Bible; that is to say, based on the revival of Jewish faith from within and against the idolatrous concepts surrounding it. See Yehezkel Kaufmann, *The Religion of Israel* (Chicago: University of Chicago Press, 1960).

Maimonides's discussion of idolatry in the different possibilities of atheist, idolatrous, and polytheist heresy as a way of redefining monotheistic faith.

Methodologically and philosophically speaking, this approach is the outcome of the notion that proper faith is an endless process, and that therefore the deep meaning of idolatry is what defines the process of the refining of faith. In a profound sense, this is an in-depth interpretation of the manner in which faith is presented in the Ten Commandments. It consists of two opposite or parallel processes. The first is the respect that is given to God's explicit name and the importance of refraining from using it in vain or perhaps using it at all. The second is the extremely detailed account of the prohibitions against the diverse kinds of idolatry, in imagery, in nature, and in human acts.

In his book *Judaism and Idolatry*, Asa Kasher formulates the definition of Judaism using the language of the sages as follows: "Every person who rejects worshipping the stars is like one who has acknowledged the entire Torah."[5] If we take into account the existence of a fundamental contradiction between Judaism and idolatry, we can begin redefining Judaism; that is to say: "the rejection of all idolatry is like loyalty to the central principle of Judaism."[6] We pay special attention here to the faith-related and consciousness-related principle, which positions Jewish faith as completely contradictory to idolatry. Kasher goes one step further with his assertion that "**the Jewish religion carries the meaning of active opposition to all possible acts of idolatry**" (emphasis in original).[7] From Kasher's perspective, this definition is a key that requires significant further development in order to redefine and redescribe different aspects of Judaism as taking part in this active project: the meaning of the commandments or the interpretation of the Holy Scriptures. With the caution that is characteristic of his writing, Kasher depicts this definition not as the only meaning of the Jewish religion, and not as the positive definition of Judaism, but rather as an interpretation that enables the fundamental discussion of Judaism. By means of this definition, he embarks upon a close reading of the commandment that prohibits the worship of idols:

> "You shall not make for yourself an image in the form of anything in heaven above or on the earth beneath or in the waters below. You shall not bow down to them or worship them...." (Exodus 20:4–5) Three components: identification of certain objects;

---

5   Asa Kasher, *Judaism and Idolatry* (Tel Aviv: Ministry of Defense, 2004), 27 [Hebrew].
6   Ibid., 27.
7   Ibid., 27.

> identification of a certain human approach to these objects; an imperative to refrain from demonstrating this approach to these objects.[8]

Kasher describes a process from the historical dogmatic context of the worship of objects that are considered to be idols to an account of the special tactical approach toward these objects—an approach summed up by the words, "you shall not worship them." However, attention must also be paid to the third step, which is decisive in this discussion, and which involves the assertion that "everything in the world that is of prominent importance in human life can serve as an idol for the person in question."[9] Moreover, it may also be possible, using Kasher, to highlight the greater claim and to provide an affirmative answer to his question: "Can everything that a person decides to view as an important aspect of his world sooner or later become an idol of that person?"[10] It is difficult to imagine "any aspect of the world—whether it be an object, a quality, a situation, or an idea," that cannot become an idol or stand at the center of a ritual.

At this point, I set aside Kasher's analysis and description of the concept of ritual, or "worship," which must be distinguished from allegiance, wonder, or even excessive appreciation, and focus on the claim that regards idolatry's role as a function that defines the process of faith.

> The Jewish religion's rejection of all possible expressions of idolatry is not passive opposition. It is not a purely emotional response of revulsion in the presence of any expression of idolatry, and it is not an absolute intellectual position negating all idolatry everywhere. The Jewish religion's rejection of all possible expressions of idolatry is meant to find expression in a person's willfulness, in both his way of life and his numerous deeds. It is meant to constitute active and practical opposition to all possible expressions of idolatry, and to all expressions of an extremely positive attitude toward any aspect of his world—the attitude of someone who assigns this aspect supreme value.[11]

---

8   Ibid., 29.
9   Ibid., 31.
10 Ibid., 31.
11 Ibid., 40.

The Psychological Aspect—the Mental Aspect

Another perspective from which to consider the issue of idolatry focuses on the mental aspect of the phenomenon. The examination I wish to recognize here considers not only the formal and practical question of the relationship between faith and the worship of gods and idols but also its spiritual and psychological elements. The deeper meaning of religious faith is a complete allegiance to the truth, which means a turn inward, to the individual's element of the "self." It is therefore not only possible, but also appropriate, to describe it as individuals' internal allegiance to themselves, and their demand for absolute honesty with themselves.

A profound and challenging problem pertaining to the issue of idolatry is manifested in the Hebrew term used to refer to the phenomenon in Jewish thought: *avodah zarah* (literally, "foreign worship"), and specifically in the word *zarah*, or "foreign." In this sense, any action that is not characterized by internal allegiance but rather by allegiance to an external force that is foreign to man and that causes man to act in contradiction of his internal values and beliefs is classified as *avodah zarah*, or idolatry. The deep meaning of idolatry is the internal action that is performed not out of internal allegiance but rather out of external compulsion.

The basic belief underlying this approach can be the religious spiritual truth that views the man bearing the "inner point," or perhaps the "spark" or the "soul," which is a "part of God above." When a person takes himself seriously as someone who bears within him the inner point, all of his honest and direct willingness to serve God is clearly linked to this divine inner point. The journey of the divine, therefore, passes first and foremost through the inner journey. In this way, man's primary attentiveness to the divine voice is his inner attentiveness to himself and his selfhood.

This metaphysical argument is not intended to blur the existential argument, which is equally as important. Shifting existential religious attention to the individual himself is also a result of inner observation regarding the religious experience. Though many view the development of this position as a solution to the hardship faced by the devout individual with the "death of God," and though some define this position as one that, in itself, also contains the fear of defrauding one's self, I regard this existential position as a deep spiritual response to the fundamental question regarding the meaning of man's existence.

I am not certain that Rav Kook would be pleased to find himself in the company of Heidegger, but it is difficult to ignore the close proximity of their positions. Rav Kook refers to a state of "I am in exile"—when the individual's I is in exile, that is, far from one's selfhood:

And I am in exile. The internal I of self, of the individual and of the public, is not revealed in his internality. [It is revealed] only according to the worth of its sanctity and purity and according to the value of supreme courage, saturated by the pure light of elevating radiance, which flares in its presence. . . .

The breath of our nostrils, the anointed of the Lord [Messiah], that valor and might is not external to us, it is our own breath, the lord our God and David our King whom we shall seek. We stand in awe before God and before his goodness. We shall seek our "I," our selves, and we shall find us. Cast off all alien gods, remove every stranger and *mamzer*, "And know that I am the Lord your God, who brings you out of the land of Egypt to be your God, I am the Lord."[12]

In a traditional sense, here we encounter the important message of *ḥazarah be-teshuvah* ("returning" to religious practice), meaning the individual return to one being oneself, or at least enabling the soul to find its rightful place as if "from ancient times." In philosophical terms, it is important to note one of the most important developments of this mental approach: the position of Martin Heidegger. The spirit of Heidegger hovers above us when we consider arguments of this kind. The analysis of man as an ongoing being, or as a constant coming into being of existence, is the core of his contention regarding the *Dasein* (coming into being) and its relationship with the *Sein* (being). The major question facing humans is the way in which they actualize being in their existence and their life. Human existence is an existence of coming into being, as we actualize being through coming into being. The key question facing humans pertains to the extent to which they bring being into existence in time, and the extent to which they evade or deny it.

The major expression instituted by Heidegger in the broad discussion that followed him is authenticity, and the question of the manner in which a person reacts to being or refrains from contact with it is related to the authentic and inauthentic modes of the individual's existence. This can truly be described as a test of existence that allows a person to live a weak life or a life that is devoid of meaning: speech that is not speech, a look toward the future that dares not observe the future, and a look toward the past that dares not touch the fundamental questions of existence and being. It is a test that finds expression in the

---

12 Taken from Abraham Yitzhak Ha-Cohen Kook, *Lights of Holiness* (Jerusalem: Mosad ha-Rav Kook, 1950), vol. 3, 140, "Seeking Our I, Our Inner Selves."

terms of existentiality at the time of being. If we can assign religious meaning to the words of Heidegger, it would pertain precisely to this topic: to the choice between the allegiance to being or denial of being. In a judgmental sense, it is a concrete expression of one's allegiance to oneself, or one's lack of such allegiance and subordination to the stranger. In the context of our discussion here, this is the deep and troubling meaning of idolatry.

As discussed by Heidegger in *Being and Time*, the concept of testimony refers to the *Dasein*'s exposure to being. After defining the *Dasein* as the mode of coming into being of the human, who is dependent on temporality, Heidegger examines the possible linkages between human and reality, and between the *Dasein* and the *Sein*. According to his approach, it is a quest for a connection to being, in contrast to the possibility of retreating into the meaningless. This connection to being is what defines the mode of authenticity.

Heidegger searches for the presence of the *Dasein* on its own and in connection with reality itself, as opposed to the meaningless, and in this way he addresses the major question of authenticity. The existential question of the *Dasein* focuses on the ways in which the *Dasein* exists: being-within-the-world, being-with, or being itself. In its manners of existence, does the *Dasein* give expression to its self or to their self?

The authentic modes of existence are closely related to one's ability to face one's own temporality and the fact of one's death. Heidegger transitions to the second part of his book with a consideration of the significance of the temporality of the *Dasein*, in which he establishes the impossibility of the ontological conception of the *Dasein* as a totality, based on the impossibility of perceiving death through the death of others. This effort to contend with the limits of finiteness and the human limits and to consider them vis-à-vis death by definition raises the question of the outstanding. In Heidegger's eyes, the human, or the *Dasein*, facing one's own death is of existential importance with regard to the ability not only to contend with the limits of the I, but with the possibility of giving authentic expression to the everyday life. The being-toward-death described by Heidegger is the *Dasein*'s ability to face its own finiteness—that which gives meaning to the temporality of its life. Here, we note that the *Dasein*'s existence is the existence of being within temporality. Put more simply, the essence of human existence is the ushering of being itself into a time-contingent reality, and for this reason the human ability to hold significance must involve contending with the temporary nature of our being. This, in turn, is dependent on our ability to cope with our being-toward-death. This intellectual step is difficult not only due to the strict philosophical phenomenological discussion it requires, but also, and primarily, due to the uncompromising demand it makes on authentic existence. On this basis, and in accordance with Heidegger, I highlight the existential project of the authentic existence of being-toward-death.

The consciousness of the *Dasein* is born at the moment of this Heideggerian connection, because it raises the question of testimony, or what Heidegger refers to as the *Dasein*'s testimony regarding the authentic potentiality of being.[13] Deep understanding of these unique phenomena enables us to think anew about the *Dasein*, and understanding that recognition of the finiteness of the *Dasein*—the fact of its death, in the mode of existence of being-toward-death—enables a person to leave his or her own circle toward reality. In a profound Heidegerrian manner, it is the possibility of leaving a meaningless existence for an existence of meaning. But about whom is the witness testifying in the testimony about being? This is the question that troubles Heidegger, and it is the question with which he begins: "We are looking for a potentiality-of-being of *Dasein* that is attested by *Dasein* itself in its existential possibility."[14] In a tone that is both proximate and distant, we see the manner in which Jean-Paul Sartre goes about discussing the concept of authenticity by means of the importance of the concept of freedom and the actualization of existentialism as an actualization of humanism. In an extreme manner, Sartre asserts that "Hell is other people," meaning that responsiveness to the expectations and judgements of others implies a coercive other that makes things difficult for the I.

The line of thinking that lies at the foundation of this discussion pertains not to the issue of faith and religion, but rather to the question of man's authenticity and one's ability to be attentive to oneself and one's selfhood. This approach, which was initially formulated by Spinoza in his book *Ethics* and which highlights the serious danger of the human being influenced by their surroundings and by the ideas of others, became virtually a motto—whether meaningful or empty of content—regarding one's effort to know oneself and to be attentive only to oneself. In such a description we can sense a spirit of cynicism, as the use of man's attention and man's obsessive engagement with man's own self can lead to narcissism and egoism. This argument, however, may actually be aimed at facilitating man's encounter with the self.

---

13   Martin Heidegger, *Being and Time*, vol. 1.
14   Ibid., §54.

The Spiritual Aspect

The next aspect of idolatry I wish to discuss here is the potential for a person's religion to play this role. That is to say, there is a spiritual-religious danger that, through a relatively simple dialectical process, our religious commitment itself can become a kind of idolatry, as manifested in the manner that spiritual commitment becomes institutional commitment and commitment to material objects. This is the spiritual danger that is spoken about by the mystics. The dangerous side of holiness is that the sanctifying approach, in itself, becomes immanent and therefore idolatrous.

In a philosophical analysis of the phenomenon of religion, Levinas describes the Jewish religion as "a religion for adults," which seeks to establish a conceptual system regarding sanctity that differs from all other religious conceptions:

> But all its effort—from the Bible to the closure of the Talmud in the sixth century and throughout most of its commentators from the great era of rabbinical science—consists of understanding this saintliness of God in a sense that stands in sharp contrast to the numinous meaning of this term, as it appears in the primitive religions wherein the moderns have often wished to see the source of all religion. For these thinkers, man's possession by God, enthusiasm, would be consequent on the saintliness or the sacred character of God, the alpha and omega of spiritual life. Judaism has decharmed the world, contesting the notion that religions apparently evolved out of enthusiasm and the Sacred.... It denounces them as the essence of idolatry.... This somehow sacramental power of the Divine seems to Judaism to offend human freedom and to be contrary to the education of man, which remains *action on a free being*.[15]

Ostensibly, Levinas's interpretation constitutes the proposal of an alternative: religion as an adult concept that is not based on the God-man dialectic that annuls human freedom. However, the opposite is true: the concept of a religion that is separate from all the foundations of religion discussed above condemns

---

15 Emmanuel Levinas, "A Religion for Adults," in his *Difficult Freedom: Essays on Judaism*, trans. Seán Hand (Baltimore, MD: Johns Hopkins University Press, 1990), 11–23, here 14.

man to freedom in an absolute sense, or, to use Levinas's words: "atheism is worth more than the piety bestowed on mythical gods...."[16]

As far as Levinas is concerned, Judaism views itself as closely related to Western philosophy, and numerous attempts at synthesis have sought to forge a link between Jewish and Greek wisdom. From Levinas's perspective, this marks the transition from engagement with divine revelation to engagement with content that meets mental and intellectual criteria.

Philosophical inquiry sets forth from the position of Totality in order to achieve its entry into the Infinite. In terms of the religious question, Levinas moves onward from the atheistic to the ethical position. This philosophical thinking must overcome the conclusion of the dialectics of religion (similar to the dialectics of the master and the slave, man determines the God by whom man wishes to be determined). Levinas's answer would be to venture forth from the dialectic in search of the role of the infinite as an Other who is not consistent with any of the categories of the subject.

The Sacred Book or the Sacredness of the Book

The Jewish model, which places greater emphasis on the Torah than on God, and on the book than on the experience, demarcates a path of deep contending with the danger of the "sacred" and the "numinousness" of religions. For Levinas, the thought that immanent sanctity exists in the sacred books amounts to the "idolatry of the Torah."[17] Sanctity does not stem from the object, but rather from specific modes of human activity that sanctify it.

To guide our discussion from the assignation of immanent sanctity to a book to the sacred modes of reading the book, Levinas distinguishes between two concepts of sanctity: sacredness, which is an expression of immanent-intrinsic sanctity; and sanctification, or the manner in which humans make certain things sacred. These two terms are representative of two different approaches to the Holy Scriptures: the Holy Scriptures as independent sacred entities—for example, as a source of religious authority or as writings that provide an experience of revelation—versus a sanctifying approach and the assignation of a status of sanctity aimed at describing or interpreting only the manner in which humans relate to the Holy Scriptures.

---

16 Ibid., 16.
17 Emmanuel Levinas, "Contempt for the Torah as Idolatry," in his *In the Time of the Nations*, trans. Michael Smith (Bloomington: Indiana University Press, 1994), 67.

Here, I summon Levinas's ethical assertion without attempting to analyze its epistemological meaning. For Levinas, every outlook of "conception" and every outlook of "desire" is a dangerous outlook that transforms the idea and the text into an object. The sacred text's significance lies in our ability to deviate from the text's subject-object relationship. In Levinasian terms, the significance of the past lies not in the fact that it is perceived as the past but rather in its capacity as a "past that was never the present." Inquiry into the text can also be a process of putting the text to death. The whole idea of the text is that one is not engaged in an object called the Torah but rather in the reading that goes beyond it.

The fact that the Torah is a book is what transforms it into a book of anti-idolatry, he explains. His view focuses not merely on the book as an object sitting on the desk of the phenomenologist, but rather on the book as a unique tool—on the book's book-ness. I think that as a result of the major fear of all things relating to books, the "ontological" human attitude toward the book, which regards books as a source of information or a "tool" for learning, or as a text for study, is not properly assessed. In truth, however, it is the mode of our being.

We need not trace the history of paganism in the context in which the Bible was written, as paganism still exists today, in modern times. The idolatrous sanctifying approach is not only a story of primitive and ancient groups and religions but rather also the idolatrous sanctifying approach of groups and religions that continue to operate in the present.

In a more explicit manner, Levinas regards the idolatrous threat as a realistic political or economic threat and as one of the temptations of idolatry. According to Levinas, idolatry is based on myths—not only myths originating in primeval stupidity or fears, but rather myths that can originate from the subconscious aspects and the stronger hidden passions of man. Herein lies the meaning of their great strength: according to Levinas, the antithesis of myths and contemporary idolatry of the Torah as a "book of anti-idolatry" is intended to advance a "logical opposition."

Levinas maintains that the fact that the Torah is written in book form also constitutes a special mode of religion that establishes opposition to idol worship. The reference here is to the Torah as a book: "But I wish to speak of the Torah as desirous of being a force warding off idolatry by its essence as Book, that is, by its very writing." The reason for this is simple: because relating to the book places man in the position of approaching the object, a book, as something that is to be read. This necessary condition of being a book attests to the reader that sanctity is not found in the Torah but rather in its reading. The Torah, as a book that is read, immediately makes its partners readers or potential readers. From Levinas's perspective, the relationship with the Torah is like the relationship with God:

"a book thus destined from the start for its Talmudic life." This teaches us that although there is a book called the Torah that does indeed have a dimension of sanctity, it immediately affirms that its real life is found outside itself, in its reading. The ways in which it is read brings it to life. As far as Levinas is concerned, these are Talmudic modes of reading. Although it is a book written in letters that are prohibited to touch, it is precisely this constancy that enables its participants to be regular commentators on the text through "permanent reading or interpretation and reinterpretation or study. . . ."[18] Reading its letters allows renewal, which is the true protection against idolatry. When Levinas uses the expression "hearing the breath of the living God in them," he is directing us toward God by means of reading beyond the letters in the direction of the infinite. This does not mean that God is embodied in the letters, but that in some way He is nevertheless written in them. The vitality of the letters is found in the lines, between the lines, and in the changing ideas of the readers interpreting them, in all places, and in all the possibilities in which the letters are echoed. All the possible readings, even the strange ones and the ones concerned with the forms of the letters, allow us to breathe life into the text and to endow it with a voice and an echo.

The fear of a hardening within the text, Levinas explains, is based on the fact that language, especially the language of the plastic arts, tends to fix and immobilize, to enclose within concepts and patterns, and to immobilize the saying (*le dire*) within the said (*le dit*). Nonetheless, he maintains, it does not do so completely, as it also contains in itself an element of that which is not said, an element of inspiration. To illustrate this notion, Levinas uses the interesting and picturesque metaphor of a musical instrument, which is made of matter—something that is stable and fixed, but that also allows the instrument to be played, facilitating a new openness of music and interpretation.

> The cello is a cello in the sonority that vibrates in its strings and its wood, even if it is already reverting into notes, into identities that settle into their natural places in gamuts from the acute to the grave, according to the different pitches. Thus the essence of the cello, a modality of essence, is temporalized in the work.[19]

This metaphor leads directly to an understanding of the Holy Scriptures as a musical instrument, the playing of which gives them life. Although the instrument

---

18   Ibid., 58.
19   Emmanuel Levinas, *Otherwise Than Being*, trans. Alphonso Lingis (Pittsburgh: Duquesne University Press, 2011), 41.

itself is made of wood, an object, the possibility of playing it gives it its spirit. This raises the question of whether the Holy Scriptures are unique in comparison to other inspirational writings. Tradition, he argues, must be seen not as ensuring the reliability and purity of the sources it conveys but rather as a place at which all the harmonics resonate: "an entire life is breathed into the letters of the text.... A text stretched over a tradition like the strings on the wood of a violin!"[20]

Though constructed from physical matter, the book's book-like quality facilitates, and perhaps even dictates, its state of being "beyond itself," always "beyond the book." Sanctity is not part of the book itself but rather of the approach to it as something that always lies beyond it. Perhaps both the Bible and the Talmud should be seen as texts that address the reader and that contain within themselves their turn to their reader. It is a model of a text that lies "beyond itself" or, to use Levinas's words, *"l'au-delà du verset"* (beyond the verse). The Talmud is interested in the existence of the text, but also in the existence of the reader. In this sense, Levinas's act of interpretation itself becomes an ethical action.

We are therefore already able to understand Levinas's unequivocal statement regarding God:

> I do not wish to define anything using God, as I know only humanity. I can define God using human relations, but not vice-versa. The notion of "God"—God knows that I do not oppose him, but when I need to say something about God, it is always out of relations between people. The unreasonable abstraction—that is God. I speak about God in terms that describe the treatment of the Other. I do not oppose the word religion. However, I accept it for the purpose of describing a situation in which the individual exists as someone who can no longer hide. My point of departure is not the existence of an extremely sizeable or powerful entity. The situation to which I am referring, if I may, is similar to that of Jonah the Prophet, who cannot escape. I refer to this extraordinary situation—in which you are always facing the Other, who has no more room for privacy—as a "religious state," and everything I subsequently say about God starts from this state, and not vice-versa. The abstract notion of God is a notion that sheds no light on any human condition. The opposite is true.[21]

---

20 Emmanuel Levinas, "The Strings and the Wood: On the Jewish Reading of the Bible," in his *Outside the Subject*, trans. Michael B. Smith (Stanford: Stanford University Press, 1993), 127.
21 Emmanuel Levinas, *Cahiers de l'Herne*.

The Ethical Aspect

The discussion in the previous section leads us directly to the focus of the present section: the ethical aspect of idolatry. The ethical position is an additional notion that gives concrete significance to the discussion of idolatry. Though its formulation may be unusual and draw attention to other aspects of the discussion, it ultimately leads us to the issue of the basic ethical commitment of being a human being. Following Franz Rosenzweig, Martin Buber, Emmanuel Levinas, and Jacques Derrida, I would like to suggest an ethical position face the question of Idolatry. Although it is a philosophical position par excellence and a modern position that can also be considered postmodern, it contains certain aspects that bring the discussion back to the subject of idolatry and to its biblical and even mythological foundations.

When we consider the fundamental philosophical positions of our time, we take note of the significant tension that exists between immanent positions and transcendental positions. In the discourse that Levinas begins for us, the natural foundation of the immanent positions is the foundation that precedes the I and the ego, that precedes all, and that finds expression in the significant danger posed by total positions. It is the unified, general, all-encompassing position, then, that can be considered the greatest form of idolatry.

If we formulate this idea in terms of idol worship, the result is modern paganism as described by Heidegger: the natural approach that introduces order to reality, that establishes hierarchies of reality, and that endows existing reality with the foundations of order and rule. There is no need to seek out this position in Heidegger alone or in the related ideological positions, as it is widespread in the religious views. It is the Stalinist risk of all religious positions: the risk that the formative total position will put an end to all differentiation and the uniqueness of all others.

The total position constitutes the danger of modern idolatry, whether it envisions the totality of the state, the totality of ideology, or the totality of society. Deconstruction of the idea of totality, which is a necessary precondition for the struggle against idolatry, is found in the infinite obligation of one person to another. In an effort to develop an alternative position on the social contract and the state, Levinas borrows the concept of "the pact" from the Biblical and Talmudic language. Although the Talmudic discussion of the pact depicts a formative event in Jewish law,[22] the discussion is broken down into ethical questions

---

22 Levinas's discussion is based on the proposal of a philosophical reading of the Talmudic text in BT *Sotah* 37.

regarding the ethical meaning of the manner in which the pact is established: "face-to-face"—people facing one another, even within the public at large. But the Talmudic account expands the event of the establishment of the pact to include a large number of formative events and laws: not a single general constitution, but rather a large number of pacts that together, in their mutual solidarity, constitute the "pact." Levinas refers to this general coming together as a coming together of law and philosophy. Society does not accept a formative constitution of one great faith, but rather creates an infinite collection of obligations toward each individual human being. Summing up, we can say that if we compare the community or the People as a whole to a circle of points, then Levinas's conception of the pact is that of a network of threads that connects the different points, as opposed to all the points being connected to the center of the circle, which is the binding law.

Levinas says the following about this: "The general spirit of the legislation must be extricated from it. The spirit of the law must be investigated. Philosophy is not prohibited, and the intervention of wisdom is not unnecessary." A special relationship is required between generalizing wisdom and the individual laws that make the major ethical ideas implementable in practice. The concrete ethical aspect of the specifications of halakhah is their direction to the concrete—the personal.

> It is precisely the concrete and particular aspects of the Law and the circumstances of its application which give rise to the Talmudic dialect: the oral law is a system of casuistry. It is concerned with the passage from the general principle embodied in the Law to its possible executions and its concrete effects.... All general thought is threatened by its own Stalinism. The great strength of the Talmud's casuistry is that it ... preserves us from ideology.[23]

In accordance with this idea, we can say that the obligation's importance to the halakhic dimension is found in the obligation to not remain in the realm of abstract spiritual philosophy. However, the danger of this obligation is the new ideology it creates, which ultimately constitutes the erasure of the different individuals and all differentiation among them.

---

23 Emmanuel Levinas, "Reading, Writing, Revolution," in *The Levinas Reader* (Oxford: Basil Blackwell, 1989), 220.

On the other hand, the halakhah holds decisive importance as "the struggle with the angel." According to Levinas, it is the ethical man's personal struggle to not choose pure "angelism" that does not take the risk of practical life—to not remain committed to an ideal ideological position of principle that has no practical expression. Action is the concrete ethical response, and the metaphor of the angel depicts a position that seeks to preserve its purity as a spirit without a body. Danger, however, lies in the fact that obligation to the practical world will ultimately build us a new constitution that does not regard people as taking part in the practical world—that we may enslave individuals to a new ideology of our own making. The struggle against the angelic is given meaning by joining the individuals, and not only the general ethical principle, as joining individuals is the quest for a system that preserves the concrete, which is done in the writing that is unique to the Talmudic halakhah.

The halakhah is also important in another way that is related to the importance of the ethical aggadic interpretation. Talmudic halakhic writing struggles against general ideas and halakhic rules expressed in all-encompassing language. The Talmud directs the student's attention to the existence of "private law" and the obligation of all individuals toward everyone who joins the pact. According to Levinas, the significance of the halakhah lies not in the law in its general sense nor in the details and the fine points of the law as presented in the *Shulḥan Arukh*. Law's significance, rather, lies in the concrete obligation between one person and another, an obligation that stems from standing face-to-face with the Other. This manner of reading and learning halakhah constitutes severe criticism of all the existing halakhic codices, which must be regarded as violations of the overarching principle of there being no overarching principle. Adhering to a master plan ends in the growth of an ideology and enslavement to an ideology. Levinas seeks the individual, the Other facing the I, and in the presence of a large number of human faces an overall pact is established. It is not generalization that plays the decisive role here, but rather the mutual guarantee of the pact.

In this context, let's consider a well-known quote of Levinas regarding the intellectual and aggadic place of the halakhic argument: "It is certain that, when discussing the right to eat or not to eat an 'egg hatched on a holy day,' or payments owed for damages caused by a 'wild ox,' the sages of the Talmud are discussing neither an egg nor an ox but are arguing about fundamental ideas without appearing to do so."[24]

---

24 Emmanuel Levinas, "Introduction: Four Talmudic Readings," in his *Nine Talmudic Readings*, trans. Annette Aronowicz (Bloomington: Indiana University Press, 1990), 4.

The Question of Tolerance—Instead of a Conclusion

"How then can we choose between religion and tolerance?" asks Levinas. His answer is that when based on responsibility and obligation, religion can constitute a basis for true tolerance. The meaning of religious tolerance is the ethical obligation whose existence the discipline of the commandments has the ability to ensure:

> The fact that tolerance can be inherent in religion without religion losing its exclusivity is perhaps the meaning of Judaism, which is a religion of tolerance. . . . The welcome given to the stranger which the Bible tirelessly asks of us does not constitute a corollary of Judaism and its love of God . . . but it is the very content of faith. It is an undeclinable responsibility. . . . The Jewish faith involves tolerance because, from the beginning, it bears the entire weight of all other men. The way in which it seems to block off the outside world and to display indifference towards the idea of a mission, together with the religious war lurking within that religion, results not from a sense of pride but from the demands that one has to make on oneself.[25]

According to Levinas, religion can lead people toward the absolute, but not in the name of an imperialistic seizure of control capable of devouring all those who refuse it, but rather as an absolute demand that is turned inward toward the self and that charges it with infinite responsibility.

---

25 Emmanuel Levinas, "Religion and Tolerance," in his *Difficult Freedom: Essays on Judaism*, trans. Seán Hand (Baltimore, MD: Johns Hopkins University Press, 1990), 173–174.

CHAPTER 13

The Line between True Religion and Idolatry

Warren Zev Harvey

Idolatry is a fascinating topic and there is much to debate about it. Is it an ethical category, a metaphysical category, or perhaps an exclusively religious category? Is it a willful sin or a cognitive error? No matter how we ultimately define it, what's so bad about it?

I do not intend to try to answer all these difficult questions here, and I'm not sure I have good answers for them. I wish, however, to make only one simple but significant point. The line between true religion and idolatry does not fall between different religions, but rather *it falls inside every religion*. Every religion can be interpreted as a true religion, and every religion can be interpreted as idolatry. There are no "idolatrous religions," only idolatrous individuals.

To be sure, the condemnation of idolatry was distinctive historically of biblical religion, and it is found particularly in the three Abrahamic religions and not in most other religions. Nonetheless, the conceptual distinction between true religion and idolatry can be applied to every religion. Any religion can be true or idolatrous, depending on how it is interpreted and how it is lived.

Idolatry, like True Religion, Is Human

According to a rabbinic teaching, idolatry goes back to the very early days of humankind, beginning with the generation of Enosh, the grandson of Adam and Eve. This teaching is based on Gen. 4:6: "And to Seth was born a son and he called his name Enosh, then it was begun [*huḥal*] to call upon the name of the Lord." Now, the meaning of this verse is unclear. Was it truly the case that human beings first called upon the name of the Lord in the generation of Enosh? Didn't

Adam and Eve address God? Didn't Cain and Abel bring sacrifices to Him? The verse demands interpretation. One rabbinic homilist inserted the word "idols" into the verse, and read: "And to Seth was born a son and he called his name Enosh, then it was begun to call *idols* by the name of the Lord."[1] The verse thus does not speak about the beginning of the worship of God but, on the contrary, about the beginning of idolatry.

Rashi (1040–1105), in his commentary on Gen. 4:6, develops this rabbinic teaching in a resourceful way. He writes that the verb *huḥal* (root ḤLL, third-person passive *hufʻal* form) does not necessarily mean "was begun" but may mean "was profaned." The verse thus teaches that in the generation of Enosh the name of God *was profaned*. Rashi explains that the generation of Enosh adopted the practice "to call the names of human beings and of statues by the name of the Holy One, blessed be He, to make them into idols, and call them God."[2] Human beings appropriated the name of God and applied it to other human beings or to statues, thereby idolizing them or deifying them. They thus introduced idolatry into the world.

Maimonides (1138–1204) makes reference to the rabbinic teaching about the generation of Enosh and idolatry when he writes in his *Mishneh Torah*, Book of Knowledge, Laws of Idolatry 1:1: "In the days of Enosh, human beings erred a great error ... and Enosh was among those who erred." The error, Maimonides explains, was that they thought that God wishes that his servants, that is, the planets and the stars, be worshipped, just as a king might wish that his vassals be honored.[3]

Both Rashi and Maimonides seem to understand idolatry as the worship of the sham in place of the divine. It is our transference of the unique prerogative of God to creatures or artifacts—to planets, to stars, to statues, or to other human beings. Idolatry, according to this understanding, would seem to be treating created things as if they were God. In other words, idolatry is the deification of objects in the world.

That idolatry is worship of the world is corroborated by a famous homily recorded in M *Avodah Zarah* 4:7. If God hates idolatry, it is asked, why doesn't

---

1   See *Genesis Rabbah* 23:6–7 and 24:6; *Mekhilta* on Ex. 20:3; *Sifre*, Deuteronomy, 43; BT *Shabbat* 118b; and Targum Pseudo-Jonathan on Gen. 4:26.
2   Rashi's commentaries are found in standard rabbinic Bibles. His commentary on the Pentateuch is available in several English translations, such as *Pentateuch with Rashi's Commentary*, ed. Morris Rosenbaum and Abraham M. Silbermann, with A. Blashki and L. Joseph (London: Shapiro, Valentine & Co., 1929), Genesis, 21–22.
3   Maimonides's *Mishneh Torah* is available in many editions. A new English translation of the Book of Knowledge by Bernard Septimus is to be published soon by Yale University Press.

He destroy all the idols? The Rabbis answer: the idols include "the sun, the moon, the stars, the constellations," and so forth. In other words, they include the whole world. *Any* created thing can be turned into an idol. To destroy all the idols would mean destroying the world. "Should God destroy His world because of the fools?!"

Whatever it is, idolatry is something profoundly *human*. In Hebrew, the adjective "human" (*enoshi*) is derived from the name "Enosh." True religion goes back to Adam and Eve, and idolatry goes back to their grandson, Enosh. Both true religion and idolatry are deep-seated human phenomena, although the former is two generations older. By teaching that idolatry derives from Enosh but not from Adam and Eve, the Rabbis taught that it is not *essential* to the human condition, but is profoundly *characteristic* of it. Thus, both true religion and idolatry are found among all peoples, in all places, and at all times.

True Religion Is Found Also among the Nations

The Bible teaches that true religion is found not only in Israel, but throughout the world, "from the rising of the sun unto the going down thereof" (Mal. 1:11; Ps. 113:3). Tracing its origins to Adam and Eve, true religion is essentially human and found in all human societies throughout the world. This universality of true religion was preached by the prophets of Israel. Jeremiah exclaimed: "Who doth not fear Thee, O King of the nations? . . . For in the eyes of all the wise men of the nations . . . there is none like unto Thee" (Jer. 10:7). Malachi declared: "For from the rising of the sun even unto the going down thereof, My name is great among the nations, and in every place offerings are presented unto My name, even pure oblations, for My name is great among the nations, saith the Lord of hosts" (Mal. 1:11). Similarly, the Psalmist said: "From the rising of the sun unto the going down thereof, the Lord's name is praised" (Ps. 113:3). And again, "As is Thy name, O God, so is Thy praise unto the ends of the earth" (Ps. 48:10). True religion, according to the Bible, is found all over the world. Indeed, the biblical paradigm of piety is Job, a non-Jew from the land of Uz (see Job 1:1; 42:7–9).

Idolatry Is Found Also among Israel

If true religion is found among all the nations of the world, so idolatry is found among all the nations, and Israel is no exception. The prophets of Israel often accused the Israelites of idolatry. After Malachi proclaims that God's name is "great among the nations" and all over the world "offerings are presented to His name," he turns to the Israelites, and cries out: "But *ye* profane it!" (Mal. 1:12). The Bible records many instances of Israelites making graven images, such as the golden calf (Ex. 32:1–8), Micah's idol (Judg. 17:1–18:31), and the "calves of Samaria" (Hos. 8:6). The prophet Ezekiel is shown by God the many acts of idolatry performed by Israelites in the sacred Temple in Jerusalem (Ezek. 8:1–9:11).

That even a true divine commandment could be turned into idolatry by the Israelites is illustrated vividly by the biblical history of the "serpent of brass" (*neḥash ha-neḥoshet*). Moses, at the explicit command of God, made a brazen serpent (Num. 21:4–9). In the days of King Hezekiah, it began to be worshipped as an idol called Neḥushtan, and Hezekiah, who was known for his faithfulness to "the commandments which the Lord commanded Moses" "broke in pieces the brazen serpent that Moses had made." The pious king is praised by Scripture for stamping out the idolatrous worship of an artifact made by the greatest Jewish prophet at the explicit command of God (II Kgs. 18:1–6). Hezekiah demonstrated his faithfulness to "the commandments which the Lord commanded Moses" by destroying an artifact made by Moses at God's explicit command! In short, the rituals of the Jewish religion, like those of any religion, can be turned into idolatry.

According to one interpretation, Moses broke the two Tables of the Law because he feared they would be used in idolatry (Ex. 32:19). This interpretation is found in a thought-provoking exposition by Rabbi Meir Simcha of Dvinsk (1843–1926), the celebrated Talmudist and Bible exegete. He explained Moses's motive in breaking the Tables as follows: "he understood . . . that [the people] would exchange the calf for the Tables, and continue in their [idolatrous] error."[4] Just as the Israelites had idolized the golden calf, so they could idolize the Tables of the Law. Even the sublime Tables of the Law could be turned into objects of idolatry! The iconoclastic Moses smashed the Tables of the Law in order to prevent idolatry.

In his *The Guide of the Perplexed* 1:36, Maimonides asserts that whenever the Bible says that God is "wrathful," "angry," or "jealous," it refers to idolatry. Many such dicta refer to the idolatry of the Israelites (for example, Deut. 11:15–17).

---

4   Meir Simcha Ha-Kohen of Dvinsk, *Meshekh Ḥokhmah*, ed. Yehudah Copperman (Jerusalem: Haskel, 1974), col. 506. Cf. Nehama Leibowitz, *New Studies in Exodus*, trans. Aryeh Newman (Jerusalem: World Zionist Organization, 1986), *Ki Tissa*, 613. Cf. also Lionel Kochan, *Beyond the Graven Image* (New York: New York University Press, 1997), 34.

Some refer to *the idolatry of Moses himself*! Thus, "And the anger of the Lord was kindled against Moses" (Ex. 4:14). The notion that the greatest of the prophets of Israel could have committed idolatry is shocking. Nonetheless, this seems to be Maimonides's intimation. Even the most virtuous and pious of human beings may on occasion be guilty of idolatry.[5]

The point that the rituals of Judaism can be turned into idolatry is made by Maimonides in this same remarkable passage in the *Guide*:

> If it should occur to you that [a Jew] who believes in the corporeality of God should be excused because of his having been brought up in this doctrine or because of his ignorance ... you ought to hold a similar belief with regard to an idolater [*oved avodah zarah*], for he worships idols only because of his ignorance or because of his upbringing.... If you should say that the external sense [*ẓāhir*] of the biblical text causes people to fall into doubt, you ought to know that an idolater is similarly impelled to his idolatry by imaginings and defective representations.

Maimonides concludes that those outwardly devout Jews who affirm the corporeality of God on the basis of biblical texts are "infidels" (*kāfirīn*).[6] There is no difference between Jews who are misled by an uncritical reading of the Bible and idolaters who are misled by the "imaginings" and "defective representations" of their traditions.[7] In other words, there are potentially idolatrous elements in the traditions of every religion, including Judaism, and we are all responsible for criticizing those elements and rejecting them emphatically. Thus, Maimonides was well aware that there are Jewish idolaters, just as there are Gentile ones.

---

5   Maimonides, *The Guide of the Perplexed*, trans. Shlomo Pines (Chicago: University of Chicago Press, 1963), 82. Moses's sin is presumably found in Ex. 4:13. In explaining how Moses could have committed idolatry, the medieval commentators on the *Guide* observe: (1) the revelation at the burning bush (Ex. 3:1–4:17) took place before Moses achieved prophetic excellence; (2) with regard to great individuals, even a small transgression might be considered idolatry; and (3) "there is not a righteous man upon earth that ... sinneth not" (Eccl. 7:20).
6   Ibid., 84–85.
7   One might argue according to Maimonides's logic: if the former can interpret their problematic biblical texts in the light of true religion, so the latter can interpret their problematic traditions in that light.

Maimonides's Inconsistency

Nonetheless, Maimonides was not always consistent. It must be admitted that he held, at least in some texts, that the line between true religion and idolatry falls *between* different religions. Thus, he wrote in some places that Judaism and Islam are true monotheisms, while Christianity is idolatrous.[8] Scholars have proposed many different theories about why Maimonides held a positive view of Islam and a negative one of Christianity.[9] As for me, I imagine that he held a positive view of Islam and a negative view of Christianity because as a youth growing up in Andalusia in the 1140s he saw that the great philosophers and scientists, for example, Al-Farabi (870–950), Avicenna (980–1037), and Avempace (1080–1138), lived almost exclusively in the Islamic world and the Christian world was mired in the Dark Ages. He evidently concluded from this that Islam was congenial to philosophy and science, while Christianity was antagonistic to it.[10] In his view, a religion that did not support philosophy and science could not be a true one, since according to him the true knowledge, love, and service of God is based on the scientific knowledge of His world.[11]

However, by the time of Maimonides's death, the center of philosophy and science had shifted dramatically from the Islamic lands to Christendom. Beginning with the thirteenth century, the world's leading philosophers and scientists, such as Albert the Great (1200–1280) and Thomas Aquinas (1225–1274), were Christians living in Christian Europe. I have no doubt that if Maimonides could have seen them, he would have changed his view of Christianity. In the years following Maimonides's death, major Maimonidean philosophers, such

---

8   See Maimonides, *Commentary on the Mishna*, Avodah Zarah 1:3–4; *Mishneh Torah*, Laws of Idolatry 9:4; Laws of Forbidden Foods 11:7; 13:11; and his Epistle to Obadiah the Proselyte, in *Iggerot ha-Rambam*, ed. Isaac Shailat (Maaleh Adumim: Maaliyot, 1988), 233–241 [Hebrew]. Maimonides's exclusionist use of the category of idolatry was in part responsible for the regrettable situation today, as described by Alon Goshen-Gottstein in the Introduction to this volume: "On the whole, the category [of idolatry] serves as a means of rejecting and invalidating other religions and their adherents [and] functions mainly as a means of excluding others" (above, xx).

9   This subject is discussed in the present volume by Menachem Kellner (see xx–xx). I do not think Maimonides's objection to Christianity was ultimately theological. After all, he knew that difficult theological doctrines could always be reinterpreted, if there was a will to do so. He himself once considered writing a reinterpretation of the grossly anthropomorphic work, *Shi'ur Komah* (see his *Commentary on the Mishna*, Introduction to *Perek Ḥelek*, seventh principle).

10 See, for example, *Guide* 1:71, 177. Cf. his description at 3:48, 598, of the "country of the *faranj*," that is, Christian Europe, where "the market places and houses" are "dirtier than latrines."

11 See Maimonides, *Mishneh Torah*, Laws of the Foundations of the Torah 1–4.

as Rabbis Jacob Anatoli (1194–1256), Moses of Salerno (d. 1279), Hillel of Verona (1220–1295), Levi Gersonides (1288–1344), and Judah Romano (1293–1330), studied the works of their contemporary Christian philosophers and scientists, and sometimes collaborated with them or translated their works into Hebrew. Living among accomplished Christian scholars, they surely could not accept Maimonides's negative view of Christianity as anti-scientific.

Rabbi Menachem Meiri (1249–1310) was one Maimonidean scholar who saw that Maimonides's negative view of Christianity did not fit the reality he knew, and boldly rejected it. He ruled that all individuals who are "restricted by the ways of the religions" (*gedurim be-darkhe ha-datot*) are not idolaters. He states unequivocally: "all those among the nations who are restricted by the ways of religion and worship God in some way, even if their faith is far from our faith, are not included among [the idolaters] but are exactly like Jews in these matters."[12] His broad definition included Christianity, Islam, and also other religions. According to one recent study of Meiri's thought, his "distinction [between restricted by the ways of the religions and not restricted by them] ... crosses national and religious lines, and focuses on the moral-religious-universal aspect ... creating complete equality ... between Jew and gentile."[13] In simple language, the line between true religion and idolatry does not fall between different religions, but rather *it falls inside every religion*. It may be disputed whether this radically egalitarian reading of Meiri accurately represents his doctrine. However, it definitely represents accurately the view I am advocating here. Maimonides was regrettably inconsistent when he asserted—in some of his writings—that the line between true religion and idolatry falls *between* different religions and not *inside* every religion, but he was corrected by later Maimonideans, including Meiri.

---

12 Meiri, *Bet ha-Beḥirah* on *Bava Kamma*, ed. K. Schlesinger (Jerusalem: privately published, 1967), folio 113b, 330. See Gerald Blidstein, "Menahem Meiri's Attitude toward Gentiles," trans. Z. Brody, *Binah* 3 (1994): 119–133; Moshe Halbertal, "Ones Possessed of Religion," trans. J. Linsider, *The Edah Journal* 1 (2000): 1–24; and Alon Goshen-Gottstein, *Same God, Other god: Judaism, Hinduism, and the Problem of Idolatry* (New York: Palgrave Macmillan, 2015), 45–46, 107–126.

13 Gedalya Oren, "Rabbi Menahem ha-Meiri's Attitude toward the Other," *Da'at* 60 (2007): 34 [Hebrew].

Conclusion

While the condemnation of idolatry is found particularly in the three Abrahamic religions, the conceptual distinction between true religion and idolatry is applicable to every religion. All religions—not only Judaism, Christianity, and Islam, but also Hinduism, Jainism, the Greco-Roman religions (known as "paganism"), Zoroastrianism, Shintoism, Buddhism, Taoism, Sikhism, the African religions, the Native American religions, and other religions—prescribe reverence for the divine, and distinguish between the divine and the sham. If we borrow the definition of Rashi and Maimonides, according to which idolatry is worship of the sham in place of the divine, then we can apply it to all religions equally. All religions can be true and all can be idolatrous. Adherents of any religion can be either pious or idolatrous. The line between true religion and idolatry falls *inside* each religion.

Postscript

Once it is agreed that all religions can be true or idolatrous, the question inevitably arises: What *is* wrong with idolatry? Is it so bad to worship created things instead of the Creator? Is it so bad to prefer the sham to the divine? Why not idolize the fake, the bogus, the ersatz? Here one can do no better than quote the Psalmist: "Their idols are silver and gold, the work of human hands. They have mouths, but they speak not. Eyes have they, but they see not. They have ears, but they hear not.... *They that make them shall be like unto them*, yea everyone that trusteth in them" (Ps. 115:4–8). One defines oneself by what one loves and reveres. Worship of silver and gold turns one into a materialistic person, worship of the insensitive makes one insensitive (see also Jer. 2:5).

CHAPTER 14

Thinking Idolatry with/against Maimonides: The Case of Christianity

Menachem Kellner

1. Thesis

My thesis is simple. Without exception, rabbinic authorities who convict Christianity of *avodah zarah* rely on Maimonides to do so. Intellectual honesty would then demand that they must also convict Nachmanides, Kabbalists, Hasidim, followers of R. Haim of Volozhin (that is, much of the so-called Lithuanian yeshiva world), among many others, of *avodah zarah*.[1] Rephrasing: my argument here is that Maimonides's views on the nature of *avodah zarah* are problematic for anyone who subscribes to those aspects of contemporary Judaism that are infused with Kabbalah. Most aspects of contemporary Judaism (not just Orthodoxy!) are infused with Kabbalah. The question arises: Why condemn Christianity as *avodah zarah* on Maimonidean grounds while giving a pass to Kabbalah-inflected Judaisms?

Not giving such Judaisms a pass is a heavy price to pay for the "pleasure" of condemning Christians as idolaters. I will show that if we follow Maimonides in convicting Christians of idolatry, we cannot avoid convicting all those listed just above. I personally have no interest in condemning Christians (or Kabbalists) of idolatry. It is not that I am in particular an admirer of Christianity as such, or that I think that it is true and Judaism false (heaven forfend!), or that I am some

---

1 I will briefly treat Nachmanides and other Kabbalists below. For R. Haim, see his *Nefesh ha-Chayyim* (Bnai Brak, 2009), Gate 1, chap. 3 (p. 4), chap. 9 (p. 33), chap. 22 (p. 75), and Gate 2, chap. 6 (p. 105) (among many, many examples).

sort of religious pluralist;[2] rather, for a number of reasons I see no point in calling Christianity idolatry. We will see below that the Talmudic sages themselves realized that idolatry as understood in the Bible was no longer a live option or a real threat. If that was true then, it is all the more so true today. Idols of wood and stone are not the challenge we face today, nor is star worship. However, worship of false ideals certainly is.[3] Our struggle with idolatry should focus on that, not on followers of Jesus of Nazareth, however mistaken we find them to be.

Beyond that, I will show here, almost no one actually follows Maimonides in his thinking about the nature of God and of faith in God.[4] It is such thinking that led him to denounce Christianity as idolatry—but it would also lead him to denounce almost all living Jews who take their Judaism seriously as idolaters. If you do not want to follow Maimonides there, how in good conscience can you follow him in seeing Christianity as idolatry?

The general question, what constitutes idolatry, is of great contemporary relevance in Israel: growing ties with Hindu India raise questions about the relevance of classic views of idolatry; the constantly growing contributions of evangelical Christian organizations to Israeli Jewish institutions raise questions about whether or not Christianity should be treated as idolatry.[5] I know

---

2   See Menachem Kellner and Jolene Kellner, "Respectful Disagreement: A Response to Raphael Jospe," in *Jewish Theology and World Religions*, ed. Alon Goshen-Gottstein and Eugene Korn (Oxford: Littman Library of Jewish Civilization, 2012), 123–133.

3   See Kenneth Seeskin, *No Other Gods: The Modern Struggle against Idolatry* (New York: Berhman House, 1995).

4   Aside from paying lip service to his views, how many Jews really follow the consequences of Maimonides's views on the nature of Jewish faith? The clearest proof that few do is that while David Berger's attack on Habad is clearly on the mark in Maimonidean terms, no other rabbi has publicly supported him. For details see Menachem Kellner, *Must a Jew Believe Anything?*, 2nd ed. (Oxford: Littman Library of Jewish Civilization, 2006), 145. The project of paying lip service alone to Maimonides's doctrines (especially his Thirteen Principles) began almost immediately. See Menachem Kellner, *Dogma in Medieval Jewish Thought: From Maimonides to Abravanel* (Oxford: Oxford University Press, 1986), 207–213. Further on this, see Marc Shapiro, *The Limits of Orthodox Theology: Maimonides' Thirteen Principles Reappraised* (London: Littman Library of Jewish Civilization, 2004).

5   The question of whether or not Christianity is *avodah zarah* usually arises in the following contexts. May one enter a church? For one detailed discussion—published under the auspices of the Orthodox Union's Israel Center—see the sources found under the title "Entering Churches and Mosques," www.rabbimanning.com, accessed August 7, 2018. May one participate in a Christian ceremony (see the previous source)? May one accept financial support from Christians and Christian institutions? This latter issue comes up often in Israel today. Prominent opponents include R. Shlomo Aviner (see forty-two [!] separate pages on his extreme opposition to Christianity at: "Shiurim of Rabbi Shlomo Aviner" [Hebrew], http://shlomo-aviner.net/index.php/%D7%A7%D7%98%D7%92%D7%95%D7%A8%D7%99%D7%94:%D7%A0%D7%A6%D7%A8%D7%95%D7%AA_(%D7%9E%D7%90%D7%9E%D7%A8%D7%99%D7%9D); and R. Eliyahu Zini who devoted a whole book to denouncing

nothing about Hinduism and will leave that discussion to experts who know what they are talking about (such as Rabbi Professor Daniel Sperber and the editor of this volume). Here I wish to deal with the claim that Christianity (in all or some of its many, many forms[6]) is to be considered *avodah zarah* ("alien or foreign worship"). It should be emphasized that this is not a light matter in Jewish eyes: *avodah zarah* is one of the three so-called "cardinal sins" of Judaism: it is settled law that one must submit to martyrdom rather than engage in *avodah zarah*, murder, or commit certain forms of gross sexual immorality.[7] Whether or not Christianity is considered *avodah zarah* is also not a light matter considering the vast numbers of Jews who over the generations who were murdered by Christians (as Christians) or who chose martyrdom over forced conversion to Christianity.[8]

---

the practice, *Ḥesed le-Umim Ḥatat* (Haifa: Yeshivat Or Vishua, 2018). Rabbi Eliezer Melamed (an Israeli Orthodox rabbi and the *rosh yeshiva* of Yeshivat Har Bracha, rabbi of the community Har Bracha, and author of the book series *Peninei Halakhah*) published three articles in the (Settler's) newspaper *Ba-Sheva* (see Eliezer Melamed, "Rabbi Melamed: It is allowed to Receive Funding from the Friendship Foundation," *Ba-Sheva*, June 11, 2014 [Hebrew], accessed August 7, 2018, https://www.inn.co.il/News/News.aspx/277905) in which he uses quotations from Rav Kook to support a basically universalist approach to non-Jews. His main concern is to argue that philo-Jewish Evangelicals are sincere and that Jews may accept financial support from them. Catholics, he maintains (correctly), do not treat statues in their churches as idols, and do not pray to them. He goes so far as to surmise that even Maimonides would be lenient with respect to Protestants. His articles was subjected to detailed, even ferocious criticism by Rabbi Yehonatan Simhah Blass (*Teḥumin* 34 [Sivan 5774/June 2014]). Strictly speaking, if Christianity is *avodah zarah*, then no business may be conducted with Christians in Israel on Sundays, or three days before Sunday (M *Avodah Zarah* 1). I know of no rabbi who actually decides halakhah in this fashion. Many of the most strident opponents of accepting financial or other assistance from Christians (because Christianity is idolatry) claim to be followers of Rav Kook the elder. For an analysis of his actual views see Karma Ben-Johanan, "Wreaking Judgment on Mt Esau: Christianity in R. Kook's Thought," *Jewish Quarterly Review* 106, no. 1 (2016): 76–100 and the sources cited there. The views of his son, Rabbi Z. Y. Kook, are presented in *Judaism and Christianity*, ed. Shlomo Aviner (Jerusalem: Sifriyat Hannah, 2001) [Hebrew].

6   I will ignore the fact that there is no such thing as "Christianity" *simpliciter*—in this I follow most of the many rabbis to whose writings I will allude here.
7   On the three "cardinal sins" see Maimonides, *Mishneh Torah*, Laws of the Foundations of the Torah 2.
8   It ought to be noted that a minority of Orthodox rabbis (some of them quite prominent) argue that Christianity is not *avodah zarah*. See, for example, Chief Rabbi Isaac Herzog's article, *Teḥumin* 2 (1981): 169–199; and Marc Shapiro, "Is It Permissible to Enter a Church? First Publication of a Responsum by Ha-Ga'on R. Eliezer Berkovitz on the Matter," *Milin Havivin* 4 (2011): 43–50. Note further the views of Nachum Rabinovitch, *Melumedei Milḥamah* (Ma'aleh Adumin: Ma'aliyot, 1992), 145); David Shapiro, *Studies in Jewish Thought*, vol. 2 (New York: Yeshiva University Press, 1981), 272–275. It may not be a coincidence that all four of these figures reached rabbinic maturity outside of Israel. See further the "Orthodox Rabbinic Statement at Christianity," Center for Jewish–Christian Understanding

Let me begin by making a number of meta-halakhic points. First, despite what many Orthodox rabbis will tell you, halakhah has a history. Second, as such, it is not a mathematical science, but halakhic decisions reflect the ideological commitments of those making them. This last point is reflected in Blu Greenberg's famous (if perhaps exaggerated) comment that "Where there's a rabbinic will, there's a halakhic way."

2. Christianity/Idolatry?

Such being the case, questions concerning the claim that Christianity is idolatry immediately arise: First, our contemporaries *could* choose to follow the widely accepted dictum that the ancient rabbis destroyed the evil inclination for idolatry.[9] This being the case, there is no real idolatry anymore—rather, contemporary "idolaters" are simply aping, as it were, their forbears, not actually worshipping idols or other false gods. Second, one *could* choose to follow the views of Menachem Meiri (1249–1310) who made something like the following argument: true idolatry always involves morally corrupt behavior; our Christian neighbors are not morally corrupt; therefore, Christianity is not true idolatry.[10] In effect. Meiri anticipated Martin Luther King, Jr.: people should be judged by the content of their characters, not by the church that they attend. Meiri moves the discussion from idolatry to idolaters, from a class to individuals. Individuals whose religion makes them brutal, or allows them to be brutal, are idolaters and their religion is therefore idolatry. People whose religion does

---

& Cooperation, December 3, 2015, http://cjcuc.org/2015/12/03/orthodox-rabbinic-statement-on-christianity/.

9 BT *Avodah Zarah* 17a–b; BT *Sanhedrin* 64a; BT *Yoma* 69b. Compare BT *Sanhedrin* 102b, which implies that the evil inclination for idolatry was strong during the period of the First Temple, but not since its destruction. See further Yitzhak Melamed, "Idolatry and Its Premature Rabbinic Obituary," in *Jewish Philosophy Past and Present: Contemporary Responses to Classical Sources*, ed. Daniel Frank and Aaron Segal (New York: Routledge, 2017), 126–137, here 127. On the expansion of the dictum mentioned here (which originally referred only to idolaters in the Land of Israel), see Jacob Katz, "The Vicissitudes of Three Apologetic Statements," *Zion* 23 (1959): 174–193, esp. 186–193 [Hebrew].

10 The literature on Meiri is vast. It is sufficient here to recommend Alon Goshen-Gottstein's treatment and the sources he cites and discusses in *Same God, Other god* (New York: Palgrave Macmillan, 2015), 107–131; and, in addition, Gerald Blidstein, "Menachem Meiri's Attitude towards Gentiles—Apologetics or Worldview?" *Zion* 51 (1985): 153–166 [Hebrew]; Moshe Halbertal, "'Ones Possessed of Religion': Religious Tolerance in the Teaching of the Meiri," *The Edah Journal* 1, no. 1 (2000); and Gedaliah Oren, "R. Menachem ha-Meiri's Attitude toward the 'Other,'" *Da'at* 60 (2007): 29–49 [Hebrew].

not make them brutal, or allow them to be brutal, are not idolaters, and their religion is not idolatry.[11] This contrasts with the view of Maimonides, who, in many of his writings, focuses on the theology of idolatry, and less on the practice of idolatry. Maimonides changes the focus of idolatry from forbidden behavior to philosophical error.[12] This is, of course, consistent with his attempt to "theologify" Judaism (an attempt that, to my mind, has had unfortunate consequences). Meiri, on the other hand, replaces a theological criterion with a moral criterion. It is not my place here to decide who is more "correct," Maimonides or Meiri, only to point out that both views are found in the tradition. Personally, I have argued (in *Must a Jew*) against Maimonides's attempt to turn Judaism into a "synagogue of true believers," but that issue need not detain us at this point—we simply need to be aware of what he is doing.

With respect to the first of these questions, the issue should be quite simple; the Talmud teaches us that contemporary idolaters are not really idolaters, since the evil impulse of idolatry has been extirpated from the cosmos. But, and there is always a but, that is not the way halakhah works. Relatively isolated aggadic statements such as the one about the extirpation of the idolatrous impulse are often ignored or explained away (unless they involve discrimination against women, in which case they are made core values of Judaism, dating back to Sinai, as it were), but "hard-core" halakhah is not so easy to ignore, especially when it makes cultural and historical sense.

A propos Meiri, a huge amount of energy has been invested in arguing that he did not really mean what he wrote. On the face of it, this has involved generous portions of special pleading and disingenuous argumentation.[13] I will not

---

11 Meiri ignores Christians who behave brutally. One can make the reasonable argument that since some Christians behave morally and some immorally, Christianity is not the decisive factor in their behavior, whatever they themselves might think. A similar argument must be made with respect to brutal and immoral Jews.

12 This is the overall thesis of my *Must a Jew*. In the context of idolatry, see Moshe Halbertal and Avishai Margalit, *Idolatry* (Cambridge, MA: Harvard University Press, 1992), 31: for Maimonides heresy is the opposite of knowledge, not the opposite of belief. Contrasting Maimonides's relatively benign view of the nature of Muslim practice (such as throwing stones with the Kaaba in Mecca), with his condemnation of Christianity without reference to its rituals, sharpens my point here. On Maimonides's exoneration of Islam from the charge of idolatry, see his responsum to Obadiah the Proselyte, cited and discussed in James Diamond, *Converts, Heretics, and Lepers: Maimonides and the Outsider* (Notre Dame: University of Notre Dame Press, 2007), 11–31.

13 The earliest example of this with which I am familiar is an article by J. David Bleich, "Divine Unity in Maimonides, the Tosafists, and Me'iri," in *Neoplatonism and Jewish Thought*, ed. Lenn Goodman (Albany: SUNY Press, 1992), 237–254. It might be argued that since Meiri was largely unknown to the halakhic tradition until only recently, that there is no reason for halakhic decisors to factor his views into their positions. But many of the rabbis who reject

involve myself in that argument here; instead, I refer the reader to what I take to be convincing refutations of these attempts.[14]

Further, as Eugene Korn has shown, the vast majority of medieval and early modern decisors in Ashkenaz found a middle path, originally charted by the Tosafists: Christianity is *avodah zarah* when practiced by Jews, but not when practiced by Gentiles.[15] Alan Brill put the matter well: on this view "Christianity is monotheistic enough for Gentiles."[16]

What appears to follow from all this is that contemporary rabbinic figures who condemn Christianity as idolatry are not *forced* to do so; they *choose* to do so. Why? It seems to me that the answer is obvious. By any measure, Christianity is closer to Judaism than Buddhism is. Christianity has a personal God, thinks of itself as monotheist, and acknowledges the sanctity of Tanakh. In North America, at least, Buddhism appears to be a greater challenge to Jewish continuity than does Xianity: there are certainly far more JUBUs (Jewish Buddhists) than Jews for Jesus. In the Jewish community, the former usually arouse no more than a tolerant smile, while Jews for Jesus arouse great anger. Why? The reason appears to be clear: how many Jews were murdered in the name of Buddha as opposed to those murdered in the name of Jesus? Further, Buddhism does not present itself as the fulfillment of Judaism, and Buddhists do not claim to be *verus Israel*.

3. Christianity/Idolatry—Maimonides

I assume that most of you reading this essay will find this explanation convincing. However, halakhah does not work in this fashion. Precedent must be found for halakhic decisions. As it turns out, there is a very clear precedent for the claim that Christianity is idolatry in the writings of the greatest halakhist of all

---

    Christianity as idolatry belong to the (allegedly) more modern camp (as opposed to the Haredi world, which has a hard time integrating Meiri into their worldviews). Thus, they *could* use Meiri as a precedent vis-à-vis Christianity. They *choose* not to.

14 See above, note 10.

15 Eugene Korn, "Rethinking Christianity: Rabbinic Positions and Possibilities," in *Jewish Theology and World Religions*, ed. Alon Goshen-Gottstein and Eugene Korn (Oxford: Littman Library of Jewish Civilization, 2012), 189–215, here 196–197.

16 See Alan Brill, *Judaism and Other Religions: Models of Understanding* (New York: Palgrave Macmillan, 2010), 179.

time, Maimonides. All the sources I have found which claim that Christianity is idolatry begin their analyses with Maimonides.[17]

Thus, even though it was Maimonides, the Andalusian, who convicted Christianity of idolatry, his decision was widely (but not universally) adopted in an Ashkenazi Europe whose Jews suffered great persecution on the part of Christendom, and who were familiar, to one degree or another, with aspects of Christianity.[18]

While I cannot claim to have made an exhaustive survey of every rabbinic authority who condemns Christianity as idolatry, I have certainly examined quite a few. I have yet to find an exception to the following statement: Maimonides is the halakhic authority upon whom all others base their claim that Christianity is idolatry—and those who deny that Christianity is idolatry are forced to contend with Maimonides.[19] Maimonides, however, does not explain his position at all.[20] He simply repeatedly states that Christianity is idolatry and accepts the halakhic consequences of that view (including not conducting business with Christians three days before Sundays—their idolatrous holiday—using wine touched by Christians, entering their places of worship, and so forth), but he never explains why he condemns Christianity as idolatry.

It is, of course, not hard to understand why he would do so: the *doctrines* of incarnation, trinity, virgin birth are enough in themselves to explain why Maimonides (and not only Maimonides) would likely view Christianity as out-and-out idolatry. Added to that the fact that he was probably aware of Christian *practices* such as image worship, veneration of relics, and so on, it easy to understand why he would condemn Christianity as *avodah zarah*.

There are, however, a number of texts from which one can deduce the reasons for Maimonides's opposition to Christianity. I propose to examine them, one by one, in chronological order. These texts are not part of the standard yeshiva syllabus and are often ignored by halakhists.

---

17 For an exhaustive survey for places in which Maimonides treats of Christianity, see Dror Fixler and Gil Nadal, "Are Christians Today Idolaters?," *Teḥumin* 22 (2002): 68–78 [Hebrew].
18 Here is a good place to inform readers that Maimonides himself knew more about Christianity than is ordinarily thought to be the case. See Daniel J. Lasker, "Rashi and Maimonides on Christianity," in *Between Rashi and Maimonides: Themes in Medieval Jewish Thought, Literature and Exegesis*, ed. Ephraim Kanarfogel and Moshe Sokolow (New York: Yeshiva University Press, 2010), 3–21.
19 Maimonides does not view Christianity solely through the lens of idolatry. He saw Christianity as part of God's plan to prepare the world for the coming of the (true) Messiah; see his *Mishneh Torah*, Laws of Kings 11:4 (in the uncensored texts).
20 As noted by Fixler and Nidal, "Are Christians Today Idolaters?," 70, 71.

4. Objection

At this point note should also be made of a possible objection to the line of argument I am developing here. According to that argument halakhists after Maimonides ignored his own reasons for his positions, and treated them as technical precedents without reference to why Maimonides arrived at them himself. (This parallels my argument, in *Dogma* and in *Must a Jew*, to the effect that Maimonides's principles of faith were accepted—to the extent they were accepted—shorn of their philosophical basis.) Might it not be countered that in his halakhic writings Maimonides does precisely what I accuse subsequent halakhists of doing, namely, deciding halakhah technically according to accepted rules, with no reference to the philosophic basis that (possibly) motivated the halakhic opinions adopted? This is a large issue, and here I can only deal with it schematically.

First, unlike in "standard" halakhah, in the two cases here mentioned (principles of faith, status of Christianity), Maimonides breaks new ground and is not simply applying standard decision procedures (*kelalei ha-psak*). It therefore makes excellent sense for halakhists also to wonder why he arrived at his positions.[21] Second, it is not the case that Maimonides's halakhah is divorced from his philosophy: witness the first four chapters of *Mishneh Torah* (Laws of the Foundations of the Torah 1–4); the final paragraphs of each of the fourteen volumes of the *Mishneh Torah*;[22] the evidence adduced by Marc Shapiro for the influence of philosophy/science on Maimonides's halakhot concerning what we would call superstition;[23] and generally the investigations of David Hartman and Isadore Twersky on the interplay of law and philosophy in Maimonides's writings.[24] Furthermore, I have argued at great length in my book *Maimonides' Confrontation with Mysticism* that many of Maimonides's philosophical *and*

---

21 But, in fact, they do not, at least so far as I could determine. It is not much use to examine those of his commentators who searched for his precedents, since printed editions of the *Mishneh Torah* generally have "idolaters" (*aku"m*, "worshippers of stars and constellations") where Maimonides wrote "Christians." Those copyists and printers who replaced "Christians" with *aku"m* apparently thought that Christianity was *avodah zarah*.
22 The subject of Menachem Kellner and David Gillis, *Maimonides the Universalist: The Ethical Horizons of Mishneh Torah* (Oxford: Littman Library of Jewish Civilization, forthcoming).
23 Marc Shapiro, *Studies in Maimonides and His Interpreters* (Scranton: University of Scranton Press, 2008).
24 David Hartman, *Maimonides: Torah and Philosophic Quest* (Philadelphia: Jewish Publication Society, 1976); and Isadore Twersky, *Introduction to the Code of Maimonides* (New Haven: Yale University Press, 1980), chap. 6, "Law and Philosophy."

halakhic positions reflect his opposition to what I there call "proto-Kabbalah."[25] I further show there that Maimonides, on philosophical grounds, adopted a form of halakhic nominalism.[26] His philosophy definitely affected his halakhah, and there is no reason to think that such would not be the case with respect to his views of Christianity.

5. So What is Idolatry for Maimonides?

In *Mishneh Torah*, Laws of Idolatry 2:1, Maimonides explains that the essential definition of *avodah zarah* is the worship of any entity other than God.[27] It behooves us therefore to investigate what might count for Maimonides as an entity other than God for purposes of worship. Before beginning a survey of such texts, I will cite one text from near the end of the *Guide of the Perplexed* (3:51, trans. Pines, 620) to set the scene for our discussion (and, by the by, to help us understand what Maimonides means by perfect worship):[28]

> So I'll return to this chapter's theme: having come to know God as I've described, gaining the strength to focus on Him alone. This is the special worship of those who apprehend reality. The more they focus on Him and on abiding in His presence

---

25 Menachem Kellner, *Maimonides' Confrontation with Mysticism* (Oxford: Littman Library of Jewish Civilization, 2006).
26 See Yochanan Silman, *Bein "Lalekhet be-Derakhav" u-"Lishmo'a be-Kolo": Halakhic Instructions as Guiding Principles or as Commands* (Alon Shvut: Herzog College, 2012) [Hebrew]; Yochanan Silman, "Commandments and Transgressions in Halakhah—Obedience and Rebellion, or Repair and Destruction?," *Dine Israel* 16 (1991): 183–201 [Hebrew]; Yochanan Silman, "Halakhic Determinations of a Nominalistic and Realistic Nature: Legal and Philosophical Considerations," *Dine Israel* 12 (1986): 249–266 [Hebrew]; Yochanan Silman, *Kol Gadol ve-Lo Yasaf: Torat Israel bein Shelemut ve-Hishtalmut* (Jerusalem: Magnes Press, 1999); and Yochanan Silman, "Introduction to the Philosophical Analysis of the Normative-Ontological Tension in the Halakha," *Da'at* 31 (1993): v–xx. The reading of Maimonides that Silman and I present has recently been given extensive grounding in a wide variety of texts in Yohai Makbili, "Consciousness and Community: Ritual Impurity and Purity in Maimonides's Thought" (PhD diss., University of Haifa, Haifa, 2018) [Hebrew]. The nominalist understanding of halakhah has been traced back to rabbinic sources in Christine F. Hayes, *What's Divine about Divine Law? Early Perspectives* (Princeton: Princeton University Press, 2015).
27 See also Alon Goshen-Gottstein, *Same God, Other god*, 47–57.
28 I cite the felicitous new translation of Lenn Evan Goodman and Phillip Lieberman (Stanford: Stanford University Press, forthcoming). I also cite the page numbers in Shlomo Pines's translation (Chicago: University of Chicago Press, 1963). My thanks to Lenn Goodman for sharing the translation with me.

the more profound their worship. But one who has all sort of notions about God and has much to say about Him without real knowledge, pursuing some fantasy or someone's dogma, is not just outside the palace and far removed from it but, in my view, does not really speak or think of God at all. For what he speaks of and fancies corresponds to nothing whatever. It's a figment of his imagination, as I explained.

Thus, worship of an entity which is not one and unique in every sense of the term, to which corporeality attaches in any sense of the term, an entity susceptible of passions, an entity which can be changed or swayed, an entity which can love (the Jewish people), an entity which has needs—such worship is *avodah zarah* according to Maimonides.[29] On this account, there are very few Orthodox Jews who are not worshippers of *avodah zarah*!

Technically speaking, for Maimonides *avodah zarah* means worshipping any created thing, even if the worshipper knows that behind or above the worshipped entity, there exists God the Creator (*Mishneh Torah*, Laws of Idolatry 2:1). However, Maimonides also treats idolatry generally as denial of the "great principle" upon which all depends (*Mishneh Torah*, Laws of Idolatry 2:6 and Laws of the Foundations of the Torah 1:6—the nature of that great principle will be treated below). Beyond that, Maimonides holds belief in God's corporeality to be worse than idolatry (*Guide* 1:36), since such belief denies God's unity.[30] He also expands the notion of idolatry to include magical practices, such as the use of talismans, the belief in spirits that can be caused to descend and impact upon us, demons, desert ghouls, and other such phenomena (*Guide* 3:29, trans. Pines, 517–518).

---

29 While Maimonides devotes much attention to the obligation to love God, I have seen only one place where he mentions God's love of any of His creatures (drawn to my attention by Zev Harvey): *Mishneh Torah*, Laws of Idolatry 1:3 near the end). This is quite remarkable in light of the prevalence of expressions of God's love for His people in the Jewish liturgy, not to mention in the blessings of the Shema. Maimonides was consistent in denying to God any human affections.
30 Harry Wolfson, "Maimonides on the Unity and Incorporeality of God," *JQR* 56 (1965): 112–136; and *Guide* 2:31: idolatry is forbidden in order to protect God's unity (trans. Pines, 539).

6. Maimonidean Monotheism

Let us now turn to our survey. In his commentary to the Mishna Maimonides famously presents his thirteen foundations of faith.[31] He puts them forward as dogmas in the strictest sense of the term.[32] The first five all relate to God.

- The first foundation is the existence of the Creator, may He be praised. . . . He is self-sufficient. . . .
- The second foundation is God's unity, may He be exalted; to wit, that this One, Who is the cause of [the existence of] everything is one. . . . Rather, He, may He be exalted, is one with a oneness for which there is no comparison at all. . . .
- The third foundation is the denial of corporeality to Him; to wit that this One is neither a body nor a force within a body. None of the characteristics of a body appertains to Him, either by His essence or as an accident thereof. . . .
- The fourth foundation is God's precedence;[33] to wit, that this one who has just been described is He who precedes everything absolutely. No other being has precedence with respect to Him. . . . .
- The fifth foundation is that He, may He be exalted, is He whom it is proper to worship and to praise; and [that it is also proper] to promulgate praise of Him and obedience to Him. This may not be done for any being other than Him in reality. . . . Do not, furthermore, seize upon intermediaries in order to reach Him but direct your thoughts towards Him, may He be exalted, and turn away from that which is other than He. This fifth foundation is the prohibition against idolatry and there are many verses in the Torah prohibiting it. . . .[34]

The upshot of these five dogmas is that God is absolutely one, unique, incorporeal, creator of the cosmos (and as such wholly unlike creation), and, crucially for our purposes, to be worshipped directly, without intermediaries. Prayers may not be addressed to angels (as in the Friday eve hymn Shalom Aleichem),

---

31 For the full text and extensive discussion, see my studies cited above in note 4.
32 See his statement at the end of the principles (*Must a Jew*, 173–174) and my analysis of that text in chap. 4 of that book.
33 In the original version of this foundation, Maimonides spoke only of God's logical precedence to the cosmos (the view of Aristotle); later in his life, he added a sentence explicitly referring to creation. For details, see Kellner, *Dogma*, 54–61.
34 I cite the translation as brought in *Must a Jew*, 164ff.

to *sefirot*,³⁵ and certainly may not be addressed to God via various types of rabbis, *rebbes*, miracle workers, and so on.³⁶

In his *Mishneh Torah* Maimonides restates his principles and, in so doing, adds to our understanding of his notion of idolatry. The first of these places is indirect, but very important. It is the very opening of the work as a whole:

> The foundation of all foundations and the pillar of all sciences³⁷ is to realize that there is a First Being who brought every existing thing into being. All existing things, whether celestial, terrestrial, or belonging to an intermediate class, exist only through His true Existence. If it could be supposed that He did not exist, it would follow that nothing else could possibly exist. If, however, it were supposed that all other beings were non-existent, He alone would still exist. Their non-existence would not involve His non-existence. For all beings are in need of Him; but He, blessed be He, *is not in need of them nor of any of them.* . . .³⁸

God's existence is necessary, that of all created things, contingent. By definition, therefore, God is not and cannot be in need of anything outside of God. Worshipping a god for whom the commandments of the Torah are a need (*mizvot tzorekh gavoha*)³⁹ is to worship an entity other than God, that is, to engage in *avodah zarah*.

Maimonides continues:

> This being is the God of the Universe, the Lord of all the Earth. And He it is, who controls the sphere with a power that is without end or limit; with a power that is never intermitted. For the

---

35 Moshe Idel describes *sefirot* as "manifestations that are either part of the divine structure, or directly related to the divine essence, serving as its vessels or instruments." See Moshe Idel, *Kabbalah: New Perspectives* (New Haven: Yale University Press, 1988), 112. Unless taken as entirely metaphorical (which is not the way it is generally taken in kabbalistic texts), the doctrine of *sefirot* must undermine God's unity, even without reference to the question of whether or not prayers be addressed to them.

36 For striking examples of this sort of behavior, see Joel Marcus, "The Once and Future Messiah in Early Christianity and Chabad," *New Testament Studies* 46 (2000): 381–401.

37 For a very detailed exposition of this text, see Menachem Kellner, *Gam Hem Keruyim Adam: Ha-Nokhri be-Einei ha-Rambam* (Ramat-Gan: Bar Ilan University Press, 2016), chaps. 2–5.

38 I cite here and below the translation of Moses Hyamson (New York: Feldheim, 1974), with emendations (and emphasis added).

39 See Morris Faierstein, "God's Need for the Commandments in Medieval Kabbalah," *Conservative Judaism* 36 (1982): 45–59.

> sphere is always revolving; and it is impossible for it to revolve without someone making it revolve. God, blessed be He, it is, who, without hand or body, causes it to revolve. Knowing this thing is an affirmative precept, as it is said *I am the Lord, thy God* (Ex. 20:2; Deut. 5:6). And whoever permits the thought to enter his mind that there is another deity besides this God, violates a prohibition; as it is said *Thou shalt have no other gods before me* (Ex. 20:3; Deut. 5:7), and denies the essence of Religion—this doctrine being the great principle on which everything depends.[40]

It is very important to understand the upshot of this paragraph: the first commandment of the 613 commandments of the Torah is to know something. And what is that thing? That God is Lord of all the earth. And how do we know it? On the basis of an argument relying upon the notion of an uncreated universe (as Maimonides makes clear in *Guide* 1:71). The God Who is to be worshipped without intermediaries, is the God Whose existence must be *known* on the basis of a philosophical argument. Any other object of worship is not God, but an imagining, and, once again, *avodah zarah*.[41]

Further on, Maimonides states:

> Since it has been demonstrated that He is not a body, it is clear that none of the accidents of matter can be attributed to Him.... Nor does He change, for there is nought in Him that would effect a change in Him. He does not die, nor has He life like that of an animal body. Folly is not an attribute of His Being, nor wisdom, like that of a wise man; neither passion nor frivolity; neither joy nor melancholy; neither silence nor speech like that of human beings. And so the sages have said, "Above, there is neither sitting nor standing, neither rigidity nor relaxation."

---

40 Hebrew: וכופר בעיקר שזהו העיקר הגדול שהכל תלוי בו. Note well how Maimonides converts the expression *kofer be-ikkar* from disassociating oneself from the Jewish community (as in the wicked son of the Passover Haggadah), to a theological stance. See my *Must a Jew*, 41, note 27.

41 Let it be noted that in *Guide* 1:34 (trans. Pines, 75–76) Maimonides may have modified this conclusion somewhat. There he distinguishes between fulfilling the First Commandment and satisfying the first principle of faith (knowing correctly that God exists), on the one hand, and avoiding idolatry, on the other. In that passage, one can fail to know God properly without being an out-and-out idolater. But even there, God is to be known through a study of creation (physics). See the text cited from *Guide* 1:34 below.

Change cannot affect a purely incorporeal entity, especially one that is perfect in every possible way. That being so, God cannot change in any way whatsoever. Furthermore, a changeable god is not perfect as he is, and is therefore not God. To have emotions is to change, to be *moved*.[42] A god subject to emotions like joy and melancholy is not God, as is a god who can be swayed by prayer or repentance. A true God is not one the inner workings of which can be aided, as it were, by human actions (be such actions be prayer or the fulfillment of the commandments of the Torah). A god subject to theurgy is no God, but the object of *avodah zarah*.[43]

The fourth of the five parts into which the first volume of *Mishneh Torah* is divided is Laws of Idolatry. Maimonides opens that part with a long historical disquisition on the origins of idolatry—in effect, a natural history of idolatry. This is necessitated by the fact that it is difficult to understand how idolatry arose: after all, the first humans according to the biblical account (Adam and Eve) were certainly not idolaters—so where did it come from?[44] Maimonides presents idolatry here as the outcome of a philosophical mistake. This has an important consequence for our purposes: Maimonides explains *avodah zarah* as mistaken worship, not foreign or alien worship (although such worship is definitely foreign and alien!). Thus, one who worships a god conceived incorrectly is performing *avodah zarah*.

Moving on in *Mishneh Torah*, in Laws of Repentance 3:6, Maimonides writes that "The following have no portion in the world to come, but are cut off and perish, and for their great wickedness and sinfulness are condemned forever and ever." In 3:7 he specifies one of the groups of people here mentioned:

> Five classes are termed sectarians [*minim*]: he who says that there is no God and that the world has no ruler; he who says that there is a ruling power but that it is vested in two or more persons; he who says that there is one Ruler, but that He has a body and has form; he who denies that He alone is the First Cause and Rock of the universe; likewise he who renders worship to

---

42 Note well: attributing personality traits to God is no better than attributing corporeality to Him (*Guide* 1:53, trans. Pines, 119–120).

43 On theurgy in Kabbalah, which Moshe Idel defines as "operations intended to influence the Divinity, mostly in its own inner state or dynamics, but sometimes also in its relationship to man," see Moshe Idel, *Kabbalah: New Perspectives* (New Haven: Yale University Press, 1988), 173–199. The quotation above is from ibid., 157. Maimonides seeks a God above all things human, especially emotion.

44 For the text and a detailed analysis of it, see Kellner, *Maimonides' Confrontation*, 77–79.

anyone beside Him, to serve as a mediator between the human being and the Lord of the universe. Whoever belongs to any of these five classes is termed a sectarian.[45]

On this text, Maimonides's acerbic critic, R. Abraham ben David (Rabad), writes:

> Why has he called such a person [he who says that there is one Ruler, but that He has a body and has form] a sectarian? There are many people greater than, and superior to him, who adhere to such a belief on the basis of what they have seen in verses of Scripture, and even more in the words of the aggadot which corrupt right opinion about religious matters.[46]

I do not believe that Rabad was affirming the corporeality of God (after all, those who do believe in divine corporeality are misled by Torah verses and aggadot that "corrupt right opinion about religious matters"); rather, he was affirming that one is allowed to be mistaken about that issue. But for Maimonides God's corporeality is an issue about which no one is permitted to remain mistaken, not even "little children, women, and the dull and deficient" (*Guide* 1:35, trans. Pines, 81).[47] The important point for our purposes here is that Rabad

---

45 Maimonides, *Mishneh Torah*, trans. Hyamson, 84b. Hannah Kasher subjects the terms in this paragraph to detailed analysis in *Al ha-Minim, ha-Kofrim, ve-ha-Epikorsim be-Mishnat ha-Rambam* (Tel Aviv: Hakibbutz Hameuchad, 2011). Zev Harvey points out that our paragraph parallels the first five of Maimonides's thirteen principles. See his "The Question of God's Incorporeality in Maimonides, Rabad, Crescas, and Spinoza," in *Minḥah Le-Sarah*, ed. S. Rosenberg et al. (Jerusalem: Magnes Press, 1994), 63–78 [Hebrew]. Note well, please, that Maimonides's discussion in this text relates to positions that it is forbidden to hold publicly (following M *Sanhedrin* 10:1, he introduces the various forbidden positions with the term *ha-omer*, "one who says"). For discussion, see Menachem Kellner, "Must We Have Heretics?," *Conversations* 1 (2008): 6–10, https://www.jewishideas.org/article/must-we-have-heretics.
46 I cite the text as translated by Isadore Twersky, *Rabad of Posquieres: A Twelfth-Century Talmudist* (Philadelphia: Jewish Publication Society, 1980), 282. A more moderate version of Rabad's gloss has been preserved. See my *Dogma*, 89.
47 Let it be noted that Maimonides, unlike almost all other medieval figures (Jewish, Christian, or Muslim), held women to be fully human, fully created in the image of God. See Menachem Kellner, "Misogyny: Gersonides vs. Maimonides," in my *Torah in the Observatory: Gersonides, Maimonides, Song of Songs* (Boston: Academic Studies Press, 2010), 283–304. For whatever it might be worth, Maimonides's misogyny is halakhic, not philosophical. Hannah Kasher has recently addressed this issue: see her "Maimonides on the Intellects of Women and Gentiles," in *Interpreting Maimonides*, ed. Charles Manekin and Daniel Davies (Cambridge: Cambridge University Press, 2018), 46–64.

recognizes that Maimonides does not allow for inadvertence (*shegagah*) with respect to theological matters. A sincere mistake about God is still a mistake and constitutes heresy. It follows that worship of a god about which one is objectively mistaken is *avodah zarah*.[48]

The points we have made so far are all based on texts drawn from Maimonides's commentary on the Mishna and his *Mishneh Torah*. Emphasis on the rejection of *avodah zarah* as divergences from philosophical orthodoxy, as it were, is even more clear-cut in the *Guide of the Perplexed*. Let us examine a few passages in the *Guide*:

> For nothing exists but God and His creations—everything besides God; and there's no way of knowing Him but through His creations. They are the evidence for His existence and what we should believe—what should be affirmed or denied of Him. That means one must study the world and learn all about its true nature, explore every field to gather the sure and solid premises to support our theological inquiries. . . . With cosmology and natural science, I don't think you'll have trouble seeing how vital such knowledge of the world is to understanding the real and not fanciful workings of God's rule. . . . Anyone aspiring to human fulfillment must train in logic first, then in mathematics in due sequence, then in the natural sciences, and then in theology. (*Guide* 1:34, trans. Pines, 74)

The upshot of this passage is that if a person worships God without studying God's creation (which, for Maimonides means the study of physics, *ma'aseh bereshit*, and metaphysics, *ma'aseh merkavah*),[49] then the object of that worship is not God, but a figment of the worshipper's imagination. In other words, such worship is *avodah zarah* in the strictest sense of the term. The worship of anyone who approaches God without understanding God's creation to one degree or

---

48   In his statement at the end of this thirteen principles Maimonides defines his principles as dogmas in the strict sense of the term: beliefs taught by the highest religious authority (in this case, the Torah itself), acceptance of which is both a necessary and sufficient condition both for being part of the community of Israel and for achieving a share in the world to come. Rabad clearly saw (and rejected) the implication that there is no possibility of *shegagah*, inadvertence, playing an exculpatory role here.

49   Maimonides consistently identifies *ma'aseh bereshit* with physics and *ma'aseh merkavah* with metaphysics. See, for example, his commentary on M Ḥagigah 2:1; *Mishneh Torah*, Laws of the Foundations of the Torah, ends of chaps. 2 and 4; the introduction to the *Guide* (trans. Pines, 8–9); and the introduction to part 3 of the *Guide* (trans. Pines, 415–416).

another, or who only knows God through traditional Jewish texts, or who only knows God thanks to mystical illumination (as it were) is false, alien worship, *avodah zarah*.

In *Guide* 1:35, Maimonides emphasizes that the God who is to be worshipped is indeed the unmoved mover, not only the Aristotelian sense of an uncaused cause, but in the sense of Abraham Joshua Heschel's (anti-Maimonidean) claim that God is the "most moved mover":[50]

> Don't think that all the caveats in these early chapters about how dark and deep this subject is—how hard to fathom and how rightly kept from the multitude—apply to God's incorporeality and impassivity.... God is not a body and cannot be affected. For affections are changes, and He is untouched by change....

For our purposes, the important points made here are that God is wholly impassive, untouched by change and impervious to all attempts to move God, not only in the physical sense (which is obvious) but in the emotional sense as well. Maimonides connects this imperviousness to being affected to God's incorporeality, which is itself a function of God's absolute unity. Thus, the worship of someone who believes that the commandments of the Torah fulfill a divine need is, once again, *avodah zarah* in the strictest sense of the term—the worship of an entity that is not God. Similarly, the worship of someone who believes that the Tabernacle in the desert and the Temple in Jerusalem were constructed out of divine need is, once again, *avodah zarah* in the strictest sense of the term—the worship of an entity that is not God.[51]

---

50 As long as I have mentioned Heschel, whom Maimonides would certainly have considered an idolater, see Eliezer Berkovits, "Dr. A. J. Heschel's Theology of Pathos," *Tradition* 6 (1964): 67–104.

51 See the following (to me amazing) passage in Nachmanides (on Ex. 29:46): "But Rabbi Abraham ibn Ezra explained [the verse to mean that] the purpose of My bringing them forth from the land of Egypt was only that I might dwell in their midst, and that this was the fulfilment of [the promise to Moses], *you shall serve God upon this mountain* [Ex. 3:12]. He explained it well, and if it is so, there is in this matter a great secret. For in the plain sense of things it would appear that [the dwelling of] of the Divine Glory [*ha-shekhinah*] in Israel was to fulfil a need below, but it is not so. It fulfilled a need above as in the meaning of Scripture, *Israel, in whom I will be glorified* [Is. 49:3]. And Joshua said, [*For when the Canaanites ... hear of it ... and cut off our name from the earth,*] *and what wilt Thou do for Thy great name?* [Josh. 7:9]. There are many verses which express this thought: *He hath desired it* [Zion] *for His habitation* [Ps. 132:13]; *Here I dwell, for I have desired it* [Ps. 132:14]. And it is further written, *and I will remember the land* [Lev. 26:42]." Ramban, *Commentary on the Torah—Exodus*, trans. Charles B. Chavel (New York: Shilo, 1973), 506–507 (emended). See further Nathan Laufer,

In *Guide* 1:36 Maimonides takes up the issue of God's impassiveness again and anticipates later discussions concerning the metaphorical sense in which the Torah attributes pleasure, displeasure, and anger to God.[52] Maimonides also emphasizes the importance of knowing God correctly, claiming that philosophical error about God is worse than idolatry!

> What then of one whose misbelief attaches to God Himself, who believes Him other than He is, denies His existence, or takes Him to be dual or corporeal, passive, or in any way lacking? He is doubtless worse than a pagan who takes idols for intermediaries or claims they can cause good or ill. Be advised, then, if you be such, that when you believe God to be corporeal or subject to any physical state, you have "roused His jealousy and anger, kindled His wrath," become a worse "enemy and foe," far more "hateful to God" than an idolater.

Mistakes about a topic as important as God cannot be allowed, and there is no room for inadvertence, *shegagah*: "If it occurs to you that a corporealist is to be excused because he was brought up as such or was naive or undiscerning, you must hold the same for the idolater: He too worships as he does out of ignorance or tradition: 'They follow the ways of their forebears' (BT Ḥullin 13a)." As in *Mishneh Torah*, Maimonides teaches us here that when it comes to theology, teachings about God, honest mistakes are not exculpatory.[53]

As noted above, in his terms, Maimonides had many reasons for condemning Christianity as *avodah zarah*. But, as also noted above, post-Maimonidean rabbis (and certainly those today) did not have to follow him in that condemnation, they *chose* and *choose* to do so. But, as argued throughout this essay, this comes

---

Rendezvous with God: Revealing the Meaning of the Jewish Holidays and Their Mysterious Rituals (Jerusalem: Maggid, 2016), 206. According to the picture presented here, God desires to live in the world generally, but He wants to dwell in one place more than in all others: among *am Israel* (the Jewish people), in *Eretz Israel* (the Land of Israel), in the Temple. The verse explains that owing to this desire on God's part, there was a need to redeem the Israelites from Egypt, for God could not dwell in their midst so long as they were still enslaved and mired in the forty-ninth level of impurity. On many issues, Nachmanides seems to go out of his way to reject Maimonidean positions. For important examples, see Dov Schwartz, "From Theurgy to Magic: The Evolution of the Magical-Talismanic Justification of Sacrifices in the Circle of Nahmanides and His Interpreters," *Aleph* 1 (2001): 165–213.

52 See Hannah Kasher, "The Myth of 'God's Anger' in the *Guide of the Perplexed*," *Eshel Beersheva* 4 (1996): 95–115 [Hebrew].

53 On *Guide* 1:36, see the detailed discussion in Hannah Kasher, "Between the Idolater and the Believer in God's Corporeality," *Da'at* 61 (2007): 73–82 [Hebrew].

at great expense: consistent halakhic Maimonidean who condemn Christianity as idolatry should also condemn as idolatry much of the Judaism they and their neighbors practice.

7. What to Do?

What precisely is going on here? Maimonides went to great lengths to protect Jews from idolatry, the greatest of sins. In pursuit of this aim, he depopulated the heavens, disenchanted the universe, and sought to lighten the burden of religious observance (as in *Guide* 3:47). He battled against astrology and magic, denying their efficacy, and railing against those (such as Nachmanides) who maintained that magic was forbidden *because* of its efficacy.[54] By the by, he also created Jewish orthodoxy in the strictest sense of the term, introducing the heresy hunting which is so popular a pastime in the Orthodox world (witness the recent battles against "open Orthodoxy" in North America and against non-Orthodox streams of Judaism in the Israeli Knesset).[55] Consistent with his understanding of Judaism primarily in terms of truth, he felt forced to reject as idolatrous Christianity, with its triune god, its incarnationism, its claim that the Messiah had come and that we were already living in a redeemed world. But, as we have seen in this essay, calling Christianity idolatry on Maimonidean grounds is to force one to reject as idolatry much the Judaism of the last thousand years.

A number of paths lie before the intellectually honest and consistent rabbinic decisor:

- One can ignore Maimonides, erase close to a thousand years of rabbinic *psak* on Christianity, ignore the Talmudic claim that idolatry no longer really exists, ignore Meiri, ignore the Tosafists, and find new reasons to condemn Christianity as idolatry.
- One can accept Maimonides and reject most of contemporary Judaism (especially in the Orthodox world) as idolatrous.
- One can admit that for all his greatness, Maimonides's Judaism is simply too abstract, too abstruse, too demanding for actual flesh and blood Jews: Maimonidean Judaism must be taken as an ideal to be aimed at, but not as a criterion by which to judge whether fellow Jews are actually Jewish.

---

54 *Mihsneh Torah*, Laws of Idolatry, end of chap. 11.
55 Arguing against all this is the thrust of my *Must a Jew*.

- One can say that the whole issue is irrelevant today and look for new ways to disagree with fellow Jews and with fellow monotheists, and with fellow humans who may not be monotheists at all but who are, withal, decent human beings.

No one who has read this far will be surprised to discover that I prefer the last two options over the first two.

8. Postscript: What Are We To Do With Maimonides?

I am grateful to the editor of this volume for the opportunity to flesh out the point I made above, to wit: One can admit that for all his greatness, Maimonides's Judaism is simply too abstract, too abstruse, too demanding, and too uncomforting for most actual Jews. Maimonidean Judaism must be taken as an ideal to be aimed at, but not as a criterion by which to judge whether fellow Jews are actually Jewish.

I agree with David Berger that in strict Maimonidean terms Habad is heresy, but disagree with him in that I reject the practical consequences of that view. Similarly, I do not accept the consequences of what I have shown here: that in strict Maimonidean terms almost all Jews today who think they worship God are actually guilty of *avodah zarah*. I do not believe that almost all Jews are worshippers of *avodah zarah*, and are in principle no different from Christians or polytheists. What does that say about my attitude towards Maimonides?

The simplest thing to do is to say that Maimonides was an interesting historical personage, but hardly one to be taken today as anyone's *"rebbe."* In a certain sense, that is obviously the case: no rational thinker can accept Maimonides's physics and metaphysics as adequate accounts of the world.[56] However, this is no solution for those of us for whom Maimonides makes it possible to be Jewish in the cosmos as science teaches us to know it. This view of the universe is very different from the way in which it is described in the first chapters of Genesis. This is no solution for those of us for whom Maimonides makes it possible to live with a Judaism freed of the "hyperrealism," magic, irrationalism, and downright

---

56 See Menachem Kellner, "Maimonides' Allegiances to Torah and Science," *Torah u-Madda Journal* 7 (1997): 88–104; reprinted in Menachem Kellner, *Science in the Bet Midrash: Studies in Maimonides* (Boston: Academic Studies Press, 2009), 217–231.

racism of so much of kabbalistically inflected Judaism.[57] This is no solution for those of us for whom Maimonides makes it possible to practice a Judaism characterized by universalism, rationalism, and the study of God's created cosmos as an integral part of Jewish practice and, indeed, worship. For such Jews, Maimonides is simply indispensable.

A number of approaches suggest themselves for other kinds of Jews. They can ignore what Maimonides actually wrote in favor of what they would have liked him to have written.[58] They can reinterpret him to make him unobjectionable (to them).[59] Hardly an approach available, I assume, to most of the readers of this volume.

Honesty demands that I admit that I pick and choose among Maimonides's positions. As noted, I do not accept his science. I wrote a whole book against his introduction of theological orthodoxy into Judaism. I certainly do not identify with his intellectual elitism.[60] As is clear from this essay, I reject his understanding of *avodah zarah*.

---

57 On "hyperrealism" see Y. Tzvi Langerman, "Science and the *Kuzari*," *Science in Context* 10 (1997): 495–522, here 495. On racism in many (but not all) Kabbalistic texts, see Moshe Hallamish, "The Kabbalists' Attitude to the Nations of the World," *Jerusalem Studies in Jewish Thought* 14 (1988): *Joseph Baruch Sermonetta Memorial Volume*, ed. Aviezer Ravitzky, 289–312 [Hebrew]; and Elliot Wolfson, *Venturing Beyond: Law and Morality in Kabbalistic Mysticism* (Oxford: Oxford University Press, 2006). Two additional and very important studies on this subject are Jerome Gellman, "Jewish Mysticism and Morality: Kabbalah and Its Ontological Dualities," *Archiv fuer Religionsgeschichte* 9 (2008): 23–35; and Hanan Balk, "The Soul of a Jew and the Soul of a Non-Jew: An Inconvenient Truth and the Search for an Alternative," *Hakirah: The Flatbush Journal of Jewish Law and Thought* 16 (2013): 47–76.

58 See, for example, Menachem Kellner, "*Farteitcht un Farbessert* (On 'Correcting' Maimonides)," *Me'orot* 6, no. 2 (2007), http://library.yctorah.org/files/2016/07/Kellner-on-Rambam-FINAL.pdf.

59 This is the burden of the essays collected in James Diamond and Menachem Kellner, *Reinventing Maimonides in Contemporary Jewish Thought* (London: The Littman Library of Jewish Civilization, 2019).

60 Hearing me talk about his elitist views once so annoyed my wife that I posted a list of Maimonides's mistakes on our refrigerator, so she would be angry with him, not me. On his elitism, see Kellner, *Maimonides' Confrontation*, 15–17; and Daniel Rynhold and Michael J. Harris, *Nietzsche, Soloveitchik, and Contemporary Jewish Philosophy* (Cambridge: Cambridge University Press, 2018), 268–277. Maimonides's elitism was intellectual, not social: there is much evidence that he suffered fools, if not gladly, at least patiently. See, for example, his account of his daily schedule in his famous letter to Samuel ibn Tibbon, translator of the *Guide of the Perplexed* into Hebrew, and, for another example, Paul Fenton, "A Meeting with Maimonides," *Bulletin of the School of Oriental and African Studies* 45 (1982): 1–5. The letter to ibn Tibbon may be found in Maimonides, *Iggerot ha-Rambam*, ed. Y. Sheilat (Jerusalem: Ma'aliyot, 2007), 530–554; and in English in Maimonides, *Letters of Maimonides*, ed. Leon D. Stitskin (New York: Yeshiva University Press, 1977), 130–136.

Does that make me any the less a Maimonidean? On the contrary, accepting Maimonides's teachings uncritically would perhaps be the least Maimonidean thing I could do. Maimonides was not searching for *hasidim*. It is his example, not his teachings, that should be our lodestar. His is the example of an extremely learned Jew (to put it mildly!) who is devoted to Torah and to the people of Israel (in the narrow and also in the messianic sense of the term); who is unwilling to close his eyes to the simple teaching of Torah that all human beings are equally made in the image of God; who is unwilling to turn off his brain; and who is unwilling to give in to the siren call of magic and irrationalism.[61]

---

[61] My thanks to Karma Ben-Johanan, Yehudah Gellman, Alon Goshen-Gottstein, Raphael Jospe, Jolene S. Kellner, Eugene Korn, Avrom Montag, Ido Pachter, Daniel Rynhold, Kenneth Seeskin, and Zephaniah Waks for perceptive comments on earlier drafts of this essay. Full disclosure: I am a signatory to "Dabru Emet—A Jewish Statement on Christians and Christianity," http://www.jcrelations.net/Dabru_Emet_-_A_Jewish_Statement_on_Christians_and_Christianity.2395.0.html. Further full disclosure: Upon our *aliyah* in 1980, my wife and I were surprised to discover that the line "they bow down to vanity and emptiness," which had been censored from the *Alenu* prayer, had been reintroduced in the prayerbooks used in our community (*Rinat Yisrael*). We chose not to say those words, then, and now. A revised version of this chapter appeared in Menachem Kellner, *We Are Not Alone: A Maimonidean Theology of the Other* (Boston: Academic Studies Press, 2021).

CHAPTER 15

Return of the Gods: A Jeux d'Esprit on Idolatry in Judaism[1]

Norman Solomon

Introduction

The Bible is vehemently and consistently dismissive of what it castigates as idolatry; for all its pleas for justice, compassion, and love it rarely expresses anything but outrage and contempt towards image-worship and those who practice it. Throughout Scripture, idolatry is presented as the worst of sins, the ultimate act of betrayal of God.

Some biblical prophets predict the eventual recognition of God by all but, as noted by the rabbis, they do not call for the active elimination of idolatry other than in the Land of Israel.[2] Early Christians, as hostile to idolatry as Jews were, smashed some pagan images, turned others into icons of saints, and from time to time reverted to smashing even those, as in the iconoclasm of the eighth and ninth centuries or, more recently, in Puritan England. Muslims have been more consistent in their rejection of image-based worship.

Should we still turn to Bible or Talmud for guidance in our relationships with "idolaters"? In practice, prudence or self-interest may dictate how to behave. Most Jews today not only embrace the values of tolerance and inclusiveness on which modern, secular society is based, but draw on traditional texts—if questionably

---

1 Much of the material in this essay is shared with Chapter 11 of Norman Solomon, *Making Sense of "God"* (Eugene, OR: Wipf and Stock, forthcoming).
2 "Scripture says, 'You shall destroy their name from that place' (Deut. 12:3)—you are commanded to pursue them in the Land of Israel, but you are not commanded to pursue them beyond the Land" (*Sifre, Re'eh* 61).

interpreted—to endorse them. In an interconnected world, where all nations depend for survival on the ability to cooperate peacefully, it would be madness to rekindle the animosities and violent conflicts of a bygone age. So far as *practical* politics is concerned, Deuteronomy's call to smash idols is rightly ignored.

This settles the socio-political issue but leaves the religious self-understanding in a quandary. Should I look on the Hindus, or the Christians with their image-based worship, let alone the image-shunning Muslims, as fellow-seekers after truth, with access to profound religious truths, if with a way of articulating them different from my own? Or should I, while working with them in the common interest in the public sphere, continue to regard them privately as deluded enemies of God and religion? If, as is the case, I unhesitatingly take the former path, how do I square this with my tradition?

Interesting as that question is, the one I am going to address is more personal. The Bible contains far more condemnation of the idolatry of the Israelites than of that of the "nations"; Jeremiah (2:11) even censures Israel for being less faithful to God than the nations are to their false gods. So I shall turn the spotlight inwards, to ask whether idolatry in some form is still to be found within myself and my fellow-Jews. Had I been among the Israelites who left Egypt and heard the voice of God at Sinai, would I have joined a few weeks later in the worship of the golden calf?

The Talmud poses a similar question. It is said that when Rav Ashi, the great fifth-century Babylonian teacher, spoke disparagingly of the idolatrous king Manasseh, Manasseh appeared to him in a dream with the rebuke, "Had you been [where I was], you would have taken hold of my coattails and run after me!" (BT *Sanhedrin* 102b).

Ezra or his contemporaries, the Sages tell us, prayed that the *yetser ha-ra* (evil inclination) for idolatry be removed from Israel (BT *Arakhin* 32b; BT *Sanhedrin* 64a). Were they suggesting that human nature had changed, or just that the circumstances were different? Either way, no-one today is likely in the literal sense to worship a golden calf; it doesn't appeal, it doesn't even make sense to us. Human nature may not have changed, but human understanding of the world has moved on; idolatry now will not take the same forms as it did when our ancestors danced around the golden calf or ran after Manasseh, king of Israel, to worship idols.

Talking of Gods

Idolatry, as portrayed in the Hebrew Scriptures, is the substitution of false gods for the true God, or the representation of the true God by an image. This sounds clear enough, but it does not translate easily into today's language. Before we can assess what constitutes idolatry today we must take note of the ways in which talk about "God" or "gods" has changed since Bible times; if you cannot recognize the true God, you cannot recognize the impostor either.

In the ancient world people spoke about "great ones," or "gods" (in biblical Hebrew *elohim* carries both meanings), without raising abstract metaphysical issues about their ontological status; in the absence of firm scientific knowledge it was perfectly reasonable to imagine superhuman beings stirring up the sea or making corn grow in the fields. Against this background, Israel's claim that there was One, supreme God, was essentially a *denial*; it meant that human affairs were *not* controlled by several powerful, conflicting superhuman agents. The Bible, for the most part, does not deny that there are superhuman agents—the prologue to Job has a graphic illustration—but just that any of them possess real power; power is entirely in the hands of the One God, the only God worshipped by Israel, with whom he has a special bond. Sometimes, as in Ps. 82, the Bible portrays God as the greatest and most just of the gods; elsewhere, for instance in the final chapters of Isaiah, he is the *only* God. The theology varies, but the Bible rarely leaves room for doubt that God is *alive, alert, in control of events, righteous, and caring*. Now and then he talks to people, sometimes through a prophet or angel, but sometimes in person. Even Job, despite his sense of injustice, doesn't doubt that ultimately God is both all-powerful and just, if inscrutable; Kohelet is perhaps more skeptical.

Things changed when Greeks such as Anaxagoras, questioning their own traditions, reduced the god-talk of Homer, Hesiod, and the ancients to little more than metaphor. Medieval Jews, Christians, and Muslims absorbed Greek philosophy; they identified the personal, interventionist God of the Bible with the impersonal "First Cause" of Aristotle or the One of Plotinus. The true God became the ineffable, invisible One whose being could not be expressed in human terms; the Bible, through metaphors, conveyed his relationship with us, but not his essence, which transcends our understanding. Jews, Christians, and Muslims agreed that there was only one supreme Power, even though they gave different accounts of its revelation. Philosophers adduced rational proofs for God's existence and attempted to list the divine attributes; mystics proclaimed the inadequacy of human reason to reach God.

Enlightenment philosophy and scientific and technological progress raised new questions. Science has relieved us of the need to invoke special acts of a supernatural being to explain a thunderstorm or the changing seasons, and religious phenomena increasingly elude the modern world's grasp. At most God is "what lies behind it all," which does nothing to explain particular things. If philosophers concern themselves with God it is often not to demonstrate His superiority or to prove His existence (or non-existence), but rather to explore what people *mean* when they use the word "god." What does "god language" tell us that cannot be expressed in the purely scientific language?

What is Idolatry?

Somehow, we must get behind the conventional "god"-based language and discover the human reality that generated the impulse to idolatry. We may find that human nature has changed little; the human factors that in the past led to idolatry still operate, if not quite in the same way. How can we recognize them?

Recall the story of the *aqeda*, the binding of Isaac. God said to Abraham, "Take your son, your only son, whom you love, Isaac . . . and offer him up to me as a burnt offering" (Gen. 22:2); when Abraham was about to bring down the knife for the slaughter, a lamb was substituted for the sacrifice. Abraham had passed the test of obedience; to this day the story is retold as a paradigm of faith in God.

That, at least, is how tradition reads the story. Yet the first people to hear it would have heard it rather differently, as a polemic against idolatry, in particular against the sacrifice of children to Moloch.[3] The lesson to Abraham and through him to the world is that God wants obedience, not child sacrifice. Abraham, even though he did not actually sacrifice his son, was no less obedient or pious than people who did; but his God was one who for whom human sacrifice was an abomination.

Child sacrifice was sufficiently entrenched in ancient Israel to warrant condemnation in law (Lev. 18:21; Deut. 18:10), to be accounted the great sin of several Kings of Israel including Manasseh (2 Kgs. 16:3, 17:17, 21:6, 23:10; 2 Chron. 33:6) as well as of Israel and Judah in general (2 Kgs. 17:17), and to have generated shockwaves in connection with Jephthah's daughter (Judg. 11:34–40), the rebuilding of Jericho (1 Kgs. 16:34), and the firstborn sacrifice by Mesha king of Moab (2 Kgs. 3:27).[4] God abhors child sacrifice, it is the archetype of idolatry, the justification for Israel to dispossess the nations of Canaan: "For they perform for their gods every abhorrent act that the Lord detests; they even

---

3   Walter Burkert, *Homo Necans: The Anthropology of Ancient Greek Sacrificial Ritual and Myth*, trans. Peter Bing (Berkeley: University of California Press, 1983 [original German ed.: Berlin: de Gruyter, 1975]), chap. 5, 35–48, surveys human sacrifice in the ancient Mediterranean. Burkert underplays the ritualization of gratitude and gifting. Moloch has been identified with various Near Eastern gods, most notably Hadad (Assyrian Adadmilki).
4   See Morton Smith, "A Note on Burning Babies," *Journal of the American Oriental Society* 95, no. 3 (July–September 1975): 477–479.

offer up their sons and daughters in fire to their gods" (Deut. 12:31). Idolatry is abhorrent because of its intimate connection with injustice and immorality.

Why on earth would anyone ever have agreed, let alone desired, to sacrifice their beloved children to the gods? Shocking as it appears to us now, they might well have done so out of what, from their perspective, appeared the purest motives. Surely, people would have argued, you should not approach a god with less respect than a mortal ruler, to whom you would bring valuable gifts and be prepared to hand over your sons for his army and your daughters for his harem. Whether you wanted to express gratitude, curry favor, or avert wrath, you would offer nothing but the best. To offer your child, your precious firstborn, expresses awe, fear, obedience, and even, in its distorted way, love for the one to whom the sacrifice is offered. But it is quintessentially idolatrous, since it places those limited values over all other considerations, making of them an idol, a false god.

Much the same goes for sacred prostitution, of both males and females, another major target of Biblical writers. Love, including sexual love, is among the highest values, but removed from its proper context and elevated to independent status it becomes a false god, an abomination.

In sum, idolatry occurs when we take some idea or principle that, in a limited context, has positive value, and make it into an absolute, driving out other considerations. This remains a common feature of human activity, whether individual or collective.

The True Believer

Philosophers, *contra* Plato, rarely make good leaders; leadership demands conviction and enthusiasm, not disinterested speculation. A charismatic leader stirs a crowd to fervent chanting of *Shema Israel*, or *Allahu Akhbar*; an army marches in the name of Christ; citizens stand in solidarity as they sing an anthem; a crowd of fans on the terrace chant the slogan of a football club. Heat rather than light is generated. You declare what you stand for, where you belong; those who do not join you are the enemy, or at least the "other." You may not have a clear concept of what you are shouting or singing, but you are fully committed.

Moses Maimonides (1138–1204) wrote:

> As for someone who thinks and frequently mentions God, without knowledge, following a mere imagining or a belief adopted because of his reliance on the authority of somebody else, he is to my mind outside the habitation and far away from it and does

not in true reality mention or think about God. For that thing which is in his imagination and which he mentions in his speech does not correspond to any being at all and has been invented by his imagination.[5]

Does it matter? It is much easier to get people to assent to a creed than it is to get them to make any sense of it. Memorize your catechism first, study it later. This is how we teach children; first say and do, you will gradually come to understand (we hope!). People generally sign up to a religion because that's what their parents did before them, and that's what their peer group does. It's how they *belong*, which is very important, but calls for commitment rather than comprehension. How and why their ancestors first made the commitment has long been forgotten; it may have been out of conviction, though it was more likely because they perceived it was in their interest to follow the ruler at the time; even the Talmud (BT *Shabbat* 88a) suggests that God uprooted Sinai and threatened to bury the Israelites under it if they didn't accept his commandments. Voluntary or not, in a generation or two the commitment becomes the cherished tradition.

Unfortunately, when a tradition is cherished without understanding it becomes corrupted. The old gods return. Disguised. "This is not idolatry," they proclaim, "there are no sticks and stones!" but the essence is there even though no rule is broken. The Sages of the Talmud recognized that many forms of behavior, though not halakhically idolatry, shared its essential character: "Who averts his eyes from [giving] charity is an idolater" (BT *Ketubot* 68a); "Who appoints an unsuitable judge is an idolater" (BT *Avodah Zarah* 52a); "Who follows his base instinct is an idolater" (PT *Nedarim* 9:1, 41b); "Who fails to keep his word is an idolater" (BT *Sanhedrin* 92a). In all these cases something, or somebody (avarice, injustice, desire, falsehood) displaces God to direct our behavior. The gods return as projections of the self and its desires—not indeed as "sticks and stones," but as that which takes the place of God to govern our lives. Money, power, sex play their roles.

On the Varieties of Idolatry

Other disguises are more subtle. The prophet (Moses) has passed on. His words are preserved through an institution, created by followers to promote his vision

---

5   Maimonides, *Guide of the Perplexed* 3:51, trans. Shlomo Pines (Chicago: University of Chicago Press, 1963), 620.

and to regulate society in accordance with his teachings. Institutions are perpetuated by administration, not inspiration, and administration has its own logic, devised for its self-preservation. If you are a visionary like Moses or Isaiah and you call for submission to One-God-Creator-of-Heaven-and-Earth-and-No-Other, or if like the Buddha you reject personal gods and seek nirvana through the Four Noble Truths and the Noble Eightfold Path, once your vision becomes institutionalized (a religion, a church, a party) it will be subject to institutional pressures. Your first disciples (priests and teachers, saints and preachers) may transmit your words with understanding; their successors will repeat them, if with less understanding; the faithful masses will voice assent but at the same time cling fast to the comforting straws of image, habit, superstition, magic, and amulet ("popular religion"). The Torah scroll is reduced to a holy icon, paraded and touched and kissed while its commandments are ignored; the Haj becomes a social occasion to be enjoyed in maximum comfort and ostentation; the Hindu Temple develops as a focus for tourism and as a base for the marketing of amulets, holy water, relics, and such paraphernalia; Christmas reverts to Saturnalia and shopping. The old gods steal back, cloaked in the vestments of the new faith.

If institutions are prone to corruption, would it perhaps be better to dispense with them altogether, and to rely on prophets and visionaries? Not at all. Where all may prophesy, chaos reigns. Human society functions through leaders and institutions; they are essential for education, social well-being, cooperation in the common good. But we must constantly exercise vigilance to ensure our institutions are not corrupted. Inevitably there will be conflicting claims as to what is the correct interpretation of the original vision; compromise is essential.

Idols of the Tribe

New gods are recruited to the pantheon. For instance, Euhemerus (c. 300 BCE, he was one of the first Greeks to write about Jews) composed a fictional travelogue in which he traced the origin of personal gods, including Zeus, back to human heroes, among them Herakles (Hercules).[6] We identify with heroes, and through them aspire to immortality.

A footballer, a film-star, a singer, even the occasional politician becomes the focus of the group's existence; their opinion on any matter is the one to follow, their behavior is the model to emulate, their mode of dress dictates fashion.

---

6   I follow the interpretation given by Marek Winiacyk, *The "Sacred History" of Euhemerus of Messene* (Berlin and Boston: de Gruyter, 2013).

People talk of "gods of stage and screen," a celebrated opera singer is referred to as a "diva" (goddess), pilgrimages ae made to shrines such as Graceland as they have from time immemorial been made to the graves of saints. Of course, no one seriously proclaims modern cultural icons as gods—"only a metaphor, or a hyperbole." But perhaps that is just what the ancients were thinking when Hercules, or the Emperor Augustus, was accorded divine honors; Constantino Brumidi, when he created the fresco *The Apotheosis of Washington* still visible through the dome in the rotunda of the United States Capitol Building was not seriously proposing that Washington had become God.

In Judaism the phenomenon is most obvious in the figure of the Hasidic *rebbe*, or *tzaddik*, as possessing a specially exalted soul. The Vilna Gaon, the Chasam Sofer, the Chazon Ish, the latest fashionable *rosh yeshiva*, though not Hasidim, enjoy comparable exalted status among their followers; their rulings constitute unchallengeable *da'at Torah*, they are never to be charged with ignorance or error, their lives are taken as exemplary, pilgrimages are undertaken to their graves (if known). The price is high: criticism is muted, history falsified, change inhibited, fragmentation—since charismatic leaders differ in their opinions—perpetuated.

Footballers, film-stars, singers, politicians, *rebbes*, and *rosh yeshivas* all have significant roles to play in society, and many of them are excellent, even outstanding individuals, deserving of admiration and respect. Only when admiration and respect become slavish, exclusive and obsessive do we cross the line to idolatry.

Idols of the Theater[7]

M *Avodah Zarah* 4:7 relates that the Sages were asked in Rome, "If [your God] doesn't want the worship of idols, why doesn't he destroy them?" "They replied, 'If people worshipped things that were of no use to the world, he would indeed destroy them. But they worship the sun, the moon, the stars, and the constellations. Should he destroy his world on account of fools?' [The philosophers replied,] 'Then let him destroy [the useless] idols and leave those for which the world has need!' 'If he did that,' [responded the Sages], 'it would bolster the argument of the others, who would say, What we worship must truly be gods, for he has not destroyed them!'"

---

[7] The phrase was coined by Francis Bacon for "idols that have immigrated into men's minds from the various dogmas of philosophies" (*Novum Organum* XXXIV, XXXIX); it seems apt for ideologies in general.

The object of idolatry need not be intrinsically bad; sun, moon, and stars are declared by God himself to be good (Gen. 1). It is not the sun that makes sun-worship bad, but treating the sun, in place of, or in addition to God, as an object of worship. The sun is merely an instrument through which God brings life, one among many such instruments; to privilege it above all others and above its Maker constitutes idolatry.

Just as people make heavenly bodies into gods, they make ideas into gods. A powerful idea grips the imagination, is adopted as an ide*ology*; it is invoked as infallible guide to life and is called upon to save in troubled times. Ideologies function like gods and celebrities; "ism" tacked on to a word is a warning sign. Not that there is anything necessarily wrong with national*ism*, social*ism*, Zion*ism*, conservat*ism*, vegetarian*ism*, liberal*ism*, and the like. But the danger is there; will the "ism" become an absolute, the exclusive answer to humanity's problems, a god to be unquestioningly obeyed?

Socialism, for instance, calls for public rather than private ownership or control of property and natural resources; everyone who contributes to the production of a good is entitled to a share in it; society as a whole should own or at least control property for the benefit of all its members. Given the right circumstances, public ownership of property and natural resources can contribute to the common benefit; it is at least an option worth considering. However, the thoroughgoing Marxist ideology that denounces all other "systems" as exploitative and unjust and calls for their overthrow by revolution is another matter; in this extreme form the ideology has become a false god.

Then there are nationalist ideologies. Zionism is a specifically Jewish form, the original aim of which was to support the reestablishment of a Jewish homeland in the historic Land of Israel; it reflected the aspirations of a large section of European Jewry at a time when modern European nation-states were in the process of formation and many Jews felt excluded from the new nationalisms. Its appeal increased as a consequence of the Holocaust; with the establishment of Israel it morphed from a movement to *create* a Jewish state into a movement to *support* the Jewish state. Zionism today covers anything from goodwill towards the State of Israel to the hard doctrine that all Jews should live in the Land of Israel, the biblical boundaries should be reestablished, and there is no future for Jews outside the Land. Extreme Zionism has parallels in other exclusive nationalisms; it marks the stage at which nationalism crosses the boundary from cultural bond to false god.

The Bible is wary of the idea of Israel as a "nation like other nations." When the people were about to demand of Samuel: ". . . there shall be a king over us, so we will be like all the nations" (1 Sam. 8:19–20) God warned him, "It is not you they have rejected, but Me" (1 Sam 8:7). Why then did God nevertheless instruct Samuel to appoint a king for them? Kings and nationhood were not bad in themselves. What was wrong was the idea that Israel's success and prosperity depended on such institutions, rather than on obedience to God's word; this ideology undermined God's rule, amounting to an abandonment of him, that is, idolatry. But if king and nation remained subservient to God (as Deut. 17) such an arrangement could be, and was, accommodated.

The books of Samuel and Kings, like the Torah itself, link Israel's fortunes at any particular time to her faithfulness to God. History is cyclic, not directed to a predetermined end; there is no eschatology. David, the favorite, chosen by God, committed errors, and despite Nathan's promise "thy house and thy kingdom shall be established for ever" (2 Sam. 7:16) narrowly averted death only by his timely repentance (2 Sam. 12:12–13). God's promises are conditional.

When in late Second Temple times the idea of the once-and-for-all-time Messiah crystallized, it polarized opinion, spawned religious sects, contributed to two futile wars against Rome, and has generated—and continues to generate—false hopes and tragedies such as the Sabbetai Zevi episode. As an article of faith that offers hope and reassurance to suffering people it has been of value; it made sense at a time when people believed that the whole existence of the human race on earth would be no more than a few thousand years, most of which had already passed, and we were nearing the end. But perceptions have changed. To promote the idea nowadays that a king of Israel will take control and initiate an era of universal peace and justice to last until the end of the time is an atavistic distraction from the world's real problems; reestablishing the dynasty of David and building a Temple on Mount Zion would do nothing to avert ecological disaster or to diminish conflict among nations. Even the more nuanced nineteenth-century Reform interpretation of Messiah as the era of inexorable, universal human progress rings hollow now in the light of the horrors of the twentieth century.

Messianic ideologies nevertheless continue to abound like the idols of old, by no means exclusively or even principally among Jews, whether in the form of religious cults or political movements. People crave a simple, once-for-all solution to all their problems, and that is what Messiah promises. The gods return, with deceitful promises of salvation, while God, who merely asks that you "do justice, love goodness, and walk modestly with your God" (Mic. 6:8), is conveniently sidelined.

Magic and Astrology

Micah is just as emphatic about what God does *not* want as he is about what God *does* want: "And I will cut off witchcrafts out of thy hand; And thou shalt have no more soothsayers; And I will cut off thy graven images and thy pillars out of the midst of thee" (Mic. 5:11–12).

Magic, witchcraft, and sorcery are explicitly forbidden by the Torah (Ex. 22:17; Lev. 19:26, 31; Deut. 18:10, 11); Deutero-Isaiah roundly condemns "astrologers, star-gazers, monthly prognosticators" (Isa. 47:13). The biblical strictures on magic and astrology were in principle upheld by the Sages. Even so, some of them endorsed spells and other magical procedures for the cure of various ailments (BT *Shabbat* 66b) and demonstrated magic techniques such as the ability to fill a field with cucumbers (BT *Sanhedrin* 68a). Such matters persisted in popular Jewish culture. Hebrew and Aramaic amulets and incantation bowls from the first to eighth centuries CE have been recovered by archaeologists; "Jewish magic" was held in high repute in late antiquity, not only in Alexandria, but in Mesopotamia and Iran.[8]

Maimonides, almost alone among premodern Jewish thinkers, categorically denied the reality of magical phenomena. He identified angels "naturalistically" with the intelligences of heavenly spheres and interpreted stories of their appearance as visions. He was particularly scathing about what he regarded as superstition, including astrology. Proclaiming that all such practices were in essence idolatrous, since they ascribe power to something other than God, he wrote:

> All such matters are falsehood and deceit with which the idolaters of old misled the nations to follow them and it is not fitting that Israel, who are wise, should be attracted by such rubbish or consider that there is any use for it. . . . Whoever believes in such things and thinks that they are true and clever but that the Torah forbids them is a fool and an ignoramus and classed with women and children whose intellect is imperfect. But the wise and pure of intellect know by clear demonstration that all these things that the Torah forbids are not things of wisdom but emptiness and trash by which the ignorant have been attracted and

---

[8] Joseph Naveh and Saul Shaked, *Amulets and Magic Bowls: Aramaic Incantations of Late Antiquity*, 3rd ed. (Jerusalem: Magnes Press, 1998).

on account of which they have abandoned all the ways of truth. That is why the Torah says, when warning people against all this nonsense, "Be perfect [wholesome] with the Lord your God" (Deut. 18:13). (Mishneh Torah, Laws of Idolatry 11:16)

Despite the high respect accorded to his *Mishneh Torah by* rabbinic Jews, these remarks were largely ignored until modern times, were summarily dismissed by the Vilna Gaon,[9] and are still regarded with suspicion by many of the Orthodox, who hesitate to condemn astrology or deny demons and magic, since the Sages of the Talmud apparently believed in them.

Belief in the efficacy of magic and in alleged phenomena such as demons, possession, and the evil eye was almost universal in the premodern world and formed a significant element of popular Jewish culture; S. Ansky's (1863–1920) Yiddish play *The Dybbuk*, as well as the novels of Isaac Bashevis Singer (1904–1991), convey something of the vividness with which people, Jews included, until very recently imagined themselves surrounded by invisible beings and forces, which controlled or at least influenced their destinies. In theory, God remained in overall command, but for ordinary people angels and demons—intermediaries—were what you faced on a daily basis. How do you avoid the evil eye (*kenenhora*)? May you [be guided by] a good constellation (*mazal tov*)! When you wake in the morning, wash your hands in the prescribed way to eliminate demons of the night (*shedim*). Of course, address God directly in prayer as prescribed by the rabbis, but match your intentions to precise forms of the divine Name as mapped out by the kabbalists.

Medieval liturgists sometimes addressed prayers to angels. One of the most notable in this regard is the anonymous petition Makhnisei Raḥamim,[10] still recited by many at penitential services even though questioned, if rarely forbidden outright, by later rabbis.

Elements of the doctrine of the ten *sefirot* (emanations) through which God is manifest in the world surfaced in thirteenth-century Provence in *Sefer ha-Bahir* and the works of Isaac the Blind. Were the *sefirot* aspects of God, part of Him, separate from Him, or what?[11] The Provençal Rabbi Meir ben Simeon ha-Meʻili (mid-thirteenth century) opposed sefirotic theology as heretical,

---

9 Note 13 on *Shulḥan ʻArukh: Yore Deʻa* 179.
10 Perhaps originally *malakhei raḥamim*. Its author and date are unknown; it is included in the Siddur of Saadia Gaon (882–942).
11 Idel's phrase "intra-divine structure" obscures the difference; plurality remains.

and in particular objected to addressing prayer to the *sefirot*.[12] The practice nevertheless took root; debate continued. Not only philosophers, but even some kabbalists—notably the ecstatic Abraham Abulafia—explicitly rejected *sefirot* for reasons similar to those for which they rejected trinitarianism.[13]

The great Talmudist Rivash (Rabbi Isaac ben Sheshet Perfet, c. 1326–1408), who preferred to pray in a straightforward fashion and not get involved in controversy, offered by way of compromise the explanation he had heard in Saragossa from Don Yosef ibn Shoshan:

> Prayer is only to the Name, may he be blessed, the cause of causes. But it is like this. If someone has a dispute and seeks justice from the king, he asks him to instruct the chief justice to deal with it, not the chief treasurer . . . and if he seeks a gift he asks him to instruct the chief treasurer, not the chief justice . . . so, with prayer, which is addressed to the cause of causes, the intention is to draw down the influence of the *sefira* related to the relevant matter . . . for instance, in the blessing for the righteous it is to draw down the *sefira* of *ḥesed*, which is mercy, and in that directed against heretics the *sefira* of *din*, which is justice. (Rivash, responsum 157)

One wonders how the great Talmudist read the following:

> Rabbi Yudan in his own name: "Flesh and blood has a patron. If he gets into trouble he does not approach [the patron] precipitously, but comes and stands by the courtyard door, summons a slave or a family member, and says, "So-and-so stands at the courtyard gate." [The patron] may ask him in or may leave

---

12 Alon Goshen-Gottstein, "The Triune and the Decaune God," in *Religious Polemics in Context*, ed. Theo L. Hettema et al. (Assen: Royal van Gorcum, 2004), 165–197, sets ha-Me'ili's critique in the context of anti-Christian polemic. Tzaḥi Weiss, "'Their Heart Was Turned Away from the Uppermost': Rethinking the Boundaries of the 'Kabbalistic Literature' and the Opposition to 'Kabbalah' in the First Half of the Thirteenth Century," *Da'at* 85 (2018): 307–339 [Hebrew], argues (ibid., 309) that ha-Me'ili's critique is primarily directed against a deviant sect based in Provence. Oded Yisraeli, "Monotheism and Dualism in Naḥmanides' Kabbalistic Thought: Formation, Volte-Face and Evolution," *Journal of Jewish Studies* 70, no. 2 (2019): 298–317, has traced the development of Nachmanides's response to the issue of plurality within the Godhead.

13 "[Abulafia] accuses certain kabbalists . . . of being even worse than Christians; while the latter believe in a triune God, the Sefirotic Kabbalists believe in a system of ten distinct divine forces." Moshe Idel, *The Mystical Experience in Abraham Abulafia* (Albany, NY: SUNY Press, 1988), 8. Idel gives no source.

> him. But with the Holy One, blessed be He, it is not so. If a man is in trouble he does not cry out to [the angels] Michael or Gabriel, but "Let him cry to Me, and I will answer," as it is written, "Whoever calls on the name of the Lord shall be delivered" (Joel 3:5).[14]

The line between telling God (who absolutely does not need my advice) which of his *sefirot* to use for my benefit and between attributing independent power to the *sefirot* themselves is a fine one. If ecstatic Kabbalah seeks mystical union through manipulation of divine names, sefirotic Kabbalah seeks to manipulate the divine by correcting the balance of *sefirot* (making *tiqqunim* to correct the damage done by the sin of Adam). Kabbalists such as Menachem Recanati (1223–1290) accordingly interpret the *mitzvot* as ways of controlling deep spiritual forces, rather than offering rational, "naturalistic," interpretations in the manner of Saadia or Maimonides. On the one hand this protects halakhah, since nothing can be changed without disturbing the balance of spiritual forces; on the other hand halakhah cannot respond to changes in society, since it is placed in an independent "higher" (or "deeper") realm.

Sefirot eventually take on distinct gender[15] roles (female always being derivative and inferior); triads (trinities?) engender one another in hierarchical order, and are even described as limbs of God's "body"—meaning, not God Himself, who is *ein sof* (infinite, beyond all description), but some sort of projection (*Adam Qadmon*).

Kabbalists categorically refuse to acknowledge that any of this in any way compromises the unity or immateriality of God. To the non-kabbalist, however, it can look as if members of an ancient Greek pantheon—Athene, goddess of wisdom (*bina, ḥokhma*),[16] Nike, goddess of victory (*netzaḥ*), or Apollo, god of the arts and beauty (*tiferet*)—have returned, cloaked as abstractions rather than persons. A lot depends on how literally you read Kabbalah. If you read it as poetry, meant to capture some spiritual essence or experience, you can circumvent the criticism that you are compromising the unity or incorporeality of God.[17] You can do much the same with narratives of Athene, Nike, or Apollo.

---

14 PT *Berakhot* 9:7, 13a.
15 On the "feminization" of God see A. Green, "*Shekhinah*, the Virgin Mary and the Song of Songs: Reflections on a Kabbalistic Symbol in Its Historical Context," *AJS Review* 26 (2002): 1–52.
16 See Elliot R. Wolfson, "Hebraic and Hellenistic Conceptions of Wisdom in *Sefer ha-Bahir*," *Poetics Today* 19 (1998): 147–176.
17 Elliot Wolfson achieves this in a sophisticated manner in *Language, Eros, Being* (New York: Fordham University Press, 2005).

Torah as Idol

Torah itself, when objectified, becomes an idol. What could be more strongly identified with Torah than the Holy Ark containing the Tablets brought down by Moses? Yet when the Israelites turned to the Ark to save them instead of directly to God it saved neither the Israelites nor itself from the Philistines (1 Sam. 4:3–11).

Nor is the Land, or the City of Jerusalem, God. Despite Isaiah's assurance to Hezekiah that Jerusalem will not fall (Isa. 31:4–52; 2 Kgs. 18:30), it is not invulnerable. The assurance of salvation is conditional, and in no way contradicted by Micah's (3:12) or Jeremiah's (26:18–19) later assurances of destruction.

The Ark and the Land can be debased into idols; they are physical objects. But what of the Word? The words of Torah, too, can become an idol when detached from the context in which they were uttered; words live only in contexts.

Surely there are eternal, unchanging laws? Maybe, but this is the wrong question. Ask, rather, whether eternal laws can be articulated in human language. "Do not murder," in the Ten Commandments, sounds as if it might be an eternal law.[18] But is it? It cannot function without a precise legal definition of what constitutes "murder" as opposed to legitimate killing (for instance, in defense), and that definition can only be given in specific social and historical contexts. Is judicial execution permissible? Is there such as thing as a "just war"? "Do not murder," insofar as it is eternal, is incompletely defined; once defined, it is related to a specific society, hence not eternal.

This conundrum affects the whole of halakhah, since law always relates to society, and society changes. What a law, as actually formulated, said to one society is not what it says to another. For instance, Deuteronomy lays down that if a man dies childless his brother should marry the widow; if he refuses, she has legal redress (Deut. 25:5–10). In ancient Israelite society such a law expressed both the value of patrimony and the virtue of providing for a widow. By the rabbinic period the same words and the same institution gave out a different message: "Here is an opportunity to get rich from your brother's estate"; this raised the question of whether ḥalitza (the ceremony of freeing the widow) was preferable to marrying her, a position eventually endorsed by Isserles.[19] Today, the same

---

18 In Hebrew, *tirtzaḥ*, as opposed to *taharog*, is a legal term; KJV "Thou shalt not kill" is an incorrect translation.

19 Rama Isserles on *Even Ha-Ezer* 165:1, deriving from BT *Yevamot* 39b: מצות יבום תנן התם: קודמת למצות חליצה—בראשונה שהיו מתכוונין לשם מצוה, עכשיו שאין מתכוונין לשם מצוה אמרו: מצות חליצה קודמת למצות יבום.

words and the same institution make even less sense. Have the words become a lifeless idol? Yes, if read without regard to context; no, if lessons are derived from them appropriate to our own society. Such considerations of meaning and historical context underlie major sectarian divisions among Jews today.

Rabbinic tradition, however, has always claimed that "the Law" is perfect, unchanging, eternal. In the last century, Rabbi Joseph B. Soloveitchik (1903–1993) drew a powerful analogy between halakhah and the a priori system of mathematics. If this analogy were valid, Torah, like mathematics, would be unaffected by social or historical context. However, halakhah as actually formulated is *not* an independent metaphysical object that somehow "confronts" society; it comprises rules that have meaning only within the structures of real societies located in time and space.[20] Something akin to this thought underlies the Talmudic story of how Moses trumped the angels' claim to Torah by demonstrating that it was meaningful only in a human context (BT *Shabbat* 88b–89a).

Society evolves. Talmudic halakhah on idolatry is articulated in terms that don't match the Christian, Muslim, and increasingly secular worlds in which most Jews now find themselves. Already in the Middle Ages economic pressure led to adjustments with regard to commerce (such as charging interest to non-Jews contrary to the Talmudic ruling) and *yeyn nesekh*,[21] yet non-Jews collectively are still routinely referred to in halakhah as idolaters. Perhaps the laws on idolatry have simply become a means of separating Jews from all others, idolatrous or not.[22]

Can an "ideal," changeless Torah ever be articulated? Not in human language. It is a chimera, an impossible beast. Rabbi Joshua declared of the *actual* Torah, *lo ba-shamayim hi*—"it is not in heaven" (BT *Bava Metzi'a* 59b); in any particular society, it can only be Torah-as-interpreted. The passage of time, the growth of knowledge and the emergence of new social structures mean that even the most constantly relevant values or general laws need adjustment. When this is denied, and a particular form of words is taken as valid regardless of context, we slip into idolatry of the word. Torah is life, not stone; to set it in stone turns it into the very idol it is intended to replace.

---

20 Joseph B. Soloveitchik, *Halakhic Man*, trans. Lawrence Kaplan (Philadelphia: Jewish Publication Society, 1983), 19–20. The matter is dealt with more fully in chap. 18 of my *Torah from Heaven* (Oxford: Littman Library of Jewish Civilization, 2012).
21 Haym Soloveitchik has given an excellent account of the process in several works, including "Pawnbroking: A Study in 'Ribbit' and of the Halakah in Exile," in his *Collected Essays*, vol. 1 (Oxford: Littman Library of Jewish Civilization, 2013), 57–166.
22 See Adi Ophir and Ishay Rosen-Zvi, *Goy: Israel's Multiple Others and the Birth of the Gentile* (Oxford: Oxford University Press, 2018).

Conclusion

We talk of God, and hence of idols, in the vocabulary of our ancestors, but worldviews have moved on and words no longer function as once they did; "worship of sticks and stones" no longer defines idolatry.

Prophets and other biblical figures saw around them injustice, immorality and corruption, in Israel as well as in the surrounding nations. They called on Israel to be different, to abandon such practices. For a nation to be different it must tell a different story and the Bible provides one. Stories of quarrelsome gods, subject to jealousies and favoritism, creating humans to serve their needs, were no longer to be told in Israel; such were the narratives of the surrounding nations, who not merely indulged in evil practices but, through story and ritual, sanctified them. Israel's narrative, to the contrary, told of just One God, creator of heaven and earth, who demanded that his creatures should conform to the highest standards of holiness, justice, and morality; he selected Abraham, Isaac, and Jacob because they followed his way; he rescued their descendants from slavery in Egypt and graced them with his laws.

The Ten Commandments, as Judah Halevi notes in his *Kuzari*, open with a historical and practical statement: "I am the Lord your God who brought out of the land of Egypt—don't have other gods, and don't make images of me"; they do not speak of causes of existence or abstract principles of belief. The Bible's story line is about what happened to Israel when it obeyed or disobeyed God's laws.

Historical research, cosmological and scientific progress make it difficult nowadays to receive that narrative as an objective historical account, but it retains its power as foundational myth of the Jewish people. Indeed, it is more powerful than ever, since a non-literal reading allows us freedom to redefine in contemporary terms the kind of target the prophets might have had in focus had they been alive today, in a world where the old gods have largely disappeared.

Being human, we still seek the satisfaction of selfish desires (power, sex, ambition, money); we put our faith in hollow ideologies, idolize cult heroes and pander to superstitions and pseudoscience; even when we "meditate day and night" on the Law we are prone to overlook the essentials and make a fetish of inconsequent details.

Forty days after the great revelation at Sinai Moses had still not come down the mountain. The people were frustrated, disappointed, restless. With Aaron's grudging approval, they thronged to a grand celebration and dance at which a real, tangible golden calf was to stand in for the invisible "god of Israel." Not being much of a party man I doubt I would have joined in. But what about you?

CHAPTER 16

The Value of Idolatry

Menachem Fisch

Introduction

In their seminal *Idolatry*,[1] Halbertal and Margalit trace and analyze a series of models of idolatry, especially in Judaism, the different concepts of God and religious obligation and faithfulness that they premise, and the forms of inappropriate worship that were deemed idolatrous in their time. They note, as Alon does in his introduction to the present volume, that the rabbinic term *avodah zarah* replaces the biblical equivalents of idolatry—the making and worship of graven images, the adoption of other deities instead or in addition to the One True God of Israel. They choose to translate *avodah zarah* as "strange worship,"[2] and stress the term's twofold connotation: worshipping of strange gods, or the adoption of strange, that is, inappropriate forms of worship, even of the true God, as was the fatal sin of Nadab and Abihu the sons of Aaron who died for sacrificing with strange fire, *esh zarah*. But the central connotation of *zarah* in this context is not the strangeness of the form or the object of worship per se, but their *inappropriateness*, which owes to them being foreign (*zar*), rather than strange (*muzar*).

But foreignness (like strangeness for that matter) comes in a variety of forms and shades. Not every gravely inappropriate, firmly prohibited form of worship or conception of the divine counts as *avodah zarah*. And those that do, play no real role today. For many[3] observant followers of Maimonides's ruling that

---

1 Moshe Halbertal and Avishai Margalit, *Idolatry* (Cambridge, MA: Harvard University Press, 1992).
2 Ibid., 3 and *passim*.
3 Many, but by no means all. As we shall see below in the teachings of Rabbi Abraham Yitzhak Ha-Cohen Kook, Christianity is upheld *sui generis*, as a uniquely and unredeemably venomous form of idolatry, to which the normal categories of *avodah zarah* do not apply. For a thorough analysis of Kook's complex attitude to Christianity, see Karma ben Johanan, "Wreaking

Christianity is *avodah zarah*,⁴ it would still make very little difference if someone were to introduce a Muslim or Christian prayer in the course of, say, the Shabbat service in their synagogue, or attribute divine significance to the words of Mohammad or Jesus in his sermon. Both would be deemed equally outrageously inappropriate and profoundly wrong to the same degree, just as Jewish conversion to Islam would not be felt less of a religious betrayal by the orthodox community than converting to Christianity. The fact that they consider the latter to be *avodah zarah* makes no meaningful difference. As a category of halakhically prohibited conduct for Jews, *avodah zarah* makes little difference, if any. It is in that respect virtually a dead letter that, in my opinion, does not merit rehabilitation.⁵

And the same, I believe, can largely be said of the *political* halakhic consequences of *avodah zarah*, when considered by Jews, not as a category of religious conduct prohibited for *them*, but as a category of prohibited religious conduct per se; a category of *Gentile* conduct to which Jews are halakhically obliged to respond if and when they have the power to do so. This would seem to be a more serious matter, even when wholly impractical, because of how it might inform Jewish attitudes toward idolatry and idolaters at a personal level, even when they lack the power to take legal or political action against them. But here again, the very long history of living in close proximity to both, from pagan Greece and Rome to Christian Europe (for those who regarded Christianity idolatrous⁶) has left its mark, rendering the term *avodah zarah* inconsequential of itself with respect to the boundary lines and demarcational practices by which Jews separated themselves from Gentiles in general.⁷ To put the point more concisely,

---

Judgment on Mount Esau: Christianity in R. Kook's Thought," *Jewish Quarterly Review* 106, no. 1 (2016): 76–100, and for the influence it has had on his followers, see her *Jacob's Younger Brother: Christian-Jewish Relations after Vatican II* (Cambridge, MA: Harvard University Press, 2022), chap. 6.

4   See, for example, Maimonides, *Mishneh Torah*, Laws of Idolatry 9:4.
5   As Alon Goshen-Gottstein reminded me in private communication, the prohibition against entering Christian places of worship, nonetheless, remains interestingly more severe for several halakhists than that against entering a mosque.
6   With the one exception, again of R. Kook and his followers (above, n. 2), to which I shall return.
7   I seriously doubt that Maimonides's ruling prohibiting taking positive action to save an idolater from death (*Mishneh Torah*, Laws of Idolatry 10:1) to the inclusion of Christians ever caused even those who followed him to discriminate between Christians and, say, Muslims in this regard. Even in Israel today, where his ruling on Christianity is enjoying a dramatic and worrying revival. Rudely dismissing centuries of Ashkenazi halakhic grappling with the problems of living within Christian society, as motivated by fear of Christian retaliation, these rabbis now rally round Maimonides's rulings loudly celebrating the Jews' newly found power by telling Christians what Judaism really thinks of them. (For detailed analyses of their

inappropriate otherness trumps idolatry as the category that informs relations to other religions, rendering the difference between idolatrous and non-idolatrous religions largely insignificant.

All of which is equally true of futuristic halakhic rulings, especially those following in Maimonides's footsteps,[8] concerning the time when Israel will enjoy "the upper hand" (*yad Yisrael takifa*, to use Maimonides's expression). Here too, *avodah zarah* per se, though mentioned, seems not to play any role, even in principle. In Maimonides's eschatological vision, no Gentiles will be allowed even temporary residency within the Jewish kingdom unless they earn the status of resident alien, *ger toshav*, by committing themselves to the so-called seven Noachide commandments[9] and acknowledging them as God-given (by the Jewish God, that is). However, as Maimonides goes on there to note, since the very category of *ger toshav* has been irreversibly annulled (due to its linkage to the Jubilee, a count that, in principle, can no longer be restored), the sharp dividing line, as in Ezra and Nehemiah's Jerusalem, runs between Jew and non-Jew, whether idolatrous or not, rendering the category of *avodah zarah*, again, inconsequential in itself.

However, it is liable to become very consequential in a different way and to make an halakhic difference that so far (thankfully) it has not. Many followers of Maimonides hold that, because still dependent on others, the State of Israel cannot be said to fully enjoy the upper the hand, and that although idolatrous, Israeli Christians should, therefore, be granted full civil rights for the sake of peace (*mipnei darkhei shalom*). Their source is the famous Talmudic ruling that "In a city populated by Jews and Gentiles, Jewish and Gentile administrators are appointed, and taxes are collected [equally] from Jew and Gentile, [from which] the needs of the Jewish and Gentile poor are [jointly] supplied."[10] One should not discriminate between the Jewish and Gentile sick, the text goes on to rule, one should attend equally to the dead of each community, pay equal respect to their respective mourners, and return the lost property of both—all in the interest of peace. However, as the Palestinian Talmud (Yerushalmi) goes on to

---

writings and reasoning, see Ben Johanan, *Reconciliation and Its Discontents*, chaps. 5–6.) So far, despite their decisive, and in the case of R. Kook's school, exceedingly derisive tone, they have had negligible effect on Israeli attitudes, individual and institutional, toward coming to aid of Christians in danger or in need in comparison to anyone else. However, as I shall argue further down, it is a categorically new development not to be taken lightly.

8   Maimonides, *Mishneh Torah*, Laws of Idolatry 10:6.
9   On the Noachide laws see David Novak, *The Image of the Non-Jew in Judaism: An Historical and Constructive Study of the Noahide Laws* (New York: E. Mellen Press, 1983).
10   PT *Demai* 6, 24a. See also PT *Gittin* 5, 47c; and Maimonides, *Mishneh Torah*, Laws of Idolatry 10:5.

explain, halakhic multiculturalism, to risk an anachronism, stops short of interreligious cooperation. "Does that mean," a common worker asked Rabbi Emi, "that for the sake of peace we should also participate in their religious feasts? Under no circumstances is this allowed, he answered, because doing so would be to permit their idolatry!"[11]

The joint authorities of the mixed city are to actively and equally assist Jews and Gentiles in their time of need. The Gentiles of the city are assumed to be idolaters, and there is no ban on their idolatrous worship. In the mixed polis, idolatry is passively tolerated for the sake of peace. However, participation in their festivals and feasts is prohibited for Jews, even at the price of peace, as is actively attending to the needs of their idolatrous institutions and practices.

In principle, as I have argued elsewhere,[12] halakhic Judaism comes well-equipped for tolerating peaceful forms of life that it regards as sinful, even gravely so—such as secular Jews who openly violate the Sabbath, the gay community, and Gentile idolatry. For the sake of the peace within their shared locales, as in the Talmud's mixed city, halakhah, though incapable of acknowledging such communities a *right* to their way of life, certainly sanctions a healthy tolerating policy of live and let live.

All of which works well from the perspective of an observant Jewish community *sharing* social and political space with others. However, from the point of view of the municipal and governmental bodies *governing* such shared spaces, toleration is not enough. Members of the Israeli government, for instance, are responsible for the well-being, security, and flourishing of all of Israel's legally recognized communities, the secular, gay, and Christian communities included. Just as it is Israel's Minister of Education's responsibility to make sure that the extensive Sabbath violations involved in the weekend activities of Israel's secular schools and youth movements are properly planned and funded, the Minister of Religious Affairs is responsible to actively ensure that the Christian churches, shrines, schools, and cemeteries are properly functioning and in good repair. From a purely halakhic point of view, systematic violations of the Shabbat and dietary laws, and institutional idolatrous worship, can be tolerated in neighboring communities for the sake of peace, but under no circumstance are Jews permitted to serve in the capacity of *active enablers* responsible for their flourishing! But that is precisely what the Zionist return to state politics requires. The

---

11 PT *Demai* 6, 24a.
12 See, for instance, Menachem Fisch, "A Modest Proposal: Toward a Religious Politics of Epistemic Humility," *Journal of Human Rights* 2, no. 1 (2003): 49–64.

problem is real and pressing for any observant member of an Israeli governing body, and has nothing to do with the separation of religion and state.

It concerns all forms of halakhically tolerated, yet seriously disapproved forms of life, and bears no special reference to *avodah zarah* in particular. But because it is a problem that will inevitably come to the fore with disruptive force, and because of the noted alarming rise in rabbinic voices condemning Christianity as an especially repulsive form of *avodah zarah*, it is a problem that needs to be addressed preemptively. To do so, I would like now to turn to a grossly understudied aspect of the Talmudic literature's attitude to idolaters: the fact that they are engaged with as extremely valuable, real and imagined, partners to highly significant religious dialogue.[13]

The Babylonian Talmud's (Bavli) insistent dialogism is legend. It registers a broad and largely unadjudicated array of contrasting Amoraic readings of each Mishnaic ruling to which it attends, which are then presented as partaking in passionate and highly detailed dialogic exchanges, in the course of which their initial positions are greatly developed and enriched.

The Bavli is wholly unique in this regard. The effort it invests in fabricating its keen imagined discourses, in which seven synchronically flattened generations of Palestinian and Babylonian *amoraim* are made to energetically engage one another, is enormous, and by no means self-evident. In former work I have argued that the Bavli's dialogism owes to an understanding, attributed to the Hillelites,[14] who considered it the solemn duty of each generation of halakhists *not* to receive the rulings of his forebears as a binding dictate, but to subject them resolutely to the test of their own circumstances and understanding, and change them accordingly. But at the same time, they were acutely aware of how difficult it is to create normative critical distance from one's own halakhic heritage and very way of life. This can only be achieved, they insisted, by exposing oneself to the normative critique of people committed very differently.[15] This explains

---

13   The following argument is dealt with more fully in my "Judaism and the Religious Value of Diversity and Dialogue: Drafting a Jewish Response to *Nostra Aetate*," in *Diversität—Differenz—Dialogoizität: Religion in Pluralen Kontexten*, ed. S. Alkier, M. Schneider, C. Wiese (Berlin and Boston: de Gruyter, 2017), 375–392; and in the latter part of my "Gulliver and the Rabbis: Counterfactual Truth in Science and the Talmud," *Religions* 10, no. 3 (2019).
14   See especially my "Deciding by Argument *versus* Proving by Miracle: The Myth-History of Talmudic Judaism's Coming of Age," *Toronto Journal of Theology* 33, no. 1 (2017), 103–127; and chap. 1 of my *Covenant of Confrontation: A Study of Non-Submissive Religiosity in Rabbinic Literature* (Ramat Gan: Bar Ilan University Press, 2019) [Hebrew].
15   In the recent decade I have devoted two book-length studies to the philosophical problem of normative self-criticism, and the indispensable transformative potential of external normative critique. See Menachem Fisch and Yitzhak Benbaji, *The View from Within: Normativity*

the Bavli's relentless (and decidedly non-Socratic[16]) dialogism, and it is in this context that Gentile idolaters make their appearance!

The Bavli "records" many rabbinic dialogical encounters with Roman aristocracy and simple folk, ranging from emperors, government officials, military commanders, judges, matrons, and philosophers, to a broad array of pagan farmers, merchants, robbers, sailors, tax collectors, and common laborers, all the way out to those fiercely independent, rich, enticing, exotic, and world-wise prostitutes of Rome, who are presented time and again as having something religiously significant to teach the sages reputed to have knocked on their doors.[17] But I want to focus here on two specific such dialogical moments situated most significantly at the very pinnacles of rabbinic Judaism's two main scales of perfection: that of halakhic rethinking, and that of repentive self-cleansing.

First to rethinking halakhah. The two Talmuds perform the lion's share of their critical halakhic work by reinterpretation, which is often radical. But sometimes harsher methods are required, especially when entrenched normative framework assumptions are involved. The Mishna's law of damages states that owners are responsible for injuries inflicted by their oxen on other oxen. However, in the case of first offenders, as it were, the ox is regarded "innocent," and its owner is charged for only half the damage. Owners of oxen with violent histories are expected to be more cautious and must pay the damage in full. But this applies only to Jews, states the Mishna (in anticipation of a time when Gentiles will be subject to Jewish law). "Where an ox belonging to an Israelite gores an ox belonging to a Gentile, there is no liability at all, whereas if an ox belonging to a Gentile gores an ox belonging to an Israelite, whether *tam* (innocent) or *mu'ad* (with a history), compensation is to be made in full."[18]

"How can this be?" asks the Bavli.[19] Either the law of damages applies to Gentiles or it does not (that is, either Gentiles under your jurisdiction are counted among your "brethren" as the biblical source of law is phrased, or they

---

       and the Limits of Self-Criticism (South Bend, IN: The University of Notre Dame Press, 2011); and my *Creatively Undecided: Toward a History and Philosophy of Scientific Agency* (Chicago: The University of Chicago Press, 2017).

16 On my disagreement with Boyarin in this regard see my "Deciding by Argument," n. 6 and *Covenant of Confrontation*, chap. 4, §2.

17 See most recently, Noam Zion, *Prostitutes, Rabbis and Repentance*, vol. 3 of his multi-volume *Talmudic Marital Dramas: Passion and Miscommunication, Intimacy and Spirituality, Love and Law* (Cleveland and Jerusalem: Zion Holiday Publications, 2018).

18 M *Bava Kama* 4:3.

19 BT *Bava Kama* 38a.

do not). If it does, then, in the case of injury to their oxen, they should be compensated like anyone else; if it does not, then they should not be required to compensate others when their oxen are to blame. However, the Bavli implies, you cannot have it both ways.

Both Talmuds start their discussion of the Mishna's ruling by offering two alternative answers that are based on earlier sources.[20] The law, they both insist, is indeed not merely inconsistent but blatantly and intentionally unfair to non-Jews. They deserve to be mistreated and their wealth given to Israel, because they failed, according to one, to comply with the seven Noachide laws they were given, and because they were offered the Torah and refused it, according to the other. Jewish law, in other words, is seen as commanded by God to collectively penalize Gentiles for failing to live up to His expectations.

At this point both Talmuds, like the earlier Tannaitic source on which they build, introduce without any forewarning a story about two legal experts sent by Rome in former times to assess Jewish law. Here is the Yerushalmi's far more direct version of the exchange:

> It so happened that the [Roman] government sent two legal assessors to learn Torah from Rabban Gamliel,[21] and they learnt from him Scripture, Mishna, Talmud, halakhah, and aggada.
>
> When they had completed their studies they said to him: Your entire Torah is agreeable and admirable except for its following two rulings: [First] that "an Israelite woman should not act as midwife to a Gentile woman," yet "a Gentile woman may act as midwife to an Israelite woman," [and that] "an Israelite woman should not suckle the child of a Gentile, but a Gentile woman may suckle the child of an Israelite women in her presence."[22] And [second], that it is forbidden to steal from an Israelite, but to steal from a Gentile is allowed.
>
> At that hour, Rabban Gamliel ruled that it was forbidden to steal from a Gentile because it is a profanation of the God's name [*mifnei ḥilul hashem*].

---

20 Cf. *Sifre, Deuteronomy* §348.
21 Presumably Rabban Gamliel II of Jabne, who was active immediately after the destruction of the Jerusalem Temple in 70 CE.
22 M *Avodah Zarah* 2:1, a ruling that is more religiously separationist than ethnically discriminatory.

> As for the ruling concerning the compensation due for goring oxen belonging to Israelites and Gentiles, they said, this we shall not report back to the [Roman] authorities.
>
> Even so, before they arrived at the Ladder of Tyre,[23] they forgot everything!

What makes this brief fictional interlude so special, is, first, how, after being exposed to the initial chauvinistic rhetoric of theologically justified Gentile discrimination—which, incidentally, bears far more broadly on the question of Jewish entitlement to Gentile possession than this or that detail of the laws of damages!—it invites us to imagine how it must sound to Gentile ears.[24] And the two learned Roman legal experts we are asked to imagine, seriously studying an earlier version of our law and way of life at the feet of a truly great rabbinic sage of old, truly curious, deeply appreciative, and in no way antagonistic to it, serve as imagined living refutations of the dismal collectivist portrayal of Gentiles as lawless and dismissive of Torah offered by the two rabbinic justifications of their discrimination.

But the main point the story is meant to convey is, of course, the profound transformative effect their criticism is reported to have had on the ethics of Jew-Gentile relations reflected by halakhah. I say this because the Yerushalmi clearly implies that had Rabban Gamliel (along with the latter-day readers of the story) *not* been exposed to the Roman assessors' external critique, the deeply discriminatory normative commitment undergirding the two formerly cited rabbinic justifications would have remained firmly in place, and, with it, the legal license to unscrupulously rob Gentiles of their possessions whenever possible.

Moreover, the story is attributed to an early phase in the history of Tannaitic halakhah dating 150 years before the final framing of the Mishna and Tosefta, and at least 350 years before that of the Yerushalmi, in which there remains no trace of a law allowing Jews to rob Gentiles. The Yerushalmi, hence, keeping in mind its informed readers, tells the story of a major normative halakhic reform that would not have been possible but for the imagined exposure of the halakhic system to the trusted scrutiny and critique of idol-worshipping yet civilized Romans!

---

23 The Ladder of Tyre is Israel's most northern mountain range that reaches the Mediterranean at Rosh ha-Nikra, about twenty kilometers south of Tyre.
24 For another even more surprising Talmudic exercise of this kind, see the detailed account of the biblical history of Jewish-Gentile relations, drawn up by Ahasuerus's advisors on the basis of their reading of the biblical story, in *Esther Rabbah* 7:13.

What the Yerushalmi, by the end of the day, leaves subtly and unspokenly unresolved is the Mishnaic ruling on which it comments. How are we to now treat the bona fide Tannaitic ruling that so rudely discriminates against Gentile ox owners? The answer, I believe, is obvious. Just as Rabban Gamliel rose to the occasion and ruled the permission to steal from Gentiles to be a profanation of the divine name, the Yerushalmi strongly implies that we too should imagine how this law would sound to the ears of serious Gentiles, and to, therefore, firmly follow Rabban Gamliel's example and treat it too as a law never to be heeded to for the very same reason.

Finally, this brief, yet potent passage is rendered even more powerful when compared to the earlier Tannaitic version of the episode from which it clearly takes its cue. *Midrash Tannaim* on Deut. 33:3 reads the verse as teaching that:

> The Holy One blessed be He holds Israel in higher esteem than all the peoples of the world. For so we have learnt: If an ox belonging to an Israelite has gored an ox belonging to a Gentile, there is no liability, but if an ox belonging to a Gentile gores an ox belonging to an Israelite, there is full liability; an Israelite woman should not act as midwife to a Gentile woman, but a Gentile woman may act as midwife to an Israelite woman; an Israelite woman should not suckle the child of a Gentile, but a Gentile woman may suckle the child of an Israelite women in her presence; that it is forbidden to steal from an Israelite, [but allowed to steal from a Gentile; and that the lost property of an Israelite must be returned] but not the lost property of a Gentile.

In other words, the full list of discriminating laws against Gentiles[25] are proudly cited as *living proof* of God's favoritism toward Israel. And at this point the story of the two legal assessors is introduced, but to a very different end.

> A story was told of two legal assessors who were sent by the Kingdom [of Rome]. They were to told: Go study the Jews' Torah and report its content back to us. They went to Rabban Gamliel at Usha and learned from him midrash, halakhot, and aggadot.

---

25 Attesting to the existence of an earlier stage of halakhah, in which stealing from Gentiles was explicitly allowed.

When their time came to leave they said to him, Our rabbi, your entire Torah is agreeable and admirable except for that which you say: If an ox belonging to an Israelite has gored an ox belonging to a Gentile, there is no liability, but if an ox belonging to a Gentile gores an ox belonging to an Israelite, there is full liability; an Israelite woman should not act as midwife to a Gentile woman, but a Gentile woman may act as midwife to an Israelite woman; an Israelite woman should not suckle the child of a Gentile, but a Gentile woman may suckle the child of an Israelite women in her presence; that it is forbidden to steal from an Israelite, [but allowed to steal from a Gentile; and that the lost property of an Israelite must be returned] but not the lost property of a Gentile.

However, we shall not report these things to the authorities.

According to the Yerushalmi's adaptation of the story, Rabban Gamliel's response was "at that hour" to immediately declare the obnoxious laws a profanation of the divine name. Here, however, introduced by the very same phrase, he is said to have done exactly the opposite: to protect the God-willed discriminatory rulings by causing the Roman assessors to forget them!

At that hour, Rabban Gamliel prayed that they will remember nothing of this, and they did not.[26]

Exposure of our deepset normative commitments to the normative critique of others (especially to those against whom they discriminate), is liable to give rise to one of the two responses we have witnessed. It may either prompt us to hunker down defensively in self-congratulating defense of what we take God's will to be, in the hope that its embarrassing disclosure will be ignored or swiftly forgotten, as in the *Midrash Tannaim* version. But it might also serve to set in motion a self-critical process of normative rethinking and halakhic reform, as in the Yerushalmi's use of the very same imagined scenario. It is more than telling, I believe, that both Talmuds, so keenly devoted to rethinking and further developing Tannaitic halakhah, opt so powerfully for the second option, assigning, in so doing, an indispensable role to civilized pagan opinion in their halakhic undertaking! Nor is it accidental, I believe, that for both Talmuds, it takes the

---

26 Midrash Tannaim Deuteronomy, 33:3.

universal moral instincts of a truly universalist religious culture, such as pagan Rome (and later Christianity), to throw into sharp relief the potentially chauvinistic microethical sensitivities bred of a religion of chosenness such as ours.

Just as the content of Jewish law, however well-justified, is liable to be deemed a profanation of the divine name, so is personal conduct, even when well intended. The key passage in this regard is found in BT *Yoma* 86a, a tractate devoted to the Day of Atonement. The discussion sets forth from a Tannaitic text that vividly describes four levels of sinfulness and the means available at each for personal, deontic self-cleansing.

It is a scale of transgressions that culminates in the very gravest of religious offences—worse than murder, worse than adultery, worse even than idolatry—the profanation or desecration of God's name, which is set up *sui generis* as a category of misconduct to itself, positioned far above all other capital offences. "But what is meant by *ḥillul hashem*, in what does it consist?" the Bavli asks. Four different answers are given of which the fourth, proposed by Abaye, is the most significant.

> Abaye explained: As it was taught: "And thou shalt love the Lord thy God" (Deut. 6:5), namely, that you should cause the Name of Heaven be loved.[27] If someone who studies and re-studies Torah and attends on the disciples of the wise is honest in business and speaks pleasantly to persons, what do people then say of him? "Happy is the father who taught him Torah, happy is the teacher who taught him Torah; woe unto people who have not studied the Torah; for this man has studied the Torah look how fine his ways are, how righteous his deeds!" Of him does Scripture say: "And He said unto me: Thou art My servant, Israel, in, whom I will be glorified" (Isa. 49:3). But if someone studies and re-studies Torah, attends on the disciples of the wise but is dishonest in business and discourteous in his relations with people, what do people say about him? "Woe unto him who studied the Torah, woe unto his father who taught him Torah; woe unto his teacher who taught him Torah! This man studied the Torah: Look, how corrupt are his deeds, how ugly his ways"; of him Scripture says: "In that men said of them: These are the people of the Lord, and are gone forth out of His land" (Ezek. 36:20).

---

27 He achieves this by subtly reading the word *ve-ahavta* (and thou shalt love [God]) as *ve-ihavta* (and thou shalt render [Him] beloved).

The "people" to whom Abaye refers throughout the passage, as the two cited verses clearly indicate, are not fellow Jews but Gentiles looking in observing one's conduct from outside. The verse from Isaiah is addressed explicitly to "the peoples of afar" (the Hebrew actually reads "nations," *le'umim*), and the verse from Ezekiel refers to the "nations" among whom Israel was scattered (Ezek. 36:19). The difference between sanctifying and desecrating God's name is not about how learned one is in Torah or how close one adheres to its teaching, nor is it about one's reputation within the Jewish community. It has all to do with how one's conduct resonates within the wider Gentile society. Because he is known to be "someone who studies and re-studies Torah, and attends on the disciples of the wise," then if *they* deem his ways to be fine and his deeds righteous, they will come to deeply appreciate the Torah, He who gave it, and those who study it. But if they deem his ways to be ugly and his deeds to be corrupt, they will come, for the same reason, to despise Torah, the God who gave it, and those who study it. What renders this text so centrally relevant to the present study is that the evaluative vocabulary of the thin normative terms "fine," "righteous," "corrupt," and "ugly," to which Abaye refers is that of the Gentile! One commits the gravest transgression of the Jewish religion, according to Abaye, if one's conduct is judged negatively by non-Jews.

The important point is that one cannot afford to wait for them to make their assessment but must do one's best to anticipate their reaction in advance. And this requires of all God-fearing Jews to constantly and prudently *imagine* how they might be judged by the surrounding Gentile population—which in Talmudic times was (certainly from a Maimonidean perspective) idolatrous through and through!

In other words, just as in the case of halakhah, at the highest rung of Judaism's scale of normative self-cleansing, we are required to imagine our commitments and conduct being normatively scrutinized, not by God nor by our God-fearing fellow Jews, but by the imaginary presence of a civilized, idolatrous, and, certainly in the case of Rome, not always philosemitic Gentiles.

****

Much has changed since these texts were composed, to which I shall return in a moment. But their underlying master idea has not. Our inability, in principle, to create normative self-critical distance from the very norms we employ in self-reflection merely by talking to ourselves, remains unchanged. And the Hillelite conviction, that, I believe, self-consciously animates the Bavli's entire undertaking, namely, that the only way to do so is by seeking the potentially self-transformative force of *external* normative censure, remains as true today as it was then, if far less appreciated than it was then. This crucial and philosophically pregnant insight, as to the normative limits of a culture's capacity for self-reflection and its profoundly pluralist remedy, is to my mind the greatest resource rabbinic Judaism's formative canon, the Bavli,[28] has to offer.

Maimonides clearly understood this in wryly observing that "he who resents rebuke, shies away from critics and fails to hark to their critique, will persist in doing wrong, *because he believes he is doing right!*"[29] However, though evidently aware that the limits of normative self-critique can only be breached by external criticism, nowhere does Maimonides consider seeking such criticism beyond the gates of the Jewish community, as in the Bavli. The need he marked for such critical input in the *teshuvah* (repentance) process just as the criteria he set for ḥillul hashem, remain firmly confined to the critique of fellow Jews. This is also the case in his well-known moral critique of the laws of slavery, which is explicitly based on internal considerations.[30] His engagement with the Gentile civilized world, in other words, was firmly limited to philosophy and science. The firm line drawn by Maimonides, perhaps the post-Talmudic rabbinic authority most open to the intellectual achievements of the non-Jewish world (whether idolatrously Greek or non-idolatrously Muslim), between welcoming its philosophical and scientific offerings while allowing no role to its normative or theological critiques, has come to set the upper standard of halakhic Judaism's openness to the world. Hence, the emphasis I lay on the Talmudic example, which in this respect remains unique.

Ḥillul hashem might be thought to be different. Jews have been constantly aware and worried about how they resonate in Gentile eyes. But I believe that it has had far less, if at all, to do with the type of confident, rational, reflective, and, most of all, welcoming Hillelite awareness of their need to be normatively challenged from without, of which I've been speaking, than with fear of Gentile

---

28 On the notion of formative canon, and the Bavli as such a canon, see Moshe Halbertal, *People of the Book: Canon, Meaning and Authority* (Cambridge, MA: Harvard University Press, 1997).
29 Maimonides, *Mishneh Torah*, Laws of Repentance 4:2.
30 "It is permitted to work a Gentile slave with rigor. However, although such is the law, it is the quality of piety and the way of wisdom that a man be merciful and pursue justice and not make his yoke heavy upon his slave or distress him.... Nor should the master heap upon the slave physical or oral abuse and anger, but should rather speak to him softly and listen to his claims.... *Cruelty and aggression are found among heathen idolaters, but the descendants of Abraham, the people of Israel upon whom God has bestowed the benefits of Torah with its just and righteous statutes and laws, that are merciful to all,* and in this way emulate God's own attributes, as it says: 'And His mercy is on all His works' (Ps. 145: 9)" (Maimonides, *Mishneh Torah*, Laws of Slavery 9:7–8, emphasis added).

resentment. That ḥillul hashem is in this regard not what it used to be is attested to by how the State of Israel's *disregard* for what others think of its policies and actions has dramatically grown in direct proportion to the confidence it feels in its strength and stability. (Similar, and not unrelated to the surge in Religious Zionist anti-Christian sentiment and halakhic legislation.[31])

What has also changed profoundly since the Talmudic texts we have looked at were written is the paradigm of the civilized, external, non-Jewish point of reference, in relation to which a true Hillelite of old would hold his value system in normative check. It is no longer imperial Rome, but, at least since the late middle ages, the Christian West. Idolatrous in the eyes of Maimonides (though by no means as idolatrous as pagan Rome), with a dark record of anti-Judaism (similar to Rome), it is to the Christian West that we exclusively owe the scientific revolution, and, until very recently, when Jews and others began to join the fray, the entire development of modern science. It is also to the Christian West that we owe the foundations of all areas of modern philosophy—ethics, political philosophy, philosophy of language, self, and agency, epistemology, metaphysics, and even religious philosophy; as well as all modern forms of government, citizenship, human rights, women's liberation; and, again, until Jews entered the fray late in the nineteenth century, all great contributions to Western literature and art![32]

And from the nineteenth century on, Jews not only joined the fray and contributed decisively to all branches of Western science, thought, and culture, but also fashioned their own philosophy as well as their own revolutionary political return to state politics in intense and fruitful conversation with them.

Modern Jewish philosophy is a case in point. As noted, Maimonides developed his own system of religious thought in intense conversation with Aristotelian and Arab philosophy, but he engaged *Islamic* theology and religious philosophy per se to a far lesser extent, if at all. In Modern Europe, by contrast, Jewish philosophers from Maimon and Mendelsohn to Soloveitchik and David Hartman

---

31 For a comprehensive survey of the new anti-Christian rabbinic rhetoric, see Ben Johanan, *Jacob's Younger Brother*. For a pointed example of a firm halakhic ruling along these lines, see Israeli former Chief Rabbi Bakshi-Doron's ruling against catering for the religious needs of Christian pilgrims to the Holy Land (*Teḥumin* 14 [1994]: 11–19), analyzed in my "Modest Proposal."

32 Needless to say, we also owe to that same predominantly Christian West the profound twentieth century barbarity of two world wars, Stalinism, Hiroshima, and more.

developed their thinking in intense and explicit interaction with, and response to, Christian theology and religious philosophy proper.[33]

Neither the massive revival in Jewish philosophy nor the Zionist revolution could have been achieved without intense engagement with the enormous achievements of the civilized Christian West.[34] It is a conversation from which halakhic Judaism cannot afford to insulate itself, especially in the political context of Zionism. For here, especially in relation to the halakhic problem of sovereignty alluded to above, Talmudic pluralism offers us an important *political* corrective to liberalism.

Liberalism is a solemn commitment to acknowledge, guarantee, and safeguard the fundamental right of citizens to live the life of their choice. However, what is ultimately valued is a community's liberty to *choose* the life of its choice, not the life it chooses. Liberals per se are committed to *tolerating* ethnic, cultural, and religious diversity, and to go out of their way to ensure it. But *qua* liberals, they are not pluralists. They do not view cultural or ethnic diversity as an ideal to be desired and sought for, only as a reality, which when realized, they are committed to defend.

Liberalism obligates one to defend the right of others to live as they see fit, but not to take the least interest in their choices, let alone value their otherness. The liberal state will justly allocate the space and means for its various communities to flourish undisturbed, but it lacks the ability to build a nation, to create *from* them a cohesive and especially solidary national collective, which for a young and diversified country as Israel, is of vital importance. This is what I believe motivates the Torah's intriguing vision and firm command with respect to the *ger*, the Gentile minorities who will dwell amongst us when we reach land. Their status, the Torah commands, will be identical to your own: "you shall not mistreat them. The stranger dwelling among you must be treated as your native-born (Lev. 19:33–34). The original Hebrew for "native-born" is *ezraḥ*, the word used today for citizen: "כאזרח מכם יהיה—לכם הגר הגר אתכם" "A citizen like yourself," we would now say, "shall be the stranger who dwells amongst you." The next verse, however, goes an important step beyond the formalities of equal citizenship: "*Love [the stranger] as yourself*," it commands, "for you were strangers in the land of Egypt. I am the Lord your God" (Lev. 19:34; and Deut. 10:19).

---

33 Christian Wiese and I have embarked on a project devoted to this "dialogical turn" in modern Jewish thought, in the course of which we intend to publish a series of monographic studies of the transformative impact engagement with Christian theology and philosophy had had on the developing thinking of several such writers.

34 Christian in the same sense that the civilized Greco-Roman world was pagan.

It is as if the whole point of the cruel enslavement of Israel in Egypt was for its painful memory to fuel a firm moral resolve never to so treat others, and as former strangers themselves, to develop toward their own alien subjects feelings of empathy and sympathy. But how is such an emotion developed, fostered, and maintained? Martha Nussbaum's solution to the problem[35] involves cultivating joint feelings of belonging to a shared national home by means of inclusive national rituals, both festive and reflective. Interestingly, the Torah too steers in that direction by welcoming the "stranger," the Gentile Israeli, into the Temple to offer personal sacrifices in the same manner, and in accord with the same protocols as Jewish Israelis (Num. 15:13–16). However, joint rituals per se do not foster respect, worth, or love of the other, and certainly do not render otherness or real diversity in any way desirable in themselves.

Karl Popper's *The Open Society*[36] goes an important step in a more promising direction that steers close to the Talmud's ideal. Popper's master idea is that diversified societies are preferable to the more monolithic variety, because of the mutually enriching challenge posed by interacting and sharing political space with serious *Lebenswelten* significantly different from one's own. However, writing under the heavy cloud of World War II, the Jewish Viennese refugee devastatingly exiled to New Zealand, which he loathed, devoted the lion's share of his massive book less to developing the idea of the open society than to criticizing its totalitarian enemies, who occupy all but its very last chapter in which his own positive solution is barely sketched.[37]

Here lies Talmudic Hillelism's great political resource. Unlike Popper's briefly *asserted* pluralism, the Talmud practices it on every page, and in such pregnant passages as those we have looked at, bravely displays the enormous *religious* value it attributes to civilized diversity, wholly oblivious to the halakhic impropriety of their way of life. Unlike modern liberalism, halakhic Judaism is incapable of recognizing the *right* of a community to live a life that halakhah deems to be gravely sinful. And yet, as we have seen, it is nevertheless capable of viewing it as a greatly valued religious asset to be seriously studied and engaged.

---

35 Martha Nussbaum, *Political Emotions: Why Love matters to Justice* (Cambridge, MA: Harvard University Press, 2013).

36 Karl R. Popper, *The Open Society and it Enemies*, 2 vols. (Princeton, NJ: Princeton University Press, 1945).

37 Popper rightly locates the true value of real difference not in what diverse cultures find they share, but in the critical challenge they pose one another. But he leaves it at that, oblivious to why anyone would seek for such challenges, as to the question of how transformative dialogue is at all possible across great normative divides. Indeed, he spent a lifetime convincing himself that in science normative diversity was a myth. See his *The Myth of the Framework: In Defense of Rationality and Science* (Abingdon, Oxon: Routledge, 1994).

Here is a brief example of such an attitude with which I have dealt elsewhere,[38] concerning homosexuality rather than idolatry. Some years ago, the Israeli daily *Haaretz* published a detailed profile and long interview with an ultra-Orthodox American woman who worked as a "rabbinic pleader," that is, a barrister to the rabbinical courts, in New York City. The interview focused on the built-in halakhic biases against women, and the ways of legally reasoning round them in the rabbinic courts. At one point, in the course of addressing various gender-based asymmetries with regard to rabbinic conceptions of marriage and divorce, she noted emphatically how, due to the growing number of same-sex couples in the city, she had come to realize how serious couples can maintain perfectly equal and symmetrical relationships of a kind she formerly did not think possible! Now, this is not an argument in favor of homosexuality, the gay community, or same-sex marriage legislation. In fact, I am sure that given her ultra-Orthodox commitents, she most probably considered them profoundly sinful. Nonetheless, however sinful and religiously loathsome she took them to be, there was something vitally important *religiously* that she admitted the gay community was able to teach her, which had it not existed she would never have learned! Homosexuality remained for her a terrible sin, and a form of life for which nobody could be considered as having a religiously sanctioned *right* to live. Yet, thank God for same-sex marriages!—she all but exclaimed, for they challenge us by their very otherness. This is Talmudic Hillelism's political lesson in a nutshell: the gay way of life can be at once denounced as profoundly sinful, while valued and engaged with for the profoundly valuable religious lesson it is able to teach us; a way of life wholly rejected, while deeming its challenging presence a rare and unique blessing!

With the crucial exception of Christianity, the forms of "strange" worship deemed to be *avodah zarah*, belong today in the same category of such profoundly inappropriate, yet serious and thoughtful otherness, which, while we are firmly prohibited from adopting, can nonetheless be deemed valuable and enriching resources for challenging our religious commitments and sensibilities. Hinduism, as addressed in Alon Goshen-Gottstein's recent book subtitled *Judaism, Hinduism and the Problem of Idolatry*,[39] belongs within this category: a religion Jews are prohibited from adopting, yet one they could profit enormously from engaging in religious and normative discourse. However, if the Talmudic Roman example proves anything, it is that to so profit from engaging

---

38 See my "Drafting a Jewish Response to *Nostra Aetate*."
39 Alon Goshen-Gottstein, *Same God, Other god: Judaism, Hinduism, and the Problem of Idolatry* (New York: Palgrave Macmillan, 2015).

a different religion, there is no need at all to find ways to reduce its levels of religious inappropriateness.[40]

But the swiftly developing animosity toward Christianity in the writings and rulings of Religious Zionism's halakhic authorities, especially of the Kook school, is different. Unlike any other current form of "strange worship," which even when hailed idolatrous, is merely forbidden to Jews, the Maimonidean rhetoric of the new anti-Christian campaign within the State of Israel poses an exceedingly pressing problem that is quite the reverse of anything we have known in the past. Unlike Maimonides, who had no contact, and no real knowledge of Christianity to speak of, and unlike the many medieval Ashkenazi halakhic authorities writing from a position of insubordination and dependence on the Christian societies in which lived and hued their limited trades, the reactionary view of Christianity taken by Israeli halakhists is adopted from a position of force and sovereign power.

Coupled to Maimonides's political fantasy of a self-sufficient Israeli sovereignty cleansed of Gentile presence, deeming Christianity, not merely idolatrous, but as determined to "break in to turn Judaism's holy form into a monster" seeking "always to suckle on the abundance of the Torah, to deform [Israel's] divine structure, to deny it its heavenly grace, to defile it completely,"[41]

---

40 As Goshen-Gottstein rightly notes: The medieval rabbinic "decision as to whether Christianity should or should not be considered Avoda Zara [had] far-reaching ramifications on the daily life of Jews in Christian society. If Christianity would be considered Avoda Zara, the strict application of talmudic law concerning commerce with idolaters would effectively preclude any possibility of commerce, hence of making a livelihood, in a Christian milieu," (*Same God Other Gods*, 81) in which many Jews made their living from manufacturing candles, robes, altar covers, and even crosses for many of Europe's churches, abbeys, monasteries, and convents. The definition of Christianity in this context was thus not a purely theological matter, but also a matter of developing strategies for Jewish survival. This was achieved at the time, as he shows (ibid., 82ff.), by the idea of *shituf,* namely by acknowledging that Christianity worships the same God as Israel, in (Trinitarian) association with other beings, which although prohibited for Jews, is allowed for Gentiles. The problem with Hinduism today, to which Goshen-Gottstein proposes to apply the same category, has far less to do with commerce and ensuring Jewish livelihood, than with acknowledging it a legitimate and meaningful partner to religious dialogue. To this end, I believe, strategies like *shituf* are superfluous, and the Talmudic example would suffice.

41 R. Abraham Yitzhak Ha-Cohen Kook, *Shemonah Kevatzim* (Jerusalem: Mosad Harav Kook, 2003–2004), 5:238. Kook deems Christianity to be the lowest of idolatrous faiths for the way it rudely idolatrizes sacred elements of Judaism itself (for example, ibid., 7:140, 366), and one of universal corruptive force described repeatedly in the vilest of terms (ibid., 5:166–167, 238; 7:28, 221, 298, 356). For a pioneering analysis of Kook's complex attitude to Christianity, see Karma ben Johanan, "Wreaking Judgment on Mount Esau," 92, and for the way it permeates those of his son R. Zvi Yehuda Kook, and several of the latter's followers, her *Jacob's Younger Brother,* chap. 6. See also Gideon Aran, *Kookism: The Roots of Gush*

presents a serious and immediate threat to the delicate fabric of Israeli society, and the even more delicate fabric of Israel's growingly uneasy relationship with the West. Hence my decision to focus on Christianity, for which the example of the Talmud's attitude to Rome, we can now appreciate, is crucially relevant.

The civilization of pagan Rome represented for the rabbis more than an imagined normative standard to reckon with in theory. It was a civilization with which the Jews at the time shared their land, as well as the world power with which to contend as a self-ruling community. In viewing that civilization as a religiously inappropriate form of life, yet as highly valued for its normative civilizing challenge, rabbinic Judaism's formative canon offers a powerful antidote to the explosive, no longer theoretical, coupling we are witnessing today between what is merely wrong for us and what is considered wrong per se.

However, over and above questions of *ḥillul hashem* and the related benefits of external normative critique, both of which are relatively powerless in the face of religious zealotry, the Talmudic passages we have examined, especially those to do with halakhic rethinking, are highly relevant to the situation swiftly evolving in Israel today, exactly because they envisage it. As noted above, the Mishnaic ruling regarding the Gentile ox owner's liability, like the earlier rulings cited regarding Gentile property rights in general all imagine situations in which non-Jews are subject to Jewish legislation. They also make cruelly explicit the type of self-justifying rhetoric we are liable to enlist in defense of their abuse now we are in power. Halakhah is changed there not for fear of Roman retaliation or because Jews are perceived as not yet possessing sufficient power, but because it was deemed to have been wrong!

Today, Maimonides is being read in the heartland of Religious Zionism as licensing theologically justified institutional and legal abuse of the rights of Israeli Christians to their property, their livelihood, their institutions and very form of life. Nowhere else in the world does the problem of idolatry raise its head as it is beginning to do here, and the only Jewish authoritative source I know of that is capable of holding up a mirror to its ugly face, are the Talmudic texts we have examined.

Emunim, Settler Culture, Zionist Theology, and Contemporary Messianism (Jerusalem: Carmel Publishers, 2013), 191–187.

Concluding Observations: The Discourse on Idolatry

Alon Goshen-Gottstein

The project description in the introduction focused on the contents of the project, on its subject matter. The summary of our project examines the dynamics of the project: the types of argumentation, the relationship between contemporary positions and classical positions, their potential implications for views of other religions. These concluding observations, then, focus on what we have studied, with an eye to stating the principles, methodology, and ultimate significance of a contemporary discourse on idolatry. I would like to begin by reviewing our project in relation to the initial concept note, that served as an invitation to the project. What aspects of that concept note were addressed by our authors?

Avodah Zarah or **Idolatry**

One question raised in the invitation letter was the relationship, or possible tension, between the terms *avodah zarah* and "idolatry." I do not believe that the conversation has advanced as far as possible clarification of the difference of appealing to one or the other term. All our authors refer to idolatry. Only four of them refer to idolatry and not to *avodah zarah*. In other words, for the most part, our authors use the terms interchangeably without considering possible differences between the appeal to one or the other term. No author offers an analysis of what constitutes idolatry, let alone one that is based on a semantic analysis. By contrast, several authors (Pedaya, Kimelman, Ben Pazi, Fisch) consider the meaning, emergence, and history of the Hebrew term as having significance for our reflections. Of all authors, Magid is the only one to explore both terms, suggesting the authors whom he studies actually discuss idolatry and not *avodah zarah*. What this tells us is that while the two terms are used mostly interchangeably, Jewish thinkers will prefer to enter into an analysis of *avodah zarah* and its associations with *zar*, strangeness, as a way of addressing wherein lies the problem with idolatry. Put differently, while for the most part the terms are not differentiated, when one seeks to probe the concepts by means of terminological analysis, the Hebrew term carries greater weight.

Medieval and Contemporary Uses

Same God, Other god set forth several key strategies that characterized medieval views of idolatry. Which of these have found a fresh restatement among the contemporary contributions featured in our project? Two insights emerge, when we pose the question in this manner.

A. Almost all classical uses are echoed in contemporary uses. There is, in fact, great affinity between the earlier uses and contemporary uses. Our authors either apply the definitions directly to the present situation or seek principles that go to the heart of what idolatry is about and apply it to the present situation. The one classical perspective that is not echoed in our project is the energetic perspective, that was presented in the name of Nachmanides. Perhaps it is because our authors are more philosophically and conceptually oriented than experientially, mystically or magically. Even the mystical voices in the project—Fishbane, Pedaya, and others—still seek out the conceptual parameters of appropriate approach to God, thereby showing some indebtedness to Maimonides and to the philosophical tradition. In fact, most of our contributors do come from the domain of philosophy and Jewish thought, early or late. It could, therefore, be a reflection of who accepted the invitation to contribute to our project. Alternatively, modern or contemporary sensibilities may be less receptive to energetic perspectives.

The only way one might consider energetic uses to appear in our studies, and this may be a stretch in relation to authorial intention, is when we consider human behavior that is harmful to the environment as a form of energetic consequence. While it may not be energetic in the original kabbalastic sense, it is nevertheless a way of arguing that our actions have negative, and even measurably negative, impact upon reality in concrete ways. There is, however, a procedural reversal. Earlier uses analyzed the harm that idolatry brings about in energetic terms. If we consider ecological consequences as an extension of such a perspective we must remember that we are applying the opposite procedure. What is visible to us is not idolatry but the negative, harmful consequences of our actions. These are then dubbed idolatrous in a way that is borrowed from, and extends, earlier uses.

B. A major function of the application and designation of *avodah zarah* is identitarian. A boundary is established, by means of which self and other are distinguished. The work that *avodah zarah* does in relation to establishing identity is discussed extensively in *Same God, Other god*. One of its expressions is in the view that different criteria for idolatry apply for Jews and non-Jews. This is expressed in the *shituf* principle. In this view, the dividing line that *avodah zarah* seeks to establish falls between Jews and non-Jews. None of our authors put forward a modern-day articulation of a *shituf*-based understanding of *avodah zarah*.[1] Significantly, this extends to the moral domain as well. There is, for example, no claim that Jews are to live by a higher moral standard that somehow reflects Judaism's anti-idolatrous stance.

Much of the battle over *avodah zarah*, then, is a battle over identity. How much of this carries over to the contemporary reflection on idolatry? Here a striking fact emerges. I believe without exception all our authors resist a contemporary approach to idolatry that is identity-based or related to identitarian concerns. Combating idolatry is ultimately a quest for pure and correct religion and this quest cuts across religious divides. While the focus may be more specifically on Judaism, the definitions, analyses, and applications could, and, I believe, for our authors also should, be applied equally to other religions. The rejection of idolatry thus becomes a global feature of good or proper religion and a rejection of lower and inadequate forms of religion, however these may be defined. It is a quest shared ideally by all faiths, and Judaism operates alongside other religions, not in opposition to them, in realizing whatever the present-day battle against idolatry is considered to entail.

Maimonides and Meiri

What we remain with, then, are two main lines of accounting for the problem of *avodah zarah*. The two point back to two figures: Maimonides and Meiri. The former emphasizes the theological/religious/ritual problem of *avodah zarah*. The latter emphasizes the moral dimension that provides a bridge between religion as it shapes our relations with God and within society. This corresponds to the distinction proposed in my initial concept note between the theological and moral dimensions of *avodah zarah*. One important difference between medieval and present discussions is the shift in emphasis. Whereas in the Middle Ages, Meiri's was a lone voice, among contemporary thinkers his voice, and its various secondary expressions, gain in prominence. This reflects, in part, the lowered interest in issues of idolatry, described by Eisen, and the subsequent

---

1   Krygier comes closest, but doesn't really make the point fully.

channeling of the category to moral concerns. Shaul Magid's essay conceptualizes several contemporary applications of idolatry in light of the dual positions of Maimonides and Meiri. This is a helpful analytical tool that can be applied across our project. Magid considers that modern Jewish thinkers offer a combination of the Maimonidean model that views idolatry as a category error and Meiri's model that idolatry can be deduced by the kind of society created by a particular religious tradition.

There is one important distinction between medieval and contemporary uses. For the medievals, *avodah zarah* was a category that revolved around God, identifying true and false god. In my reading, this is also true for Meiri, who uses the moral criterion for theological purposes, and not as self-standing. With reduced concern with the status of other religions as idolatry, the notion of idolatry is expanded from God to the religious life more broadly. Accordingly, it becomes a means of distinguishing true from false religion, true religious idealism from petrified idealism, reference to living Torah from an ossified Torah. The expansion of idolatry from God to religion is broader than a possible discussion over the preferred reading of Meiri and whether his criteria are moral or theological. The essays in this volume show multiple points at which religion in its various aspects comes under scrutiny, rather than *avodah zarah* in a narrow sense. It is possible that precisely such an expansion is facilitated by the ambiguity of *avodah zarah* and idolatry. Critique of religion and fixity, for example, draws more readily on an understanding of idolatry than on the precedents for defining *avodah zarah*. Eisen's reference to the ways in which idolatry is applied, given the lowered interest in *avodah zarah*, illustrates the point well. Harvey's appeal to true religion, as a broader category than *avodah zarah*, is representative of this broader shift. The age-old view of Torah standing in for God and representing him is, in fact, extended not only to Torah as the object of idolatry, as expounded by Marmur and Flohr, but to religion in its entirety.

Between Maimonides and Kabbalists

The question of medieval authorities and their continuing contribution to a present-day statement of the meaning of *avodah zarah* leads us to consider who are the authorities that inform the reflections of our authors. Having already noted the two theoretical poles of Meiri and Maimonides, we must now take note of just how powerful a presence Maimonides has in our project. In fact, there is no personality that comes close to occupying the central position that Maimonides occupies, either by means of his halakhic rulings or his philosophical works. He is cited in all essays, save one. Kellner's essay proves the point more than anything. The entire essay is dedicated to an analysis of the consequences of Maimonides's ruling on Christianity and how intellectual honesty requires adopting the same criteria when we examine Judaism in and of itself. The issue is not whether one follows Maimonides or another figure. The point is just how influential Maimonides is and the degree to which he shapes discourse. He provides the categories that authors extend into different domains and he provides the foil against which other positions are framed. He also provides the justification for some of the socially and ideologically problematic applications of idolatry in Israeli society, as Menachem Fisch notes. When we consider the four approaches to idolatry spelled out in the opening essay, we realize that in fact two of them owe to Maimonides. The core definition that idolatry is the worship of something besides God, that is echoed time and again, owes to his halakhic discussion in *Mishneh Torah*. The concern for proper knowledge of God and how this defines the discourse of idolatry is grounded in his philosophical understanding, spelled out both in the *Mishneh Torah* and in the *Guide of the Perplexed*. Maimonides's negative theology and apophatic approach is echoed time and again by authors, and is used as a means of criticizing various internal developments within Jewish religion. This ends up feeding criticism of holy places and people, on the one hand, and shaping feminist Jewish thought, on the other.

Noting what sources are used leads us to consider what sources do not play a central role in shaping the contemporary thoughts articulated in our project. Biblical and rabbinic sources are used by some authors for terminological explorations. They also provide precedents for what *avodah zarah* means. But, significantly, they do not provide resources for developing new approaches for today. In theory, a return to the most foundational sources could be an important resource for contemporary reflections. One example for this, discussed in *Same God, Other god*, is the work of Ben Sommer, whose contribution to biblical thought has proven helpful to my own reflections on the religious imagination, as this relates to other religions. The earlier, foundational sources—biblical and rabbinic—are not only the most authoritative. They are also the most pliable. If our authors do not turn to these sources in order to gain fresh insights and to open new theoretical possibilities, this may well speak to the profile of our contributors. Most of them come from the discipline of philosophy, many from modern philosophy. A biblical/rabbinic scholar like Michael Fishbane sets out the biblical background, only to draw constructive resources for his theologizing from hassidic literature. In fact, the second corpus of significance, in terms of the extent of its impact on the theological reflections offered in our project, are hassidic sources and, to a lesser extent, kabbalistic sources. If from the halakhic perspective the key tension was between Maimonides and Meiri, from the theological or theoretical perspective it is between Maimonides and Jewish mystical (Hasidic and kabbalistic) literature. That Maimonides features in both axes is testimony to his towering presence and how it shapes Jewish discourse on idolatry.

Revisiting Other Religions

The starting point of our project was that there are strategies by means of which all, or nearly all, contemporary religions could be cleared of the charge of idolatry. This does not mean that the category is no longer relevant to a view of other religions. As Fisch makes us aware, the State of Israel could become a major global site for acting out the negativity that is derived from the proclamation of another faith as idolatry. Yet, in theoretical terms, tools exist and positions have been articulated that allow us to view other religions as non-idolatrous. There are various consequences to such a view. As Meiri already deduced, this establishes commonality and fraternity among religions. It makes them partners in broader global, social and even spiritual pursuits. Clearing other religions of the charge of idolatry is only the first step towards redefining relations and restating the divine purposes in the existence of multiple faiths.

Our exercise in stating the contemporary meaning of idolatry independently of stated positions in relation to other religions is seemingly irrelevant to present-day views of other religions. Yet, as we reflect on positions and views our authors take, we find ourselves revisiting how other faiths ought to be approached and viewed. Let us consider Kellner's call for methodological consistency and honest application of principles. Kellner's point is that the declaration of Christianity as *avodah zarah* is a matter of choice, not of necessity. Under alternative social or political conditions, the same theological choice meets with a different outcome, when phenomena internal to Judaism are considered. The argument could go in one of two ways. It could lead to a condemnation of certain Jewish views. More likely, an honest appraisal of the data would force a reevaluation of the view of Christianity as *avodah zarah*. The view from within, considered objectively, impacts the view of the religious other.

Similarly, Rosenzweig, cited by Marmur, teaches us that idolatry comes from the way in which an object is worshipped and not from the thing itself. While the thrust of Marmur's argument is internal, the argument could also be reversed. If we take this position seriously, then the dividing line between idolatrous and non idolatrous religious practices does not run between religions but within them. Judaism, like other religions, could harbor idolatry or its opposite. It is all a matter of attitude and approach to the object being worshipped.

More extreme is the conclusion that the very attribution of "idolatry" to other religions might itself be an expression of an idolatrous attitude. One way of making the argument would be to associate idolatry and intolerance, a move I also suggested in *Same God, Other god*. According to Levinas, tells us Ben Pazi, religion can lead people toward the absolute, but not in the name of an imperialistic seizure of control capable of devouring all those who refuse it, but rather as an absolute demand that is turned inward toward the self and that charges it with infinite responsibility. The implication of this understanding, it seems to me, is tolerance, the lack of which would be considered idolatrous.

A similar point emerges from Krygier's essay. Following his presentation of what constitutes idolatry, he poses the question of how Jewish people should relate to the plurality and corporeality of the divine manifestations to which other peoples or communities are committed. Krygier moves from within outward. The capacity for internal acceptance of multiple conceptions of God that can exist within should be extended to other religious groups possessed of other spiritual or philosophical convictions. Judaism's purpose is to encourage the nations of the world to commit themselves to the Supreme God by seeking out the light of God's face as refracted through their own prisms. Taking the point further, the charge of idolatry is turned towards monotheism itself. In his analysis, monotheism has the capacity to foster dehumanization. Through the lens of dehumanization we return to the question of attitudes to other religions, leading to a reversal of perspectives wherein the lens of idolatry is turned upon monotheism itself. This is, perhaps, the most extreme instance of idolatry within, tying together a view of other faiths, a criticism of religion within and a consideration of the danger and price paid by the discourse of monotheism, and its correlate—the discourse of idolatry.

Magid's polemic with Art Green leads him to offer a novel, kabbalistically based, anti-Maimonidean understanding of idolatry, which has consequences for the view of other religions. For Magid, stasis within divinity, appealing here to a notion of fixity within the divine itself, is the basis of an idolatrous view. Idolatry occurs when the cascade of infinitude somehow becomes ossified in ways that create unmovable hierarchies. Magid appeals to a notion found in Rav Kook, called "progressive revelations of a preexistent ideal," an idea that innovation can be a new unfolding of revelation. In Rav Kook's mind, this serves as a metaphysical justification for changing ideas in the infinite body of Torah. Magid suggests that this can also serve as a model for the infinite possibility of Torah's manifestations and its alternative constitutes a form of idolatry.

Consequently, the ossification of divine hierarchies, making one refraction superior to another, is idolatrous. On this reading, the notion that divine truth exists exclusively in one iteration of the divine, only *here*, a view that easily slides into exclusivity, becomes itself a form of idolatry. It seems to me that in fact Magid is suggesting that the view of exclusive truth and considering other religions as idolatrous can itself become a form of idolatry.

All this has consequences not only to how other religions are defined and whether or not they are considered as *avodah zarah*. If other religions are not viewed as *avodah zarah* and if *avodah zarah* has been redefined, the new formulation would apply equally to Judaism and other religions. I have already noted that one of the characteristics of our contributions is that the same criteria are offered for Judaism and other religions, once idolatry has been reframed. Haviva Pedaya is explicit on this matter. Her presentation works towards establishing a common framework for all religions, as distinct from classical reference to *avodah zarah*. With *avodah zarah* redefined, she states, common awareness of God, beyond the particular narratives of different religions, will lead to a perfected and purified human spiritual existence. Thus, going beyond earlier applications of idolatry points to common spiritual ground and to the common spiritual quest that should define relations between religions.

The Enduring Vitality of Idolatry

When I set out to solicit contemporary voices that would reflect on the meaning of idolatry, I was not sure that much would turn up. In fact, quite a number of individuals to whom I turned claimed that they did not have much to contribute to the project. Yet, when we review the project in its entirety, one incontestable conclusion is that idolatry, or *avodah zarah*, maintains its vitality. A range of contemporary issues are seen through the lens of idolatry, that offers a new nuance and new perspectives on issues of contemporary concern, on configurations of present-day life, as well as on the enduring classical concerns of idolatry, that in some way remain as relevant today as they ever were. I believe it is fair to sum up our collective efforts with the realization that while *avodah zarah* may not be the most useful or appropriate lens by means of which to view religions today, certainly not as the default, knee-jerk attitude as practiced in some sectors of the Jewish world, the category can still operate in significant ways. One need not have another religion in view when considering *avodah zarah*, and idolatry is an important category by means of which our religion, our person, and our community can be purified.

Index

Aaron, 43, 81, 180, 215, 328–29
Abravanel, Isaac, 139, 145n10, 252
Abaye, Yose bar, rabbi, 234, 339–40
Abba, Ḥiyya bar, rabbi, 48
Abel, 283
Abihu, 43, 215, 329
Abraham, 52, 62, 146, 153–54, 166, 251, 315, 328, 341n30
Abrahamic religions, 137, 139, 199, 282, 289
Abraham, rabbi, 227
Abulafia, Abraham, 324
Adam, 52, 54, 64, 98, 114, 137, 139, 153n6, 241–42, 247, 282–84, 303, 325
Adler, Rachel, 128, 130, 134
Akiba, rabbi, 145
Albert the Great, 287
Albo, Yosef, rabbi, 145n9
Aleinu, 66–69
alienation
    and capitalism, 158, 241–43
    and idolatry, 21, 158, 241–43
    and feminism, 126, 128, 132, 139
    from tradition, 261
America, 188–89, 198–201, 203, 208, 295, 308
Amos, 147n14, 249
Anatoli, Jacob, rabbi, 288
Anaxagoras, 314
angel, 141–43, 154n9, 211, 280, 300, 314, 322–23, 325, 327
anger, 162, 241, 341n30
animals, 64–65, 138, 175, 177–78, 180, 214n2
anthropocentric view, 29, 34, 168, 170, 178, 180, 184, 254, 259

antisemitism, 32, 55, 58–61, 64, 135
Apollo, 39, 155, 325
apophatic theology, 228–29, 353
apostasy, 78, 116, 124n77
Aquinas, Thomas, 111, 287
Arendt, Hannah, 107, 134
Aristotle, 94n3, 148n17, 300n33, 314
Ark, 36, 49–50, 215, 326
art, 102, 107, 137, 239, 342
Artson, Bradley Shavit, 189
Ashi, Rav, 313
Assmann, Jan, 114, 119
astrology, 308, 322–23
atheism, 55, 136, 191, 193, 202, 216, 220, 267, 274
Augustus, emperor, 319
Austin, John Langshaw, 80
Avempace, 287
Avicenna, 217, 228–29, 287
Avimelekh, king, 146
Aviner, Shlomo, rabbi, 291n5
Avital, Yemima, 163

Ba'al Shem Tov. *See* Ben Eliezer, Israel
Babylonia, 44n5, 54, 130, 313, 333
Bacon, Francis, 319n7
Baeck, Leo, 97
Barfield, Owen, 28, 241, 243–46
Barth, Karl, 29, 138n29, 253–54
Batnitzky, Leora, 235, 237
Beatles, the, 152
Ben Azzai, Simeon, 145
Ben David, Abraham, 216, 229, 304, 305n48
Ben Eliezer, Israel, 24, 40, 51, 90–91, 112, 166

Ben Gershon, Levi, rabbi, 139
Ben Isaac, Solomon, 138, 149–50, 174–75, 182, 283, 289
Benor, Ehud, 97n20
Ben Pazi, Hanoch, 16, 25–26, 35, 37, 349, 355
Ben Sheshet Perfet, Isaac, rabbi, 237n13, 324
Ben Shlomo, Joseph, 109n42
Berger, David, 291n4, 309
Bible, the,
    anthropomorphic depictions of God in, 17, 92
    concept of multiple supernatural forces in, 4, 51, 78, 93–4, 143, 146
    connection between idolatry and immorality in, 96
    centrality of revelation in, 51, 86
    contrasting idolatry to Israelite worship, 107, 154, 238
    definition of foreignness in, 214
    ethics in, 146, 154, 178–80, 264, 281, 284
    fashioning Judaism, 108, 151, 194, 266n4, 273, 277, 304, 314, 320, 328
    and feminism, 130, 133
    idolatry and historical context of writing, 275, 291, 313
    image of anti-Christ in, 59n46
    image of Israel in, 74
    image of Moses in, 57–58, 285
    lack of tolerance for idolatry, 112, 117–8, 124, 151–2, 312
    moral and social critique in, 54, 144–5, 173, 178–80, 186, 316
    relational God in, 51–2, 143, 146, 149, 153–4, 166, 195
    promise of liberation in, 130
    sacred vs. sanctifying approach to, 37–38, 238, 274
    study of, 335, 339
    theological implications of, 77–78, 83, 267, 276–77, 285–6, 304, 306n51
    understanding idolatry as worship of humans in, 26
Blass, Yehonatan Simhah, rabbi, 292n5
blasphemy, 55n33, 57, 59n46, 141, 193
blessing, 21, 144, 176, 207–8, 210, 241, 243, 299n29, 324, 345
blood, 46, 50, 61, 74, 308, 324
Bloom, Harold, 239
body,
    evil inclination in, 241, 247
    of God, 40, 142, 236, 325
    of god, in Ancient Egypt, 74
    incorporeality of God and angels, 280, 300, 302–4, 306
    masculine and feminine, 126–7, 129, 134, 137
    sensual perception, 76, 84
Bohnen, Michael, 69n75
Bonhardt, Simhah Bunem, rabbi of Peschishke, 85–86
Boyarin, Daniel, 135, 334n16
Boym, Svetlana, 259
Brenner, Athalya, 134
Brill, Alan, 295
Broner, Esther, 132
Brumidi, Constantino, 319
Buber, Martin, 24, 83n23, 109n44, 111n50, 121, 138, 191, 193n20, 196, 203, 206, 258, 262, 278
Buddha, Buddhism, 188, 197, 216, 227, 264, 289, 295, 318
    JUBU (Jewish Buddhists), 295
Burkert, Walter, 315n3

Cain, 283
Caligula, Gaius, 56, 62n57
Calvin, John, 203
Cardozo, Abraham, 124n77

Canaan, Canaanite deities, 78, 130, 216, 315
capitalism, 59–60, 100, 103n33, 105–6, 151, 158–159, 160–62, 166–67, 175, 225
Cardozo, Isaac, 124n77
Catholic feminists, 129–30
Chasam Sofer, the. *See* Sofer, Moses
chauvinism, 32, 36, 103, 113–14, 120–21, 148, 221, 247–48, 336, 339
Chazon Ish, the. *See* Karelitz, Avraham Yeshaya
Christianity,
    Jewish dialogue with, 116n59, 199–200, 209, 343
    Jewish opposition to, 59, 94–95, 98, 117n62, 252, 264, 291–7, 307–8, 329–31
    images in, 47n15, 55, 57, 197, 252, 292, 346n40
    in Israel, 252, 332
    moral failings in, 56, 162, 224, 293
Cicero, 57n37
Civil War, the, 209
Clinton, Bill, 103n33
Cohen, Hermann, 23, 83, 97, 116n59, 153n7, 235
colonialism, 184, 220–22
commandments
    and ethics, 168, 173, 180–3, 216n6, 225, 267, 281, 317, 326, 331
    and feminism, 133, 139
    forgetting about, 36, 214, 318, 328
    and God's nature, 301–3, 306
    and Jewish learning, 255, 257–58
    mystical understanding of, 325
    as spiritual preparation, 88, 144–5, 171, 179, 229, 249
Communism, 55, 58–59, 100, 102–3, 105–6, 203, 220

community,
    and ethics and responsibility, 28, 103–6, 171–2, 217, 223, 230–1, 279, 331–2, 340–5, 355–56
    identity, 46, 72, 99, 115–7, 120, 188, 197, 199, 201, 206, 209, 214, 226, 257, 263, 302n40, 305n48, 330, 347
    and learning about God, ix, 37, 254–60
    object of idolatry, 7, 20, 148, 188, 205, 218
    and feminism, 132, 135
compassion, 25, 34, 152, 163–64, 169, 174, 179, 182, 206, 312
conscience, 18, 145, 148, 172, 291
consciousness,
    developing a false consciousness, 17, 73, 77–8, 81, 125–6, 129, 153n4
    evolution of, 19, 25, 76, 80, 181–2, 243, 265–67, 272
    hierarchy of values in, 13, 28, 91, 157, 204
    interaction with worldly images in, 17, 89, 92, 142
    internalized image of God in, 26, 153–4n7
    and the public/social sphere, 30, 104, 133
Cordovero, Moses ben Jacob, 108–9
covenant, 24, 86n28, 99, 113–14, 117, 120, 144–45, 148, 166, 188, 196, 199, 203, 213, 229, 234, 246, 260
COVID, 189, 208, 222–23
creation, 87–8, 90–1, 169, 217, 223, 262
    capitalist culture and disintegration of self, 156–1, 165, 166–7, 203
    creating identity, 74
    and diversity, 70
    and divine sovereignty, 34, 64–6, 68, 73, 79, 84–5, 94n3–4, 142–3,

153, 177–181, 188–191, 239, 300–2, 305, 328
  feminist criticism of the concepts of, 126, 128–129, 131–4, 137–9
  human powers to create, 64, 79, 82, 107, 165, 166, 172, 184, 208, 237
  individualist turn in, 29, 158, 180, 182, 222, 253–4, 256–57n12
  and importance of difference, 342, 344n37
  in God's image, 18, 26–7, 29, 33–4, 64, 76, 100–2, 105, 119, 121, 137–9, 145, 189–90, 253
  and Jewish cultural heritage, 135–6, 165, 196, 198–9, 206, 232, 322, 323, 341, 342
  and Jewish monotheism, 133, 150, 196, 264, 339, 341
  and language, 82, 86, 237
  object of worship, 16, 28, 53–4, 62, 156, 161, 162, 168, 171, 200–1, 283–4, 289, 299, 305, 310
  presence of God in, 35–6, 111–3, 116, 119, 122, 153, 162, 164–165, 170, 183–4
culture,
  popular culture and idolatry, 27, 29, 151–2, 202
  scientific impulse in understanding, 92, 186, 202, 260

Daly, Mary, 129–30
Daniel, 48, 237
Darwin, Charles, 189
Davis, Ellen, 179
dehumanization, 18, 133, 141, 145–46, 148, 355
deification,
  in ancient Egypt, 74
  of emperors in Rome, 56–7
  of objects, 283
  of pop culture figures, 201
  of self, 28, 245, 173
  rejection of, in Jewry, 56
deity (other than God), 14, 39, 46–47, 74, 80n20, 94, 112, 114, 141–2, 170, 186, 188, 192, 194, 197, 204, 216, 228, 240, 246, 302, 329
democracy, 100, 102–4, 176, 200
Derrida, Jacques, 255n9, 278
Descartes, René, 253
destruction, 21, 57–58, 61, 74, 119, 147, 168, 175, 180, 184, 189, 215, 225, 242, 293n9, 326, 335n21
devekut, 119
devil worship, 94n4
Dionysus, 155
disbelief, 33, 100n27, 102, 196
discipline, 18, 104, 155, 182, 214–15, 281, 353
disenchantment, 83, 186, 211, 244
divinization, 18, 32, 54, 56, 62, 145
doctrine,
  and the prohibition of idolatry in Judaism, 141, 268, 288
  as illusion or idol, 291n4, 299, 319
  becoming separated from lived practice, 238, 257
  becoming separated from living relationship with God, 143–4, 154–55
  reinterpretation of, 287n9
Douglas, Mary, 215

Eckhart, Johannes, 217, 228–29
ecology, 25, 35, 162, 167, 171, 179–181, 175, 189–90, 211, 225, 230, 321, 350
economics,
  and Marxism, 58n45
  and antisemitism, 60–1
  in Jewish sources, 215, 327
  in Levinas, 275

in postmodernity, 102–3, 159, 161, 165, 169, 173–7, 178, 184
patriarchal, 128–9
education,
and *avodah zarah*, 1
as object of infastructure, 160–1, 318, 332
and liberation, 167, 259, 273
in Rosenzweig, 259–262
Egypt,
correlation of tyranny and idolatry in, 55, 62–63, 68, 132, 174
connection of deities with nature, 74, 147, 180
and the commandment of loving strangers, 343–4
helping establish God's relation with Israel, 58, 75, 81, 144, 270, 306–7n51, 328
liberation from, in every generation, 13, 113, 115, 166, 213, 217, 313
protecting Israel against, 45
Eibeschutz, David Solomon, rabbi, 247–48
Einstein, Albert, 181, 189
Eisen, Arnold M., 20, 22, 24, 28, 30, 32, 351–52, 351
Eisenstadt, Oona, 233
Eisenstadt, Shmuel Noah, 263n33
Elisha, prophet, 147
Emi, rabbi, 332
empire, 56, 60n48, 189, 219, 226
Enlightenment,
defeat of, 103, 222, 260
and individualism, 258
and monotheism, 97, 103
and skepticism about religion, 196
promotion of learning, 37, 254, 260–1, 314
Enosh, 25, 282–84
enslavement, 62, 133, 242, 280, 344
entertainment, 57, 256, 262

Ephraim of Sudilkov, Moshe Chaim, rabbi, 90
epistemology, 83, 87–88, 91, 253, 342
Erlewine, Robert, 98nn23–24
ethnic group/particularity, *see also* Christianity, gentile, interreligious dialogue
and collective responsibility, 105–6, 116
hierarchy of worship, 142
pluralism, 30, 187, 334, 343
separationism, 117, 335–6
transcendence of, 116
Euhemerus, 318
Eve, 135, 138–39, 242, 282–84, 303
exile, 56, 135, 176, 269–70, 344
Exodus, 13, 38, 45, 62–63, 75, 132, 140, 143, 180, 206, 234, 238, 265, 267
Ezekiel, prophet, 130, 174, 242, 285, 340
Ezra, 313, 331

Fackenheim, Emil, 98, 110, 186, 192, 209n57, 244–46
faith, *see also* idolatry, Maimonides, Thirteen Principles, monotheism
centrality of God in, 5, 190–1, 207
and ethics, 22, 26, 186–7, 210, 269, 272, 281
and evil, 192
and Jewish exceptionalism, 58–59n45, 61, 105, 117, 219
and Jewish heritage, 254, 262
and Jewish observance, 30, 94–95, 99, 131–132, 147, 148, 186–7, 189, 191–94, 196, 198–200, 202–3, 205–7, 211, 217, 219, 305n48, 316, 323, 328
living, as opposed to idolatry, 25–6, 52, 266–8
and loyalty, 130, 144, 149, 186, 285, 315, 321

and modern condition, 28, 105,
    151–7, 160–62, 173, 177,
    202–3, 211, 214, 222–3, 230,
    246
  object and subject of, 18, 21, 141
  and personalism, 112
  reflecting human nature, 26, 269
  and selfishness, 328
  and social laws, 279
  and superstition, 318
  vs. science, 189–90, 196–7, 211
  ultimate importance of, 202, 264
family, 105, 168, 172, 205, 224, 324
Farabi, al-, 229, 287
Farians, Elizabeth, 129
Fascism, 100, 102–6, 172, 203
feminine, 128–31, 134–35, 137–39
feminism, 126, 128, 130–1, 132, 135,
  138–9
Feuerbach, Ludwig, 125, 204
Finkelstein, Louis, rabbi, 200
finitude, of human, 138, 262
Firestone, Shulamith, 129
Fisch, Menachem, 31, 349, 353–54
Fishbane, Michael, 13, 17, 24, 33–34,
  350, 353
Flavius, Josephus, 145n10
Formstecher, Salomon, 158
Francis, Pope, 178
Freedberg, David, 197
freedom,
  of the Divine, 24, 163, 236
  and fight against idolatry, 21
  foundation of new community, 115,
    126, 140, 242–3, 254, 328
  foundation of religion, 98
  and human becoming, 132, 138,
    157, 163, 165, 242–3, 272–4
  illusion of, in modernity, 159
  as opposed to fundamentalism, 104,
    172
Freedman, Marcia, 132

Freudenthal, Gideon, 238
Friedan, Betty, 129
Friedman, Dov Ber, rabbi (Maggid of
  Mezeritch), 87–90, 181
Fromm, Erich, 21, 158, 162n27, 241–42,
  244–46
fundamentalism, 100, 104–6

Gabriel, 325
gender, 65, 130, 135–36, 172, 208, 345
gentile,
  applicability of the category *avodah
    zarah* to, 286, 295, 330
  coexisting with gentiles, 199–200,
    288, 331-2, 334–8, 341,
    343–44, 346–47
  in contrast to Jews, 120, 147n14,
  tolerating Jewish culture, 30, 187,
    198, 340, 341
Gersonides, Levi, 288
globalization, 8, 100–1, 103, 106, 190
Glory, 50, 66, 88, 90, 181, 306n51
God
  aḥor, 88–91
  agency, 79, 88, 126n2, 131n11,
    169
  anthropomorphic images, 17, 52,
    82, 92, 143, 189, 195, 287n9,
    307
  countenance (*panim*), 88–91,
    192–93
  disclosure of, 88
  emanation, 74–75, 84, 323
  embodied in all creatures, 87–9,
    116–7, 165, 182, 197
  exclusivity, 4, 23, 37, 314
  fluidity, 46n12
  and history, 136, 192, 208, 314
  human forgetfulness of, 64–65, 79,
    176, 182
  incarnation, 98, 121, 137, 296, 308
  in letters of Torah, 38, 276

(in)corporeality, 39–47, 143, 148, 195, 197, 286, 299, 300, 303–4, 306, 325, 355
indivisibility of God, 120, 153–5, *see also* kabbalistic tradition, *sefirot*
ineffability, 84, 90, 195, 314 goddess, 27, 153, 319, 325
infinitude, 82, 123–4, 245–6, 355
immanence, 25, 50, 67, 73, 88, 90–91, 117, 119n67, 135, 207
manifestation, 82, 87, 90, 91, 92n49, 122, 124, 142–143, 148, 301n35, 355
metaphorical images of, 44–46, 51, 68, 120, 176, 246, 314
names of, 68, 81, 84–85, 110, 190, 207
negative theology, 229, 266
ontologization of, 87–89, 91n42, 110
polymorphism, 22–24, 44, 45–47, 48n18, 50–51, 68–69, 90, 122, 148, 191
transcendence, 17, 50, 67, 73, 76–77, 79, 81–83, 86–90, 92, 109–10, 117, 119n67, 121–22, 207, 254, 258, 263n33
unity of, 155, 300, 301n35, 302, 323
Goffman, Erving, 28, 203–4
Goldman, Emma, 126
Gordon, Aaron David, 153, 165
Goshen-Gottstein, Alon, 69n75, 94, 96, 116n59, 118n65, 205, 215n5, 287n8, 293n10, 311n61, 330n5, 345
Gottlieb, Lynn, 135
Graceland, 27, 319
Green, Arthur, 19, 32, 36, 97n22, 98–100, 108–22, 124, 201, 355
Greenberg, Blu, 128, 293
Greenberg, Irving (Yitz), 115–16n59
Greer, Germaine, 127
Gross, Rita, 17, 24, 195–96
Gutenberg, Johannes, 256

Habad, 109, 291n4, 309
Hadot, Pierre, 262
Hadrian, king, 56–57, 61, 131
Haim of Volozhin, rabbi, 290
Ha-Kohen, Meir Simcha of Dvinsk, rabbi, 35, 285
halakhah,
historical development of, 293–95, 325–7, 332, 334–8, 347
as idol, 163
and Kabbalah, 325
and Maimonides, 20, 294–8
and personal responsibility, 178, 279–80
regarding dealings with non-Jews, 292n5, 327, 332, 334–8, 340, 344
Halbertal, Moshe, 96, 187, 195n26, 232–33, 329
Halevi, Judah, 235, 237, 328
Ha-Meʻili, Meir ben Simeon, rabbi, 323, 324n12
Ḥanina, rabbi, 49–50
Hartman, David, 297, 342
Harvey, Zev, 25, 35, 37, 299n29, 304n45, 352
Hasidism, 40, 108–10, 113, 119, 217, 224
Hasidim, 290, 311, 319
Hayim of Volozhin, rabbi, 290
heaven,
as created object, 73, 74, 76, 84, 94n4, 318, 328
and dimensions of God, 49–50, 190
not place of Torah, 327
as place of God, 53, 54, 182, 188, 208
as place of idols, 308, 320
as place for other creatures, 94, 142, 322
stimulating awareness of God, 66
Hefter, Herzl, 8n9
Hegel, Georg Wilhelm Friedrich, 98, 110, 241

Heidegger, Martin, 169, 269, 270–72, 278
Heine, Heinrich, 158
Herakles, 318–19
Heschel, Abraham Joshua, rabbi, 24, 27, 31–32, 34, 51, 131, 175, 184, 192–97, 200–1, 206, 209, 245, 247–51, 306
Heschel, Susannah, 128, 132
heresy, heretics, 95, 267, 294n12, 305, 308–9, 324
Hesiod, 314, 333, 340–42
Hezekiah, king, 285, 326
Hillel, 171
Hillel of Verona, 288
Himmler, Heinrich, 63
Hinduism, 2, 11, 96n11, 197, 227, 264, 289, 291–92, 313, 318, 345, 346n40
Hirsch, Samuel, 98, 110
Hirsch, Samson Raphael, rabbi, 158, 171, 179
Hitler, Adolf, 55–56, 58n45, 59n47, 63, 192, 200, 209
holiness, 18, 38, 144, 197, 214, 228n29, 249, 273, 328
Holocaust, 186, 191–92, 208, 221, 320
Homer, 314
Horowitz, Isaiah, rabbi, 240
Hosea, prophet, 78, 80n20, 130
humanism, 97–108, 122–3, 272, *see also* ethics, monotheism, morality
Hume, David, 101, 104
humility, 85, 90, 92, 180, 182, 246, 254
Humphrey, Hubert, 103n33
Husseini, Haj Amin el-, mufti, 59n45

Ibn Ezra, Abraham ben Meir, rabbi, 142n4, 306n51
Ibn Gabbai, Meir, rabbi, 51
Ibn Shoshan, Don Yosef, 324
Ibn Tibbon, Samuel, 310n60

iconoclasm, iconoclast, 36, 62, 110–11, 126n2, 131–2, 240, 285, 312
Idel, Moshe, 301n35, 303n43, 323n11
idolatry, 6, 17, 155–6, 194, 201, 230–1, 247, 302n41, 303–4, 307
and absolutes, 16, 35, 122, 278, 316
articulating otherness, 94–95
consequences to human, 21, 80–1, 99, 141, 146–8
focus on, in biblical commandments, 1, 35, 77, 170, 267
fluidity of category, 166, 207, 232, 238
and God's responsiveness, 145, 251, 299, 301, 303, 306
going against internal allegiance and belief, 269
expressed as fixity, 8, 14–17, 23–24, 32, 35–37, 46, 114, 120, 122, 124, 233, 352, 355–6
expression of group divisions, 200–1, 243
and ideologies, 99, 118, 209, 217–19, 250
and Jewish opinion about people of other religions, 98, 286, 288, 290–7, 312, 327, 330–4, 341, 346
logical mistakes in, 79, 97
and personal insecurity, 156, 160–7, 275, 316
reduction of world to usable things, 85, 246
rejection of, in biblical commandments, 53, 74–5, 112–3, 131, 133, 137, 139, 239, 285
and relativism, 155
substitution of God, 21, 31, 162n27, 202, 240, 245, 302, 317, 322
and tyranny, 68
withdrawal from Israel's covenant with God, 145, 312

idoloclasm, 125–26,130, 132, 135, 137
ignorance, 17, 78, 125, 183, 286, 307, 319
image, *see also* Christianity, God, iconoslasm, kabbalistic tradition, prayer, prophet, reverence
and definition of idolatry, 94, 99, 233, 235–7, 241, 285,
fixity, 14, 16, 24, 44–8, 52, 131n11, 139–40, 237
graves (images), 27, 319
icons, 36, 57, 126n2, 170, 226, 312, 318
and ignorance of masses, 125, 318
in Ancient Greece, 47, 155
in Christianity and Islam, 57, 95, 197, 296, 312–3
in internet, 223, 226
instrument of cognition, 76, 86–7, 243–4
of leader, 55, 62
possessing artificial life, 17, 25, 79–80, 125–7, 135
prohibition to worship, 27, 76, 82–3, 86, 92, 93, 133–4, 137, 181, 187, 194–5, 216–7, 267, 312–3, 322, 328, 329
stimulating imagination, 17, 52, 237
substitution of God, 81–2, 110, 131, 132, 134, 138, 139, 141, 170, 196, 239, 244, 313
and visuality, 197, 208–9, 238, 257
imagination,
and cognition, 84, 86–7
and creativity, 70, 79, 91, 159, 184
and ideology, 320
and illusions, 60–1, 125, 134, 225–6, 246, 286, 299
in modernity, 222–3, 230
in Talmud, 333–40
in theology, 52
purification of, 44

vs. reason, 194, 299, 302, 305, 314, 316–7
individualism, 101, 103–4, 177, 258
interpretation, 79, 86, 89–90, 148, 267, 276–77, 280, 334
interreligious dialogue, 19, 150, 187, 205–6, 227–30, 251, 262–3, 264, 281, 288, 332–4, 351, 354
Iran, 57, 61, 75n8, 322
Isaac, 166, 251, 315, 328
Isaac the Blind, 323
Isaiah, prophet, 50, 53, 78–79, 82, 174, 176, 181, 188, 211, 223, 314, 318, 322, 326, 340
Islam, Muslim, 7n7, 55, 57–61, 75n8, 95, 101, 112, 200, 217, 220, 224, 226n27, 227, 229, 241n26, 287–89, 294n12, 304n47, 312–14, 327, 330, 341–42
Israel, 317, 326, 328, 334–38
exclusivity of, 7, 58–61, 109, 112–5, 117, 120–3, 144, 281, 320–1
faithfulness to God, 285, 321
Israelites, the, 35–36, 44–45, 49, 107, 131, 149–50, 186, 188, 194, 215, 247, 285,
Land of Israel, 15, 131, 192–93, 199, 208, 221, 234, 293n9, 307n51, 312, 320–2
State of Israel, the, 8, 30, 186–87, 191–92, 201, 221, 320, 331, 342, 346, 354
Isserles, Moses ben Israel, 326

Jacob, 116, 147, 149, 166, 251, 262, 328
Jainism, 289
Janowitz, Naomi, 233, 237
Jephthah, 315
Jeremiah, prophet, 53, 78, 80, 176, 284, 313, 326
Jerusalem, 54, 60, 69n75, 142n4, 149, 252, 285, 306, 326, 331, 335n21

Jethro, 74
Job, 46n12, 207, 284, 314
Johanan, rabbi, 1
Johnson, Elizabeth, 129
Jordan, Michael, 152
Joshua, 306n51
Joshua, rabbi, 327
Jonah, prophet, 146, 277
Jonas, Hans, 169
Judah, rabbi, 234

kabbalistic tradition
    Arthur Green's reimagining of, 108–11, 119
    divine body in, 40, 236
    eliciting divine response in, 51, 88, 303n43, 352
    elevation of sparks, 31
    interconnectedness of world in, 183,
    polemics about the idolatry of, 39–40, 122, 217, 224, 236–7, 290, 298, 323–5
    sefirot, 39, 110, 120, 122, 143, 236, 301n35, 324–5
    eyn sof, 120, 122–3, 228–9
    understanding of creation, 84–5, 91n42, 109–11, 113, 143
    understanding of idolatry in, 16–7, 142n4, 353–4
    racism in, 309–10
Kafka, Franz, 204
Kant, Immanuel, 89n35, 258
Kaplan, Mordecai Menahem, rabbi, 189, 198–99
Karelitz, Avraham Yeshaya, 39, 319
Kasher, Asa, 16, 267–68
Kasher, Hannah, 266, 304n45, 304n47
Kaufmann, Yehezkel, 194n21, 266n4
Keller, Catherine, 195–96
Kellner, Menachem, 39, 287, 353–54
Kimelman, Reuven, 15, 19–20, 23–24, 26, 29, 32–34, 40, 349

King, Martin Luther, Jr, 200, 251, 293
Kiewe, Amos, 60n49
Klein, Naomi, 175
Kohelet, 314
Kook, Abraham Yitzhak Ha-Cohen, rabbi, 123, 269, 292n5, 329n3, 346n41, 355
Korah, 43
Korn, Eugene, ix, 295, 311n61
Krygier, Rivon, 18, 23, 351n1, 355

Laban, 147
Lamm, Norman, 178
Lavi, Shimon, rabbi, 84n25, 142n4
leader
    abuse of power by, 21, 218, 224, 226, 228
    democratic, 176
    disconnection from God, 162, 182
    idolization of, 21, 55–57, 61, 200, 209–10, 241, 318–9
    Jews as disruptors, 59–61
    responsibility of, 211, 225, 229, 316
Lehrhaus, 260–62
Leibniz, Gottfried Wilhelm, 253
Leibowitz, Yeshayahu, 38, 158, 236–37, 240, 249, 254, 262
Leiner, Mordechai Yosef, rabbi (Izhbitzer), 86
Levi, rabbi, 47
Levin, Ira, 129
Levinas, Emmanuel, 37–38, 97, 273–81, 355
liberalism, 103–4, 106, 250, 320, 343–44
liberation,
    as alternative to idolatry, 77, 126, 152, 162, 164, 166–67
    foundation for Israel's identity, 115, 144
    and gender, 126–130, 132, 133, 135, 137, 139, 342
    and postmodernity, 121, 223

Lichtenstein, Aharon, 117n62
liturgy, 24, 46, 66, 252, 299n29
Luria, Isaac, rabbi, 120–21, 123, 219
Lurianic Kabbalah, 88, 109, 111, 118–20, 122–24
Luzzatto, Samuel David (Shadal), 145n10
Lyotard, Jean-François, 158–60

Machiavelli, Niccolò, 157
Maggid of Mezeritch (Friedman), 87–90, 181
Magid, Shaul 16–17, 19, 22, 27, 30, 32–34, 36, 40, 349, 352, 355–56
magic, 130, 147, 181, 194, 206, 227, 299, 308–9, 311, 318, 322–23
Mahdi, Muḥammad ibn al-Ḥasan al-, imam, 61
Maimonides,
    and conception of oneness, 99, 109, 119, 121–22, 300
    dialectics of love and awe, 180
    encouragement to learn, 305
    founder of rationalistic Judaism, 39–40, 141, 291, 297–8, 311, 322, 325, 350, 352
    ideas as idols, 17, 125–6
    idolatry as error, 5, 96–7, 118, 141, 142n4, 217, 229, 283, 294, 301–4, 305, 307, 316–17, 352
    idolatry within Judaism, 39, 309–10, 341
    idolatry as worshipping anything other than God, 4, 23, 154, 168, 235, 237, 283, 289, 298–9, 302, 306
    laying down the framework for understanding idolatry, 1, 13, 16–17, 20, 25, 157, 248n44, 254, 266–7, 303, 354, 355
    and Muslim tradition, 217, 228, 229, 287, 294n12, 330, 341–2
    politics towards gentiles, 340–2, 346–7
    rituals as foci of idolatry, 37, 286
    struggle against images and personalization of God, 52, 83, 109, 122, 142, 216, 285–6, 302–4
    Thirteen Principles, 44, 291n4, 300–2, 305n48
    and Western tradition, 94n3, 148n17, 217, 228, 287–8, 290–2, 295–6, 297, 307–8, 329–31, 341–2, 346–7, 353
    and understanding of women, 138, 304
Malachi, prophet, 147, 205, 284–85
Malik, Yakov, 58–59n45
Manasseh, 313, 315
Mao Zedong, 55, 200, 209
Margalit, Avishai, 96, 187, 195n26, 232–33, 329
Marmur, Michael, 16, 21, 23, 28, 31, 34, 36, 39, 352, 354
martyrdom, 95, 292
Marx, Karl, 59n45, 125, 158, 160n25
Marxism, 58n45, 104, 241, 320
masculinity, 135–36, 163
media, 152, 165, 190, 220, 223, 226
mediator, 16, 154, 156, 161, 304
Meinecke, Friedrich, 259n18
Meir, rabbi, 49
Meiri, Menachem, rabbi, 6, 20, 22–23, 25, 95–97, 99, 105, 118, 122–23, 288, 293–94, 295n13, 308, 351–52, 354
Meister Eckhart. *See* Eckhart, Johannes
Melamed, Eliezer, rabbi, 292n5
Menachem Mendel, rebbe of Kotzk, 124
Mendelssohn, Moses, 36–37, 97, 198, 235, 238, 254–55, 256n12, 257
Mendes-Flohr, Paul, xi, 17–18, 29, 37–38, 253, 352

Merleau-Ponty, Maurice Jean Jacques, 90n37
Mesha, king, 315
Messi, Leo, 152
messianism, 38, 58–60, 101, 140, 193, 218, 221, 228, 254, 270, 296n19, 308, 321
metaphor, 152, 157n15, 183, 195, 245–6, 314, 319, *see also* God, image
metaphysics,
    in Aristotle, 94n3
    in Arthur Green, 115, 118–120
    in continental philosophy, 253
    kabbalistic, 122–124
    in Maimonides, 305
    in modernity, 259, 262
    and halakhah, 327
Micah, prophet, 149, 285, 322, 326
Midrash,
    divinization of humanity in, 54, 56–8
    evil inclination in, 241–42
    idolatry in, 133, 170, 223, 234–35
    images of God in, 45–6, 48–9, 142–3, 169, 183–4
    Israel and gentiles in, 337–38
    perfection of God, 52
    women in, 130–2, 135, 242
Mishneh Torah, 5, 97, 168, 180, 216, 248n44, 283, 287n8, 292n7, 296n19, 297–99, 301, 303, 305, 307, 323, 353, *see also* Maimonides
modernity, *see also* postmodernity
    destruction of idolatry, 104, 107, 118, 128
    and humanism, 100–7, 122–3
    loss of values in, 101–2, 223, 244, 263
    nationalism, 31, 59n48, 61, 105–6, 218–19, 222
    and the new Judaism, 96, 98–9, 101, 125, 237–8, 263
    understanding of idolatry as ideology, 17, 72, 126
    reason and individualism, 258–9
    relationship to nature, 34, 100, 102, 246
    relationship to history, 99–100, 119
    secularism, 33, 101
Moloch, 201, 315
money, 5, 8, 16, 22, 160–63, 166, 201, 215, 224, 317, 328
monotheism, 71, 108, 196
    and aesthetics, 107
    in Ancient Greece, 47, 94n3
    contrast to idolatry, 93–4, 99, 100–1, 112, 118, 267
    development in Judaism, 32, 66–7, 73, 76–8, 95–7, 101, 105, 110, 113–4, 116–7, 121, 122, 143, 149, 188, 194, 196–9, 202, 217, 229, 232, 287, 295, 300
    dangers of, 113–4, 119, 122, 130, 146–7, 264, 355
    distinctions between God and human, 108–12, 186
    and divine transcendence, 77, 83, 86, 87–8
    ethics in, 22, 33, 97–9, 100, 102–7, 118–9, 123, 136, 149–50, 186, 188, 199, 202, 246–47, 309
    idolatry in, 32, 71, 118, 146–8, 355
    and image worship, 47, 62
    and nature, 108, 189
    negative theology, 229, 266
    and patricularism, 146, 187
    and Reformation, 97, 100
Mopsik, Charles, 143
morality, *see also* ethics
    abuse of power, 224
    connection to *avodah zarah*, 3, 6, 18, 32, 96, 188, 201, 213, 224, 292, 316, 328
    decline with secularization, 203

and humanism, 158n21, 328
and religious observance, 258, 292
and sexual discrimination, 130
Moses, 35–36, 49–52, 57–58, 63, 76, 81, 131, 170, 183, 222, 234–35, 238, 285–86, 306n51, 317–18, 326–28
Moses of Salerno, rabbi, 288
Muhammed, 55–57, 330
Munkacs, Rebbe of, 220
Murphy, Zen Roshi Susan, 177
mysticism, 40, 87, 89–91, 99, 111, 219, 227, 229, 236
mystics, 84, 121, 123, 229, 237n13, 273, 314
myth, 104, 113–14, 169, 242, 244, 274–75, 328, 344n37
mythic plenum, 73–77, 87
mythology, 59, 109, 151, 153, 194n21, 207, 228, 278

Naaman of Aram, 147
Nachman, Samuel bar, rabbi, 234
Nachmanides (Moses Ben Nachman), 6, 142n4, 145, 217, 290, 306–7n51, 308, 324n12, 350
Nachman of Breslev, rabbi, 160n25
Nachum, Menachem, rebbe of Chernobyl, 176
Nadab, 43, 215, 329
narcissism, 21, 31, 162, 242, 246, 252, 272
Nathan, biblical figure, 321
nationalism, 14–15, 29–31, 40, 60–61, 105–6, 203, 218–22, 224–25, 230–31, 250, 320
Nazism, 55, 58–59, 97n21, 209n57, 222, 245, 249n45
Nebuchadnezzar, king, 54, 237
Nehemiah, rabbi, 234
Nehemiah, biblical figure, 331
Neḥushtan, 285
Nietzsche, Friedrich, 29, 155, 157–60, 253

Nimrod, biblical figure, 61–62
Nimrod, Naomi, 132
Noachide, 145, 147, 331, 335
Noah, 153, 156, 161, 165
Nobel, Anton Nehemiah, rabbi, 260nn21–22
North Korea, 55, 61
Novak, David, 24, 147n14, 196, 209, 247, 250–51
Novick, Leah, 135
Nussbaum, Martha, 344

Obadiah the Proselyte, 287n8, 294n12
objectification, 326
of the divine, 50, 82, 109, 136
and group identity, 230
of ideas, 17, 83, 90, 92
of the natural world, 79
of products, 79, 83
and women, 127
Orthodoxy, 132, 205, 290, 305, 308, 310
Ozick, Cynthia, 133–34, 239–40

paganism, 154, 289, 343n34, *see also* polytheism
conception of gods in, 74–5, 94n4, 134, 152, 158–9, 186, 194, 197
and humanism, 30, 146–8, 334, 338–9
and imagination, 244
in modern world, 157–60, 188–9, 193, 275, 278
opposition of Judaism to, 99, 150, 188, 191–2, 201, 266, 307, 312, 330, 342, 347
vs. rationalist theories, 196
pandemic, 35, 189, 190, 208, 210, 222
panentheism, 87, 99, 108–11, 117, 119
pantheism, 110–11, 119n67
particularism, 9, 31, 100, 106, 114, 117, 190, 248, 252, *see also* Israel, exclusivity of

patriarchy, 126–27, 129, 132, 134, 139, 195
Paty, Samuel, 57n40
Pedaya, Haviva, 13, 16, 19, 21, 30–31, 33–34, 40, 349–50, 356
personhood, 40, 59, 109n44, 121–22, 133, 191
Pessoa, Fernando, 259
Pharaoh, the, 29, 55, 62–63, 132, 146, 174–75, 180
phenomenal world, 76–77, 89–91, 136, 142, 275, 314
    and idolatry, 253
    magic and superstition, 299, 322–3
    and science, 243
Philo of Alexandria, 56, 116n61, 146n10
philosophy,
    God of the philosophers vs. living God, 24, 196
    and ethical monotheism, 97–8, 148, 196
    and defense of democracy, 158, 200, 316
    and feminism, 128
    and interreligious dialogue, 287–88, 342–3
    philosophical error, 307
    and rational cognition, 83, 141, 194, 217, 314, 324
physics, 190, 302n41, 305, 309
piety, 56, 129, 131, 260n21, 274, 284, 341n30
Plaskow, Judith, 128, 130, 134–36
Plato, 155, 316
Plotinus, 47n14, 314
pluralism, 148, 198, 259n19
    among American Jewry, 30, 187, 193, 198
    in dialogue with Christianity, 116n59, 343
    and liberalism, 343–44
polemics,
    against "other," 71–3
    defining Jewish God against other deities, 74–77
    criticizing Christianity as new idolatry, 95, 324n12
    criticizing idolatry within Jews, 78–80, 315
    within Judaism about
        avodah zarah, 5, 7, 38–40, 51
        God's attributes, 44n5, 207, 216, 355
        rationalism and mysticism, 235, 237, 262, 324
        referring to God, 17, 187, 195, 208
    in modern climate, 72, 210
    on racism and Zionism, 59n45
politics,
    and control over nature, 6–5
    and group division, 201, 207, 209, 218, 245, 262, 346–7
    and group coexistence, 313, 332, 342–5
    and growth, 165, 230
    historical-political understanding of idolatry, 8, 19, 20, 55, 124, 187–8, 198, 217, 242–3, 275, 330
    and ideas of hatred, 57–64
    and ideology of femininity, 128–30, 132, 135
    and idolization of the national feeling, 30–1, 32, 218–9, 221, 224, 231, 262
    and Jewish tradition, 211, 248–51
    and messianism, 193, 321
    in modernity, 102–3, 106, 107, 126, 211, 218–9
    monotheism as politics, 68, 75, 100, 109, 118–9
    totality, 16
    and worship of leaders, 23, 26–7, 29–30, 54–8, 318–9

polytheism, 100n27, 186, 188, *see also* paganism
  in ancient Egypt, 147–86
  and elected condition, 144
  and demand for exclusive worship, 4
  and humanism, 101, 148
  and polyphony of God, 49–50, 71
  and transcendence, 33, 81, 102, 185
Popper, Karl Reimund, 344
possession, 127, 273, 323, 336
postmodernity, postmodernism, 33–34, 100–2, 105–8, 121–2, 218, 221, 223
prayer,
  and awareness, 176, 183
  as communal activity, 255
  component of worship, 5
  definitions of idolatry in, 66–67, 311n61
  fluidity of, 120, 123
  idolatry in, 237n13, 300–1, 303, 323–24, 330
  images of God in, 76n10, 109n45
  options for women, 128
  personal communication with God, 166, 179
  preparation for, 123, 164n32
prophet, 277
  critique of idolatry, 239, 249, 265
  critique of immorality, 32, 186, 201, 250
  critique of Israel, 78, 80, 125, 130, 147, 187, 188, 211, 284–6
  critique of neighboring kingdoms, 8, 54, 80, 125, 146–7, 174
  and direct contact with God, 312, 317–8
  iconoclasm, 130–1, 236
  image of Moses, 57, 286n5
  and images of God, 76n10, 195, 236
  impulse for social justice, 125, 127, 130–1, 133, 147, 173, 175, 211, 328

messianism, 101, 149–150, 191, 205, 284, 312
Psalms, 52–53, 80, 178, 184, 214, 265, 284, 289
psychology, 19, 22, 77, 123
punishment,
  Holocaust as, 192–93
  for Israel's following other gods, 130
  personal fear of, 154, 182, 186, 223
  of the woman and the man, 64–65,

Rabad. *See* Ben David, Abraham, rabbi
Rabban Gamliel II of Jabne, 335–38
Rabinowitz, Ya'akov Yitzhak, rabbi, 85
Racism, 29, 31–32, 59n45, 200–1, 247, 250, 310
Ralbag. *See* Ben Gershon, Levi, rabbi
Rambam. *See* Maimonides
Ramban. *See* Nachmanides
Raphael, Melissa, 17, 19, 27, 29
Rappoport, Shloyme Zanvl, 323
Rashi. *See* Ben Isaac, Solomon, rabbi
rationalism, 194, 210, 235–7, 314, 341
  in Hermann Cohen, 83, 194
  in Deuteronomy, 186
  in Erich Fromm, 158n21
  and Holocaust, 192
  in Niccolò Machiavelli, 157
  in Maimonides, 39, 83, 235, 309–10, 325
  in Moses Mendelssohn, 254–5
  and modern dangers of, 83, 186
  in Eliezer Schweid, 104, 106
  in Max Weber, 185, 189, 211
Rauschning, Hermann, 58n45
Recanati, Menachem, 325
redemption,
  coming from idols, 79, 321
  as expression of universal relation to God, 67, 112, 172, 223, 144, 326
  and feminism, 132

field for coexistence of Judaism and Christianity, 200
from ignorance, 17, 125
as an idol, 38, 219, 225, 254
as self-acceptance, 167
and Zionism, 219
Reformation, 100–1
reification, *see* objectification
relativism, 22, 155, 187, 260
religion, *see also* Christianity, interreligious dialogue, monotheism, polytheism, panentheism, pantheism
classification as *avodah zarah*, 2, 7, 11–5, 18, 38, 196
choice of, 172
and politics, 30–1, 187–8, 198–9, 209, 262, 264–5, 354
repentance (teshuvah), 35, 170, 260n22, 270, 303, 321, 341
representation
in culture, 90n37
of the divine, 75, 216, 233
in idolatry, 18, 23–4, 47, 81, 94n4, 96, 110, 141, 170, 235–6, 245, 286, 313
in Kabbalah, 236
pictorial vs. linguistic, 187, 195n26
with metaphors, 45
multiplicity of, 24, 44–5, 46–7, 155
rejecting the possibility of, 44, 73, 75–7, 79–80, 82, 187, 243–4
of human, 216, 235
via institutions, 172, 204, 210
of the other, 71, 82, 263
woman as, 138
reverence,
before divine, 180, 289
through images, 197
before nature, 179, 182

before a wise man, 257
before world/reality, 90, 180, 182
ritual,
correct vs. incorrect practice, 43, 77, 80, 154, 194, 206, 207, 232, 328
directed towards the human, 28, 203–4
expressive of fluid practice, 36–37, 214, 239
foundation of shared identity, 344
made into idol, 16, 268, 285–6, 294n12, 315n3
and mysticism, 227
part of worship, 5, 154, 199
as stimulus of Jewish piety, 257–258
Rivash. *See* Ben Sheshet Perfet, Isaac, rabbi
Romano, Judah, 288
Rome,
contrast to Israel, 57n37, 188–9, 210, 339–40, 342
emperor worship, 56,
influence upon Jewish conceptions of idolatry, 188–9, 330
rebellions against, 321
in Talmud, 319, 334–35, 337, 347
Roosevelt, Franklin Delano, president, 103n33
Rosenblum, Yitzhak, 218n15
Rosenzweig, Franz, 23–24, 194, 199–200, 235–37, 259–62, 278, 354
Ross, Tamar, 123
Rubenstein, Richard Lowell, 192–93, 208
Rubiés, Joan-Pau, 233
Ruether, Rosemary, 129

Saadia Gaon, 82, 323n10, 325
Sabbath, 34, 65–66, 144, 200n38, 210, 249, 330, 332
sabbatical year, 179–80
Sacks, Elias, 238n14

sacrifice, 53, 131, 144, 146, 157, 187, 190, 214, 227, 264, 283, 315–16, 344
Sade, Donatien Alphonse François, Marquis de, 157
Salerno, 288
salvation, *see* redemption
Samael, 242
Samson, 177
Samuel, 153, 320–21
sanctity,
    as different from idolatry, 214, 265
    inner quality of self, 270
    of Israel, 117n62
    of all life, 16, 28, 119, 168, 177, 180–81
    of objects vs. created by practices, 37–38, 132, 273–77
S. Ansky. *See* Rappoport, Shloyme Zanvl
Saragossa, 324
Sartre, Jean-Paul, 53, 272
Satan, 220
Satlow, Michael, 116n61
Satmar, 192, 219n17, 225
Schachter-Shalomi, Zalman, rabbi, 118n64, 132
Schelling, Friedrich Wilhelm Joseph, 158
Scholem, Gershom, 73n4, 81, 106
Schopenhauer, Arthur, 110
Schweid, Eliezer, 22, 30, 33–34, 96, 98–108, 118, 122–24
scientism, danger of, 83, 104, 185, 202, 344n37
science,
    and fragmentation of values, 185–6, 189, 190, 196–7, 208, 211, 243, 314–5, 328
    as an idol, 202
    in Islam and Christianity, 287–8, 341–42
    and knowledge of God, 176, 301, 305
    and nature, 181, 243
    and promise of unification, 190, 200, 287, 301, 305, 309
    rabbinical science, 273, 293, 297, 309–10
    object of sale, 161
Scripture. *See* Bible
Scruton, Roger, 86n28
secularity, 33, 99–103, 105, 107, 158n21, 214, 217
Seeskin, Kenneth, 246–48, 311
sefirot, 39, 109–10, 120–21, 143, 237n13, 301, 323–25
self, 27–8, 168–70, 181, 229, 246
    and awareness, 26, 70, 269, 272
    and communal heritage, 171–3
    and creative work, 140, 165
    and fear, 70, 165, 278
    and individualism, 8, 28, 203, 223–24, 240, 245, 258
    in Levinas, 254
    and liberation, 22
    and patriarchy, 132, 163
    and separation, 183, 241, 269
Sennacherib, king, 54
Seth, 282–83
Shamir, Eilon, 13, 16, 21–22, 27–28, 30, 33
Shapiro, Dovid, rabbi, 69n75
Shapiro, Marc, 297
Sharansky, Anatoly, 182
Shekhinah, 135, 143, 306n51
Shintoism, 289
Sikhism, 289
Silman, Yochanan, 298n26
Simlai, rabbi, 170, 183
Simon, rabbi, 234
Sinai, mountain, 47–48, 75–76, 81, 86, 114, 117n62, 170, 183, 234, 294, 313, 317, 328
Singer, Isaac Bashevis, 323
Six Day War, the, 193

slavery, 22, 65, 74, 126, 132–33, 139, 165–66, 175, 274, 324, 328, 341
Sofer, Moses, 39, 319
society, 6, 16, 25
    and capitalism, 160, 162
    and ethics, 20–22, 36, 95–7, 99–100, 103–5, 165, 171, 172, 174–5, 243, 279, 312, 326, 344, 351–3
    and idolatry, 36, 97, 133, 160, 213, 224–6, 278, 318–20, 351–53
    around Jews, 95, 104, 198–9, 201, 325–7, 330n7, 340, 346n40, 347
    and Jewish woman, 134
    and nature, 33, 102, 160, 162
    postmodern, 102, 166
    totalitarian, 61
Socrates, 262
Solomon, king, 36, 48
Solomon, Norman, 17, 19, 21, 27, 29–31, 36, 38–39
Soloveitchik, Haym, 327n21
Soloveitchik, Joseph Ber, rabbi, 138, 192, 193n20, 203, 327, 342
Sommer, Benjamin, 93, 353
soul, 92
    and ethics, 174, 210
    forgotten about due to idolatry, 21–22
    image of God, 26, 29, 137, 153–154, 165, 253, 269–70
    inner life, 26, 126, 134, 253
    integrity and history of idolatry, 153–159, 163, 166, 210
    psychological understanding of, 21, 70
    special in *tzaddik*, 39, 319
    in women, 126, 134, 137–8
Sperber, Daniel, 292
Spinoza, Baruch, 110–11, 198, 253, 272
spirituality, 3, 6, 12, 19, 108, 132, 145, 182, 260

Stalin, Joseph, 55–56, 200, 278–79, 342n32
statue, 141, 148, 220, 229, 283, 292n5
Steiner, George, 258–59
Stern, David, 52, 57n37
Stoicism, 47
Strauss, Leo, 203
Streicher, Julius, 58n45
suffering, 20, 148, 157, 175, 180, 321
superstition, 232, 238, 257, 297, 318, 322, 328

Tablets, the, 35–36, 234–35, 326
Talmud, 147n12, 175, 180, 215, 234, 240–41, 260, 273, 277, 280, 294, 312–13, 317, 323, 331, 335, 344
Talmud Torah, xi, 37, 254–56, 257n12, 258–60, 262–63, 275
Tammuz, 130, 216
Tanchum, Miriam Bat, 131
Tanḥuma, 146
Taoism, 289
Taylor, Charles, 203, 244
technology, 33–34, 100, 102, 104–5, 160–61, 165
Temple, 44n5, 56–57, 130, 147, 215–16, 226, 285, 293n9, 306, 307n51, 321, 335n21, 344
Tertullian, the Church Father, 94
Thanatos, 240
theurgy, 303
Tiamat, 153
Tillich, Paul, 13, 28, 173, 202–3, 250
Titus, 56n36
tolerance, 118–19, 124, 175, 281, 312, 355
Tosafists, the, 295, 308
totality,
    and God, 34–35, 87, 122, 136, 274
    and idolatry, 16, 35, 122, 278
    and life, 183, 241, 271
triumphalism, 60

Trump, Donald John, 30, 162, 201
truth, 155
    and ethics, 5, 128, 130, 137, 160, 162, 183, 197, 209–10, 217, 222, 251, 255
    and faith, 26
    and knowledge of God, 82, 86–7, 111, 112, 124, 126n2, 240, 253, 258, 263, 265, 269, 323, 356
    perception of reality, 70, 88
    and reason, 37, 99, 194, 196, 254
    in religions, 98, 112, 197, 240, 308, 313
Twersky, Isadore, 297
tyranny, 54, 61, 68, 131, 175

United Nations, the, 58, 61, 192
United States, the, 200–1, 209, 319
universalism, 78, 101, 113, 114, 119, 223, 246, 247–48, 292, 310, 339
Usha, 337
Uzzah, biblical figure, 215

Van Winden, Jacobus Cornelis Maria, 94n4
Vilna Gaon (Elijah ben Solomon Zalman), 39, 319, 323
Voltaire, François-Marie Arouet, 233n3

Washington, George, 319
Whitehead, Alfred North, 82
Weber, Max, 22, 83, 92n44, 185–90, 196, 198, 205–7, 209–11, 215
Weisblum, Elimelech rabbi of Lizhensk, 164n32

Weiser, Meir Levush ben Yechiel (Malbim), 145n10
Wiese, Christian, 343n33
Winnicott, Donald Woods, 218
wisdom, 57, 80, 166, 174, 179, 208–9, 212, 237, 257, 262, 274, 279, 302, 322, 325, 341n30
Wittenberg, Jonathan, 16, 19, 20, 25, 27–29, 34–35, 40
Wolfson, Elliot, 39–40, 93n1, 109n44, 121, 236, 325n17
wonder, 75, 83–85, 90, 92n44, 92n49, 111, 180, 182, 261, 268
World War I, 185, 187, 210, 260n21, 342n32
World War II, 103, 342n32, 344

Yocheved, Moses's mother, 131
Yochanan, rabbi, 67n68, 234
Yose, the son of Ḥanina, rabbi, 49
Yudan, rabbi, 324

Zachariah, prophet, 150
Zephaniah, prophet, 150
Zeus, 155, 318
Zevi, Sabbetai, 124n77, 321
Zini, Eliyahu, rabbi, 291n5
Zion, 50–51, 149
Zionism, 31, 59n45, 59n48, 101, 103–6, 219, 221, 225, 320, 343, 347
Zohar, 33, 40, 84–85, 109, 181, 202, 236–37, 241n26
Zoroastrianism, 289

"*Idolatry* is a profound, probing yet engaging exploration of human misdirection whose roots are as ancient as human yearning. This book springs from history and scholarship but it speaks to our society and to the individual heart."

— Rabbi David Wolpe, Max Webb Senior Rabbi, Sinai Temple, Los Angeles

"This remarkably rich anthology—beyond disabusing anyone who might still be operating under the notion that the biblical injunction against idolatry can be limited to worship of 'sticks and stones'—suggests many thought-provoking extensions of the traditional injunction against false gods both within Judaism and without. The efforts of an impressive array of contributors to pin-point in contemporary terms just what is problematic about this deviant form of worship not only revive the theological relevance of this ancient prohibition: the wide variety of perspectives that they introduce also bear important implications for current attempts at interfaith dialogue, subtly shifting the nature of the discourse from rarefied debates regarding the precise doctrinal imperatives of monotheism to broader moral interests and concerns, questions of pluralism and tolerance, social theory, education, and politics. In spelling out the multitude of theoretical and practical dimensions of this discussion, *Idolatry: A Contemporary Jewish Conversation* powerfully challenges Jews and non-Jews alike to revisit the notion of idolatry, and rediscover its importance as a critical category of thought."

— Tamar Ross, Professor Emerita, Department of Jewish Philosophy, Bar-Ilan University

"Alon Goshen-Gottstein has put together a sterling volume of outstanding contributors for new directions for the concept of 'idolatry' in Jewish thought. For Goshen-Gottstein the traditional interest in idolatry for rejecting other religions has largely been surpassed. So, this volume aims to retrieve 'idolatry' as a live concept for our age. This book is both an intellectual and spiritual diamond."

— Jerome Yehuda Gellman, Professor of Philosophy Emeritus, Ben-Gurion University

"The discussion of idolatry is surely of tremendous importance. Nearly all religions and philosophies consider it awful. But what is idolatry and why is it 'awful'? That debate is the core of this fascinating book. Is it wrong when we do not put God at the center of the universe and our lives? But what is really the problem? Does God really mind? Or is idolatry forbidden because it is the source for great evil and immorality? If so, what about idol worship or atheism that does not lead to evil and in fact encourages the good? Or is this a contradiction in terms? Rabbi Dr. Alon Goshen Gottstein has managed to pull together some of the greatest religious thinkers of our time to try to respond to these questions. Intriguing: I could not put this book down once I started."

— Rabbi Dr. Nathan Lopes Cardozo, Dean of the
David Cardozo Academy Jerusalem

www.ingramcontent.com/pod-product-compliance
Lightning Source LLC
Chambersburg PA
CBHW072038160426
43197CB00014B/2543